C000069744

CHART PATTERNS:
AFTER THE BUY

The Wiley Trading series features books by traders who have survived the market's ever changing temperament and have prospered—some by reinventing systems, others by getting back to basics. Whether a novice trader, professional or somewhere in-between, these books will provide the advice and strategies needed to prosper today and well into the future. For more on this series, visit our Web site at www.WileyTrading.com.

Founded in 1807, John Wiley & Sons is the oldest independent publishing company in the United States. With offices in North America, Europe, Australia, and Asia, Wiley is globally committed to developing and marketing print and electronic products and services for our customers' professional and personal knowledge and understanding.

■ Also by Thomas Bulkowski

Encyclopedia of Candlestick Charts, the definitive reference book covering 103 types of candlestick patterns and their performance.

Encyclopedia of Chart Patterns, **Second Edition,** a reference book reviewing 53 chart and 10 event patterns packed with performance information, identification guidelines, failure rates, trading tactics, and more.

Fundamental Analysis and Position Trading: Evolution of a Trader, a primer about value investing and adding market timing to a buy-and-hold strategy using position trading.

Getting Started in Chart Patterns, **Second Edition,** a popular, low-cost choice for learning about chart patterns.

Swing and Day Trading: Evolution of a Trader, explains how to use chart patterns to swing and day trade, including major reversal times for day traders, plus the opening range breakout and opening gap setups.

Trading Basics: Evolution of a Trader, discusses money management, stops, support, resistance, and offers dozens of tips every trader and investor should know, in an easy-to-read and understand book.

Trading Classic Chart Patterns provides a simple-to-use scoring system to improve the selection of chart patterns that work.

Visual Guide to Chart Patterns, an easy-to-use guide which shows how to recognize chart patterns, understand why they behave as they do, and what their buy and sell signals mean, presented on color charts.

CHART PATTERNS: AFTER THE BUY

Thomas Bulkowski

WILEY

Cover image: Finance background © isak55/Shutterstock; Abstract background © Click Bestsellers/ Shutterstock; Soft colored abstract background © Pixel Embargo/Shutterstock
Cover design: Wiley

Copyright © 2016 by Thomas Bulkowski. All rights reserved.

Published by John Wiley & Sons, Inc., Hoboken, New Jersey.
Published simultaneously in Canada.

No part of this publication may be reproduced, stored in a retrieval system, or transmitted in any form or by any means, electronic, mechanical, photocopying, recording, scanning, or otherwise, except as permitted under Section 107 or 108 of the 1976 United States Copyright Act, without either the prior written permission of the Publisher, or authorization through payment of the appropriate per-copy fee to the Copyright Clearance Center, Inc., 222 Rosewood Drive, Danvers, MA 01923, (978) 750-8400, fax (978) 646-8600, or on the Web at www.copyright.com. Requests to the Publisher for permission should be addressed to the Permissions Department, John Wiley & Sons, Inc., 111 River Street, Hoboken, NJ 07030, (201) 748-6011, fax (201) 748-6008, or online at www.wiley.com/go/permissions.

Limit of Liability/Disclaimer of Warranty: While the publisher and author have used their best efforts in preparing this book, they make no representations or warranties with respect to the accuracy or completeness of the contents of this book and specifically disclaim any implied warranties of merchantability or fitness for a particular purpose. No warranty may be created or extended by sales representatives or written sales materials. The advice and strategies contained herein may not be suitable for your situation. You should consult with a professional where appropriate. Neither the publisher nor author shall be liable for any loss of profit or any other commercial damages, including but not limited to special, incidental, consequential, or other damages.

For general information on our other products and services or for technical support, please contact our Customer Care Department within the United States at (800) 762-2974, outside the United States at (317) 572-3993 or fax (317) 572-4002.

Wiley publishes in a variety of print and electronic formats and by print-on-demand. Some material included with standard print versions of this book may not be included in e-books or in print-on-demand. If this book refers to media such as a CD or DVD that is not included in the version you purchased, you may download this material at http://booksupport.wiley.com. For more information about Wiley products, visit www.wiley.com.

Library of Congress Cataloging-in-Publication Data:

ISBN 978-1-119-27490-2 (Paperback)
ISBN 978-1-119-27491-9 (ePDF)
ISBN 978-1-119-27492-6 (ePub)

Printed in the United States of America.

10 9 8 7 6 5 4 3 2 1

To Donna McCormick.

Abundant intelligence,
A kind soul,
A giving heart,
Wrapped in a frail body.

She is discovered treasure.

CONTENTS

I used to think chart patterns were the footprints of the smart money. Now I believe the definition should include the dumb money, too, and everyone in between.

When I trade a stock, others are doing the same. We move price up or down, depending on how strongly we want to buy or sell. If enough of us buy a stock with enthusiasm and continue to buy, we force the stock to trend upward. Prolonged aggressive selling forces the stock down. That buying and selling creates patterns on the price chart, patterns that we see repeatedly.

Chart patterns have been around for decades. I expect them to be around in the coming decades, too, because the forces of buying demand and selling pressure will still be present to shape the charts. Machines may change the dynamics, but human emotion will still be there to leave the footprints.

The idea for this book came in the form of a question. What happens *after* I buy a stock showing a chart pattern?

Answering that question for 20 chart patterns took two years. The result is this reference book.

Most books focus on what triggers a buy. Fewer books focus on what happens next. I used 43,229 chart patterns pulled from bull markets to uncover the secrets to what happens after buying a stock. The results help select better buy signals so you have an increased chance of making money and avoiding disaster. All you have to do is match your setup to one of the configurations illustrated in this book.

Most chapters follow the same layout so using this reference book is easier, too. The **Behavior at a Glance** section illustrates how a chart pattern behaves, with the most important performance statistics right on the charts.

Identification Guidelines follow so even people new to chart patterns will know what to look for. And with almost 370 stock charts and illustrations, you have plenty of examples.

Next comes the **Buy** and **Sell Setups**, backed by statistics that describe how well they work.

The **Best Stop Locations** tell how often a stop in a chart pattern will trigger. That alone is worth the price of this book.

The section on **Configuration Trading** shows how your setup is likely to behave in the future. It is the heart of the book.

The **Measure Rule** tells how to set price targets and how often you can expect price to reach those targets for both up and down breakouts.

The **Trading** section gives examples of how to use the information and discusses actual trades.

You will find the **Setup Synopsis** charts at the end of each chapter to be invaluable. The charts combined the ideal setups in one location, making it easy to match your trade with what could happen after you buy.

Each chart includes labels for points of interest. Too many authors forget this step and leave you wondering where that price spike they are talking about really is.

Not so with this book.

I never leave you guessing.

But wait. There's more.

Not only do I cover the most common and popular chart patterns, I include other patterns as well. Earnings misses, price mirrors, price mountains, and straight-line runs are just a few of the chapters that fill this book.

Whether you are new to chart patterns or are an established professional, this book has the information you need to better select trades that work. This book will give you the edge that all traders and investors need in today's markets.

ACKNOWLEDGMENTS

Thanks to Dr. Tom Helget, Ross Hall, and Ronda Palm for their suggestions and help with molding this manuscript.

Thomas Bulkowski is a successful investor with 35 years experience trading stocks. He is considered to be a leading expert on chart patterns and an internationally known author.

Bulkowski is a frequent contributor to *Technical Analysis of Stocks & Commodities* magazine and has written for the following magazines: *Active Trader*; *Stocks, Futures and Options*; *The Technical Analyst*; *Traders*; and *The Trader's Journal*, and his articles have appeared on numerous websites.

Before earning enough from his investments to retire from his day job at age 36, he was a hardware design engineer at Raytheon and a senior software engineer for Tandy Corporation.

His website address is www.thepatternsite.com. There you will have free and open access to hundreds of original articles, research, and blog posts written by Bulkowski.

CHAPTER 1

Big M

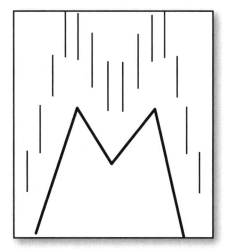

I fired up my computer and typed "big M chart pattern" into a search engine and my website (thepatternsite.com) came up first on the list. That tells me not a lot of research has been done on the big M.

You might think that the big M is a burger joint, but in technical analysis, it is a variation of a double top chart pattern. The difference between a double top and a big M is that the big M has tall sides (when it works). When it fails, the left side remains tall, but the right side is amputated.

Let us take a closer look.

Figure 1.1 shows the typical behavior after a big M chart pattern forms. The big M is shown in a slightly thicker line.

The launch price is where the uptrend begins that leads to the big M. Often the run up to a big M is a straight-line affair, not a rounded turn. The climb lasts as long as bullish enthusiasm drives price higher. Eventually, however, the stock peaks and retraces. That retrace forms the first peak of the big M.

Bulls gather and attempt a new high, but price stalls at or near the price of the first high and drops back. This up-and-down movement forms the second peak.

When price closes below the valley between the two peaks, it confirms the chart pattern as a valid one and signals a breakout. Timber!

Price drops an average of 17% below the breakout price, but that is for more than 1,300 perfect trades. Do not expect to duplicate those results. You might hurt yourself.

Comparing the ultimate low with the launch price, we find that 60% of the big Ms see price returning to or dropping below the launch price. That also means 40% remain above the launch price.

■ After a big M, the stock returns to the launch price 60% of the time.

Pullbacks

Figure 1.2 shows what happens to big M patterns 63% of the time.

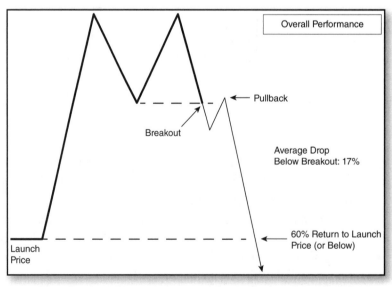

FIGURE 1.1   This is the typical behavior of a big M chart pattern.

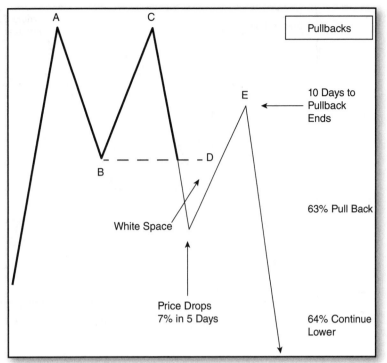

FIGURE 1.2 Statistics related to pullbacks.

A big M appears as peaks AC with B marking the lowest valley between the two peaks (the so-called confirmation, or breakout price). A close below the price of B means a downward breakout. If price closes above the highest peak (A or C) *before* closing below the breakout price (B), then you do not have a big M.

D represents a pullback when the stock returns to the breakout price within a month after the breakout. The one-month window is arbitrary, but it serves as a good benchmark. I prefer that white space appear between the breakout and pullback as shown in the figure.

After a downward breakout, price drops an average of 7% in 5 days. Price reverses and retraces the drop for 5 more days (10 calendar days total since the breakout) until it peaks again at the top of the pullback (E).

Thirty-six percent of the time price continues higher, often leaving traders with a loss on their ledgers. However, the vast majority of the time (64%) price continues lower.

■ A pullback occurs 63% of the time and price continues lower 64% of the time.

Busted Tops

Figure 1.3 shows the performance of busted big M chart patterns. A pattern busts after a downward breakout when price drops less than 10% before reversing and closing above the top of the chart pattern.

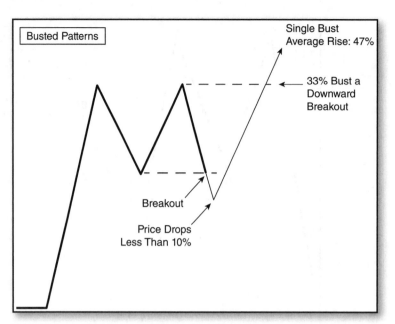

FIGURE 1.3 The average performance of big Ms that bust a downward breakout.

I found that 33% of big Ms will bust a downward breakout in a bull market. That means 1 in 3 trades will likely lose money. However, if you see a busted big M, then buy it. The average rise for a single busted chart pattern is a mouthwatering 47%. Of course, a single bust can turn into a double or triple bust, too. That is a risk. I will explain double and triple busts later or you can visit the glossary, which shows a picture (see Figure G.1).

- Big Ms bust 33% of the time.

Identification

Figure 1.4 shows an example of a big M chart pattern. The launch price is at A. The bulls get excited about the stock and bid it up, day after day, so that a straight-line run forms and takes price much higher, to the first top (B).

The first peak's shape can vary from rounded looking (as in this case) to a one-day needle ready to draw blood. Following the first peak, price tumbles to C when the bears take charge of the stock, often forming a V-shaped turn. The BC drop averages 10%.

The bulls counterattack and force the price back up. Those buying the stock near the first peak say, "as soon as I get my money back, I'm selling." And they are as good as their word. That forms peak D near the same price as B. The two peaks need not match the same price exactly. However, I found that the average price difference between the two is about 1%.

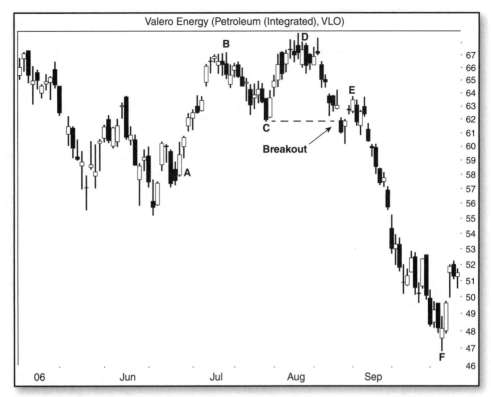

FIGURE 1.4 This big M looks like a double top with tall sides.

When people sell near the second peak, that selling pressure forces the stock lower. When it closes below the price of the valley between the two peaks (C), it breaks out and confirms the chart pattern as a valid big M. In this case, price pulls back to E before continuing lower.

Table 1.1 shows the identification guidelines for finding big Ms.

Rise. Price should rise quickly, often in a steep, straight-line run leading to the first peak. The move from A to B in Figure 1.4 shows an example of a typical move higher.

Avoid selecting potential big Ms with a rounded turn on the rise leading to the first peak. I show an example of that in **Figure 1.5**. BD is a double top, not a big M. The inset shows the difference between the two chart patterns.

■ Avoid selecting potential big Ms with a rounded-looking turn leading to the first peak.

The rise from A to B starts as a nice straight-line run, but it is not long enough when compared to the size of the drop from the first peak (B) to the valley floor (C). The AC price distance is shorter than CB.

TABLE 1.1	Identification Guidelines
Characteristic	**Discussion**
Rise	Price makes a steep move higher, often in a straight-line run, leading to the first peak.
Height	The height from the launch price to the first peak should be extensive, often twice as tall as the distance from the first peak to the bottom of the valley between the two peaks.
Twin Peaks	Two peaks top out near the same price but allow variation. The average price difference between the two peaks is about 1%.
Breakout	When price closes below the lowest valley between the two peaks, a breakout occurs and you have a valid big M. If, instead of breaking out downward, price first closes above the highest peak, then you do not have a big M.
M Shape	The chart pattern should look like an M once it completes.

FIGURE 1.5   The ABCD pattern is a double top and not a big M because of the rounded turn leading to peak B.

For valid big Ms with peaks spaced months apart, the rise to the first peak is often more sedate (less vertical) than for big Ms with narrower peaks. Use common sense when looking for big Ms.

Height. The height of the big M is an important feature. Consider the big M in **Figure 1.6**. The launch price is at A1, and the stock flies up quickly to C1. The run is straight, almost vertical, not curved like that shown in the approach to A in Figure 1.5.

Look at the inset of Figure 1.6. The horizontal line at B marks the valley floor between the two peaks of the big M. The price difference from A to B should be at least as big as the move from B to C.

The measure is like playing horseshoes or tossing hand grenades: close is what counts, but allow variations. On the stock chart, the price change from A1 to B1 is about the same as the change from B1 to C1.

Take care when comparing the move visually. The logarithmic price scale can make a visual examination difficult. Either switch to the linear scale or whip out your calculator and tabulate the price difference if it concerns you.

■ Beware using a log scale when visually inspecting a chart pattern.

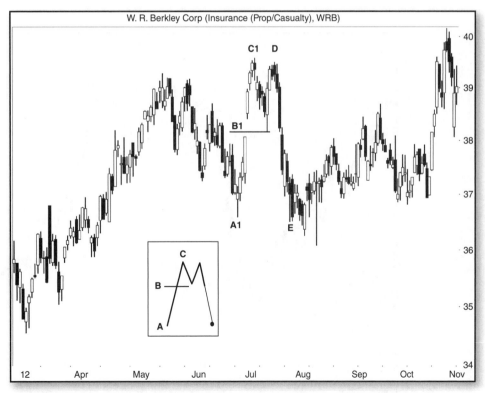

FIGURE 1.6 A swift move higher from A1 to C1 forms a big M pattern when price closes below B1 on the way to E.

Twin Peaks. Price should form two peaks in the big M. The peaks can be any shape from gently rounded turns to needle-thin spikes. Both peaks should top out near the same price.

Breakout. A breakout occurs when price *closes* below the valley between the two peaks. In Figure 1.6, that means a close below the price of B1 as the stock drops on the way to E. When a breakout happens, it changes squiggles on a price chart to a valid big M chart pattern. If price first closes above the top of the big M (C1, the taller of the two peaks in this example) before confirmation (before price closes below B1), then you do not have a big M.

M Shape. Finally, look for the overall pattern to resemble an M with tall sides. Figures 1.4 and 1.6 show this.

Identification Variation

Figure 1.7 shows an identification variation I saw many times as a big M formed. In this case, after price climbed off the March low (A), it paused and retraced for a few weeks, forming what I call a handle. Then price resumed its climb to the first peak (B), dropped some, and climbed back to the second peak (C), before plunging to E and completing the big M.

FIGURE 1.7 Price pauses on the way to forming a big M.

Handles on the way up to the first peak are rare and may obscure identification of a big M. If another handle forms on the drop to D, which mirrors the one on the left, then you probably have a complex head-and-shoulders top chart pattern. That would be a pattern with two heads and two shoulders. In such a case, you should treat it not as a big M, but as a complex head-and-shoulders top.

- A handle sometimes forms on the rise to the first peak.

- A handle on both sides of the big M means the pattern is a complex head-and-shoulders top and not a big M.

■ Buy Setup 1

The following setups use bull market data (only) from August 1996 to May 2014. I found 1,323 big Ms in 501 stocks.

Look at the inset of **Figure 1.8**. Price forms a big M (A–E) with a valley at C. Price breaks out downward and drops to E. However, the price of E is less than 10% below C. After E, the stock rises. When it closes above the top of the big M, it busts the pattern. That is the buy signal.

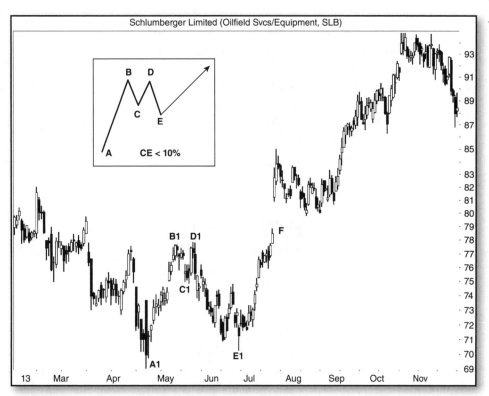

FIGURE 1.8 A busted big M leads to a good move higher.

The stock chart shows an example of a busted big M at A1 to E1. The drop from C1 to E1 measures 6% in this example, within the 10% window for busted patterns. When price climbs to F, it closes above the taller of the two peaks (D1) and busts the pattern. Since price rises more than 10% above D1 (the taller of the two peaks), it completes a single busted big M. The rise ended in July 2014 at almost 119.

Here are the steps to use this setup.

1. Qualify the chart pattern using the identification guidelines shown in Table 1.1.
2. The stock must confirm the big M by closing below the price of the valley between the two peaks (below C in Figure 1.8).
3. Price must drop less than 10% below the valley before reversing (the C to E drop).
4. Price rises and closes above the taller of the two peaks of the big M.
5. Buy at the open the next day.
6. Place a stop-loss order a penny below the bottom of the chart pattern or at a location of your choice.

Table 1.2 shows a few statistics for busted big M patterns.

1. Percentage of busted big Ms. Of the 1,323 big Ms I looked at, 33% of them busted. That means a third of the time price fails to drop more than 10% after a breakout before closing above the top of the big M. The number suggests that if you are looking for a large decline (more than 10%), then you have a 33% failure rate to start, which is huge.

2. Average rise after busting. The average rise of all types of busted big Ms (meaning single, double, and triple+ busts) is 31%.

3. Average rise after single bust. This is where busted chart patterns shine. After a big M busts, the average rise from the top of the chart pattern to the ultimate high is 47%. That gain is for big Ms that single bust only.

TABLE 1.2 Busted Big M Statistics	
Description	**Result**
1. Percentage of busted big Ms	33%
2. Average rise after busting	31%
3. Average rise after single bust	47%
4. Percentage of single busts	62%
5. Percentage of double busts	17%
6. Percentage of triple+ busts	20%

4-6. Percentage of single/double/triple+ busts. Sorting the 33% of big Ms that bust into single, double, and triple busts, we find that 62% of them bust once. Double busts cross the finish line at 17%, and three or more busts (triple+) finish at 20%.

In other words, your chance of having a single busted pattern is quite good.

■ Four Sell Setups

Figure 1.9 shows four setups, two you should look for and two you should avoid. I will discuss the performance statistics in a moment.

The trend start is the highest high or lowest low before which the stock drops or rises, respectively, at least 20%. Look for the trend start *before the launch price* of the big M. See the glossary for more details on finding the trend start.

Look at Setup 1 in the upper left of the figure. From the trend start to the first peak of the big M, the stock makes a small rise that takes a long time to reach the big M. That combination of small price rise and a long time is bad for post-breakout performance.

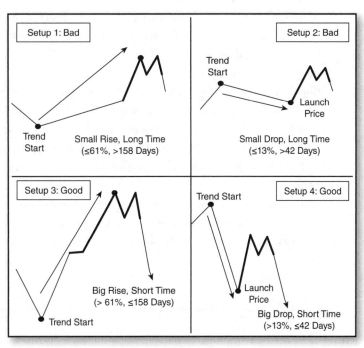

FIGURE 1.9 Four sell setups for big Ms.

Setup 2 shows another bad combination of price and time. This one has price trending *lower* to the launch price. The drop from the trend start to the launch price is small, representing a shallow decline, but it takes a long time.

Setup 3 is the first of two good variations. Look for a rising price from the trend start to the first peak in the big M. The rise should be short and yet the percentage gain should be large. That combination of short and steep can lead to a large decline after the breakout.

Similarly, Setup 4 shows a big drop in a short time from the trend start to the launch price. Those types of downdrafts tend to pull the stock lower after the breakout.

Setups 1 and 3 have price rising from the trend start and Setups 2 and 4 have it declining. A rising or falling inbound trend is important to the setups.

Setup Numbers

I measured the median time for the stock to *rise* from the trend start to the first top (158 days). The median percentage rise over that time from the low at the trend start to the high at the first top was 61%.

Using these two numbers as benchmarks, I mapped how well big Ms performed post-breakout, and **Table 1.3** shows the results. The differences between the numbers may seem minor, but a 19% drop is 46% bigger than a 13% drop. When traders speak of having an "edge," this is what they are talking about.

To reach the first peak of a big M, patterns that took longer than the median 158 days and climbed more than the median 61% showed price declining an average of 16% after the breakout.

Big Ms that had a large rise but took less time, showed the largest drops in the table: 19%. That combination corresponds to Setup 3 in Figure 1.9. When looking for big Ms that will outperform, search for a big rise (more than 61%) in a short amount of time (less than or equal to 158 days). After the breakout, the stocks tends to give back more of that rise than the other combinations of rise and time.

Since more samples will likely change these numbers, be flexible. Concentrate not on the numbers but on the shape: A big rise in a short time leads to a larger post-breakout decline. It will not always happen, of course, but that is the way to bet.

TABLE 1.3 Rising Inbound Trends: Average Loss versus Time and Percentage Drop		
Description	Big Rise (>61%)	Small Rise (≤61%)
Long time (>158 days)	−16%	−13%
Short time (≤158 days)	−19%	−17%

The worst performance comes after a small rise (less than or equal to 61%) after a long time (more than 158 days) leading to the first peak of a big M. Big Ms with that combination showed post-breakout drops averaging 13%. I show that combination in Figure 1.9, Setup 1.

To put this finding in a positive light, if you own a stock long and wish to hold onto it, then the smallest decline comes from big Ms with a small rise in a long time leading to the first top.

Table 1.4 shows the performance numbers when the inbound trend *declines* from the trend start to the launch price.

I found that the median drop was 13%, and it took 42 days for price to decline from the high at the trend start to the low at the launch price. Once I had those numbers, I could map the performance of big Ms, which Table 1.4 shows.

For example, stocks that made a big drop (more than 13%) in a short time (less than or equal to 42 days) leading to a big M, saw price decline the most after the breakout: 23%. That scenario corresponds to Setup 4 in Figure 1.9.

The worst post-breakout performance was a drop of 16%. That happened when stocks dropped less than or equal to 13% (small drop) and took longer than 42 days to reach the launch price of a big M. That combination appears as Setup 2 in Figure 1.9.

Again, use the numbers as guidance of what to look for, but pay attention to the shape of the inbound trend: short or long, steep or shallow.

Although the numbers in Tables 2.3 and 2.4 show results close to each other, give yourself an edge and trade big Ms with the best performance and avoid the worst performers. The trade may still fail, but the probabilities suggest you will do better by trading the right combination of time and price drop consistently.

Here are the steps for using the best performing setups (3 and 4).

1. Qualify the big M using the identification guidelines shown in Table 1.1.
2. Find the trend start. The trend start is the highest peak or lowest valley before which price falls or climbs (respectively) at least 20%.
3. If the trend start is above the launch price (Figure 1.9, Setup 4), then look for a steep drop of more than 13% in 42 days or fewer from the trend start to the launch price (between the black dots in the figure).

TABLE 1.4 **Declining Inbound Trends: Average Loss versus Time and Percentage Drop**

Description	Big Drop (>13%)	Small Drop (≤13%)
Long time (>42 days)	−17%	−16%
Short time (≤42 days)	−23%	−19%

4. If the trend start is below the launch price (Figure 1.9, Setup 3), then look for a steep rise from the trend start to first peak (between the black dots in the figure). The rise should be more than 61% but takes 158 days or less.
5. If both steps 3 or 4 do not apply, then the probability of a losing trade increases. Consider looking for a different big M.
6. The stock must confirm the big M by closing below the price of the valley between the two peaks.
7. Short at the open or sell a long holding the day after a breakout, or place an order to short/sell a penny below the valley between the two peaks.
8. Place a stop-loss order a penny above the top of the big M or at a location of your choice.

■ Best Stop Locations

If you trade a big M, where is the best place to put a stop-loss order in case the trade blows up? **Table 1.5** shows how often price hits two stop locations.

1. **Penny above the pattern.** Placing a stop a penny above the highest peak of the big M means the chance of being stopped out is just 1%. The average loss is 9%, and those missed trades would go on to drop 16% below the breakout price. All of the numbers are averages.
2. **Within the pattern.** Stops placed somewhere between the tallest peak and lowest valley of the big M means a 69% chance of the stop being hit. The loss is small, 3%, and those trades went on to lose an average of 17%.

The numbers suggest that a stop placed a penny above the top of the big M is the best stop location, providing you can stomach a 9% loss.

I suggest you measure the potential loss from the breakout price (use the low price of the valley between the two peaks) to the stop location. If that distance represents too large of a loss, then choose a more suitable location.

■ Place a stop-loss order a penny above the top of the big M and trail it downward as price drops.

TABLE 1.5	Stop Locations for Big Ms		
Description	Chance of Being Hit	Average Loss	Missed Trades, Loss
1. Penny above the pattern	1%	9%	16%
2. Within the pattern	69%	3%	17%

■ Configuration Trading

I gleaned the configurations in this section from visual inspection of 283 big Ms on the weekly charts, sorted by the largest decline in bull markets.

To trade these configurations, follow these basic guidelines.

1. Find a big M on the *daily* chart that obeys the identification guidelines shown in Table 1.1.
2. On the *weekly* scale, compare what you see on your chart to find a configuration that matches.
3. The day after a breakout (daily chart), short at the open, sell a long holding, or place an order to short/sell a penny below the valley between the two peaks.
4. Place a stop-loss order a penny above the top of the big M or at a location of your choice.
5. Ideally, the stock will drop to just above the launch price before the trend reverses. Close out your position then or if the stock finds substantial support along the way down. Do not let a pullback flush you out of the trade prematurely.

Figure 1.10 shows the first configuration that happened 41% of the time in the stocks I looked at.

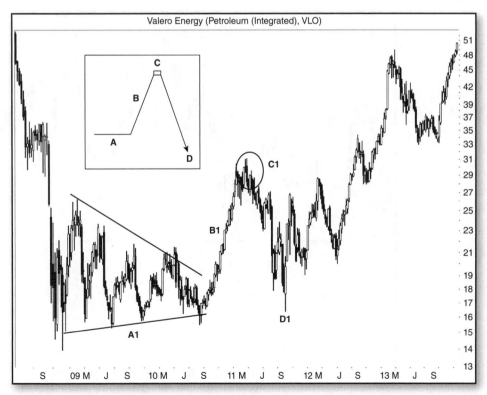

FIGURE 1.10   This is the most popular big M configuration that led to a large decline.

The ideal conditions begin at launch price A, but the trend does not have to be flat like that shown. Sometimes the price trends downward and sometimes it trends upward, so be flexible.

At B, however, often a straight-line run takes price higher, eventually forming a big M at the end of the run, C (shown as a rectangle for convenience). The run is steep and forms a straight line (few consolidation regions) most of the time, but allow exceptions. I did not put time restrictions on this since they varied all over the place.

After a downward breakout from the big M, price drops. The extent of this decline (D) varies. Price may stop above the launch price (A) to below it (I show below it in the inset).

The stock chart shows an example of this configuration. At A1, price trends up, down, or even sideways, depending on how much alcohol is in your system and which trendline you wish to use. This horizontal movement corresponds to trend A in the inset.

The B1 rise takes price higher in a nice straight-line run, heading to the big M.

At C1, buried in the weekly data, a big M appears. Price returns to earth at D1 before taking off again.

Chart Pattern Big Ms Figure 1.11 shows the next configuration. I show three variations in the inset as A, B, and C. Version A is a double top with the big M represented by the rectangle. Notice that the big M is on the second peak, not the first one.

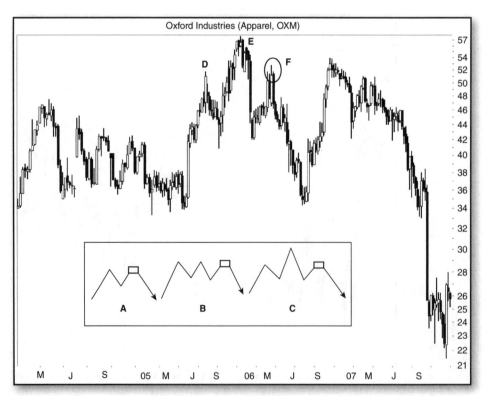

FIGURE 1.11   Big Ms form ending three types of chart patterns.

Version B is a triple top with the big M appearing on the third peak, and type C is a head-and-shoulders top with the big M on the right shoulder. The topping shape (double top, triple top, head-and-shoulders top, and so on) can be most any chart pattern, but a big M forms to end the pattern. The three shown are the most common patterns.

In these variations, price climbs to overhead resistance and forms a reversal pattern like that shown in the inset (the big M is the small box). That reversal completes and sends price tumbling. I found this configuration in 41% of the big Ms I looked at.

The stock chart shows an example. DEF is a head-and-shoulders top on the weekly scale. The big M appears buried at F, circled, but you cannot tell from the figure. Price drops after F, returning to the launch price of the DEF pattern (near 34).

The Downtrend Variation **Figure 1.12** looks like a complicated setup, but it is not. Price peaks at A and then starts a long downward trend. The stock bottoms (B) at the launch price of the big M (C). The stock rises, forms the big M, and then drops (D). Sometimes the stock will return to the launch price, reverse just above it, or go below it as I show in the figure.

The stock chart shows an example of this variation. Price makes a strong push higher to A1. There is a big M tucked in there, but that is not the big M I wish to discuss.

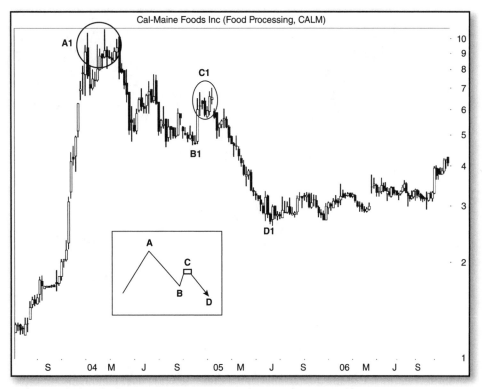

FIGURE 1.12 This big M variation occurs in a downward price trend.

Rather, price drops to B1, the launch price, and then rises to C1 where it forms a big M. When price breaks out downward, it joins with the existing downtrend (A1 to B1) and the stock digs a hole on the way to D1.

This setup is rare, happening 18% of the time.

Downward Breakout Failures

Not all configurations work as expected. Here are the ones that fail to see price drop at least 10% after the breakout from big Ms.

Figure 1.13 shows the first of two failure types. Price peaks at A, backtracks for a time, and then forms a second peak, B. B is where the big M appears. Price drops but only to C, less than 10% below the bottom of the valley between the two peaks of the big M, before a recovery ensues. The stock climbs to D, busting the big M.

The rise to D may be long or short, but (single or triple) busted patterns often perform well. The stock chart shows an example of this configuration where the stock double busts and kills a long upward gain.

After the 2009 bear market ended, the stock climbed until hitting overhead resistance, eventually forming peak A1. A big M took shape at the two peaks to the right

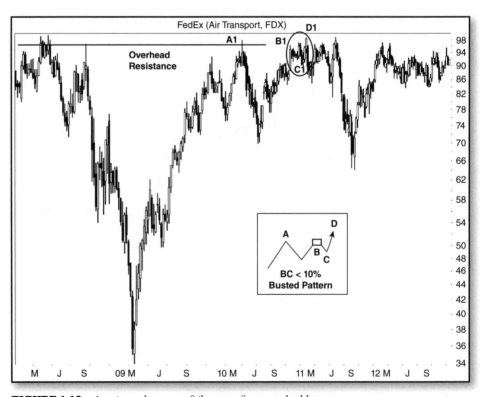

FIGURE 1.13   A twin peak pattern fails to confirm as a double top.

of B1, but it is difficult to see it on this weekly chart. A downward breakout sent the stock lower to C1, before the bulls pushed it back up to D1. In this case, the stock busted the big M and then double busted it when price closed below the bottom of the big M.

Notice that this inset is a variation of Figure 1.11, A. In Figure 1.11, the stock forms a double top that sees price make a dramatic swing lower. In Figure 1.13, the stock's bullish enthusiasm stops the decline and busts the big M just for grins. Overhead resistance kills the upward momentum, sending the stock declining.

■ This variation occurs most often: 54% of the time.

Uphill Run Not Over **Figure 1.14** shows a configuration different from the prior figure. Price makes a sustained move higher from A to B. At B, the big M acts as a reversal and sends price lower. The stock drops a short distance to C (less than 10% below the breakout) before moving higher to D. The CD move busts the downward breakout from the big M. This configuration occurs 44% of the time.

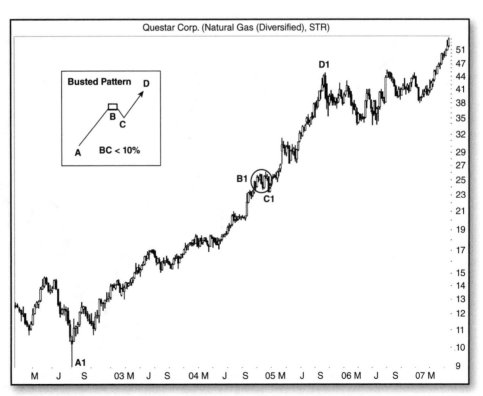

FIGURE 1.14 The upward run is not over when the big M appears.

The stock chart shows an example, but it is difficult to see on the weekly scale. Price starts the upward move at A1. That move takes the stock to B1, where it forms a big M in a large congestion region, circled.

Traders might think that after such a long uptrend, the upward move *must* be over. After the downward breakout, they know they are right and pile in. Once everyone has sold the stock short, there is no one left to push the stock lower (C1). Bullish buying whips the stock upward, launching another stage on its rise to the sky (D1). A buying frenzy unfolds when the shorts cover their losing positions.

Figure 1.14 is similar to Figure 1.10 except that price dropped from C to D in Figure 1.10. In Figure 1.14, the stock has enough bullish momentum to bust the big M and soar.

■ Measure Rule

The measure rule is not a rule at all, but a guideline that suggests how far price might decline below the breakout.

Figure 1.15 shows an example of how the measure rule works.

FIGURE 1.15   Use the height of the big M to help gauge the decline.

The big M appears at AB with C forming as the lowest valley between the two peaks. A is the higher of the two peaks, and it has a high price of 57.00. C is the lowest valley, and it has a low price of 53.30 for a big M height of 3.70.

Subtract the height from the valley (C) to get a target: $53.30 - 3.70$, or 49.60. I show the target as D. In this example, the stock easily reaches the target, but that is not always the case. In fact, this rule works just 57% of the time.

For a more dependable target, use half the height in the computation. Thus, the new target would be $53.30 - 3.70/2$, or 51.45. The half-height works 82% of the time.

Rather than rely on a computation, I prefer to search for areas where the stock might stall or rebound. I use the measure rule to give me a target, but then I look for nearby support where the stock might run aground and stop sinking.

Also, consider the launch price as a target. I found that the big M will decline to or below the launch price 60% of the time. To be safe, add a margin onto the launch price. In other words, do not depend on the stock dropping all the way down to the launch price. In my trading, I found a target above the launch price to work well.

- The measure rule works 57% of the time.

■ Trading

Let us divide trading tactics into trading styles. For people who like to buy and hold, also known as investors, a big M is nothing to worry about. The average drop below the breakout price is 17% and the median is 14%.

A prudent long-term investor should monitor his or her holdings. If price makes a significant decline, such as when a company is on the way to bankruptcy, then consider exiting the position. Use fundamental analysis to confirm the dire situation and act accordingly.

You should avoid shorting a stock showing a big M when holding for the long-term unless conditions at the company are desperate. The 17% average drop is for 1,323 perfect trades. You may get in late and exit early, cutting the trade's profit and risking a loss.

Instead, why not buy a busted big M? I cover that next.

Position Traders

How often does a big M lead to a large drop? A trend change (from rising to falling) means a drop of at least 20%. In a bull market, 33% of big Ms see price drop more than 20% after the breakout. Thus, if you are long the stock and a big M appears, then you could suffer a big hit to the wallet or purse a third of the time, on average.

If you are short the stock, then 2 out of 3 trades (67%) will not make a large (greater than 20%) decline. I do not think that big Ms represent a good chart pattern to short just by themselves. To make money, your timing has to be exquisite or the company's situation is precarious. Look for additional factors that would cause the stock to drop by a large amount.

A better strategy is to find a big M that busts and take a long position when price closes above the top of the chart pattern. Recall that the average rise after a single bust is a mouthwatering 47% (but the median is only 32%, which is still tasty). Yum.

Figure 1.16 shows a big M that appears at AC (the peak-to-peak price variation is just 3%), and it confirms as a valid big M when price closes below B.

The stock drops to D (a decline of 7% below B) and then reverses. A buy signals the day after E. E is where price closes above C, the highest peak in the big M.

Look at how far price soars in this example! Not all busted patterns will perform this well, of course.

Swing and Day Traders

For swing and day traders, a big M is tailor made. Place a sell-short order a penny below the breakout to get in when the chart pattern confirms. Place a stop a penny

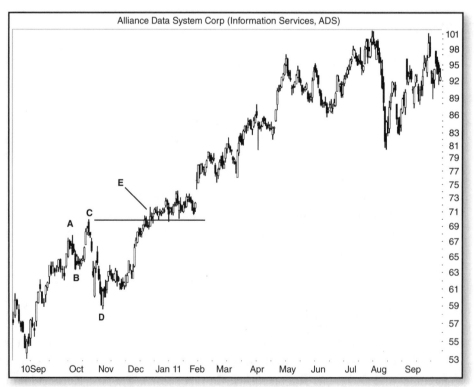

FIGURE 1.16   This is an example of trading a busted big M.

above the top of the big M and lower the stop as price drops. Then ride the stock down.

Watch for a pullback, which happens 63% of the time. Do not get shaken out of the trade because of it. Because pullbacks happen frequently, you may want to wait for a pullback to occur and short after the pullback ends. **Figure 1.17** shows an example of this.

The big M appears at CD and it confirms at E when the stock closes below the horizontal line. Notice that this big M has a handle (B). I discussed that in "Identification Variation."

Suppose that you were on vacation or missed the opportunity to short the stock on the breakout (E). Recognize that the ultimate low happens 36% of the time between the breakout and the pullback (between E and G). I would be concerned with the depth of the plunge during the pullback (F), because the stock makes its way down to support before rebounding.

A pullback sucks price back up to G. I would wait for price to close below the low of the valley between CD, just to confirm that a downtrend is happening. That occurs the day before H.

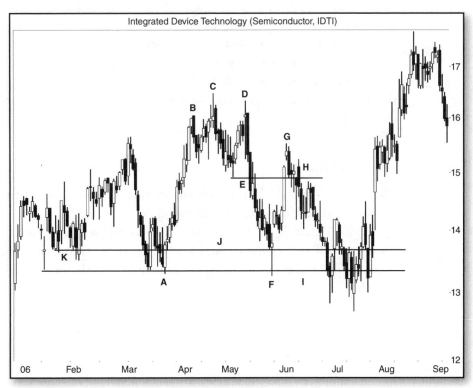

FIGURE 1.17   Short after a pullback completes.

Before placing the short, measure the distance from the entry and exit points to determine whether the stock is worth the risk of a trade. The risk would be a close above the top of the big M. That is the location where a stop order should be (or a close location of your choice). As price drops, trail the stop lower.

What about the target? Since line I is also drawn at the launch price, I would place my cover order above this (many times the stock will stop dropping just above the launch price, hence the desire to exit above line I in this case).

I drew line J where I would cover the short. The line begins at the bottom of congestion area K and extends to the right.

In this example, the stock dropped through line J, reached line I, and kept going down for a time in July before making a sustained rise.

■ Closing Position

The view from the top of a big M provides an exciting glimpse of the price landscape. By using the launch price as a target, you can determine how far the stock will decline and be correct 60% of the time (see Figure 1.1).

By using the information in this chapter, you can further refine the price movement to include pullbacks and busted patterns. You will know not to worry when a handle appears on the left side of a big M.

After finding the trend start and comparing your situation to Figure 1.9, you can gauge how well your big M will perform after the breakout. That information could save you money, allowing you to sell now instead of suffering through the decline, or it could give you the confidence to hold on and weather the brief downturn.

Setup Synopsis

The charts in **Figure 1.18** may help you identify the various types of trading setups. See the associated figure for an explanation.

"Occurs" in the figure means how often I found the configuration in the stocks I looked at. If two configurations apply to your situation, then the one with a more frequent occurrence (a higher percentage) is the one you should choose to follow.

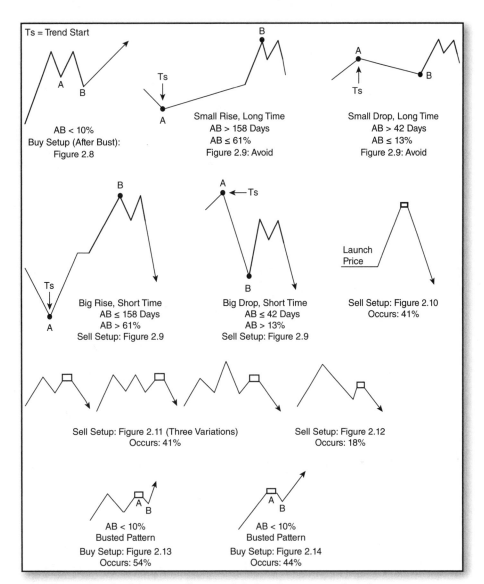

FIGURE 1.18 This figure is a collection of ideal trading setups and configurations.

CHAPTER 2

Big W

O n the basis of an average rise of 45%, the big W chart pattern sounds like it has something extra to offer traders and investors. However, the details tell the truth. The median rise is much lower: 30%. That is still a terrific gain, but it is like a platoon leader yelling "Charge!" and running toward the enemy well ahead of his platoon. What do you think will happen to him?

Picture two valleys that bottom near the same price. The left side going into the pattern is unusually tall. The hope is that the right side will also be tall. That configuration, a twin bottom with tall sides, is a big W. It acts as a reversal of the downward trend.

Figure 2.1 shows the typical behavior after a big W chart pattern ends.

Price is the solid line forming the twin bottom pattern. The launch price is the location where the trend down into the big W begins. Often the decline is a straight-line affair with few or no pauses (ideal case) leading to the first bottom.

Price bounces twice near the same price, forming two valleys, and climbs to the breakout. When the stock closes above the price of the center peak, it is called a breakout, and it confirms the big W as a valid chart pattern.

After a breakout, a throwback occurs frequently (more about that in a bit).

In the ideal case, price continues rising until reaching the launch price, which happens 77% of the time. The average rise is 45% above the breakout price.

■ Price returns to the launch price an average of 77% of the time.

Throwbacks

Figure 2.2 shows a big W as ABC although it also includes the tall left side.

A throwback begins almost immediately after the breakout when the stock returns to the breakout price. By convention, this looping action must occur within a month.

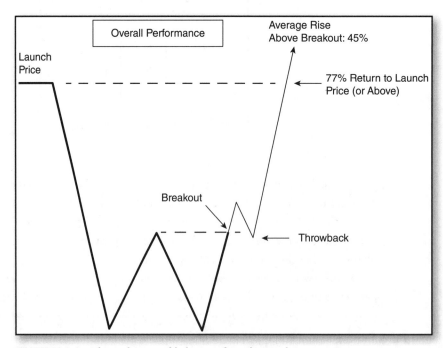

FIGURE 2.1   This is the typical behavior after a big W chart pattern.

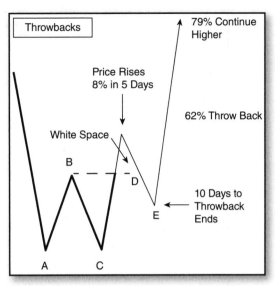

FIGURE 2.2　Over half the time a big W will see a throwback.

A breakout happens when price closes above the peak (B) between the two bottoms (AC). In 62% of big Ws, a throwback occurs. The profile of a throwback sees price rise an average of 8% in 5 days. Then the stock returns to the breakout price and often goes lower before the decline ends (D to E). On average, a throwback takes 10 days to complete (measured from the breakout day).

After a throwback ends, 79% of the time the stock continues higher, closing above the breakout price (B).

■ A throwback occurs 62% of the time and price continues higher 79% of the time.

Busted Big W

Figure 2.3 shows the performance of busted big W chart patterns.

A big W busts when price fails to rise at least 10% above the breakout, reverses, and closes below the bottom (the lower of the two valleys) of the big W. The 10% number is arbitrary, but it serves as a good benchmark. You can think of this movement as a throwback that got carried away.

I found that 16% of big Ws bust. The 16% number is comparatively small, perhaps because the 45% average rise is so big. In other words, big Ws tend to perform well normally, so few bust.

When they single bust, price drops an average of 22% below the bottom of the big W. That is a significant decline. Sell Setup 1 discusses how to trade a busted big W and explains single, double, and triple busted big Ws.

■ Sixteen percent of big Ws will bust an upward breakout.

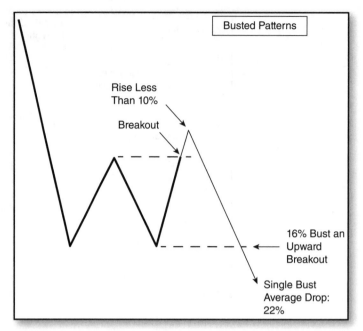

FIGURE 2.3   Performance of busted big Ws.

■ Identification

Figure 2.4 shows a terrific example of a big W on the daily scale. The launch price is at A, which is where the stock jumps off a cliff in a straight-line plunge down to the first bottom, B, with few bounces off the cliff face along the way.

At the bottom, price bounces and forms peak C before the stock collapses again and creates valley D. In this example, the stay at D is brief and price moves up, peaking at E, completing the big W shape.

The stock throws back to the breakout price (the price of C) on the way down to F before resuming the advance.

Table 2.1 shows the identification guidelines for big Ws.

Launch Price. This corresponds to point A in Figure 2.4. The launch price is where the big W begins. It is located at the top of the tall left side of the big W.

Fall. Price should plunge leading to the first bottom. An example of this is the nightmare drop from A to B in Figure 2.4. Often the drop is a straight-line run lower with few or no significant pauses along the way. The plunge should be steep, not sedate, like starting down a cliff instead of the gentile roll of a foothill.

Height. Height is one of the key attributes that separates a double bottom from a big W. Use common sense when selecting big Ws for height, but a good guideline is that the decline from A to B should be at least 1.5 to 2 times the difference between C and B.

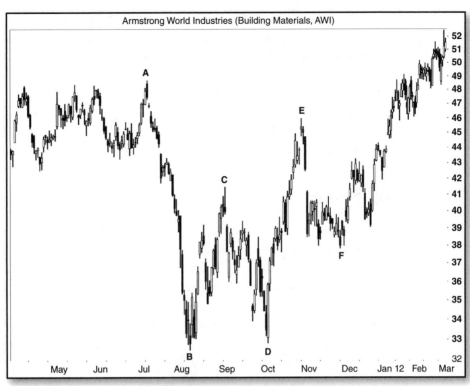

FIGURE 2.4   This big W looks like a double bottom with tall sides.

TABLE 2.1	**Identification Guidelines**
Characteristic	**Discussion**
Launch Price	The launch price is where the big W begins. It is located on the left side, at the top of the big W. It is where the swift drop into the first bottom begins. Think of it as the edge of a cliff.
Fall	Starting from the launch price, the stock makes a steep drop, often in a straight-line run, leading down to the first bottom. The ideal pattern has no pauses along the way.
Height	The height from the launch price to the first bottom should be extensive, often twice as tall as the distance from the first bottom to the peak between the two valleys.
Twin Bottoms	Two valleys bottom out near the same price but allow variation. The average price difference between bottoms is less than 2%.
Breakout	When price closes above the highest peak between the two bottoms, a breakout occurs and you have a valid big W. If, instead of breaking out upward, price first closes below the lowest valley, then you do not have a big W.
W Shape	The completed chart pattern should look like a W.

Twin Bottoms. Look for two valleys that bottom near the same price. Often the two bottoms will *not* share the same price but are usually close.

Breakout. A breakout occurs when price *closes* above the peak between the two bottoms. In other words, when price closes above C on the way to E, it breaks out. A breakout confirms the chart squiggles as a valid big W.

If price closes below the lowest valley (B in Figure 2.4) before closing above the price at C, then you do not have a big W.

W Shape. The overall shape should look like a W with tall sides.

■ Four Buy Setups

Consider the four situations shown in **Figure 2.5**. The numbers represent the median movement of stocks before a big W appears. Median means half the stocks perform worse and half better. Use the numbers as guidance, not as absolute boundaries. I will discuss the numbers in Setup Numbers.

Starting clockwise from the upper left, Setup 1 is a sheep: baaaad. Price rises from A to B (the trend start to the launch price), taking longer than 84 days but rising 46% or less. Unfortunately, the big W appears in a trend that is reluctant to move higher. The upward breakout fails and price plummets.

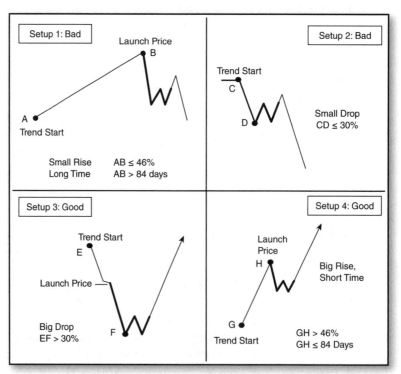

FIGURE 2.5 Shown are two setups to avoid and two worth trying.

Avoid this setup.

Setup 2 is also bad. Often you see this setup in bear markets when stocks hurtle themselves onto the ground. The initial drop is small (30% or less), from C to D, and then the twin bottoms of a big W appear. Because the C to D move is so short in both time and price, there is not much to reverse. After the big W confirms (that is, after price closes above the peak between the two bottoms), price climbs a bit but then reverses and continues down, making a long freefall.

Setup 3 is one to shop for. The drop from E to F represents an extensive percentage decline (more than 30%). When the big W reversal occurs, the downtrend is most likely over and the stock has been battered enough to want to recover. The move after the big W is a tasty reward for traders. This setup is bottom-fishing, and it represents a wonderful buying opportunity just as or just after a bear market ends.

Setup 4 also shows a winner. The rise from the trend start to the launch price (G to H) is steep (big rise in a short time) before a big W appears. After the big W, price joins the uptrend current and zips higher, making a long and rewarding advance. This is a momentum play. It works best in a *trending* bull market.

Setup Numbers

Table 2.2 shows the average gain for stocks with big Ws sorted by the time from the *trend start to the first bottom* (median 83 days) and percentage drop (median 30%). This table corresponds to Setups 2 and 3 in Figure 2.5.

Look at the results of the Big Drop column: 49% and 50%. Because the numbers are almost identical, the length of the inbound trend is not important to performance. It does not matter whether the trend lasts for 60 days or 100 days. The performance results are the same.

Performance only varies significantly when you compare the *size* of the incoming drop: big or small. That is why Figure 2.5 shows two variations, a small and a big drop.

For the best results, find big Ws where the inbound trend results in a decline larger than 30%.

■ The size of the drop from the trend start to the first bottom is more important than how long it takes to get there.

Table 2.3 shows the performance of big Ws when the trend start is *below the launch price*. In other words, when the trend rises going into the big W. That scenario appears in Setups 1 and 4 of Figure 2.5.

TABLE 2.2 Falling Inbound Trends: Average Gain versus Time and Percentage Drop		
Description	Big Drop (>30%)	Small Drop (≤30%)
Long time (>83 days)	49%	38%
Short time (≤83 days)	50%	40%

TABLE 2.3	Rising Inbound Trends: Average Gain versus Time and Percentage Rise	
Description	Big Rise (>46%)	Small Rise (≤46%)
Long time (>84 days)	42%	32%
Short time (≤84 days)	58%	51%

The best combination of percentage rise and time is for the stock to make a big move upward (more than 46%) in 84 days or less leading to the launch date. Big Ws with that combination showed post-breakout gains averaging 58%.

The worst-performing combination is a small rise that takes a long time (Setup 1) to reach the launch price. Avoid those situations.

Here are the steps for using the best-performing setups (3 and 4).

1. Qualify the big W using the identification guidelines shown in Table 2.1.
2. Find the trend start. The trend start is the highest peak or lowest valley before which price falls or climbs (respectively) at least 20%.
3. If the trend start is above the launch price (Setup 3), then look for a drop more than 30% from the trend start to the first valley of the big W (between the black dots in the figure).
4. If the trend start is below the launch price (Setup 4), then look for a steep rise from the trend start to the launch price (between the black dots in the figure). The rise should be more than 46% in 84 days or less.
5. If both steps 3 and 4 do not apply, then the probability of a losing trade increases. Consider looking for a different big W.
6. The stock must confirm the big W by closing above the price of the peak between the two valleys.
7. Place a buy order a penny above the peak between the two bottoms or buy at the open the next day.
8. Place a stop-loss order a penny below the bottom of the big W or at a location of your choice.

Sell Setup 1

The failure rate for big Ws is comparatively small, so selling short is not recommended. Even if you own a big W that busts, the *average* decline is not huge (16%). However, every loss may hurt, and a few outlier big Ws can significantly damage your wallet or purse, so let us take a closer look.

The inset of **Figure 2.6** shows how this setup unfolds in the ideal case. In 63% of the cases, the trend start (A) is above the launch price (B). That means the big W forms in a downward price trend.

The rectangle represents the big W (C). After an upward breakout, price climbs but rises less than 10% (D) before reversing and closing below the bottom of the big

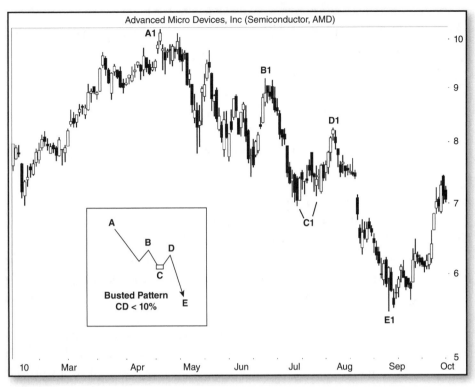

FIGURE 2.6 Wait for price to bust a big W.

W. When that happens, the stock busts the upward breakout. That is the sell signal for a long holding or a sell short signal for a new position.

The stock continues lower to single bust the pattern (E) 51% of the time.

The stock chart shows an example of this setup on the daily scale. A1 is where the trend starts. B1 is the launch price for big W C1. The stock breaks out upward from the big W and climbs to D1, a rise of 5% above confirmation.

The stock reverses and busts the big W when it closes below the lower of the two C1 bottoms. Price continues down to E1, a drop of 21% below the bottom of the big W.

If you want to avoid this situation or maybe you have a compelling desire to short this setup, here is what you should look for.

1. Qualify the big W using the identification guidelines shown in Table 2.1.
2. The stock must confirm the big W by closing above the price of the peak between the two valleys.
3. The rise above the breakout must be less than 10%.
4. Price then reverses and closes below the lower of the two bottoms of the big W.
5. Sell a long holding or short at the open the next day.
6. Place a stop-loss order a penny above the breakout price (the peak between the two valleys) or at a location of your choice.

TABLE 2.4	Statistics for Busted Big Ws	
Description		**Result**
1. Percentage of big Ws that bust		16%
2. Average drop after busting		14%
3. Average drop after single bust		22%
4. Percentage of single busts		51%
5. Percentage of double busts		35%
6. Percentage of triple+ busts		14%

Before doing any of this, look at the statistics.

Table 2.4 shows statistics for busted big W patterns.

1. Percentage of big Ws that bust. Big Ws bust just 16% of the time. That means only 16% of big Ws see price climb less than 10% after the breakout before suffering a significant loss. That may not sound like a high percentage until it happens to you. Even so, busted big Ws are as rare as seeing cedar waxwings in my backyard.

2. Average drop after busting. The average decline for big Ws that bust (single, double, and triple) is 14%. I consider that a mild decline. A large decline is more than 20% (a trend change). Those kinds of drops provide food for my nightmares.

3–6. Percentage of single/double/triple+ busts. Of the 16% that bust, 51% of those were single busts, 35% were double busts, and the remainder (14%) busted more than twice. For an explanation of single, double, and triple busts, refer to the glossary.

■ Best Stop Locations

Table 2.5 shows how often price hits two stop locations, within the big W or below it.

1. Within the pattern. If you place a stop-loss order somewhere between the lower of the two bottoms and the peak between the two bottoms, the chance of the order being triggered is 73%. That is huge!

TABLE 2.5	Stop Locations for Big Ws		
Description	**Chance of Being Hit**	**Average Loss**	**Missed Trades, Gains/Losses**
1. Within the pattern	73%	4%	46%
2. Penny below the pattern	2%	9%	47%

The average loss you will suffer is 4%, and the trades you were stopped out of would have reversed and climbed an average of 46%.

2. Penny below the pattern. A better place for the stop-loss order is a penny below the bottom of the big W. That order would be hit 2% of the time, on average, but the loss would amount to 9%. That loss is larger than I like to see (of course, I do not like to see any size loss). The missed trades would go on to make 47%.

- Place a stop-loss order a penny below the bottom of the big W and trail it upward as price rises.

■ Configuration Trading

To trade the following configurations, follow these guidelines but make adjustments as necessary.

1. Find a big W on the *daily* chart that obeys the identification guidelines shown in Table 2.1.
2. Using the *weekly* scale, match what you see on your chart to one of the configurations. Figures 2.18 and 2.19 should help.
3. Buy at the open the day after the breakout (daily chart) or place an order to buy a penny above the peak between the two valleys.
4. Place a stop-loss order a penny below the bottom of the big W or at a location of your choice.
5. Ideally, the stock will rise to the launch price before the trend reverses. Close out your position then or if the stock hits substantial resistance along the way up. Do not let a throwback cash you out of the position prematurely.

I sorted my database of big Ws according to large post-breakout gains in a bull market. The following three configurations were the most popular.

Figure 2.7 shows the variation that occurred most often, 51% of the time in the 226 patterns I looked at. The inset shows the ideal configuration. The figure reminds me of the time our car overheated on the way up a mountain. We waited for the engine to cool and then were on our way.

Price rises over the long term from A to the big W at B. The breakout is upward from the big W, of course, and it sends price higher, to C.

The stock chart shows an example on the weekly scale. The stock starts the uptrend at A1, and it rises for a long time, to B1, where a big W forms. You might think that after such a long run, the chart pattern would bust, and yet price keeps moving higher to C1. Stocks in the 1990s participated in a strong bull market so maybe that has much to do with performance, but charts that are more recent show similar behavior, too.

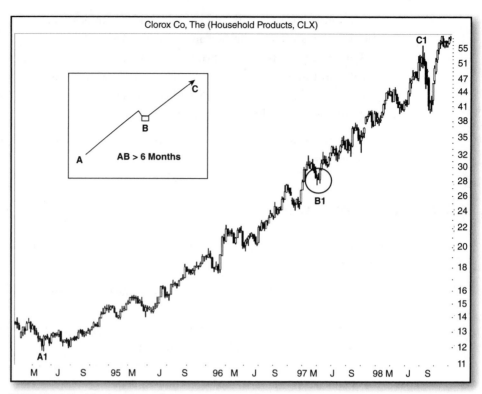

FIGURE 2.7 This big W acted as a continuation of an upward move.

If you see a big W forming after a long-term run (more than 6 months), consider buying the stock. If price reverses and closes below the bottom of the big W, then sell (or let a stop-loss order close out the position).

The Reversal

Figure 2.8 shows an example of where the big W forces a change in the downward price trend. This configuration happened 40% of the time in the stocks I looked at.

The chart is on the weekly scale, which I use to find configurations such as these. The inset shows the ideal case.

Price drops over the long term from A to B where it forms a big W. The AB downtrend can be shorter than six months, but most times, you will see it longer.

The big W breaks out upward and reverses the downtrend. Price moves up from B to C in a strong push higher.

Sometimes this configuration appears after a bear market ends, so it represents a wonderful profit opportunity.

The stock chart shows an example of this behavior. Price powers into the ground from A1 to B1. At B1, a big W appears. The downtrend reverses and price moves higher, rising to C1 before encountering overhead resistance that stops the upward run.

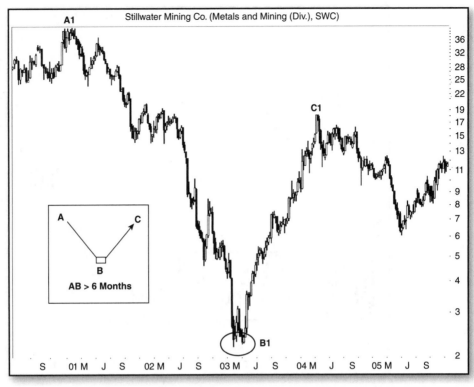

FIGURE 2.8   This big W signals a trend change.

This type of configuration works best just after a bear market ends. After a long-term downtrend, buy the stock on the breakout from the big W. Place a stop-loss order a penny below the bottom of the big W. This method will get you into an uptrend at the start of the trend.

Flat Base

I argued with myself whether to show **Figure 2.9** or not because it only happens 9% of the time. In this configuration, the stock moves sideways for a time before dipping down to the big W. I show that as the AB move.

On the weekly charts, this sideways progression is easy to spot. It is long term, often a year or longer.

After the upward breakout from the big W, the stock rises to C. I did see one instance (so it is rare) when the stock moved horizontally for several months after the big W before rising, so be flexible.

The stock chart shows an example where price is range bound at A1. I highlight this sideways movement by the two horizontal lines. The big W appears at B1 followed by a strong push higher, to C1 (weekly chart).

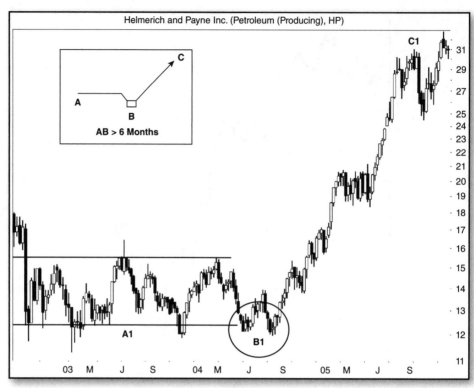

FIGURE 2.9   A sideways trend precedes a big W.

In this situation, when you see a big W, look to the left on the weekly scale and see if a flat base is present. The flat base can be irregular shaped, a rugged up and down terrain that tends to move horizontally instead of making a sustained trend higher or lower (that is, a trend that punches out of the trading range). A breakout from this trading range can lead to a big move upward, especially if the stock has been trending sideways for a year or more.

Place a stop-loss order a penny below the bottom of the big W and trail it upward as price rises.

■ 5% Failures

I found only 57 big Ws that failed to rise at least 5% after the breakout. Those failures created five varieties, but only two are worth discussing at length. Here is the first.

Figure 2.10 shows the configuration that happens 46% of the time (weekly scale) in Inset 1. The stock rises over the long term from A to B and then begins a short

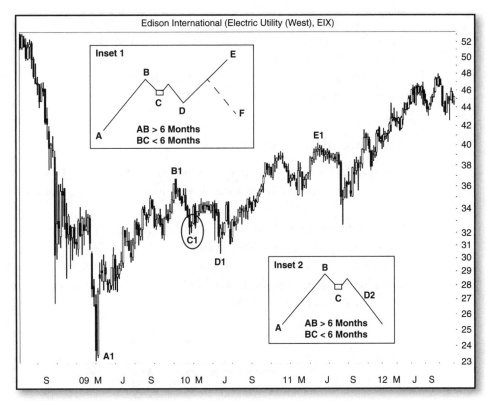

FIGURE 2.10 The uptrend ends for a time in a retrace where a big W appears.

retrace into the big W at C. The big W breaks out upward and price climbs less than 5% until peaking. The retrace resumes and price sinks to D.

The ABCD pattern reminds me of a chart pattern called the simple ABC correction. The BCD stair-step decline is the "ABC" drop in an upward price trend. We now return to your regularly scheduled programming.

After bottoming at D, the stock recovers. In 46% of the cases, the stock follows this configuration and climbs to E. However, in 11% of the configurations, the stock turns down and heads to F.

The stock chart shows an example of this configuration. Price bottoms at A1 and rises up to B1 taking over six months to get there. Then the stock reverses and drops to C1 where the big W hides (weekly chart). The upward breakout busts when the stock drops to D1.

After flushing out the bulls, the stock recovers and rises to E1, the post-bust ultimate high. That means E1 is the highest high after D1 before price drops at least 20%.

There is another variation shown in Inset 2. The stock follows the same ABC path until D2. At D2, the stock plays dead and just continues down. This configuration happens 7% of the time.

The three variations (Inset 1 path E, path F, and Inset 2), represent 64% of the patterns that failed to show large post-breakout gains.

Downtrend Reversal Failure

Figure 2.11 shows the stock trending down from A to B over the long term. The inbound downtrend is what distinguishes this configuration from the prior one.

A big W appears at B and traders think, nay, hope that the downtrend is over. Price breaks out upward and coasts to C but then reverses. Uh-oh.

Often the BC rise is small, less than 10%. When the stock continues lower to D, it busts the upward breakout. That sends bottom-fishing traders screaming their heads off. Perhaps you have heard them.

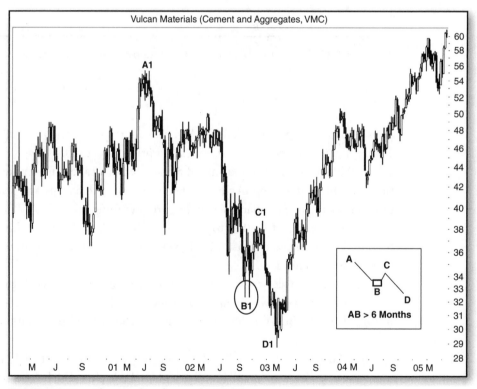

FIGURE 2.11 After trending down, a big W fails.

The stock chart on the weekly scale shows an example of this configuration. Price peaks at A1 and steps down on the way to the big W (B1). After this, the stock recovers but only to C1 before continuing lower to D1.

- This variation occurred 18% of the time.

■ The Measure Rule

The measure rule helps determine price targets for chart patterns. In many cases, the rule computes the height of the chart pattern added to the breakout price. Let us look at how the rule works for big Ws.

Figure 2.12 shows a big W that bottoms at AC and peaks at B. The height is BA. In this case, it is 20.24, or $174.41 - 154.17$. Add the height to the breakout price (B) to get a target: $174.41 + 20.24$, or 194.65. I show the target on the figure.

The measure rule works 78% of the time.

FIGURE 2.12 Use the measure rule to compute a target price.

The way I use the rule is to compute a target and then look for nearby overhead resistance. I assume that the stock will pause or even reverse at that resistance, not at the computed target.

If you wish to be more conservative, then slice the height in half, 10.12 in this case, and add that to the breakout price: 174.41 + 20.24/2, or 184.53. Price reaches the closer target 91% of the time.

■ Trading

After reviewing the charts of big Ws and confirming my ideas with statistics, I think these tactics will help you select winning big Ws or help avoid losing situations.

The Throwback Entry

Consider **Figure 2.13**. Imagine that you have found a big W in a stock that interests you. Unfortunately, you are late to spot the pattern. The big W has confirmed as a valid chart pattern and a throwback has occurred. Which setup, 1 or 2, represents the better profit opportunity?

In Setup 1, the stock has a throwback (A) that drops price below the breakout (the dashed line). Setup 2 has the stock remaining above the breakout price during the throwback (B).

The answer: Setup 2 represents the better profit opportunity. Here are the stats. Big Ws that had a throwback drift below the breakout price (Setup 1) showed gains that averaged 39%. When price remained above the breakout price (Setup 2) during a throwback, the stocks gained an average of 49%.

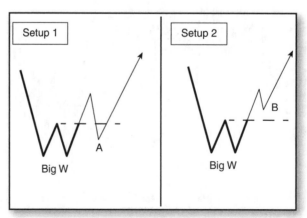

FIGURE 2.13 Setup 2 shows the better entry when a throwback remains above the breakout price.

Early Entry

Once you have selected a big W to trade, when do you buy the stock? The statistics in this chapter and, in most chapters of this book, stress that you should wait for confirmation (breakout). Once the pattern closes above the breakout price, then it confirms the chart pattern as valid, and it is safe to buy. Doing so before confirmation could lead to a loss when price reverses and fails to confirm the big W. Keep in mind that even though price confirms the pattern as valid, it does not guarantee how far price will climb. The big W could be a dud anyway.

I show the standard entry method in **Figure 2.14**. The big W begins at A and bottoms at B and C. The confirmation price is at D, a horizontal line that connects the tallest peak between bottoms B and C. Buy when price closes above line D. Often, I place a buy order a penny above the line, and it gets me into the stock in a timely manner and at a good price.

Consider a different method. This is for aggressive traders because it entails more risk but higher reward.

Draw a down-sloping trendline starting from the launch price, A, so that it touches but does not cross through the peak (E) between the two bottoms. I show that in the figure as line AG. Notice that the line touches point E but does not cross through it.

FIGURE 2.14   Two ways to buy a big W are shown.

Buy when price either closes above this line or touches it (at F). Note that you will be buying before confirmation (D), so it is possible the chart pattern will not confirm as a valid big W, likely leaving you with a loss. If it works, you will be buying into a big W at a lower price than normal.

Overhead Resistance

Notice the circled area on the drop from A to B in Figure 2.14. Try to select big Ws without such knots of congestion. Those knots represent areas of overhead resistance that could kill an upward move.

That is what happens in Figure 2.14 at H. Price bumps up against overhead resistance and reverses. H is the ultimate high, so this big W saw price climb just 14% before tumbling.

Figure 2.15 shows an ideal situation that I have come across in my trading. Price follows a trend down from A to the start of the big W at B. The big W bottoms at CD, confirms as a valid chart pattern, and climbs to E. Then it bumps up against overhead resistance setup by the down-sloping trendline AE.

I remember facing a buying opportunity in Southwest Airlines in a similar situation. A down-sloping trendline posed nearby overhead resistance, so I skipped the trade (the potential profit was too small). The stock climbed to the trendline and then tumbled, just as I predicted. A loss evaded. Whew!

Avoid such situations when bottom-fishing and overhead resistance, setup by a down-sloping trendline, looms above the stock. Look elsewhere for a more promising situation.

The difference between this setup and the one shown in Figure 2.14 is that Figure 2.15 has confirmed the big W and price has climbed to the trendline. In

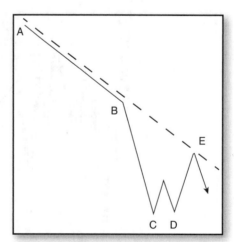

FIGURE 2.15 Overhead resistance setup by a trendline stops the rise from a big W.

Figure 2.14, you have not purchased the stock yet. You are using the trendline as an early entry mechanism.

Launch Price

What makes big Ws unique is the launch price (yes, other chart patterns have a launch price, too, but work with me here and pretend). The launch price is where the stock begins a strong downward move that leads to the first bottom of the big W.

Figure 2.16 shows an example. I use point A as the launch price because it begins a straight-line run down to the first bottom (B) without any pauses. On the return trip, when price is rising, I would expect the stock to stall at the congestion region shown at A (circled). That happens at D.

Like the measure rule, we can use the launch price as a target. Determine where the launch price is and assume that price will near it after an upward breakout. This method works 77% of the time.

Because the launch price is often a peak, congestion area, or other type of overhead resistance, it makes for a good target. Be conservative when selecting a target and assume that price will far short of the launch price. Sometimes it does.

FIGURE 2.16   Price almost returns to the launch price after the breakout.

Actual Trade

Figure 2.17 shows (on the weekly scale) a round-trip trade I made using a big W chart pattern.

The big W begins at A, the launch price, and ends at F when the stock returns to the launch price. Between those two points is double bottom BC. The two valleys do not bottom at the same price, but the W shape of the AF pattern is clear.

I started looking to buy the stock in mid-April, anticipating a 38% retrace of the climb off the March 6 low (C). If I had placed the buy order at 4.55 (near the 38% retrace value of 4.59), it would have triggered at D when the stock made a quick journey south. But I did not place the order. Instead, I waited for confirmation.

That happened at E. I bought on May 1 (the tall bar to the right of E) and received a fill at 5.94. The target was the 9 to 12 range with an option to hit 13, if I was lucky.

I sat and watched the stock rise. In late April 2010 (G), I became nervous and placed a conditional order to sell at 9.93 (the horizontal line at H). I either let the order expire or removed it because the stock eased below 9.93 in the summer, and yet I held onto the position.

FIGURE 2.17 A big W trade made 194%.

In early July, I became nervous again and used limit and stop orders to protect my position. After Intel reported their best quarter in a decade, I canceled the stop order, figuring this company will do well, too.

I learned in September that insiders sold stock in the company when price peaked in April (G). I thought the price would make for a good stop loss location.

In January 2011, I feared the stock would drop back to 13, then 12, and then 11 (which it did later in the year). A month later, I placed a stop below a minor low at 17.55.

On February 23, the stop triggered and sold at 17.5505 for a gain of 194%. The stock dropped that day on market weakness. I thought I sold too soon and expected a rebound. But the stock kept sliding. That made me smile since I sold at a peak and the stock dropped thereafter.

I bought in near the breakout of the big W and sold when the stock peaked. Few trades occur as well timed as this one and with such a large gain. I consider myself fortunate, but if you trade stocks long enough, you will have perfect trades like this, too.

Application   Let us apply the information in this chapter to Figure 2.17.

Setups 1 and 4 from Figure 2.5 do not apply because the stock drops from the trend start to the launch price. Those setups require the inbound trend to rise, not fall.

The drop from the trend start to the first bottom measures 81%, eliminating Setup 2. Only Setup 3 applies. The drop from the trend start to the first bottom is about six months long. Table 2.2 shows that combination of drop (81%) and time (six months) gives an average rise of 49%, the second highest in the table. That is good news.

The configuration shown in Figure 2.6 applies only to busted big Ws. Our big W did not bust.

The only other configurations that have downward price trends are Figures 2.8 and 2.11.

The bear market ended in March 2009, but many stocks started turning bullish sooner, including this one (in November 2008 after the first bottom).

The stock made a higher second bottom, suggesting this was an ugly double bottom chart pattern. I do not cover that chart pattern in this book, but it is one that reliably signals the end of a downtrend. Even if you did not know that, the bullish situation becomes clear as price rises 96% from the first bottom to confirmation.

Because we can expect a strong upward move after a bear market ends, that eliminates Figure 2.11, leaving Figure 2.8. In fact, the stock chart shown in Figure 2.8 is remarkably similar to our situation. That is also good news because the figure suggests a good gain.

If you need a better reason for booting Figure 2.11 aside, it only occurs 18% of the time compared to 40% for Figure 2.8.

The information in this chapter suggests good performance from the big W shown in Figure 2.17, and that is what happened.

■ Closing Position

The launch price for a big W is even sweeter than the one for a big M. It correctly predicts a minimum target 77% of the time (Figure 2.1).

Knowing that a throwback will occur 62% of the time allows you to hold onto the stock during the brief downturn and then ride price higher.

By matching your situation to one of the configurations, you can better plan how the trade will unfold. You can be selective and trade only the best setups, giving yourself the highest likelihood of success.

You may find trades in the big W are like hating lima beans, but eating them anyway because you know dessert awaits. The dessert is the big W.

Setup Synopsis

Figure 2.18 may help you identify the various types of trading setups.

"Occurs" in the figures means how often I found the configuration in the stocks I looked at. If two configurations apply to your situation, then the one with a more frequent occurrence (a higher percentage) is the one you should choose to follow.

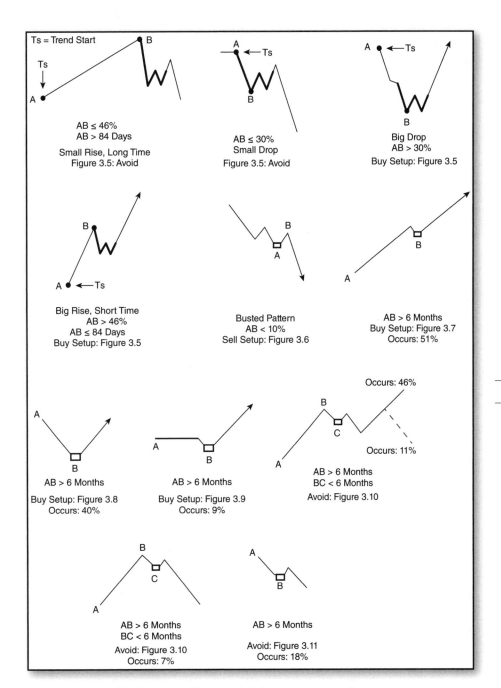

FIGURE 2.18 This figure is a collection of ideal trading setups and configurations.

CHAPTER 3

Broadening Bottoms

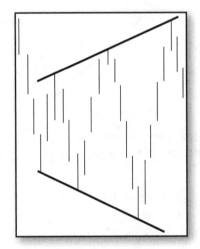

Broadening patterns are rare, regardless of whether they are tops, bottoms, wedges, or right-angled. However, new identification guidelines help traders and investors avoid selecting patterns that are just squiggles on the price chart.

Of the six varieties of broadening patterns, we begin discussing broadening bottoms, those patterns in which price trends downward into the start of the chart pattern. (Broadening bottoms have nothing to do with weight gain.)

■ Behavior at a Glance

Figure 3.1 shows the average performance of broadening bottom chart patterns. I found 820 broadening bottoms in 520 stocks from July 1991 to August 2014. After removing bear market samples, I had 251 patterns in bull markets with downward breakouts and 386 with upward breakouts.

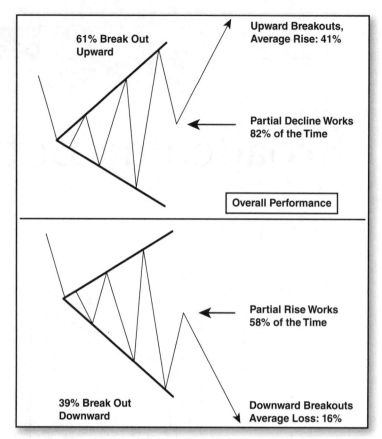

FIGURE 3.1   The average behavior of broadening bottom chart patterns.

The top half of Figure 3.1 is for upward breakouts, and the lower half is for downward breakouts. Clever, yes?

Price breaks out upward from a broadening bottom 61% of the time and rises an average of 41%. A partial decline correctly predicts an upward breakout 82% of the time.

What is a partial decline? A partial decline is a dip that can appear once a broadening bottom is established (price has touched the trendlines enough times to become valid and it satisfies the other identification guidelines) and before the breakout. The downward plunge of the partial decline does not touch or come that close to the bottom trendline. An immediate upward breakout follows (when it works, that is). The figure shows an example.

Downward breakouts occur 39% of the time from broadening bottoms. The average drop measures 16% before price makes a significant move higher (a trend change).

A partial rise correctly predicts a downward breakout about randomly: 58% of the time. A partial rise is the same as a partial decline except upside down. A peak occurs after the pattern is established, and it predicts a downward breakout. Price in the partial decline must not touch the top trendline or come that close.

- A partial rise works 58% of the time and a partial decline works 82% of the time.

Throwbacks and Pullbacks

Figure 3.2 illustrates the performance of stocks after the breakout from broadening bottoms. For upward breakouts (top half of the figure), price throws back to the top of the chart pattern 45% of the time. On average, it takes 5 days to rise 8% before price begins the return trip to the broadening bottom.

Price may stop declining in the throwback slightly above the breakout price or continue much lower, but the average says it will take 10 days to complete the trip. After completion, the stock resumes its upward rise and closes above the top of the broadening bottom 72% of the time.

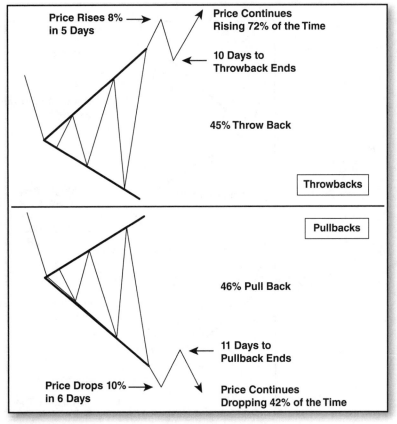

FIGURE 3.2 Typical throwback and pullback behavior of broadening bottoms.

Downward breakouts (bottom half of Figure 3.2) show a similar pattern except for the breakout direction. Price drops an average of 10% in 6 days. Then a pullback begins that sucks price upward until it peaks 11 days after the breakout. Once the upward move ends, price drops and closes below the bottom of the broadening pattern 42% of the time. A pullback occurs 46% of the time.

■ Broadening bottoms throw back 45% of the time and pull back 46% of the *time.*

Busted Bottoms

Figure 3.3 shows statistics related to busted broadening bottoms. A busted upward breakout occurs when price fails to rise at least 10% above the breakout price before the stock plunges and closes below the bottom of the chart pattern. A busted upward breakout (top half of the figure) occurs 25% of the time.

I explain single busted patterns in the glossary and mention them later. The average drop for single busted patterns is 24% below the bottom of the chart pattern. That statistic uses just 54 single busted patterns, so the numbers are likely to change.

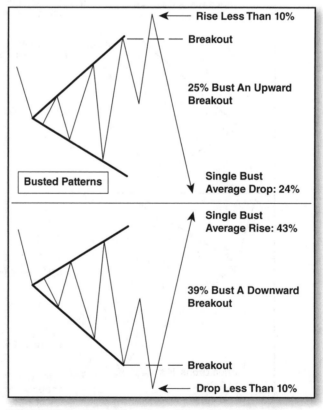

FIGURE 3.3 The performance of busted broadening bottoms.

Downward breakouts also bust. Price drops less than 10% after the breakout, reverses, and closes above the top of the chart pattern. That scenario happens a massive 39% of the time. Because this is based on just 97 busted broadening bottoms, I would expect the 39% number to change after the addition of more samples. Still, it suggests traders should avoid shorting broadening bottoms with downward breakouts (in bull markets).

If you do find a busted downward breakout from a broadening bottom, the average rise is a tasty 43% as measured from the top of the chart pattern to the ultimate high.

I drew a partial rise and decline in the figure but only because it tickled my toes. Do not expect to see a partial rise or decline preceding a busted pattern.

- Price busts a broadening bottom with upward breakouts 25% and downward breakouts 39% of the time.

■ Identification

Figure 3.4 shows an example of a broadening bottom (B) with an upward breakout (C) in a stock that no longer trades (it was bought out by AT&T in July 2015).

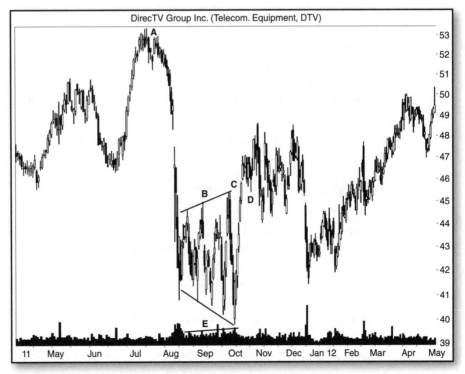

FIGURE 3.4 This broadening bottom has an upward breakout, but price struggles to climb.

Price begins the journey down from the peak at A and finds bedrock at the broadening bottom. The stock moves horizontally, bouncing between two diverging trendlines that bound the chart pattern.

Eventually, the stock closes above the top trendline and stages a breakout at C. The first *close* outside either the top or bottom trendlines constitutes the breakout.

In this example, price throws back to the breakout price at D and then struggles to find traction going forward. Notice that volume (E) trends upward. It does this 61% of the time (for both breakout directions).

Table 3.1 lists the guidelines for identifying broadening bottoms.

Downtrend. Deciding if the broadening pattern is a top or a bottom is perhaps the hardest element of finding a broadening bottom. To qualify as a bottom, price should *trend* downward going into the chart pattern. I ignore undershoot and overshoot that commonly appear before the start of the chart pattern. I show an example of undershoot in Figure 3.5 (point B).

Shape. Price should make higher highs and lower lows, forming a megaphone appearance. The two trendlines should diverge from one another with the top trendline sloping up and the bottom one sloping down.

Touches. I now require at least five trendline touches to qualify a broadening bottom. That means three or more touches of one trendline and two or more of the opposite one. The broadening bottom can have more touches as Figure 3.4 shows.

Volume. Usually trends higher from the start of the chart pattern to the breakout.

Breakout. A breakout occurs when price closes above the top trendline or below the bottom one.

Figure 3.5 shows another example of a broadening bottom. Price peaks at A in a double top pattern and then plummets to B. The brief decline (B) in the week before the start of the broadening bottom (C) is what I call undershoot. Price drops below the start of the pattern briefly and then recovers. Although price climbs into

TABLE 3.1 Identification Guidelines

Characteristic	Discussion
Downtrend	Price should trend down leading to the start of the broadening bottom. Ignore any overshoot or undershoot that occurs in the week or so before the start of the chart pattern.
Shape	Price takes on a megaphone appearance, sandwiched between two diverging trendlines. The top trendline slopes up and the bottom one slopes down.
Touches	Price must touch the trendlines at least five times: three touches on one trendline and two on the other.
Volume	Trends higher from the start of the chart pattern to the end.
Breakout	A close outside either of the trendlines represents a breakout.

FIGURE 3.5 This broadening bottom has undershoot leading to the start of the chart pattern.

the broadening bottom from below, the overall trend from A is downward, leading to 51 on the lower right of the chart. I consider the overall trend when determining whether the chart pattern is a broadening bottom or top. This one is a bottom since the prevailing trend is downward from A.

The broadening bottom pattern at C has four minor high touches of the top trendline and two minor low touches of the bottom trendline. A partial decline at D incorrectly predicts an upward breakout. Instead, a downward breakout occurs at E.

Sometimes trying to determine where the breakout is can be a problem. If you extend the bottom trendline down to F, you see that price finally closes below the bottom of the broadening bottom. But that would make the pattern look weird. I chose E as the breakout price.

One way around this dilemma is to count three touches of one trendline and two of the other. Once you have five touches, total, consider the next touch as the breakout. I do not know if this method works, so test it yourself. Just looking at a hundred patterns will sharpen your identification skills in any case. Or put you to sleep. Do not hunt for chart patterns while operating heavy machinery.

If you apply the five touch method to Figure 3.5, the broadening bottom will have an upward breakout that busts.

■ Buy Setup 1

Let us discuss busted chart patterns as the first trading setup. **Figure 3.6** shows the ideal example of a busted downward breakout, with the broadening bottom represented by the box (A).

Price breaks out downward from the broadening bottom at A and drops less than 10% before turning upward at B. The stock moves higher and eventually closes above the top of the broadening bottom (C). When that happens, it busts the downward breakout. Many times the stock will make a strong push higher but not always.

The stock chart shows an example of this setup. The downtrend begins at D and stumbles to form a broadening bottom at A1. Price breaks out downward at E and declines to a low at B1. The decline from E to B1 is 8%, which is within the 10% window required for a busted pattern.

The stock recovers and closes above the top of the broadening pattern at C1. When that happens, it busts the downward breakout. Unfortunately, this stock is not finished busting breakouts. The second bust occurs when price closes below the bottom of the broadening pattern. The stock continues down to F, which is less than 10% below the bottom of the broadening bottom and then recovers. The

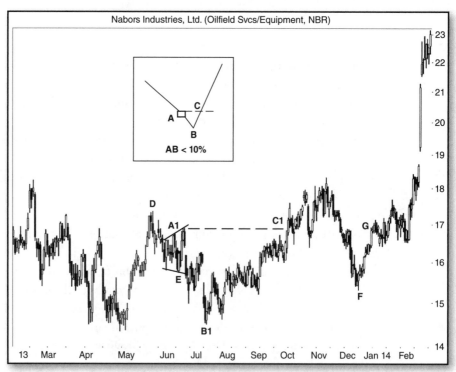

FIGURE 3.6 A busted broadening bottom can lead to a good gain.

third bust occurs at G when price closes above the top of the broadening bottom. After that, the busting ends when price soars more than 10% above the top of the chart pattern.

Here are the steps to use this setup:

1. Qualify the broadening bottom using the identification guidelines shown in Table 3.1.
2. After a downward breakout, price must drop less than 10% below the breakout before reversing and moving up.
3. Price closes above the top of the broadening pattern.
4. Buy at the open the next day or have a buy order waiting a penny above the top of the broadening bottom.
5. Place a stop-loss order a penny below the bottom of the broadening pattern or at a location of your choice.

The triple bust shown in Figure 3.6 is unusual. How unusual is it, you ask? **Table 3.2** shows the answer.

1. Percentage of broadening bottoms that bust. Over a third (39%) of broadening bottoms with downward breakouts will bust the pattern. That is huge.

2. Average drop after busting. Once the stock busts the pattern, the average rise from the top of the broadening bottom to the ultimate high is 34%.

3–6. Percentage of single/double/triple+ busts. Broadening bottoms that bust split into one of three varieties: single, double, and three or more busts. Of the 39% of broadening bottoms that bust, single busts occur 74% of the time, double busts happen 9%, and the rest bust three or more times (16%).

Buy Setups by the Numbers

Table 3.3, shows broadening bottom statistics for *upward* breakouts according to two parameters as measured from the trend start to the start of the chart pattern: short or long term ("Term") and percentage move (close to close, "Move").

TABLE 3.2	Statistics for Busted Broadening Bottoms with Downward Breakouts
Description	**Result**
1. Percentage of broadening bottoms that bust	39%
2. Average rise after busting	34%
3. Average rise after single bust	43%
4. Percentage of single busts	74%
5. Percentage of double busts	9%
6. Percentage of triple+ busts	16%

TABLE 3.3 **Performance of Broadening Bottoms with Upward Breakouts**

Term: 65 Days	Move: 16%	Average Rise	Count	5% Failures
Short	Big	48%	59	5%
Long	Small	42%	59	12%
Long	Big	40%	133	10%
Short	Small	38%	133	14%

By selecting patterns with a short term and a big move, you can increase your chances of a winning trade.

Short or long term in this case means less or more than the median 65 days from the trend start to the start of the broadening bottom. The median percentage decline was 16% over that period. See the glossary for a definition of the trend start if needed.

I sorted the table by the average rise column. The best performance after an upward breakout from a broadening bottom came from patterns that took fewer than 65 days but dropped more than 16% from the trend start to the pattern start. The 59 patterns that qualified under those conditions saw price climb an average of 48% with 5% of them failing to see price rise at least 5%.

Look at the last row in the table. This row shows the worst average rise: 38%. That is still respectable. Price trended downward and dropped less than 16% in fewer than 65 days before the broadening bottom. The average rise post-breakout was 38% from the 133 patterns that qualified, but 14% failed to rise at least 5%.

You can use Table 3.3 to help determine how successful a broadening bottom may be after the breakout. Because the results are averages of perfect trades and samples are few, your performance may vary.

If you wish to trade using these findings, follow these steps.

1. Qualify the broadening bottom using the identification guidelines shown in Table 3.1.
2. Measure the time (calendar days) from the trend start to the start of the chart pattern. Is it shorter or longer than 65 days?
3. Measure the drop from the trend start to the start (first trendline touch) of the broadening bottom. Is it bigger or smaller than 16%?
4. Use the answers to items 2 (short or long) and 3 (big or small) to find the corresponding row in Table 3.3. That will give you some idea of how perfectly traded broadening bottoms perform.
5. If you decide to trade the broadening bottom, wait for price to close above the top of the broadening bottom.

6. Buy at the open the next day or have a buy order waiting a penny above the top of the broadening bottom.

7. Place a stop-loss order a penny below the bottom of the broadening bottom or at a location of your choice.

■ Sell Setups by the Numbers

Table 3.4 shows the various combinations of term and move for *downward* breakouts, according to my statistics on broadening bottoms.

The term is "long" for durations more than the median 67 days from the trend start to the start of the broadening bottom, otherwise the term is "short."

Similarly, the move is "Big" if it is more than the median 17% drop from the trend start to the pattern start, otherwise the drop is "Small."

Look at the row with a 19% average drop. This is the average decline of 47 broadening bottoms from the breakout price to the ultimate low. I found that 4% of the patterns failed to see price drop at least 5% after the downward breakout.

Look at the last row. The decline took longer than 67 days leading to the start of the chart pattern and yet the drop going into the chart pattern was small (less than 17%). The average decline post-breakout was 12% and the 45 patterns involved showed that 20% of them failed to decline at least 5%.

Remember, the numbers are for perfect trades. Because the sample counts are small, expect the statistics to change with additional samples.

If you wish to trade using the findings, follow these steps:

1. Qualify the broadening bottom using the identification guidelines shown in Table 3.1.

2. Measure the time in calendar days from the trend start to the start of the chart pattern. Is it shorter or longer than 67 days?

3. Measure the percentage drop from the trend start to the start of the broadening bottom. Is it bigger or smaller than 17%?

4. Use the answers to items 2 (short or long) and 3 (big or small) to find the corresponding row in Table 3.4. That will give you some idea of how perfectly traded broadening bottoms perform.

TABLE 3.4 Performance of Broadening Bottoms with Downward Breakouts

Term: 67 Days	Move: 17%	Average Drop	Count	5% Failures
Short	Big	19%	47	4%
Long	Big	18%	77	14%
Short	Small	14%	79	20%
Long	Small	12%	45	20%

5. If you decide to trade the broadening bottom, wait for price to close below the bottom of the broadening bottom.
6. Short at the open the next day or have an order in place to short a penny below the bottom of the broadening pattern.
7. Place a stop-loss order a penny above the top of the broadening bottom or at a location of your choice.

■ Best Stop Locations

Table 3.5 shows how often price hits two locations for upward and downward breakouts.

1. Penny below the pattern. For upward breakouts, a stop-loss order placed a penny below the broadening bottom has a 3% chance of being hit. If the stop is hit, the average loss would amount to 10%, but trades stopped out would go on to make an average of 37%. The 37% number suggests that price hits the stop, reverses, and makes a strong push higher.

2. Within the pattern. If the stop is placed somewhere within the broadening bottom, there is a 79% chance of it being hit. However, the average loss is narrower, just 5%, and the stopped out trades would go on to make 42%.

3. Within the pattern. For downward breakouts, placing a stop within the broadening bottom results in a 73% hit rate, creating a loss of 3%, and the missing trades would see price drop an average of 16%.

4. Penny above the pattern. A stop placed a penny above the top of the broadening bottom would be hit 1% of the time, resulting in a 10% average loss, and the stopped out trades would drop an average of 16%.

The table shows that the best stop locations are a penny above or below the broadening bottom, for downward and upward breakouts, respectively, providing you can tolerate the size of the loss. You may wish to use a stop location closer to the entry price. However, doing so increases your risk of a loss.

TABLE 3.5 Stop Locations for Broadening Bottoms

Description	Chance of Being Hit	Average Loss	Missed Trades, Gains/Losses
1. Penny below the pattern	3%	10%	37%
2. Within the pattern	79%	5%	42%
Up Breakouts Above, Down Breakouts Below			
3. Within the pattern	73%	3%	16%
4. Penny above the pattern	1%	10%	16%

- For the best results, place a stop-loss order a penny above the top for downward breakouts and a penny below the bottom of the broadening pattern for upward breakouts.

■ Configuration Trading

When using broadening bottoms to buy a stock, allow variations, but try to fit what you see to one of the setups discussed here. They may help you decide to attempt a trade, make a long-term investment in a promising stock, or walk away.

To trade the following configurations, begin with these guidelines.

1. Find a broadening bottom on the *daily* chart that obeys the identification guidelines listed in Table 3.1.
2. On the *weekly* scale, match what you see on your chart to the appropriate configuration in this chapter. Figures 3.20 and 3.21 should help.
3. Buy at the open (daily chart) the day after the breakout or place an order to buy a penny above the top of the chart pattern (upward breakouts) or below the bottom of the pattern (downward breakouts).
4. Place a stop-loss order at a location of your choice.

Figure 3.7 shows the most common trading setup. Of the 305 broadening bottoms I scanned for trading setups (in both bull and bear markets), this configuration occurs 41% of the time.

Price climbs to the first peak at A. Peak A is not just another tree in the forest. Rather the peak represents a significant turning point, perhaps a new yearly or multiyear high.

The drop from A to B is short, less than six months. The short drop (time) is a key component that distinguishes this setup from others. The percentage decline varies, so I did not focus on it.

The broadening pattern appears at B as a reversal of the downtrend. After an upward breakout from the chart pattern, price attempts to make a new high (C). Sometimes it falls well short of the price of A. Sometimes it exceeds A by up to 10% but rarely more. Often it stops near the same price as A or just short of it. Then the stock tumbles, dropping more than 20% from C or D to E.

Since this setup occurs so often, it can be an attractive trading opportunity. However, as price climbs from B to C, it faces overhead resistance. That resistance stops the climb. Thus, you have to be alert to a reversal, especially as price closes in on the price of A.

This setup is best for swing or day traders, those people willing to buy at a breakout from the broadening bottom and ride price higher until they get bucked off.

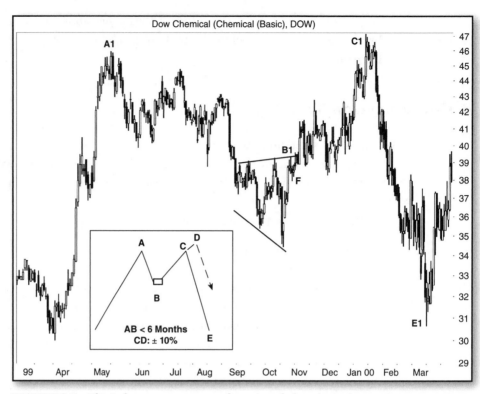

FIGURE 3.7 This is the most common configuration of a broadening bottom in a price series.

The stock chart shows an example of this setup. Price peaks at A1 and then stair-steps lower. Eventually, it finds footing and creates a broadening bottom (B1). Yes, this broadening bottom is a stinker. A well-formed broadening pattern would have the first bottom touch closer to the start of the trendline.

A partial decline (F) signals an immediate upward breakout.

Price breaks out of the chart pattern when it closes above the top trendline (to the right of B1). Then the stock fights its way up to C1 where it stalls just above the price of the prior peak, A1. After that, traders were not given much time to sell their stock before it tumbled to E1, forming a big M type pattern.

Continuation Patterns

Figure 3.8 shows a broadening bottom configuration that occurs 15% of the time, but it is one worth searching for. In the ideal case, price rises slowly from A to B, taking at least 6 months. The slope of the rise is often gentle for the best gainers, but slopes up to 45 degrees are common, too. Avoid trading trends steeper than about 45 degrees (shallower is better).

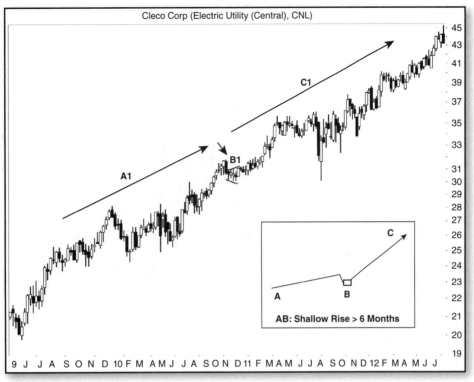

FIGURE 3.8 This is the second most common configuration for broadening bottoms, and it leads to tasty gains.

Price drops quickly, maybe a month or so of downtrend, until a broadening bottom appears (B). The breakout from this chart pattern sends price moving higher. Soon, the stock is making new highs (C).

What is important with this setup is the lack of overhead resistance. When price breaks out upward from the broadening bottom, it easily pushes to an all-time high (no overhead resistance). After that, off the stock goes, shooting for the moon.

The stock chart shows an example of this configuration on the weekly scale. Price climbs following trend A1. Then it stumbles briefly (about a week) and forms a broadening bottom (B1). The upward breakout from this chart pattern (B1) takes time to appear, as if the stock is reluctant to venture higher. The march to new highs follows as the stock climbs trend C1.

On the daily chart, with my aspect ratio (the ratio of screen width to height), trend A1 is a gentle rise but shown here on the weekly scale, it appears steeper.

Zigzag Variation

Figure 3.9 shows a zigzag variation. This is nearly the same configuration as Figure 3.7 but with a few twists. Price makes a long-term move (over six months)

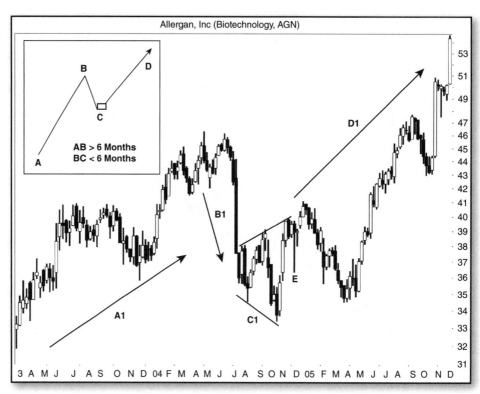

FIGURE 3.9 This variation sees price make a substantial gain.

from A to B, forming a major turn at B. Then price drops and forms a broadening bottom within six months (B to C). The breakout from the chart pattern is upward and off price goes, rocketing to D. The stock has enough strength to power through overhead resistance setup by areas along the ABC route.

In Figure 3.7, price can reverse up to 10% above the prior peak (C to D, above A), but in this setup, the stock continues higher. If it pauses at the price of B, eventually it will resume the uptrend.

This configuration occurs 10% of the time, so it is best to use Figure 3.7 as the template and not depend on this setup happening. If the stock continues making new highs instead of reversing near the price of peak B, then good for you. Enjoy the climb. I recommend bottled oxygen for higher altitudes.

The stock chart shows an example of this configuration on the weekly chart. It is clearer on the daily chart, but the layout would not fit on the page.

Price trends higher following line A1, making a climb that is more than six months long. It peaks and reluctantly begins a retrace that takes price down to the broadening bottom (C1). This retrace (B1) is shorter than six months.

At E, the stock makes a partial decline, suggesting an immediate upward breakout, which happens. The climb to D1 is treacherous in this example. Notice that it pauses in September 2005 near the old high of April 2004 before working its way higher. After that, the stock just powers its way upward.

The only thing I can find that distinguishes this setup from Figure 3.7, is that this one is rare. Do not depend on the stock making a major move higher.

Shallow Setup

Figure 3.10 shows a setup similar to Figure 3.8 only the inbound trend (AB) slopes downward in this setup. The AB trend is at least 6 months long, but the drop is minor, about 5% to 10%. It may be hard to distinguish whether price is trending up, down, or sideways until the quick drop (often less than a month long) leading to the broadening bottom (B).

After an upward breakout, the stock makes a new high quickly, and with no overhead resistance, price keeps rising (C). This setup occurs 9% of the time.

The stock chart on the weekly scale shows an example of this setup. The long-term inbound decline follows trend A1. Notice that it is a shallow decline from peak to peak. Then price makes a quick drop to the broadening bottom (B1).

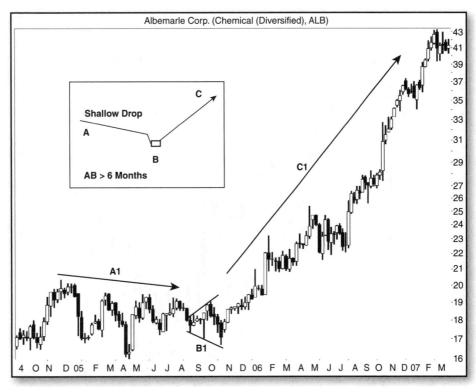

FIGURE 3.10 A shallow drop leads to a broadening bottom reversal that sends price higher.

After price reverses, it moves higher and breaks out of the clouds with no resistance to impede an upward climb (C1). This climb is an example of what makes the mouths of buy-and-hold investors salivate.

To trade this configuration, set a buy stop a penny above the top of the broadening pattern, so you get in as soon as possible. Place a stop below the bottom of the pattern, just in case.

Downtrend Retrace

Figure 3.11 shows the next setup that occurs 8% of the time.

Price toboggans downhill from A to B, taking longer than six months before the airbags deploy. Do today's toboggans come with airbags? Anyway, if you own the stock on the way down to B, the ride would sicken you as well as drain your wallet or purse.

Price does not just bounce at B, it makes a substantial rise from 10% to 50% or even more (C). Then the run ends when overhead resistance piles on top of the trading euphoria and the trend changes. Price sinks to D and continues down.

The risk with this setup is to buy into the stock as early as possible and sell just as price changes direction at the top. That is easy to say but hard to do.

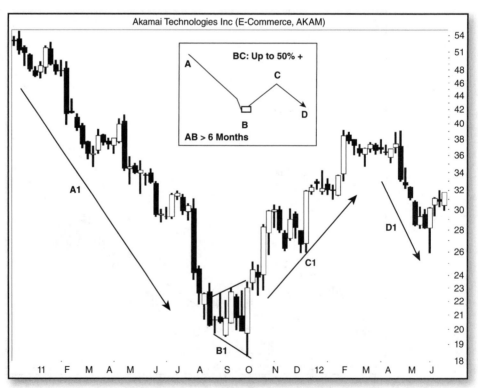

FIGURE 3.11 This high-risk setup is appropriate for swing traders.

The stock chart shows an example on the weekly scale. This setup has price trending downward over the long term (more than six months, A1). Then the broadening bottom reverses the downtrend (B1). Price rises and makes a substantial move higher (C1) until a trend reversal occurs. Price drops thereafter (D1).

Buy on or soon after the upward breakout from the broadening top. Use the weekly scale and an up-sloping trendline drawn below the valleys as price rises, as a warning signal to sell. When price closes below the trendline, consider dumping the turkey (selling).

■ Sell Setups

Sell setups happen when price breaks out downward (usually) from a broadening bottom chart pattern. If you own the stock, should you sell? A timely sale can mean the difference between capturing most of the profit or watching the stock ease lower day by day, torturing traders and investors worried about protecting their investment.

Figure 3.12 shows what happens all too often, and yet I found it occurs just 7% of the time. This setup is similar to the last one. Price makes a long-term decline (AB), reaches a broadening bottom (B), and reverses. However, climbers stumble

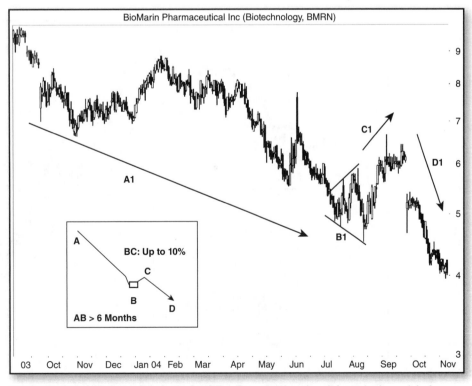

FIGURE 3.12 Price drops over the long term, reverses but then fails to climb much before tumbling again. Avoid this setup unless you like to short a stock.

getting off the bottom (C) and price drops. The rise after the broadening bottom (BC) is often near 5%, but it can be higher (10% or so, but nothing like 50%).

If you bought the stock expecting a yummy gain, you would be staring at a loss when the stock continued lower. The inset is an example of the perils of bottom-fishing.

The stock chart shows an example on the daily chart. Price makes a long-term decline (A1) and forms a broadening bottom (B1). An upward breakout gives the stock hope that a major turn has come and price rises (C1). But the rocket runs out of fuel, stalls, and the stock collapses (D1).

This type of behavior is common during a bear market or in stocks with deteriorating fundamentals.

Downtrend Continuation

Figure 3.13 shows the next configuration, which occurs 11% of the time in the stocks I looked at. It is rare but can result in a large drop, often 15% to 20%, and sometimes more than 40%.

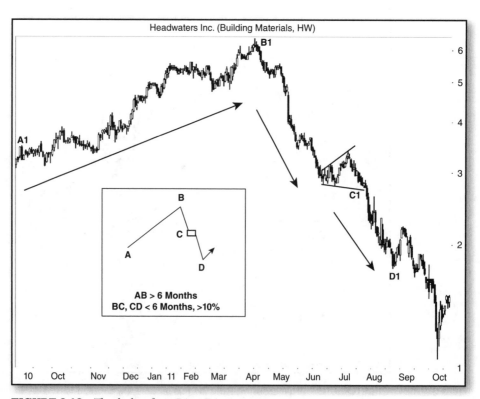

FIGURE 3.13 The decline from B1 to D1 is extensive.

The climb from A to B is long term (more than 6 months). The length of moves BC and CD are less than 6 months, each. The price decline from B to C is extensive (typically measuring 20%), but it can be larger, more than 50%.

Traders looking for this configuration will find it difficult to distinguish this setup from the next one (a failure). In this setup, after a downward breakout from the broadening bottom, the drop can be breathtaking. But it is also rare.

The stock chart shows an example (daily scale) of this variation starting with a long uptrend, A1, going into peak B1. Then price tumbles. Although it might not look like much, the drop is a whopper according to the price scale: 56%. A broadening bottom at C1 calms things down but only for a time.

After the breakout, price tumbles again, falling 36% until price bounces at D1, sending the stock higher by at least 20% (a trend change). Point D1 marks the ultimate low even though the stock drops farther.

Trade this configuration by shorting a stock or selling a long holding when it breaks out downward from the broadening bottom. Be careful. More likely is that this setup will turn into the failure scenario described next.

Downward Breakout Failures

Here are the most common setups that fail to see price make a substantial decline after a downward breakout.

Figure 3.14 shows an ideal representation of the most commonly occurring sell setup for broadening bottoms. It happens 26% of the time in the 122 broadening bottoms with downward breakouts I looked at.

This configuration is the same as the prior one, except the drop from C to D is less than 10% in this setup.

The rise from A to B takes longer than 6 months. Then the trend reverses. The decline from B to C is short term (less than 6 months), and yet the stock makes a steep drop that ranges between 10% and 30%, usually hovering around 15%.

At C, a broadening bottom with a downward breakout appears. The CD drop is tiny, less than 10%, and it is a quick one, too, less than 6 months long. It is common for the drop to be about 5% and taking just a month or so.

Because the drop from C to D is small, this is a case when holding onto the stock can be a good choice for many (long side) traders and investors. Of course, there is no guarantee that the stock will make a small decline after the breakout, but the odds suggest it will. That is especially true if the general market is zipping higher.

The stock chart shows an example using the weekly scale. The A1-B1 rise takes longer than 6 months. Price declines from B1 to C1 in about 2 months and finds the start of the broadening bottom (C1) 21% lower.

The breakout from the broadening bottom to the low at D1 takes less than a month and sees price drop about 10%. After that, the stock recovers.

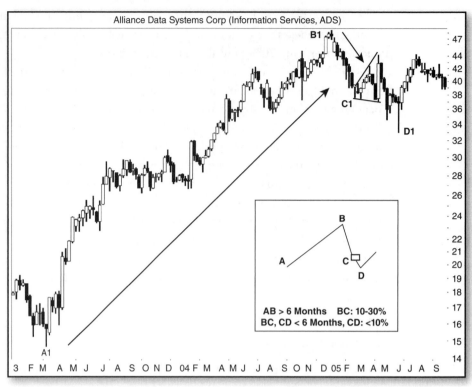

FIGURE 3.14 This broadening bottom appears in a simple ABC correction chart pattern.

Downtrend Failure

The following configuration occurs 17% of the time in the stocks I looked at. **Figure 3.15** shows the ideal configuration in the inset.

The stock makes a long-term decline (AB) that takes longer than 6 months, and price makes a substantial drop, too. The drop ranges from 15% to 60% or more but is often about 40%.

Because the decline is big in both time and price, the appearance of a broadening bottom is a signal that the drop is ending. Oddly, the stock breaks out downward from the broadening bottom and continues lower but only for a short time (less than 6 months) before price reverses after dropping less than 10%. When price closes above the top of the broadening bottom, it busts the pattern.

This setup is not good for shorting because the BC decline is meager. Rather, it is better to wait for price to bust the broadening bottom (on the rise after C) before going long.

The stock chart is an example of this variation, shown on the daily scale. The stock suffers a turbulent, long-term decline from A1 to B1, and then the broadening bottom appears.

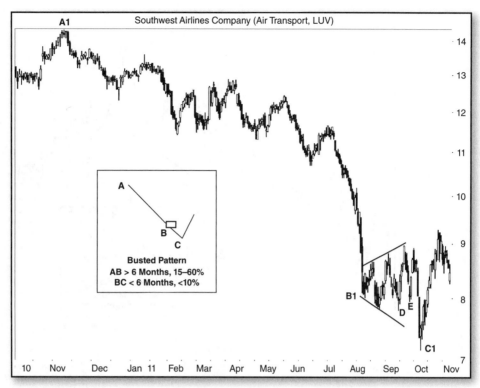

FIGURE 3.15   The stocks busts a downward breakout.

The broadening bottom has a partial decline, but is it D or E? The broadening bottom has to be complete before we start the search for a partial decline, meaning it has the correct number of trendline touches. That happens only at E. So E is the partial decline, except that it fails to predict an upward breakout this time. Go figure.

The breakout move from the bottom of the chart pattern to the low at C1 amounts to 8% and takes two trading days.

In this example, the stock zips back above the top of the chart pattern, busting the downward breakout. Not shown is that the stock continued to wobble up and down, busting the chart pattern multiple times before deciding on an upward move that eventually took the stock much higher (over 24).

This stock chart reminds me of all of those nightmares when I was learning to invest. I would buy a stock, worry as it dropped each day, and then get so fed up with the dog that I would sell within a week or two of the bottom. Oops.

Short Retrace

The last configuration is a variation of Figure 3.14 except that this setup is rarer, occurring 12% of the time, and the BC drop is smaller, too. **Figure 3.16** shows the ideal configuration.

FIGURE 3.16 After a long-term rise, price retraces but not much.

The stock makes a long-term climb from A to B that takes more than 6 months. A reversal occurs at peak B, but price drops less than 10% in just a few months before the broadening bottom appears (C).

The broadening bottom acts as a continuation pattern when price breaks out downward. The drop is another short one both in time (less than 6 months) and extent (less than 10%). Often the BC and CD drops are about 5% and take a month or two.

This configuration is an example of a broadening bottom in a bullish stock. The downward breakout from the chart pattern is a trap for those believing that the BD drop will retrace a significant portion of the AB move. Instead, price recovers after the turn at D.

The stock chart shows what this configuration looks like in the flesh. Price rises over the long term from A1 to B1. The drop from B1 to the start of the broadening bottom is quick (two weeks) and small (8%).

Then the broadening bottom appears (C1). The breakout from this pattern is downward and price drops but not far (5%, D1). It does not take long either (about 5 weeks).

The difference between Figure 3.14 and this setup is the BC move. In a bullish move such as that shown in Figure 3.16, the amount of retrace from peak B to the start of the broadening bottom (C) is inconsequential. The stock will find support, and price will be on its way upward again.

■ Measure Rule

The measure rule serves as a tool to help traders set a price target. It is not a guarantee that price will reach the target nor does it say that once price reaches the target, it will reverse. The measure rule only gives a number. What you choose to do with that number is up to you.

Figure 3.17 shows a broadening bottom at AB. Point A is at 98.60 and B is at 94.88, for a height of 3.72. If the breakout is downward, subtract the height from the bottom of the pattern (B) to get a target. If the number is negative, then discard it. If the percentage decline is unreasonable, then throw it away.

For upward breakouts, add the height to A. Again, if the percentage move is unreasonable, then do not depend on price reaching it.

In this example, the measure rule gives a target of 102.32, which I show as C. Price touches the target several times about a month after the breakout before the stock tumbles. This time, taking profits at the target was timely.

How often does the measure rule work? Answer: 66% of the time for upward breakouts and 41% of the time for downward ones. To increase the success rate, try cutting the height in half. That boosts the success rate to 87% for upward breakouts and 72% for downward ones.

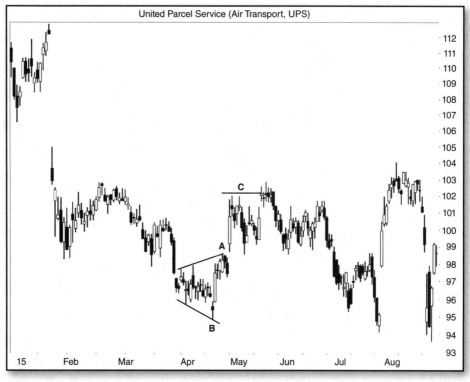

FIGURE 3.17   The measure rule helps traders set a price target.

The way I use the measure rule is to calculate a target and look for underlying support (downward breakouts) or overhead resistance (upward breakouts). If support or resistance is nearby, I assume price will reverse there.

- The measure rule works 66% of the time for upward breakouts and 41% of the time for downward breakouts.

■ Trading

If you are a position trader or investor, one that buys and holds a stock for years, should you lose sleep worrying about a broadening bottom? No. Even if it breaks out downward, there is a 27% chance that the drop will be larger than 20%. That means 73% of the time, you can get a good night's sleep.

Let us consider **Figure 3.18,** which is a complicated looking mess. Imagine that you wish to buy the stock shown during formation of the broadening bottom (B). How would you trade it?

A partial decline appears on the way to the breakout. In this case, the partial decline correctly predicts an immediate, upward breakout.

FIGURE 3.18 This stock trade results in a good gain.

Inset 1 shows the monthly chart of the stock. Notice that it has been trending down since 2012 as the arrow shows. One could argue that since the downtrend has been in existence for so long it is due to end. An end means a reversal of the downward trend—a buying opportunity. Think bottom-fishing. You are not a vegetarian, are you?

The drop on the monthly chart measures 58% from peak to valley. I computed that to see whether it was close to a Fibonacci number, such as 62%, 50%, or 38%. Sigh. It is not.

Point A is the trend start, before which the stock tumbled by at least 20%. The trend start to the start of the broadening bottom measures more than 65 days (long), and the drop is larger than 16% (big). For this combination of term (short/long) and move (big/small), Table 3.3 for upward breakouts shows the average rise of 40% with a 10% failure rate. Placing third in the list, it is not the ideal combination.

Considering the various configurations, Figures 3.11 and 3.12 are both possibilities. Figure 3.12 describes a busted pattern, but those happen 25% of the time (see "Busted Bottoms," Figure 3.3). In 3 of 4 trades, you will be fine. That probability of success suggests Figure 3.11 is the one to follow. The configuration associated with Figure 3.11 also occurs a bit more often than Figure 3.12 (8% versus 7%). I know the numbers are close, but work with me.

Figure 3.11 shows a large gain after the breakout. That configuration is the one traders hope to see. In fact, this stock followed that setup.

Looking at other stocks in the same industry, one was flat, six were trending higher, and eight were trending down. That suggested a weak industry or at least one in turmoil. The markets, however, were doing well, except for an August downturn, as represented by the S&P 500 Index.

The broadening bottom is at B with a breakout to the right of C. The breakout occurs when price closes above the top of the chart pattern. The height of the broadening bottom is C − B, or 67 cents. The target would be 11.52, which matches the high price at D to the penny.

If you were a swing trader, placing a sell order at the target or just below the 11.50 round number (I would use 11.47 to avoid the masses wanting to sell at a round number) to get you out would have been a timely trade. The stock returned to E in a classic throwback.

If you owned the stock and decided to hold longer, here is how I would swing trade it. After the throwback completed, the stock started moving up. At F, the company announced earnings that were better than the market expected. The stock gapped up higher on the news.

Look at Inset 2. This is a zoom-in of the FG rise (F matches F1 and G matches G1). I know that after a good earnings surprise the stock frequently rises for ten days to two weeks before giving back some of the gains (before retracing). For a short-term trade, that would be my hold time. I would want to sell when it started rounding over near the end of that period.

If you place a stop order below the prior day's low and raise it after the close each trading day (trail the stop upward, never lowering it), often you can catch the majority of these types of vertical runs. You know it has gone vertical after three consecutive higher lows appear, preferably with little overlap from day to day, and preferably with higher highs, too.

In this case, raise the stop each day, trailing it below the prior day's low. At the end of the run, when the market closes at G1, you place a stop-loss order a penny or two below the day's low. The next day, H, the stock opens lower and takes you out of the trade.

For a swing trade, you buy in at or near the price of C and exit at H. In about two week's time, you have made almost 3 points, or about 25%.

For investors (buy-and-hold), the stock wobbled in the fall, which is typical but has continued to rise during the first half of 2015. Buying this broadening bottom has turned into a winning trade with a gain of 70% (if cashed out in mid-August 2015).

Point I is the ultimate high, the highest high before the stock drops by at least 20%. If you were to sell there (a perfect trade), the gain would have been 39%. That is amazingly close to the average 40% rise for perfect trades in Table 3.3.

Actual Trade

Figure 3.19 shows a trade I made using a broadening bottom. Here is what I wrote in my trading notebook about the entry (A): "1/25/2000. I bought the stock at the market as it was moving up off the bottom of a broadening bottom formation. At 15 3/8 (unadjusted for splits), the stock is cheap and shows support at this level. Oil prices are high meaning fuel costs will continue to hurt, interest rates are rising and expected to move up 1/4 point next Wednesday at the FOMC (Federal Reserve open market committee) meeting. However, as a long term holding, it is a good price to add to my position.

"The position size is small because this could break down through the bottom of the formation and move lower. In that case, I will buy more. If fuel costs were stable, the earnings of this beast would improve, so it is a good buy even though the general market is trending lower."

The timing of the entry was superb. Just after the stock bottomed and completed a broadening pattern, I bought. But the early entry contradicts my view of waiting for confirmation before buying.

Waiting for confirmation is the safest approach. The statistics in this book assume you wait for a valid pattern to appear. However, there is nothing wrong with buying earlier, especially once a chart pattern has enough trendline touches to become valid.

Buying early increases your risk of loss. The stock could do a partial rise and drop out the bottom of the pattern (it almost did when it dropped to B). The stock could rise to the top trendline and reverse.

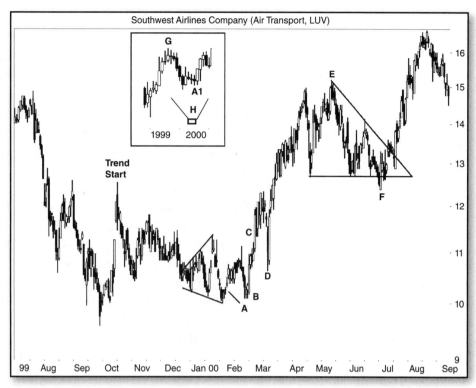

FIGURE 3.19   A perfect entry but a flubbed exit led to a 27% profit on this trade.

In other words, I got lucky on this trade.

The stock looped around and returned to my buy price (B), just as I worried it would but stopped there. Then it recovered.

The traditional buy point is at C when the stock closed above the top of the chart pattern. A throwback took the stock back down to D and presented traders another opportunity to buy the stock when it again closed above the top of the chart pattern.

The airline kicked on the afterburners and the stock shot nearly vertically, to peak at E.

Here is what I wrote about the sale (F). "6/27/00. I sold my entire holdings because the stock has pierced the support base of a descending triangle. With seasonal performance moving up in December and peaking in the spring, I missed the high by about $3/share (split unadjusted). Ouch. Oil prices are high, raising fuel costs and interest rates are still high, maybe moving up more. So, it looks like the excitement is over although today the stock is up almost $1."

I made 27% on the trade with a hold time of about five months. The timing on the exit was both good and bad. The day after the triangle broke out downward, I sold the stock. That is how chart pattern trading is supposed to work. But I left a lot of money on the table selling as late as I did. I sold exactly when the stock bottomed. Sigh. That happens sometimes, and it always pisses me off.

Application Let us apply the lessons learned in this chapter to see how this broadening bottom was predicted to do.

I show where the trend starts in October. The time between the trend start and the start of the broadening bottom is 68 calendar days and price drops 15% (high to close). According to Table 3.3 for upward breakouts, the term is long and the move is small. It rates the trade in second place for a potential rise of 42%.

If the broadening bottom were to break out downward, Table 3.4 suggests the stock would drop the least of the four choices. That is reassuring.

The configurations do not use the trend start. Instead, they use a longer-term shape of price as it meanders up and down.

The inset of Figure 3.19 shows the stock using the monthly scale. I want to show the price trend going into the broadening bottom in a small amount of space.

The broadening bottom is at A1, corresponding to point A on the other stock chart. G is where the price trend peaks and starts a long decline going into the broadening bottom. Thus, the configuration looks like the stick figure trend at H.

The G-A1 drop is longer than 6 months, the trend drops into the top of the broadening bottom (34%, so it is more steep than shallow), and price breaks out upward. Because I was not interested in trading a busted broadening bottom (that is, Figure 3.6 would not apply), the best matches are Figures 3.11 and 3.12.

Both figures could apply to this situation. However, because Table 3.3 suggests good performance, I think Figure 3.11 is the more likely candidate in this instance. I would use that one as a template for this trade.

■ Closing Position

Broadening bottoms are difficult to trade because it is seldom clear when the breakout occurs. Instead of breaking out, the stock could be racing toward a trendline only to touch it and reverse. Using a guideline like assuming a breakout will occur *after* five distinct minor high or minor low touches of the two trendlines (three on one side, two on the other) could help.

The setups and configurations described in this chapter put the broadening bottom in context, allowing you to determine the Scuds from the duds before you trade. That kind of information can be invaluable.

Setup Synopsis

Figure 3.20 may help you identify the various types of trading setups.

"Occurs" in the figures means how often I found the configuration in the stocks I looked at. If two configurations apply to your situation, then the one with a more frequent occurrence (a higher percentage) is the one you should choose to follow.

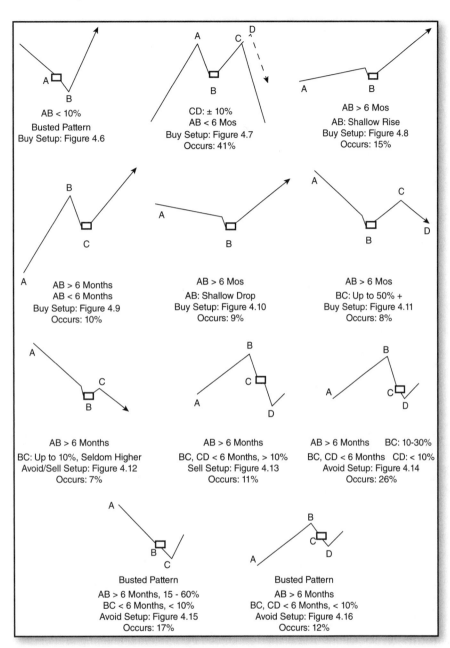

FIGURE 3.20 Various types of trading setups.

CHAPTER 4

Broadening Tops

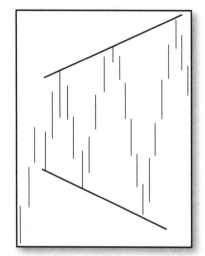

Broadening tops and bottoms share everything except the price trend leading to them. Tops have price rising into the chart pattern. Bottoms have price falling. Even the performance statistics are similar.

What I like about broadening tops is that they are more plentiful than bottoms. I found almost twice as many tops as bottoms. But does price act the same after the chart pattern ends? To answer that, we need to delve into the pattern.

■ Behavior at a Glance

Figure 4.1 shows the average performance of broadening top chart patterns. I found 1,553 broadening tops from July 1991 to August 2014, but only 1,252 of those were from a bull market.

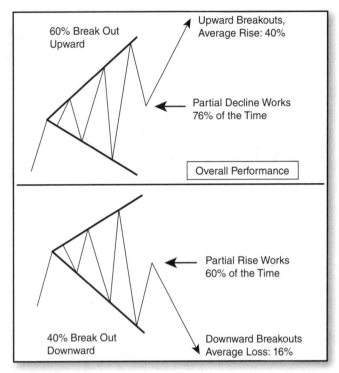

FIGURE 4.1   The average behavior of broadening top chart patterns.

Price breaks out upward from a broadening top 60% of the time. The average rise is 40%. Do not expect to make 40% on your trades. The number comes from hundreds of *perfect* trades, something no mortal can duplicate. The number does not include commissions, dividends, and fees, either.

A partial decline works 76% of the time. This is perhaps a misleading statistic because it does not count the number of times a partial decline occurs after the pattern can be recognized but well before the breakout. See the glossary for a discussion of partial rises and declines.

Downward breakouts occur 40% of the time and price drops an average of 16% below the bottom of the chart pattern. Partial rises work 60% of the time, which is slightly above random. Again, the same caution applies to partial rises: The number may be high because it excludes partial rises that flub up inside the chart pattern.

- Sixty percent of broadening tops break out upward.

Throwbacks and Pullbacks

Figure 4.2 illustrates the average short-term performance of stocks after the breakout from broadening tops. Price throws back to the breakout price or trendline boundary just over half the time: 52%.

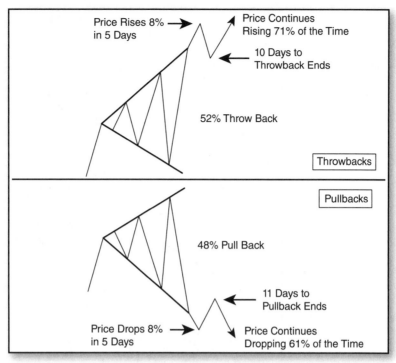

FIGURE 4.2 Throwback and pullback behavior for broadening tops.

During the average throwback, price rises 8% in 5 days (calendar days, not trading days) before peaking. Then it retraces and drops 5 more days for a total of 10. That up and down movement returns the stock to near the breakout price, completing the throwback. After that, the stock rises 71% of the time to clear the top of the broadening pattern.

Almost half (48%) of stocks with downward breakouts have pullbacks (see the lower half of Figure 4.2).

During a pullback, the stock drops an average of 8% in 5 days. A pullback carries the stock back up to the breakout price, and it peaks 10 days after the breakout. The stock closes below the bottom of the broadening top 61% of the time.

■ Price throws back (upward breakouts) to the breakout price 52% of the time and pulls back (downward breakouts) 48% of the time.

Busted Tops

Figure 4.3 shows statistics related to busted broadening tops. A bust occurs when price fails to rise at least 10% above the breakout price before the stock plunges and closes below the bottom of the chart pattern.

Busted upward breakouts happen 28% of the time in a bull market. The average decline, as measured from the bottom of the chart pattern to the ultimate low, is 23%, but that is for single busted patterns.

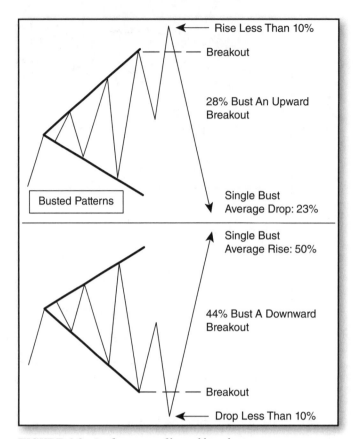

FIGURE 4.3   Performance of busted broadening tops.

Downward breakouts bust 44% of the time, which is huge. When a downward breakout busts, price drops less than 10% and then rebounds, closing above the top of the broadening top.

The high bust rate means almost half of all trades with downward breakouts will end in failure if you attempt to short the stock. It also suggests holding onto long-side positions since the decline could be meager and a large gain awaits.

After the pattern single busts, the average rise is a redeeming 50%. If you want to trade broadening tops, then buy after the stock busts a downward breakout.

- Busted upward breakouts happen 28% of the time and downward breakouts bust 44% of the time.

■ Identification

Table 4.1 shows identification guidelines for finding broadening tops, and then we'll look at an example.

TABLE 4.1 Identification Guidelines

Characteristic	Discussion
Uptrend	Price trends upward leading to the start of the broadening top. Ignore any overshoot or undershoot that may occur a week or so before the start.
Shape	Price takes on a megaphone appearance with higher peaks and lower valleys.
Touches	Price should come close to or touch the two trendlines at least five times (total), three on one trendline and two on the other.
Volume	Volume trends upward 67% of the time.
Breakout	A breakout occurs when price closes either above the top or below the bottom of the chart pattern. Upward breakouts predominate.

Figure 4.4 shows an example of a broadening top chart pattern. In this example, price overshoots (A) and plummets to undershoot (B) the entry. When determining the inbound price trend, I ignored undershoot and overshoot since they do not last long and are not important to pattern behavior. Price trends upward leading to the start of this broadening top.

The stock forms higher peaks and lower valleys creating a megaphone appearance. Two trendlines bound the price action and form a broadening top at C.

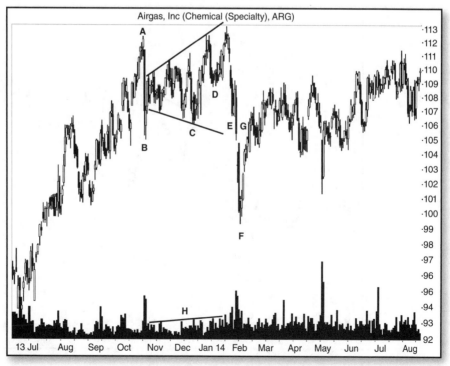

FIGURE 4.4 A broadening top with overshoot and undershoot at the start (AB) and a downward breakout.

Price leaves the top trendline and attempts to cross to the bottom of the pattern but fails at D. This is an example of a partial decline failure. In 76% of the cases, a partial decline would correctly signal an upward breakout.

The breakout occurs at E when price closes below the bottom of the chart pattern (C). The stock continues lower to the ultimate low, F, before rebounding and pulling back to the breakout price at G.

Line H shows volume trending upward. That happens 67% of the time. You get a 10% boost (better post-breakout performance) from upward breakouts with an upsloping volume trend. Tell your neighbors.

The volume trend for downward breakouts shows no performance difference.

Refer to Table 4.1 and **Figure 4.5** as I discuss identification guidelines.

Uptrend. A double bottom appears at A. Confirmation of this chart pattern sees the stock zip upward to the start of the broadening top (B). To qualify the broadening pattern as a top, price must trend upward like that shown. If there is a question as to whether the trend is up or down, switch to a longer time scale and see whether the trend is clearer. For daily charts, like that shown, use the weekly scale.

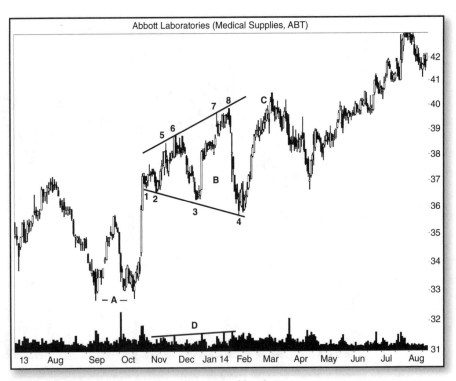

FIGURE 4.5   A broadening top with an upward breakout.

Shape. The stock should follow two diverging trendlines that look like a megaphone with the top sloping upward and the bottom sloping downward.

Touches. There must be at least five touches of the two trendlines. The one shown in Figure 4.5 has four touches of the bottom trendline (1–4) and four touches of the top trendline (5–8). Look for each touch to be a minor high (distinct peak) or minor low (distinct valley).

Volume. Volume usually trends upward as in this case (D) from the start of the broadening top to the end. Volume may show many spikes, of course. I do not let an unusual volume trend disqualify a broadening top.

Breakout. The breakout occurs at C when the stock closes above the top of the chart pattern.

One difficulty with broadening tops is determining when price has broken out. In Figure 4.5, if C were a bit taller, it would touch the top trendline, so we would have to wait several months before it became clear that price had closed above the top trendline.

It may help to search for other examples of broadening tops in the same stock to view what their breakouts look like. Or you could count five touches (three of one trendline, two of the other) and hope that a breakout will occur at the next trendline intersection. For the chart shown in Figure 4.5, that would mean buying into the pattern at touch 7 and riding down price to 4.

Maybe you should not try this at home, or at least have lots of bandages available.

■ Buy Setups

Broadening tops present several buy setups and **Figure 4.6** shows the ideal busted breakout in the inset.

Price trends up to the start of the broadening top (the box represents the broadening top) before breaking out downward at A. Price drops less than 10% (B) below the breakout, by definition, of a busted downward breakout. The trend reverses and price moves higher, eventually closing above the top of the broadening pattern, and soaring (C). The move from B to C often meanders, so do not attach any significance to my straight lines.

The stock chart shows an example of a busted downward breakout. The broadening top breaks out downward at A1 and price makes its way to B1 following a measured move down pattern (down, upward retrace, down again). The drop in this case is 9% (A1 to B1).

The stock finds support at B1 and the downtrend reverses, eventually climbing to C1.

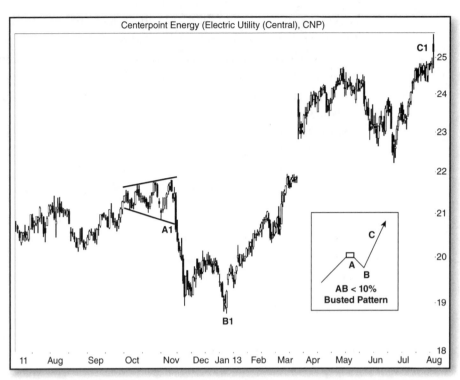

FIGURE 4.6 A busted broadening top breaks out downward but then the trend reverses.

To use this setup, follow these steps:

1. Use Table 4.1 to help identify a broadening top. For best results, look for an in-bound price trend (from the trend start to the start of the chart pattern) less than 3 months long. Single busted patterns with 3 months or less inbound price trends show gains averaging 57% (but that uses only 46 samples, so it is likely to change).
2. Price should breakout downward and drop no more than 10% below the bottom of the chart pattern.
3. Wait for the price to close above the top of the chart pattern.
4. Buy the stock at the open the next day. To enter the trade sooner, place a buy stop a penny or two above the top of the chart pattern.
5. Place a stop-loss order below the bottom of the broadening pattern or at a location of your choice.

Table 4.2 shows a few statistics for broadening tops with busted downward breakouts.

1. Of the 505 broadening tops with downward breakouts in a bull market, almost half (44%) saw price drop less than 10% before reversing trend and closing above the top of the chart pattern. That is frightening. Nearly half of all trades with downward breakouts will fail to make a meaningful decline. Wow.

TABLE 4.2	Statistics for Broadening Tops with Busted Downward Breakouts	
Description		**Result**
1. Percentage of broadening tops that bust		44%
2. Average rise after busting		36%
3. Average rise after single bust		50%
4. Percentage of single busts		68%
5. Percentage of double busts		15%
6. Percentage of triple+ busts		16%

2. The average rise is 36% for all busted patterns (single, double, and triple busts).

3. Broadening tops that single bust (only) show gains averaging 50%. That move measures from the top of the chart pattern to the ultimate high. It also represents over 200 *perfect* trades, so do not expect to duplicate that result in actual trading.

A frequency distribution of the gain shows that most of the broadening tops have gains in the 20% to 40% range.

4–6. Splitting the 44% of broadening tops that bust into single, double, and triple busts, we find that single busts predominate (68%) followed by triple busts (16%) and double busts (15%).

Buy Setup 2

Let us discuss some trading setups by looking at the length of the inbound price trend and overhead resistance.

Figure 4.7 shows price climbing out of overhead resistance (the jagged peaks to the left of A) and trending higher into the broadening top (B). A is the trend start, and B is the start of the chart pattern. The AB time must be less than six months for the best average performance (less than three months is even better).

The broadening top appears with the stock eventually closing above the top of the chart pattern at C (the breakout). In the *ideal* setup, there is no resistance above the chart pattern. That means the stock is making all-time highs with nothing to block the advance.

The stock chart shows an example of this setup on the daily chart. The trend start is at A1 when the stock bottoms. Price rises less than 6 months leading to the start of the broadening top (B1). At C1, the stock breaks out higher and begins its journey to the ultimate high (not shown), which ended in February 2014, above 41, for a gain of 58%. If you were to switch to the monthly scale, you would find that the breakout from the broadening top made an all-time high.

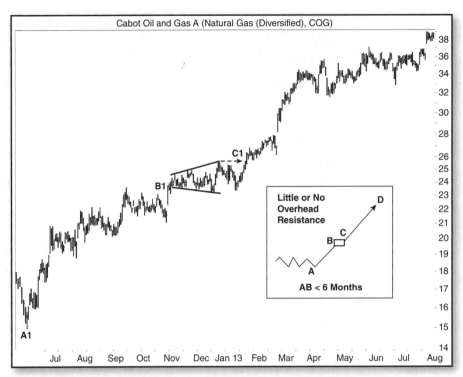

FIGURE 4.7 The inset shows the ideal broadening top setup without overhead resistance.

For the best results, here are the conditions for this setup.

1. Use Table 4.1 to help identify a broadening top.
2. The inbound price trend (from trend start to pattern start, AB in Figure 4.7) must be less than six months long (but three months is better).
3. No overhead resistance above the top of the chart pattern (price will break out to new all-time highs).
3a. Step 3 describes the ideal setup. If your situation has overhead resistance, then compute the percentage difference from the current price to the all-time high price. Use: $100 \times (\text{HighPrice} - \text{CurrentPrice})/\text{CurrentPrice}$.

   For example, if the current price is \$20 and the all-time high price is \$25, then the stock will have to climb $100 \times (25 - 20)/20$, or 25%, before it clears overhead resistance. Does the percentage seem doable? If not, then look for another setup.
4. Buy the stock at the open the day after price closes above the top of the broadening top. To enter the trade sooner, place a buy stop a penny or two above the top of the chart pattern.
5. Place a stop-loss order below the bottom of the broadening pattern or at a location of your choice.

TABLE 4.3	Statistical Analysis of Buy Setup 2	
Description	Inbound Trend ≤6 Months	Inbound Trend >6 Months
1. Occurrence, samples	28%, 178	24%, 155
2. Post-breakout average gain	62%	38%
3. Median gain	36%	19%
4. Gains over 25%	63%	42%
5. 5% failure rate	8%	12%
6. 10% failure rate	15%	30%

Table 4.3 shows the performance based on perfect trades for two different lengths of inbound price trend. Referring to Figure 4.7, the inbound price trend is the duration of the AB move, which measures from the trend start to the start of the chart pattern.

1. I found 651 broadening tops in bull markets, but when you sort them into various categories, samples become few. The two setups shown in the table occur between 24% and 28% of the time.

2, 3. For short inbound price trends, the post-breakout gain (CD in Figure 4.7) averages 62%, but the median is well below that: 36%. Large gains pull the average upward, skewing the results.

Notice that setups with shorter-term (≤6 months) inbound price trends perform better than longer ones. This makes intuitive sense. If a trend lasts a year, for example, you will make more money if you join the trend sooner rather than later.

4. A count of the number of gains over 25% range from 42% to 63% of patterns. Notice that the shorter-term trend outperforms the longer-term trend. That seems to be the case with many chart patterns in this book.

5, 6. The failure rates range between 8% and 30%. For example, 15% of broadening tops with short inbound price trends will see price fail to rise at least 10% after the breakout.

When you compare the two statistics columns, the middle column (inbound trend ≤6 months) shows superior performance.

■ When shopping for broadening tops, select those with short inbound price trends. They perform best.

Buy Setup 3

Figure 4.8 shows the last buy setup and the performance results tell why. I recommend avoiding this setup.

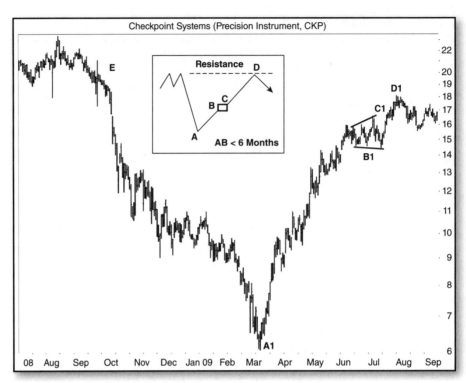

FIGURE 4.8 Overhead resistance at the ultimate high stops the rise.

The mountain range to the upper left of A represents overhead resistance. Point A is the trend start and price rises leading to the broadening top at B. The AB duration is less than six months for the best results.

Price breaks out upward at C and makes its way to the ultimate high, D. Resistance to an upward move wears the stock down, and the trend reverses at D. This setup is an example of a stock mired in too much overhead resistance that causes the stock to abandon its rise.

The stock chart shows an example of a situation you are probably familiar with. Overhead resistance is a dark cloud massing at E. The stock drops on the way to the bear market bottom, which it finds at A1.

A trend change ensues and the stock rises, moving upward when the bear market ends. By the time the stock forms the broadening top at B1 (a rise less than 6 months long), the stock has climbed from a low of just over 6 to a high of 16.61 at the top of the chart pattern, a move of almost 175%. That is a delicious return.

After the chart pattern breakout (C1), price rises to D1 (the ultimate high), but the stock is tired after climbing so far, and with overhead resistance blocking the way higher, the stock packs up its equipment and heads back down to base camp. The rise to D1 amounted to just 10%. After D1, the stock dropped more than 20% (not shown).

The rise from the top of the chart pattern to no overhead resistance (an all-time high) was 135% (the stock reached 39 back in 1996). Such a large move to clear overhead resistance suggests that Buy Setup 2 was unlikely and that this setup would occur. The broadening top happened too far up the price trend (on a percentage basis) to suggest another meaningful move high.

Here are the steps to finding this setup.

1. Use the identification guidelines in Table 4.1 to select a broadening top.
2. Overhead resistance is present so that after the chart pattern breaks out upward, it runs into that resistance.
3. Stocks with unrealistic gains from the breakout to the all-time high price (see Buy Setup 2, step 3a) are candidates for this setup. Stocks in weak industries or those that have breakouts in a weak general market are also candidates for this setup.

The rise from the breakout price to the ultimate high is meager, not always, but this is the worst performing buy setup.

The prior setup had stocks that were able to push through overhead resistance or broke out immediately to all-time highs. This setup captures the remaining ones that failed to break into all-time high territory.

Let us talk about the numbers, shown in **Table 4.4**.

1. This setup occurs most often (38%) when the price trend leading to the start of the chart pattern is less than or equal to 6 months. For longer trends, the frequency is just 11%. Combined, about half (49%) of all broadening tops will follow this setup.

2, 3. The best this setup can do is a 23% average gain and that is for perfect trades. Trends longer than 6 months have an average rise of just 11%. When compared to the prior setup's 62% average gain, this setup underperforms.

The median gain varies from 5% to 14%, depending on the inbound trend length.

4. Large gains, those over 25%, occur between 16% and 30% of the time. That frequency falls well short of the prior setup's 63% rate.

5, 6. The failure rate ranges from a yucky 17% to an obscene 65%.

TABLE 4.4 Statistical Analysis of Buy Setup 3		
Description	Inbound Trend ≤6 Months	Inbound Trend >6 Months
1. Occurrence, samples	38%, 243	11%, 69
2. Post-breakout average gain	23%	11%
3. Median gain	14%	5%
4. Gains over 25%	30%	16%
5. 5% failure rate	17%	42%
6. 10% failure rate	37%	65%

Again, because the performance is so bad, I recommend avoiding this setup. The one exception is if you can determine that price will rise far enough to overhead resistance before reversing. In visual terms, if the potential rise from C to D (see Figure 4.8) is high enough to be worth the risk of being wrong. Day and swing traders may find value in trading this setup.

■ Sell Setups

As good (or bad) as the buy setups are, the sell setups are awful. If you own the stock, the drop is often minor, too small to be worth selling. If you try to short the stock, the bulls will eat your lunch when price quickly turns and moves higher.

One way to make the best of a bad situation is to use busted chart patterns. These have upward breakouts with a price trend that flips direction. **Figure 4.9** shows the ideal configuration.

Price rises into the start of the chart pattern (A), as it should in all broadening tops. The stock breaks out upward from the broadening pattern and coasts up to B before reversing. The AB climb is less than 10%, by definition of a busted pattern. After that, the stock tumbles and closes below the bottom of the chart pattern (the dashed line). Once that happens, the upward breakout has busted and down the stock goes.

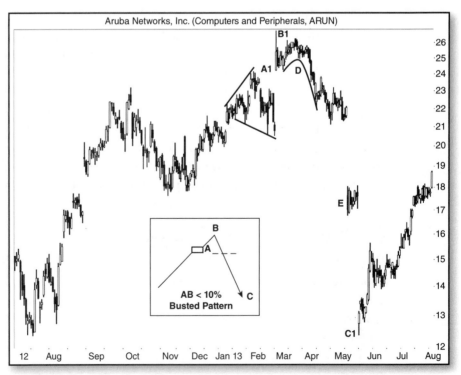

FIGURE 4.9 The ideal configuration for a busted upward breakout from a broadening top.

The stock chart shows an example of this setup. However, this stock climbs 10.8% above the breakout, so it does not technically qualify as a busted pattern. Pretend that it does. This stock stands as a cautionary tale about how difficult it can be to make money on the short side and how easy it can be to lose money on the long side.

On February 21, 2013, the company announced second quarter results. The next day (A1), the stock gapped above the broadening top and peaked the same day. That day became the ultimate high (B1).

The stock seemed to coast upward in a rounding turn (forming a descending and inverted scallop, really, at D) before beginning to head down in the next few weeks.

Almost three months after the quarterly report, the company announced preliminary third quarter results. The stock gapped down on the news (E) and then moved sideways for about a week.

The company announced final third quarter earnings and that it bought Meridian Apps, Inc. The next day, the stock gapped lower again, to C1.

Imagine that you bought the stock at A1 when the stock gapped up, thinking that such a bullish move would carry the stock higher. You would have had about a month to sell before the stock vacuumed the cash out of your pocket.

At E, the stock busted the broadening top. For those wanting to short the stock, that was the entry signal, but it was far below the bottom of the broadening pattern. Entry at E was far from ideal.

Traders shorting the stock had about a week to get into their positions before the company announced the Meridian acquisition. After that (after C1), the stock recovered quickly, leaving shorts scrambling for the exit.

The drop, as measured from the bottom of the chart pattern to the low at C1, was 40%. On paper that sounds good, but if you shorted the stock the day after E, and sold at the ultimate low, C1, you would have made 30% if you traded it perfectly.

Notice how the price of C1 sits on support setup by the prior price movement on the left side of the chart (the valleys in July 2012).

Here are the steps to using this setup:

1. Use the identification guidelines in Table 4.1 to select a broadening top.
2. Price breaks out upward but rises less than 10% before reversing and closing below the bottom of the chart pattern.
3. Look for underlying support to help gauge where price might turn.
4. Sell a long position or sell short if the anticipated drop outweighs the risk of loss.
5. For short positions, place a stop a penny above the top of the chart pattern or at a location of your choice.
6. Pray for a large decline.

Table 4.5 shows the performance of busted broadening tops.

TABLE 4.5 Statistics for Busted Upward Breakouts

Description	Result
1. Percentage of busted broadening tops with upward breakouts	28%
2. Average drop after busting	14%
3. Average drop for single busts	23%
4. Percentage of single busts	52%
5. Percentage of double busts	34%
6. Percentage of triple+ busts	14%

1. Over a quarter (28%) of broadening tops with upward breakouts will bust. If you own the stock, that statistic is scary. Imagine buying the stock the day after it closes above the top of the chart pattern (an upward breakout), only to see the stock plummet below the bottom of the broadening pattern when it busts. Ouch.

2, 3. The average drop for all busted patterns (single, double, and triple busts) is 14%. However, single busted patterns fare better: 23%, but that does not include the height of the broadening top. Thus, your loss—if you are unlucky enough to hold the stock until it reaches the ultimate low—can be considerable.

4–6. Splitting the 28% that bust into the three types of busts, we find that over half (52%) single bust, 34% double bust, and the remainder triple (or more) bust.

Sell Setup 2

I do not recommend trading this setup because the decline after the breakout is often meager. The failure of 41% to 55% of patterns declining at least 10% is startling.

Figure 4.10 shows the ideal configuration for Sell Setup 2. Price starts the upward trend at A and reaches the start of the broadening top (B) in less than 6 months. Price forms a broadening top and then breaks out downward from the pattern (C). The stock drops to the ultimate low at D where it finds support and completes a trend change by rebounding (rising at least 20%).

The stock chart shows an example on the daily scale. The trend starts at A1 and leads to the start of the chart pattern at B1. The A1-B1 move is about 2.5 months, well within the 6-month limit for this setup.

The broadening top unfolds like other broadening patterns with higher highs and lower lows. At C1, however, the stock closes below the bottom of the chart pattern, signaling a downward breakout. Price takes about two months before the downward move really begins. It ends at D1, 20% below the breakout.

People that sold at C1 would have been upset when the stock trended slightly higher from May to July. Those that shorted the stock at C1 might have closed their positions for a loss before July only to see the stock plummet.

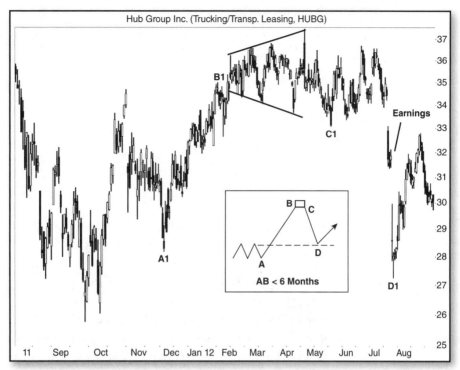

FIGURE 4.10 After rising into the broadening top, price breaks out downward and finds support at the dashed line.

This is an example of how quickly a stock can decline. The catalyst in this case was the announcement of disappointing earnings. On July 19, the company issued a press release about second quarter earnings on the date shown on the chart. Notice that the stock had already gapped down two days earlier as if someone knew ahead of time that earnings would disappoint.

Here are the steps to this setup:

1. Use the identification guidelines in Table 4.1 to select a broadening top.
2. For the best results, look for an inbound trend less than 6 months long. The inbound trend measures the time from the trend start to the start of the chart pattern.
3. Look for underlying support to help gauge where price might turn.
4. Sell a long position or sell short if the anticipated drop outweighs the risk of loss.
5. For short positions, place a stop a penny above the top of the chart pattern or at a location of your choice.

Table 4.6 shows two setups, sorted by the duration of the inbound price trend, as measured from the trend start to the pattern start.

TABLE 4.6	Statistical Analysis of Sell Setup 2	
Description	Inbound Trend ≤6 Months	Inbound Trend >6 Months
1. Occurrence, samples	60%, 290	40%, 197
2. Post-breakout average loss	15%	12%
3. Median loss	12%	8%
4. Losses over 25%	18%	13%
5. 5% failure rate	18%	22%
6. 10% failure rate	41%	55%

1. Most of the broadening tops (60%) with downward breakouts had price trends leading to the start of the chart pattern 6 months long or less.

2, 3. The post-breakout loss averages 12% to 15%. As one might expect, the median loss is lower. If you wish to trade this setup, stick to selecting patterns with short inbound price trends.

4. Losses over 25% are few, amounting to 13% to 18% of all trades.

5, 6. Eighteen to 22% of trades will see price drop less than 5% below the breakout price before rebounding. The 10% failure rate is dramatically higher, suggesting this setup will likely not lead to a large decline.

The results for inbound trends longer than six months appear in the right column, and they are inferior to the middle column. If you own a stock showing a broadening top, you are more likely to suffer a larger loss if the inbound trend is shorter than six months than if it is longer.

■ Best Stop Locations

Table 4.7 shows how often price hits two stop locations for each breakout direction.

TABLE 4.7	Stop Locations for Rectangles		
Description	Chance of Being Hit	Average Loss	Missed Trades, Gains/Losses
1. Penny below the pattern	3%	9%	42%
2. Within the pattern	79%	4%	41%
	Up Breakouts Above, Down Breakouts Below		
3. Within the pattern	76%	3%	16%
4. Penny above the pattern	3%	6%	15%

1. Penny below the pattern. For upward breakouts, price would trigger a stop placed a penny below the bottom of the broadening pattern 3% of the time, handing you a 9% loss. Those trades would go on to climb an average of 42%, leaving you picking your nose, wondering what went wrong.

2. Within the pattern. A stop placed somewhere between the top and bottom of the broadening top would trigger 79% of the time. Massive! The average loss narrows to 4%, and the stopped-out trades would climb an average of 41% if a stop were not used.

3. Within the pattern. For downward breakouts, the table shows the results. If you place a stop-loss order somewhere within the broadening top, you have a 76% chance of being taken out of the trade.

4. Penny above the pattern. Placing a stop above the top of the broadening pattern results in a significantly lower chance of the stop triggering. After being stopped out, the loss increases (to 6%) because the stop is placed farther away from the entry price than if you placed the stop within the chart pattern.

- For upward breakouts, place a stop-loss order a penny below the bottom of the broadening pattern. For downward breakouts, place a stop a penny above the top of the pattern.

■ Configuration Trading

To trade the following configurations, begin with these guidelines.

1. Find a broadening top on the *daily* chart that obeys the identification guidelines listed in Table 4.1.
2. Using the *weekly* scale, match what you see on your chart to one of the configurations. Figure 4.23 should help.
3. Buy at the open the day after the breakout or place an order to buy a penny above the top of the chart pattern (upward breakouts) or below the bottom of the pattern (downward breakouts).
4. Place a stop-loss order at a location of your choice.

I sorted my database of broadening tops according to the post-breakout gain and found 152 patterns with gains more than 35%. They formed two basic shapes, which I call configurations. The first appears in **Figure 4.11** on the weekly scale.

In a strong uptrend, price keeps trending higher for months, even years. I show that by the AB move in the inset. The AB move must be longer than 6 months. A broadening top appears (represented by the box) that gives the uptrend a pause. After an upward breakout from the broadening pattern, the uptrend resumes, climbing to C.

The stock chart shows an example. Price starts its upward move at A1 and climbs to the broadening top at B1. After an upward breakout, the stock resumes its climb to C1.

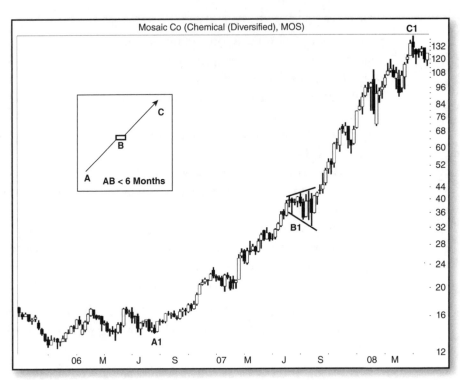

FIGURE 4.11 This broadening top acts as a continuation pattern in a long-term uptrend.

This configuration was the most popular, happening 58% of the time.

Match your chart to this configuration and buy when price closes above the top of the broadening pattern. If the uptrend is strong, a trendline that hugs price can be a warning sign of a trend change (when price closes below the trendline on the weekly chart). It might be time to sell, or it could be that the stock will continue climbing but at a slower rate.

Trend Change Rebound **Figure 4.12** shows the last configuration for large uptrend moves. Price drops for longer than 6 months (AB), turns at B, and climbs to C in a short duration move (BC is less than 6 months). The short BC move is important to catch the start of a new trend.

After an upward breakout, the stock rises (to D).

You often see this configuration after a bear market. The AB run would be the bear market decline, and the BD rise would be the bull market recovery.

The stock chart shows an example of this configuration on the weekly scale. The stock tumbled through the bear market from A1 to B1. Although the bear market ended in March 2009, this stock bottomed much earlier, at B1.

The stock made a short-duration run to the broadening top at C1, moved sideways for a time, then broke out upward and shot to D1.

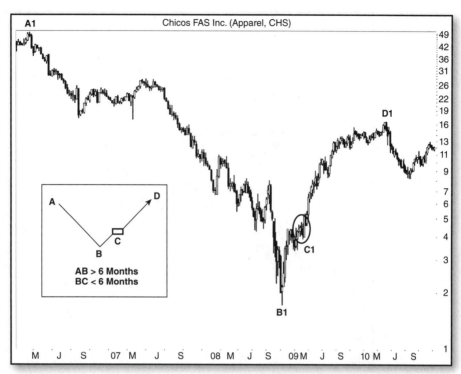

FIGURE 4.12 After a long downtrend, the stock recovers. Along the way, a broadening top appears.

This configuration appeared 34% of the time in the stocks I looked at.

Often a terrific time to buy stocks is when a bear market ends. Nearly all of the stocks will recover and recover with gusto. Price can double in a matter of weeks. Then chart patterns appear, but many of those will fail. Because a big move has already occurred, trade with caution.

This chart is an example in which the recovery was stronger than most. It started before the bear market ended and kept rising for almost 2 years.

Upward Breakout Duds

What configurations do broadening tops take that fail to perform as hoped? Here are some to consider.

Figure 4.13 shows the first of two configurations on the weekly scale. I found 145 patterns before the post-breakout rise became too high to be called a failure. This variation happened frequently: 60% of the time.

Price rises over the long term (AB) before encountering a broadening top. In many ways, it looks the same as Figure 4.7, except the move is long term, not short. The rise from the breakout (C) to where price poops out (D) is short, less than 10%.

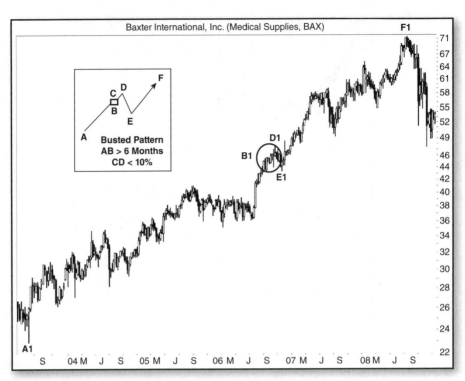

FIGURE 4.13 Price busts the pattern when the upward breakout fails to see the stock climb.

The trend reverses and price closes below the bottom of the broadening top (E), busting the upward breakout.

In many cases, the rise resumes upward to F but not always. Sometimes the stock just tumbles, from D to E and continues lower (not shown).

The stock chart on the weekly scale shows an example of this configuration. Price rises from A1 to B1 in a long-term upward climb. At B1, a broadening top appears, but it is difficult to see on this scale. The breakout from the broadening pattern is upward and price rises to D1 (less than 10%) before tumbling and making its way to E1.

After whipping the bulls out of the stock, price resumes its upward rise, to F1, double busting the broadening top. Buy when the stock closes above the top of the broadening pattern for the second time.

Overhead Resistance   **Figure 4.14** shows what happens 35% of the time. Price climbs to overhead resistance and then drops.

After rising over the long term (more than 6 months) from A to B, the stock peaks. Then it moves sideways, building overhead resistance (the dashed line). A broadening top forms at C. This one breaks out upward, and price rises to

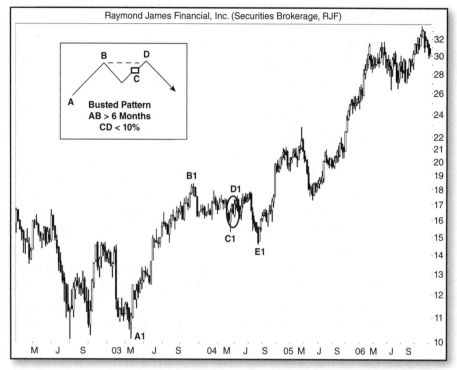

FIGURE 4.14 Price rises to overhead resistance and then drops.

the resistance area (D) before encountering trouble. The stock busts the upward breakout when it drops below the bottom of the broadening top on the way to E.

In many cases, the stock will continue this trading range behavior by forming multiple peaks before deciding on a new direction.

The stock chart on the weekly scale shows one example. The stock climbs from A1 to B1 in a long-term move. Then the stock drops to C1 before moving up to the broadening top (circled). The upward breakout carries price to D1 before it reverses and busts the pattern. In this example, another peak forms before the stock drops to E1.

In this configuration, the stock met overhead resistance that it could not plow through. In the prior configuration, the stock crested on slackening momentum. It just ran out of gas, so it refueled, and was on its way again.

If a chart pattern does not do what you expect it to do, then sell. If a broadening top busts, then it is probably best to sell immediately. If you expect a double bust, then it might be worth holding onto the stock, but do not use that as an excuse to maintain a losing position.

Downward Breakouts

Figure 4.15 shows the most frequent configuration that sends price dramatically lower. I used just 57 patterns before the decline to the ultimate low became too small. This configuration occurs 47% of the time.

Price rises from A to B in a long-term (more than 6 months) momentum play that sends the stock climbing a mountain. At the peak, B, a broadening top forms with a downward breakout. This ends the momentum move and sends price somersaulting back down the mountain (C).

The stock chart shows an example on the weekly scale. Price rises from A1 to B1 over the long term in a near straight-line run upward. It makes me salivate just looking at it. A broadening top appears hidden in the circle at B1. The downward breakout pushes the stock lower, but it takes time for the stock to reach C1.

Notice how C1 bottoms at the launch price, A1. In straight-line moves higher like the one shown from A1 to B1, the return trip can take the price back to the launch price, but often it bottoms just above the launch price and takes longer to get there. In other words, C1 bottoms just above A1, so be conservative with your price target.

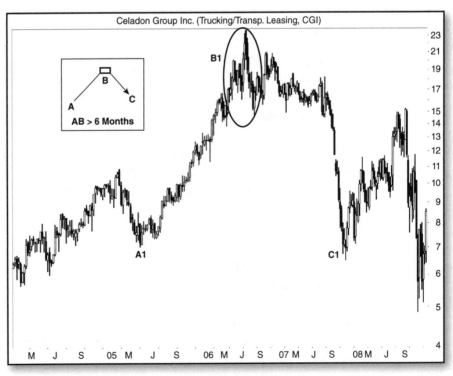

FIGURE 4.15   A downward breakout after a momentum play sends price lower.

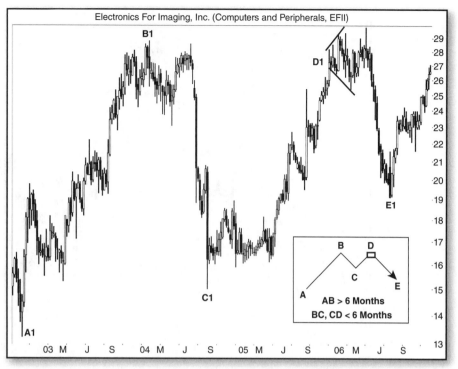

FIGURE 4.16 A broadening top completes a twin peak pattern that sends price lower.

Twin Peak Resistance   **Figure 4.16** shows a configuration that leads to a big drop, and it appears on the charts I looked at 39% of the time. It reminds me of a roller coaster.

Price rises over the long term (AB), eventually forming a peak. The stock retraces a portion of that climb (C) and then recovers to form a second peak. The BC and CD moves are frequently short term but not always as the stock chart shows.

A broadening top at D forms at overhead resistance setup by prior price action (the peak at B in this example). A downward breakout completes the pattern when the stock tumbles to E.

The stock chart on the weekly scale shows an example. Price forms the rollers with the A1 to D1 wave matching the inset's A to D move. After a downward breakout from the broadening top at D1, the stock retraces a good portion of the C1-D1 rise, when it bottoms at E1.

If you wish to short a stock showing this configuration, look for underlying support where the stock might reverse. Trade cautiously.

ABC Retrace   **Figure 4.17** shows a configuration that I found only 14% of the time. In this example, the stock heads down from A to B. Price then bounces in a

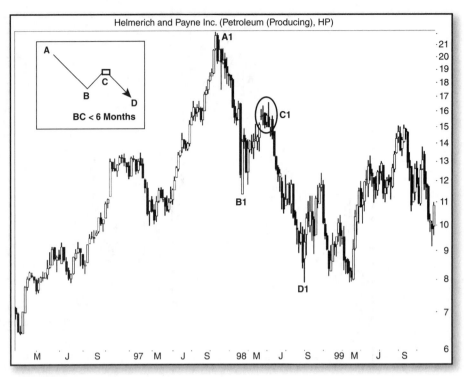

FIGURE 4.17 Price retraces a portion of the downward move.

short rise from B to C. A broadening top with a downward breakout signals that the retrace is over. Price drops to D.

The stock chart shows an example of this configuration on the weekly chart. The A1-B1 drop is short but steep. The stock hits support and bounces, retracing about half the A1-B1 drop when it rises to C1. The broadening top hidden at C1 has a downward breakout and price resumes its downward move (C1-D1) at a slightly slower pace than the A1-B1 decline.

If a broadening top appears at the top of an upward retrace (as in this example), then it could be an opportunity to short the stock. The resulting pattern might resemble a measured move down, so read the chapter on that pattern (Chapter 11), too.

Downward Breakout Failures

Figure 4.18 shows one of two versions of how downward breakouts typically fail. Your situation may be different, but this is the most common.

Price rises in a long-term uptrend from A to B. A downward breakout sends price lower, but it does not last long. Price drops by less than 10% before reversing (C).

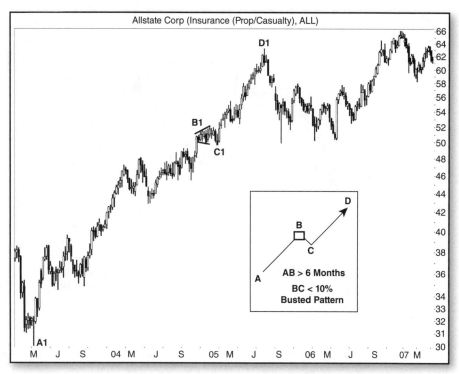

FIGURE 4.18 In a long uptrend, this downward breakout fails to drop price far.

When it closes above the top of the broadening top, it busts the downward breakout. Price continues rising to D.

One way to trade this is to wait for the broadening top to bust and then buy. Place an order to buy a penny above the top of the broadening pattern or buy at the open the day after the stock closes above the top of the chart pattern.

The stock chart shows how this scenario plays out in real life. The uptrend began at A1 and climbed to the broadening top at B1. The stock broke out downward from the broadening pattern, although it is hard to see on the weekly scale, and bottomed at C1.

The stock turned upward there and climbed to D1, the ultimate high. Anyone shorting this stock after the downward breakout would likely have suffered a loss.

This configuration happened 57% of the time in the 140 charts I looked at. The samples are few because I stopped cataloging when the post-breakout drop reached 10% (I do not consider drops larger than that a failure).

Resistance and Support Figure 4.19 shows a configuration for downward breakouts that occurs 43% of the time.

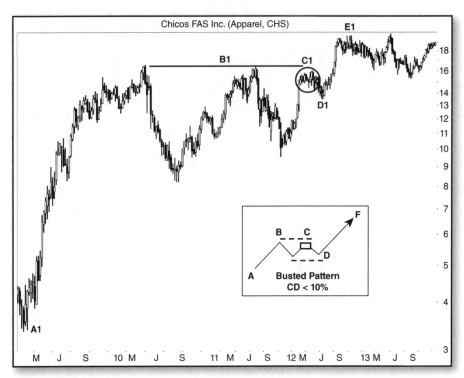

FIGURE 4.19 Overhead resistance stops the advance, but price does not drop far after a downward breakout.

Price rises from A to B and forms overhead resistance, often in the shape of a peak. Price retraces and forms another peak where the broadening top appears (C). A downward breakout sends price down but support catches the fall (D) and the stock turns higher. On the way to E, the stock busts the downward breakout.

Overhead resistance can be formed by any number of peaks, not just the one at B.

The stock chart on the weekly scale shows an example of this configuration. The stock climbs from A1 to B1. Overhead resistance (the horizontal line at B1) blunts the advance at C1 where a broadening top appears.

A downward breakout sends price tumbling to D1, but the drop is short. The stock reverses and climbs to E1, busting the downward breakout.

Once the stock busts the downward breakout, consider buying it. The move can be large, not always, but it could be a bet worth taking.

■ Measure Rule

The measure rule is a guideline to help determine how far price will climb (or drop) after a breakout. Look at **Figure 4.20** to see how the rule is applied.

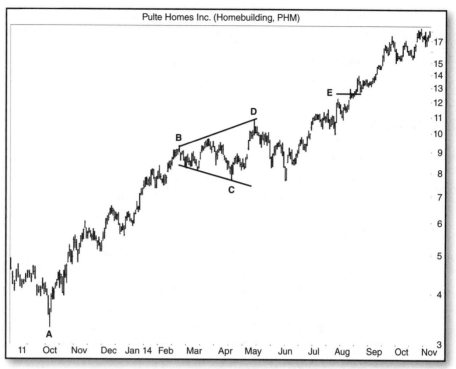

FIGURE 4.20   The measure rule applied to broadening tops.

The standard rule is to use the height of the chart pattern applied to the breakout price. In this example, the height is D − C (the last two trendline touches, at its widest). Add the height to the top of the chart pattern, D, for upward breakouts, or subtract it from C for downward breakouts.

In this example, D is 10.82 (high price), C is 7.65 (low price) for a height of 3.17. The target would be 13.99 for upward breakouts and 4.48 for downward ones.

Here is a wreck check. Take the height of the chart pattern, divide it by the breakout price, and multiply the result by 100. In this example, that is 100 × 3.17/10.82, or 29%. That percentage sounds like a reasonable amount the stock could climb. However, the same computation for a downward breakout means a drop of 41%. That is a whopper of a decline, too far to be believable because the average drop is just 16%.

Unfortunately, the full height works only 47% (downward breakouts) to 69% (upward breakouts) of the time. Cutting the height in half gives a closer target. Upward breakouts reach the closer target 88% of the time, and downward breakouts reach it 76% of the time. I show the upward breakout half-height target as E in the figure.

When I use the measure rule, I look for nearby support or resistance closest to the target to help gauge how far the stock might move. That method works well.

- The measure rule works 69% of the time for upward breakouts and 47% of the time for downward breakouts from broadening tops.

Trading

Figure 4.21 shows two potential trades. A broadening top with an upward breakout appears at C. The trend start is important to some setups, so where does it start?

From C, we look to the left (backward in time) for the lowest valley before which price rises at least 20%. That occurs at B (the low at B is 94.15, and the high at A is 114.95, or 22%, above B). So B is the trend start.

The time between B and C is about two months.

Looking back at the historical chart (not shown) shows that peak A sets an all-time high. Thus, an upward breakout from the stock would quickly push through any overhead resistance and would begin setting all-time highs. Good news!

This scenario is Buy Setup 2 (Figure 4.7), except there is overhead resistance until the stock reaches an all-time high. That setup has a short-term inbound trend (the

FIGURE 4.21 Is the broadening top at C worth an investment?

rise from A to B) and an upward breakout, the same situation as shown in the Figure 4.21 (the rise from B to C).

Just by looking at the chart, the move to clear overhead resistance is minor, so there is no need to compute the gain to see whether it is reasonable.

Two things bother me about this setup. First is the volatility. I do not care for the wide price swings each day. Second is the price. Research says that low-priced stocks, those below $20, outperform higher-priced ones.

After the breakout from the broadening top, the stock hit 181 in July 2015 (not shown).

The second broadening top appears at D. This one, however, breaks out downward, and price drops to the ultimate low at E, a drop of 9%. The stock could follow Figures 4.15 or 4.18.

If you own the stock and it drops 10% below the bottom of the broadening top, then sell (because 44% bust a downward breakout, there is a good chance the stock will not decline 10%, so if it does, it could mean a larger decline coming). That path would follow Figure 4.15. You would suffer a 10% loss, but that would be it.

If you considered selling short, look for underlying support. I show a support area around 111 that would worry me. If the stock dropped to that area and rebounded, you would be looking at a loss of less than 7%. Is that potential profit worth the risk of selling short? My answer is no.

Instead, I would trade this pattern by treating it as a potential busted broadening top (the bust is not shown). Place a buy order a penny above the top of the chart pattern or wait for price to close above the top of the chart pattern before buying at the open the next day. That would put you into the stock at about 129 (or less) for a potential gain of 40% (if sold at the ultimate high of 181). That gain represents a perfect trade.

Actual Trade

Figure 4.22 shows an actual trade I made using a broadening top. In July 2009, I was worried that price would retrace back to the bottom of the broadening top, but I bought anyway (B). The concern stemmed from the straight-line run up from the low at A. How much higher would the stock climb without retracing?

In my notes to the trade, I wrote, "New management took over in January/February so a turnaround is in place." Insiders were buying the stock and not selling (that is good news).

I thought that the small knot of congestion at B was a partial decline, so I bought before the breakout and received a fill at 10.75. My target was 17 where overhead resistance began, but I was willing to hold up to 27, too, for a longer-term trade.

Resistance at 17 appears on the monthly chart (inset) at C. D is where I bought the stock and you can see how price bumped up against that resistance a few times before I sold at F.

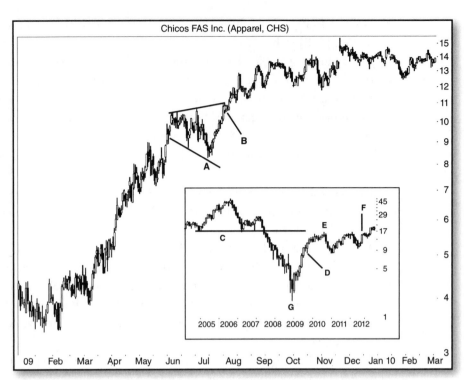

FIGURE 4.22 This trade resulted in a gain of 42%.

In April 2010, right at peak E, I placed a conditional order to sell the stock if it were to drop below 13.74 before October 1. Within two weeks, the stock was selling at 12 and change, but the order never triggered. Apparently, I canceled it.

Here are my notes about the sale. On "3/1/12, I placed a trailing stop at 1 point below the bid, good till canceled, until 7/1/12." That date is near point F.

"3/15/2012. I canceled the trailing stop at 14.64 and raised it to 14.91 because I think this is going to drop. It is a good earnings event pattern and I do not want to ride it down a buck before it moves higher. Stop placed just below support."

The good earnings event pattern is one in which the stock climbs on the announcement day and is like a ball thrown into the air. Price coasts higher for a time but then starts to ease back down in a week to 10 days after the announcement of earnings.

It is difficult to see on the monthly chart, but after I sold, the stock dropped for three months before starting a recovery. The stock almost hit 20 in the 3 years since (yawn). I made 42% (including dividends) on the trade during a hold time of just over 2.5 years.

Application How do we apply the information in this chapter to the situation shown in Figure 4.22?

Point G bottoms in mid-November 2008, and the broadening top starts in June 2009, a 7.5-month difference.

Figure 4.8 looks like the perfect match except for the AB duration is less than 6 months (ours is 7.5 months). Technically, the setup does not apply. If we ignore the AB duration requirement and concentrate on the rise from the broadening top to overhead resistance, then this setup is worth considering.

Because the buy price was 10.75, and with overhead resistance starting at 17, a 58% gain would make for a tasty reward.

Figure 4.11 is the chart that applies, because the AB move is more than 6 months, price rises going into the broadening top, and it has an upward breakout. The setup suggests a good rise, and even though I cut the trade short, I still pocketed 42%.

Figure 4.13 also applies except overhead resistance is often the cause of a busted pattern. Because the bear market ended in March 2009, four months before I bought, and with overhead resistance so far away, I would expect the bullish current to carry the stock upward. So I would discard Figure 4.13.

■ Closing Position

With 60% of broadening tops breaking out upward, it can be easier to determine when a breakout will occur. You can use the 5-touch guideline (wait for 5 distinct minor high or minor low touches, 3 on 1 trendline and 2 on the other) and assume a breakout will occur on the next touch. By that time, the broadening pattern should be wide enough that a cross to the opposite trendline would be more difficult (but not impossible, of course).

Throwbacks and pullbacks occur about randomly, but expect a retrace just in case.

Busted downward breakouts happen 44% of the time, so do not expect an extended move down. If you find a busted broadening top with a downward breakout, the move after it busts averages 50%. That is as tasty as a hot fudge banana split.

Use the setups and configurations to place the pattern in the surrounding price landscape. You do not want to buy a broadening pattern when the associated configuration suggests a losing trade.

■ Setup Synopsis

Figure 4.23 may help you identify the various types of trading setups. See the associated figure for an explanation.

"Occurs" in the figures means how often I found the configuration in the stocks I looked at. If two configurations apply to your situation, then the one with a more frequent occurrence (a higher percentage) is the one you should choose to follow.

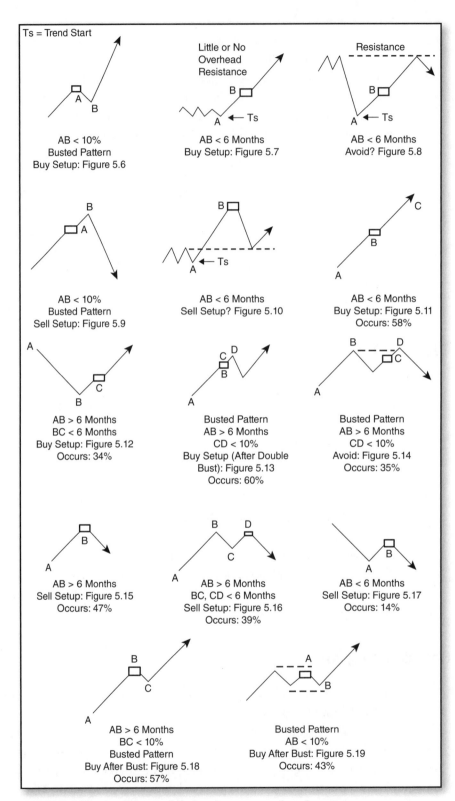

FIGURE 4.23 A collection of ideal trading setups and configurations.

CHAPTER 5

Double Bottoms

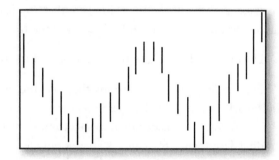

A double bottom is aptly named: two valleys hit bottom near the same price. What more is there to know? Plenty.

Double bottoms act as reversals of the downward price trend, meaning price drops and hits bottom like an alcoholic realizing he cannot live like this. After the double bottom, the hangover ends and price recovers.

That scenario is how the typical double bottom unfolds, but there are exceptions. Sometimes price trends upward, forms a double bottom, and then resumes the up-trend. Those continuation patterns are rare and performance is slightly worse, too.

Sometimes price reverses after a double bottom only to reverse again and drop to a lower bottom. Unfortunately, that situation happens too often, leaving the trader or investor with a loss. Avoiding losing situations is why I wrote this book.

Double bottoms come in four varieties, all based on the shape of each bottom (called Adam and Eve for narrow or wide, respectively). For this chapter, I dispensed with the Adam and Eve varieties and just lumped them into one category: double bottoms.

Let us look at some examples and describe their behavior.

■ Behavior at a Glance

Before I discuss double bottoms, let us explore a little-known fact I uncovered. Consider **Figure 5.1**.

I programmed my computer to find twin valleys that obey all of the identification guidelines of double bottoms except for confirmation. Confirmation occurs when price closes above the highest peak between the two bottoms (Above A). A confirmed pattern is a good egg, a valid pattern, perhaps one worth trading. An unconfirmed pattern is meaningless squiggles on a price chart.

I found 20,720 patterns from January 1970 to October 2014. Not all stocks covered the entire period. I discovered that 44% of the time, the stock closes below the lower of the two valleys (B in the figure). The other 56% of the time, the stock closes above A, the highest peak in the double bottom.

The point is this: Buying a twin bottom pattern before confirmation will be a mistake almost half the time. Imagine that you have a 44% chance of having a heart attack on the next trade. Would you take the trade?

■ Unconfirmed double bottoms fail 44% of the time.

For the 56% of twin bottoms that become double bottoms, the average rise in bull markets was 47%. That rise measures from the breakout to the ultimate high of 2,743 trades, so consider them perfect trades that you will never duplicate in actual trading. Use the performance statistics only for comparison to other chart patterns, not as a gauge of how you may do trading them.

For the following statistics, I used 2,743 double bottoms in 1,024 stocks from July 1991 to June 2015, pulled only from bull markets.

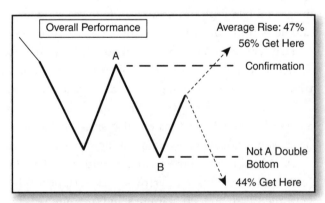

FIGURE 5.1   In 44% of the cases, the stock continues lower without confirming the double bottom.

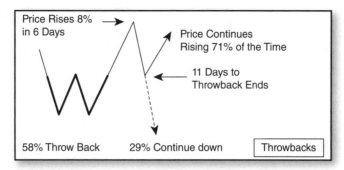

FIGURE 5.2 Typical throwback behavior after a double bottom.

Throwbacks

Figure 5.2 shows the behavior of price after double bottoms with throwbacks. By definition, a throwback occurs within a month of the breakout when price returns to or comes close to the breakout price. The breakout price is the same as the confirmation price, which is the price of the highest peak between the two bottoms. I found that 58% of double bottoms throw back.

- Double bottoms throw back 58% of the time.

The throwback sequence starts after an average rise of 8% in 6 days. Then the stock drops and returns to the breakout price. That takes an additional 5 days for a total trip time of 11 calendar (not trading) days.

After the throwback ends, the stock resumes its upward move 71% of the time. Twenty-nine percent of the time the stock will close below the bottom of the chart pattern, meaning a loss to anyone who bought after the breakout.

- Price resumes an upward move 71% of the time after a double bottom throwback.

Busted Bottoms

If you trade chart patterns often enough, you will likely buy a double bottom that sees price reverse quickly, leaving you with a hole in your pocket where the money used to be. Here are a few statistics about busted patterns.

Figure 5.3 shows how busted double bottoms typically behave. By definition, a busted double bottom sees price rise less than 10% after the breakout before reversing and closing below the bottom of the chart pattern.

I found that 19% of double bottoms bust. If the stock single busts (after an upward breakout, price reverses and drops at least 10% below the bottom of the double bottom), the decline averages 22%.

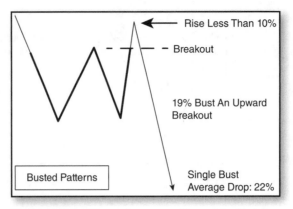

FIGURE 5.3 The performance of busted double bottoms.

If you want to short a stock, consider trading a busted double bottom. I will describe details of this setup later in this chapter.

■ Double bottoms bust 19% of the time.

■ Identification

Figure 5.4 shows an example of a double bottom. Refer to **Table 5.1** as we discuss the identification guidelines.

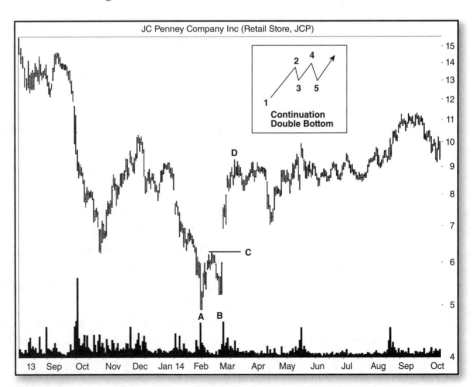

FIGURE 5.4 A double bottom in a struggling company sees the stock rise.

CHART PATTERNS: AFTER THE BUY

TABLE 5.1	Identification Guidelines
Characteristic	**Discussion**
Downtrend	Price should trend down going into the first bottom such that the double bottom acts as a reversal of the trend.
Two valleys	Price bottoms out near the same price, forming two valleys. The average price difference between the two is just 2%.
Bottom separation	The distance between the two bottoms can vary from near (several days apart) to far (several months apart). The average is 49 days apart.
Rise between bottoms	I did not set a minimum rise between the two valleys, but the average is 23%. The common standard is at least 10%.
Volume	Volume is higher on the left bottom 64% of the time.
Breakout	Price breaks out of the double bottom when it closes above the highest peak between the two bottoms.

Downtrend. Price should trend downward going into the chart pattern. One guideline I use is that the trend must start above the top of the chart pattern (above C). The figure shows the stock declining on the far left from a price of 15 to the start of the double bottom (A) below 5.

The J. C. Penney double bottom acts as a reversal. Contrast that reversal with the continuation double bottom shown in the inset. In this continuation pattern, price trends upward (1), peaking at 2. The double bottom is at points 3 and 5. Notice that price peaks at 2 but that peak is below 4. When peak 2 remains below 4, the pattern acts as a continuation pattern and not a reversal.

Continuation patterns occur just 7% of the time and performance is slightly worse: reversals see price rise by 47%, but continuation patterns show an average rise of 43%.

Two Valleys. The two bottoms can look as different from on another as a one-day price spike versus a rounded turn that takes a month to complete. I ignored the shape of each bottom for this chapter.

The guideline I use is that the two bottoms should appear near the same price, often within a few percentage points of each other. I allow variations up to 10%, especially for low-priced stocks (which are more volatile). In Figure 5.4, the two bottoms (AB) are 7% apart.

Bottom Separation. My database shows the two bottoms vary from three days to over a year apart. Both extremes are rare. Double bottoms wider than the median month outperform. Figure 5.4 shows the two bottoms 20 calendar days apart.

Rise between Bottoms. There should be an extensive rise between the two bottoms often reaching or exceeding 10%. Of course, if you have a double bottom with valleys just days apart, the rise between the two valleys will be far less than 10%.

In Figure 5.4, the measure I use is the low price at the lowest bottom (the low price at A in this case) to the high at C. The height of the double bottom in this example measures 28%.

Obviously, if you are a day trader, this measure does not apply. Just look for a rise proportional to the width of the double bottom.

Volume. Although it does not look like it, volume in the 5 days surrounding bottom A (2 days before to 2 days after) is more than twice as large as it is around bottom B. The volume spike on bottom B occurs during the breakout, not on formation of the second bottom. Volume higher on the left bottom happens 64% of the time.

Let me also offer this tidbit: Breakout volume exceeding the 1-month average does not mean a better-performing double bottom. In fact, the performance results are the same: 47% average rise. Those that claim a double bottom confirms only after a high volume breakout are wrong. Those that say a high volume breakout leads to better performance are wrong.

Breakout. The double bottom confirms as a valid chart pattern when price closes above the top of the pattern (C). A close above C is also called the breakout. If price closes below the bottom of the chart pattern (below the lower valley, A in this example) before reaching confirmation, then you do not have a double bottom. Rather, you have squiggles on the price chart.

In Figure 5.4, the stock confirms the chart pattern when it breaks out by gapping above the line at C. Price goes on to reach the ultimate high (D) by soaring 48%.

■ Buy Setups

The first buy setup is difficult to find because price must have the stamina to reach all-time high territory. If it falls short, which is likely, this setup becomes the disaster described in Buy Setup 2.

Figure 5.5 shows what to look for in the inset. A double bottom (the box at B) appears after a downward move. Overhead resistance awaits at A as price climbs after the double bottom completes. The stock will likely pause along the rise to the ultimate high (C) as it encounters resistance, but it eventually pushes through to post an all-time high.

For an example of this setup, consider the stock chart (daily scale). I show two double bottoms. The trend start for both double bottoms begins at A1. Before that, the stock drops by at least 20% (not shown, but a 20% drop is how to locate the trend start).

FIGURE 5.5 One ideal double bottom setup occurs when price pushes through overhead resistance.

According to a press release by the company on February 16, 2012, the chairman and CEO Bill Ayer announced his retirement. The next day, D, the stock peaked but began a quick drop going into the first double bottom, EF.

Price confirmed the double bottom and climbed to G before ending its uphill run with a 4% gain. This double bottom is one of those situations in which overhead resistance, company, industry, or world events conspired to beat the stock down.

Look at double bottom B1. It shares the same trend start, A1, as I mentioned. In fact, the peak at A1 represents all-time high territory. All the stock needs to do is clear that hurdle and soar. The first double bottom failed to make it to all-time high territory. Will B1?

Price confirms the double bottom at I when the stock closes above the peak between the two bottoms opposite B1. The airline stock pushes through overhead resistance and flies into virgin skies waiting just 12% above the breakout price. It continues gaining altitude, eventually posting a gain of 92% at the ultimate high (not shown).

Compare double bottoms EF and B1. Both have a twin peak (A1-D and H), leading to a quick drop that sends the stock down to the double bottom. Bottom E hits the dirt a lot faster than does bottom B1. Other than that and the retirement announcement, I do not see much difference between the two patterns. One worked and the other did not.

For best results, here are the conditions for this setup:

1. Look for a double bottom that obeys the identification guidelines listed in Table 5.1.
2. Find the price at which the stock will enter all-time high territory.
3. Compute the percentage change from the double bottom's breakout price to the all-time high price. Use: 100 × (High Price − Breakout Price)/Breakout Price. For example, if the breakout price is $20 and the all-time high price is $25, then the stock will have to climb 100 × (25 − 20)/20, or 25%, before it clears overhead resistance.
4. Does the percentage gain in step 3 seem reasonable? If not, then look for another setup.

    I measured the gain from the breakout price to the all-time high and found that the median rise was 20% and the average was 31%. If step 3 gives significantly higher numbers than those two, then consider looking elsewhere for a more promising trade.
5. Place a buy order a penny above the breakout price or buy the stock at the open a day after the breakout.
6. Place a stop-loss order a penny below the lower of the two bottoms.

Ideally, look for a setup in which the double bottom is near the all-time high. The farther the double bottom is from the all-time high, the higher the risk of Buy Setup 2 occurring.

Table 5.2 shows why this setup is worth looking for.

1. Long-term (over 6 months) inbound price trends are rare, happening just 4% of the time. The shorter term occurs more often, 20% of the time. Because the performance of this setup is outstanding regardless of the length of the inbound price trend, you can ignore the inbound trend length (that is, ignore searching for the trend start).

TABLE 5.2 Statistical Analysis of Buy Setup 1		
Description	Inbound Trend ≤6 Months	Inbound Trend >6 Months
1. Occurrence, samples	20%, 476	4%, 93
2. Post-breakout average gain	89%	88%
3. Median gain	61%	62%
4. Gains over 25%	84%	77%
5. 5% failure rate	1%	1%
6. 10% failure rate	3%	3%

2, 3. The average gain is almost 90%. The median gain is also impressive, just over 60%. The differences between the averages and the medians are that large gains pull the averages up. Additional samples would likely pull the results down to earth. Use the numbers only for comparison, not as a gauge of how your trade might do. These numbers are for hundreds of perfect trades.

4. Large gains, those over 25%, occur nearly all of the time as the table shows. Unfortunately, this setup is rare enough that overhead resistance will often kill the upward move, turning it into Buy Setup 2. Those stocks that have staying power and breakout to a new high can soar with eagles. Watch for drones up there.

5, 6. Do not be fooled by the low failure rates. This setup fails to see price climb by less than 10%. However, I found only 16 patterns that failed in the 569 samples. You may not be so lucky. More likely is that this setup will turn into Buy Setup 2 when price encounters resistance and reverses trend.

Buy Setup 2

The second buy setup occurs often, judging by the numbers in Table 5.3. This setup is one you will want to avoid. I will discuss the statistics in a moment. First, though, look at the inset of **Figure 5.6,** which shows what happens.

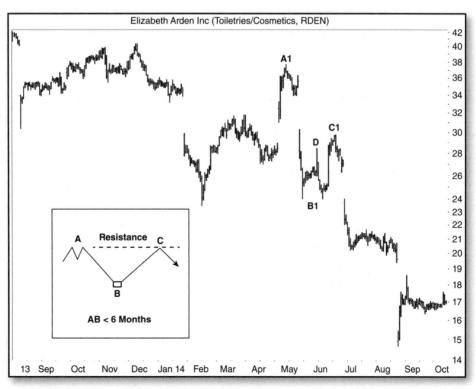

FIGURE 5.6 Overhead resistance stops the advance.

The stock forms overhead resistance that I show as a mountain range at A. For the best performance, look for a quick drop into the double bottom, B. By quick, I mean within six months from the trend start to the valley of the first bottom (B).

Price forms a double bottom, and it confirms as a valid chart pattern when price rises above the peak between the two bottoms. In this setup, however, the stock cannot push through overhead resistance (C). The trend reverses and the stock heads down.

Here are the conditions for this setup.

1. Look for a double bottom that obeys the identification guidelines listed in Table 5.1.
2. The inbound price trend (from trend start to the first bottom) is less than six months long (for the best results).
3. Find where overhead resistance will likely stop the stock.
4. Compute the percentage change from the double bottom's breakout price to resistance. Use: 100 × (Resistance − Breakout price)/Breakout price. For example, if the breakout price is $20 and overhead resistance begins at $25, then the stock will climb 100 × (25 − 20)/20, or 25%, before it hits resistance.
5. Can you make enough money with the projected gain from step 4 to outweigh the risk of failure?
6. If yes, then place a buy order a penny above the breakout price or buy the stock at the open a day after the breakout.
7. Place a stop-loss order a penny below the lower of the two bottoms and trail it upward.

The stock chart in Figure 5.6 shows an example of this setup.

The stock peaked in May 2013 (not shown) at almost 50 before entering a stairstep decline. When the double bottom appeared a year later (B1), the stock had been cut in half. You might think that when goods or services are on sale for 50% off, it represents a bargain. That is not always the case with stocks, though, as the chart shows. The stock has dropped another 62% as of January 2016, to about 9 (not shown).

In this example, the trend start is at A1, leading to a short-term decline to the double bottom at B1. Price moves higher and eventually closes above D (at C1), confirming the chart pattern as a valid one. However, the stock reversed at C1, busting the upward breakout when the stock closed below the bottom of B1. The rise from D to C1 measured a paltry 5%.

If you look at the headlines, the company cut its revenues and earnings outlook in January. That news caused the stock to gap lower. After the earnings announcement in mid-May, the stock gapped down again. Clearly, the market hated the news.

A large drop is often a clue that it will underperform in the future, especially after a dead-cat bounce (the stock drops in one session at least 15%, like it did in May and

TABLE 5.3	Statistical Analysis of Buy Setup 2	
Description	Inbound Trend ≤6 Months	Inbound Trend >6 Months
1. Occurrence, samples	63%, 1,483	13%, 317
2. Post-breakout average gain	30%	25%
3. Median gain	20%	18%
4. Gains over 25%	40%	36%
5. 5% failure rate	11%	15%
6. 10% failure rate	28%	31%

again in August). Often (38% of the time) one dead-cat bounce follows another within 6 months; 26% occur in 3 months.

As an investment, the stock was a poor choice. You should be looking for a healthy stock that stumbles or one that is punished unusually hard when the market dips. Stocks that drop most rebound fastest (I proved this), but they should have solid fundamentals, not be struggling like Elizabeth Arden.

Table 5.3 shows the performance results for this setup.

1. Of the two buy setups in this chapter, this one is the most prolific. It occurs 76% of the time, split into short and long inbound price trends.

2, 3. The post-breakout gain averages between 25% and 30%, depending on the length of the inbound price trend. The median gain is less, between 18% and 20%. When compared to the prior setup's average gain of 89%, these results are pathetic.

4. Gains over 25% are fewer than in the last setup, which is no surprise. In fact, only 36% to 40% of trades do exceptionally well.

5, 6. The 5% failure rate of this setup rests in the medium category, 11% to 15% (the best patterns show failures about 5%). The 10% failure rate is even worse, as the table shows.

Buying Opportunity Buy Setup 1 targets double bottoms near the all-time high price. Buy Setup 2 finds those farther away. In both setups, overhead resistance can stop an advance. Use that knowledge to your advantage.

Measure the percentage change from the breakout price to where you expect overhead resistance will stop the stock. If the stock performs as you expect and hits resistance, will you be satisfied with the return?

For example, if overhead resistance is a solid block of horizontal price movement at 20 with the breakout price at 17, that is a 3-point move, or 17%. Is a 17% gain worth trading? If so, then you can use a limit order to sell at, say, 19.97 and place a buy stop at 17.01. After commissions, you should net about 17%.

Should the stock show strength, you can always rescind the limit order before the sale and ride price higher.

If the stock fails to perform as expected, then sell it and look elsewhere for a more promising trade.

■ Sell Setup

There is only one sell setup for double bottoms, and that is when the pattern busts. The inset of **Figure 5.7** shows the ideal configuration.

The double bottom is at A. Price breaks out normally but rises less than 10% above the breakout price (the move from A to B). Then something goes wrong and the stock drops. When it closes below the lower of the two bottoms, it busts the upward breakout. I show that as downtrend C.

For an example of what a busted double bottom looks like, I repeated the Elizabeth Arden figure. Price rises just 5% before reversing and closing below the bottom of the chart pattern.

Another example is busted double bottom EF in Figure 5.5. If we assume traders shorted the stock when it closed below the EF bottom, the drop to the low in May measured just 7%. Anyone shorting the stock would probably have posted a loss because they would likely not have covered the short at the lowest price for the day.

FIGURE 5.7   Sell Setup 1: a busted double bottom.

To use this setup, follow these steps:

1. Use Table 5.1 to help identify a double bottom.
2. Price should breakout upward and rise no more than 10% above the top of the chart pattern.
3. Price reverses and *closes* below the lowest valley in the double bottom, busting the upward breakout.
4. If underlying support is far away, sell a long holding or sell short at the open the next day.
5. Place a stop-loss order a penny above the top of the double bottom or at a location of your choice.

Table 5.4 lists statistics related to busted double bottoms.

1. Nineteen percent of double bottoms will bust. When they do, it will be a challenge to eke out any profit at all. Your timing must be exquisite for that to happen.

2, 3. The average decline after a double bottom busts is 15%. That means the stock drops 15% below the lower of the two bottoms. Single busts drop farther, 22%.

4–6. Of the 19% that bust, they split into single busts (58%), double busts (30%), and three or more busts (11%).

Should you sell a long-side holding if a double bottom busts? Maybe. If you sell, you cap the loss immediately instead of sitting back and watching the stock go down day by day. A large loss often begins with a small one.

If you decide to hold on, like many buy-and-hold investors and position traders will do, decide how far price might decline by looking for underlying support. If support is nearby, say, 5% below the bottom of the chart pattern, then expect that the stock will punch through it.

If support is farther away, can you tolerate such a loss? If it blows through that support and continues lower, when will you sell? Determine at what price the market is saying you made a mistake. When the stock reaches that price, sell.

You can use the measure rule (discussed later in this chapter) to help determine where price might stop. Instead of adding to the breakout price the chart pattern's height (from highest peak between the two bottoms to the lower of the two bottoms),

TABLE 5.4	Statistics for Busted Upward Breakouts
Description	**Result**
1. Percentage of double bottoms that bust	19%
2. Average drop after busting	15%
3. Average drop after single bust	22%
4. Percentage of single busts	58%
5. Percentage of double busts	30%
6. Percentage of triple+ busts	11%

subtract it from the lower of the two bottoms. The result will be a target in which price might touch ground and stop reversing. Or not. The stock could be digging a grave, too.

Try changing the height into a percentage of the breakout price (or price of the lowest bottom) to see whether such a loss is tolerable to your wallet or purse.

For example, if the height of the chart pattern is 1 point and the stock has a breakout price of 10 then a drop to 8 (10 is the peak with a height of 1, so 9 is the bottom of the pattern with an expected decline of 1, to $8) for a potential decline of 1/9 to 1/10, or 10% to 11%.

■ Best Stop Locations

If your buy a stock showing a double bottom, where should you place a stop-loss order? **Table 5.5** shows how often price hits two stop locations.

1. Penny below the pattern. Placing a stop-loss order a penny below the lower of the two bottoms results in the safest of the two stop locations. The chance of the stop being hit is just 2%. If hit, the average loss would be 9%, and the missed trades will turn and rise an average of 50%.

2. Within the pattern. If you place the stop somewhere within the double bottom, the chance of being hit is 76%. You would suffer an average loss of 5%, and the stopped-out trades would go on to make 48%.

■ The best stop location is a penny below the lower of the two bottoms, but the potential loss may be large, depending on the height of the double bottom.

■ Configuration Trading

To trade the following configurations, begin with these guidelines:

1. Find a double bottom on the *daily* chart that obeys the identification guidelines listed in Table 5.1.
2. Using the *weekly* scale, match what you see on your chart to one of the configurations. Figures 6.18 and 6.19 should help.
3. Buy at the open the day after the breakout or place an order to buy a penny above the top of the chart pattern.
4. Place a stop-loss order below the lower bottom or at a location of your choice.

TABLE 5.5 Stop Locations for Double Bottoms			
Description	Chance of Being Hit	Average Loss	Missed Trades, Gains/Losses
1. Penny below the pattern	2%	9%	50%
2. Within the pattern	76%	5%	48%

FIGURE 5.8 A double bottom appears in an extensive upward trend.

The following configurations used hundreds of charts, sorted by the best performing, all using the weekly scale.

Figure 5.8 shows the first buy configuration in the inset. Price begins an upward move (A) that follows a trendline higher over the long term (more than 6 months). At B, the stock peaks and begins declining into double bottom C. This decline typically takes less than 6 months. The breakout from the double bottom sees price resume the uptrend (D).

An example of this is the A1-D1 pattern on the weekly scale. Imagine riding your bicycle up this one. Yikes!

Price makes an extensive rise at A1 to B1, lasting over a year. The stock peaks at B1 and drops to the double bottom at C1. The stock confirms the pattern and continues its rise until reaching the ultimate high at D1. After D1, the stock tumbles. Notice the log price scale.

This variant is the most common, happening 41% of the time in 167 patterns I cataloged. It depends on a robust bull market trending higher.

If you find such a configuration, place a buy stop a penny above the top of the double bottom or buy the day after price closes above the top of the chart pattern. Ride price higher and try to sell before you give back all of your profit.

Flat Base

Figure 5.9 shows the next variant in the inset. Forget the bicycle. Drive up this one.

Price moves horizontally at A, often for years. The stock can trend upward or downward slightly during the AB move, and the approach can look irregular. When I write *irregular*, I mean the stock can form mountains on the weekly scale, but the sideways trend should be obvious. If you have difficulty finding a flat base, switch to a line chart that connects closing prices with a line.

The double bottom forms at the end of the trading range. Price will drop into the double bottom (B), but the decline should be minor, often declining less than 10%. After the pattern confirms, the stock lifts off and flies to C.

The stock chart shows an example of the pattern in Mosaic. The top of the flat base, A1, is choppy but horizontal overall, and it lasts more than a year. The double bottom is at B1, and it is difficult to see on this scale. Price rises like an escalator to peak at C1, the ultimate high.

Although the upward trend continues for 6 months or so after C1, the stock drops at C1 by at least 20%, calling a statistical end to the rise. The stock peaks near 162 before tumbling during the tail end of the 2007 to 2009 bear market.

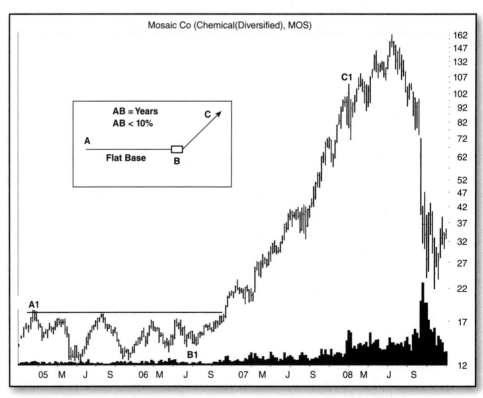

FIGURE 5.9 This flat base setup sees a double bottom form within the trading range before a large upward move.

This variant occurs 25% of the time.

Once you find a flat base followed by a double bottom, place a buy stop a penny above the top of the chart pattern or wait for price to close above the top of the double bottom. Then buy at the open the next day. That will get you into the trade near the start of the uptrend.

Flat Base Plunge

In this configuration (**Figure 5.10**), the stock moves horizontally (AB) in a flat base pattern, but the trend can look quite irregular and tilt up or down. This horizontal movement typically lasts more than 6 months.

Price makes an extensive decline (BC) below the flat base. The drop is usually short (less than 6 months long) but steep, more than 10%. Notice that the double bottom (C) is well below A.

After the double bottom confirms, price rises to D. The configuration looks like someone jumping off a diving board and then climbing up the beach.

An example of this configuration appears in the stock chart on the weekly scale. The stock forms a flat bottom at A1 that lasts over a year. The drop from B1 to C1 is large on a percentage basis (48%), and yet it happens fast. The double bottom

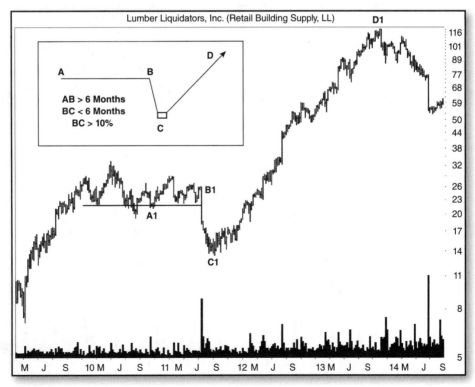

FIGURE 5.10 A flat base precedes a drop that leads to a double bottom.

(C1) rescues the stock and sends it soaring on a straight-line run up to D1, the ultimate high.

This configuration occurs 13% of the time, so it is rare.

Upward Breakout Failure

This section focuses on failures, those double bottoms with upward breakouts that fail to reach the expected potential of a big move. **Figure 5.11** shows an example.

In this scenario, the stock moves steadily higher (AB) for at least 6 months but sometimes lasting years. At the end of the upward run, the stock drops in a short-term move (often a month or two) before forming a double bottom (C). The break-out from this double bottom is upward, of course, but the new uptrend does not last long before peaking. Overhead resistance sends the stock lower, below the bottom of the double bottom. Sixty percent of the time, the stock recovers and moves up, following path D. The remaining 40% of the time, the stock tumbles, following the dashed line E.

Lumber Liquidators shows an example of this configuration. Price rises from A1 to B1. Then it drops and forms a wide double bottom at C1. The stock confirms the

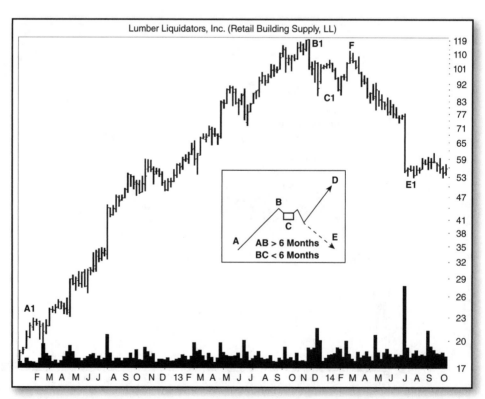

FIGURE 5.11   A long-term rise precedes a short drop into the double bottom.

double bottom when price closes above the peak between the two valleys and makes its way to F. Then the stock bangs its head on overhead resistance and tumbles to E1 (following path E in the inset).

This configuration occurs 67% of the time in the 145 charts I looked at.

After a long uptrend with overhead resistance, the double bottom may be trying to seduce you into a losing trade. Avoid trading this setup.

Downtrend Reversal Failure

The second failure type occurs in a downtrend as **Figure 5.12** shows. Price begins falling at A in a long-term decline (frequently lasting more than 6 months), leading to the double bottom at B. Price confirms the double bottom at C before the downtrend resumes, tumbling to D.

The stock chart shows an example. The stock peaks at A1 and drops to B1 where the double bottom resides (weekly scale). The stock confirms (which is hard to see in the figure) an upward breakout but reverses and tumbles to D1.

This variant occurs 19% of the time.

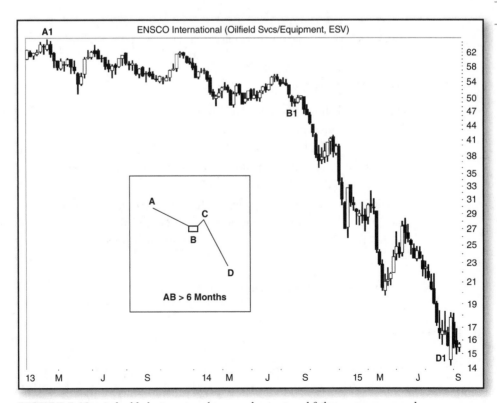

FIGURE 5.12 A double bottom in a downward price trend fails to act as a reversal.

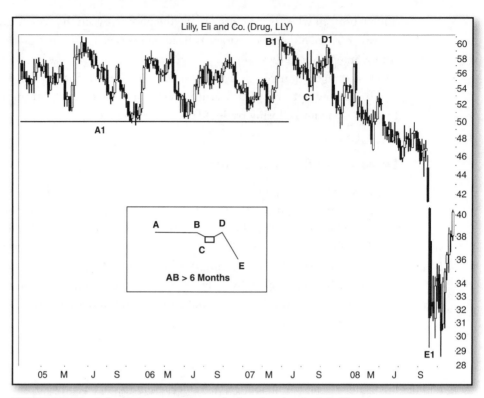

FIGURE 5.13 A double bottom follows a flat base but the rise is lackluster.

Flat Base Failure

Figure 5.13 shows the next failure configuration. Price forms a flat base from A to B. This horizontal price movement can last years, but it is at least 6 months long. In many cases, a double bottom (C) after a flat base would signal an enticing rise, but not this time. The stock peaks at D before encountering overhead resistance and reversing trend. The loss extends to E.

The stock chart shows an example of this configuration. The stock builds a flat base (A1). The top of the trading range is B1, and the drop that follows leads to the double bottom C1 (weekly scale). Price jumps up to D1 then falls through a trap door to E1.

■ This failure scenario occurs 14% of the time.

■ Measure Rule

The measure rule is a tool to help gauge how far price is expected to rise after the breakout from a double bottom. Simply put, measure the height of the double bottom and add it to the breakout price to get the target. Price hits the target 68% of

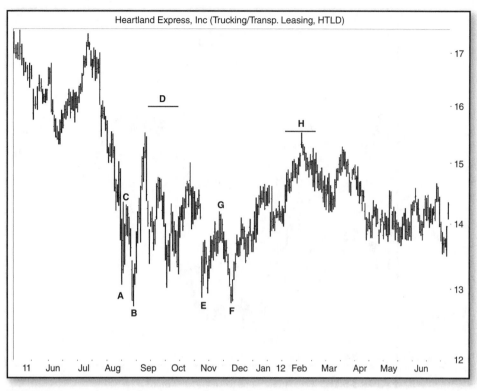

FIGURE 5.14 Shown is the measure rule applied to double bottoms.

the time. If you use half the height, price reaches or exceeds the target 86% of the time.

Figure 5.14 shows two examples of how to use the measure rule. Double bottom AB has uneven bottoms just 2% apart. The height of the double bottom is the measure from B (the lower of the two bottoms) to C, which is the highest peak between the two bottoms. Add the height to C to get target D. In this case, the stock failed to reach the target. However, if you were to take the BC height and cut it in half before adding it to C, it would have hit the target.

Use the same method to get a price target for the EF double bottom. The height is G − F added to G. The stock falls short of the target (H) by just a few pennies. The stock exceeds the half-height target easily, though.

- Price hits the measure rule target 68% of the time for double bottoms.

■ Trading

How do you use the information in this chapter to trade a double bottom successfully? Let us take the hypothetical situation shown in **Figure 5.15**, on the daily chart.

FIGURE 5.15 Price breaks out to an all-time high.

The double bottom appears at BC, and it becomes a valid double bottom when the stock closes above D. That happens at E. Point E is also the buy signal. Traders had about two weeks to uncover this double bottom and do their research on the company before buying.

Look at the monthly chart of Figure 5.15 (see inset). Point H corresponds to point A in the stock chart. It is an all-time high because the stock had never traded there before (going back to 1990 anyway). G is the double bottom, the same as BC on the daily chart.

Looking at the setups in this chapter, which ones apply? Figure 5.5 shows a situation similar to this one. Once the stock breaks out above overhead resistance (above A), the stock would be free to climb higher.

From the breakout price (D) to clear point A means a rise of 10%. That seems reasonable. The stock should be able to rise that far.

Table 5.2 shows the performance using Buy Setup 1. In this case, the trend start is at point A, so the distance from A to B (the first bottom) is about 5 weeks, well short of the 6-month boundary. Table 5.2 says to expect better performance, but the discussion warns of this turning into Buy Setup 2 (Figure 5.6).

With resistance just 10% away, I would feel comfortable that the stock could make it to all-time high territory.

Figures 6.8 and 6.11 also apply. Both of those are configurations, which do not use the trend start.

The stock chart of Figure 5.8 shows the same situation as this one. The stock had been rising for over a year before a short downturn brought it to the double bottom. The post-breakout rise shows the stock continuing to move up.

Of the configurations with upward breakouts and big moves, the setup occurred 41% of the time, the most common.

Figure 5.11 shows a cautionary tale. The rise leading to the double bottom is also a long-term affair followed by a short-term drop. As the stock chart shows, this setup did not end happily. Of the stocks that failed, this setup occurred 67% of the time. Ouch.

Which figure best fits our situation? Figure 5.6 is bullish and so is 5.8 but 5.11 is bearish. That is two to one for a bullish outcome.

I looked at the angle that price made over the long term. I pulled up the charts of Figures 5.6, 5.8, and 5.11. Bullish Figures 6.8 and this figure, 6.15, have shallow angles. Bearish Figure 5.11 has a much steeper angle.

From my research with trendlines (see my book *Trading Classic Chart Patterns*), I know that as the angle of the trend drops (becomes shallower), performance improves. Steeper trends end quicker than do shallower ones. The two bullish figures have shallower uptrends. Thus, I would tend to believe that the outcome from this trade would be bullish and not bearish.

Returning to Figure 5.15, the stock confirmed the double bottom by breaking out upward. This would be a dangerous buy signal. Why? Because earnings were due to come out at F.

In this case, the stock made a massive climb higher on better-than-expected earnings, but the stock could have dropped if earnings disappointed. I have learned to avoid buying a stock within three weeks of an earnings announcement, so I would not have traded this stock.

Preservation of capital is more important than a quick gain. I could have bought the stock and married the position with put options to protect the down side.

Actual Trade

Figure 5.16 shows a trade I made in a stock I no longer follow.

The 2007–2009 bear market was not kind to many stocks, including this one. I do not show the entire decline, but the swift drop from A to the first bottom of the double bottom (CD) is dramatic in its severity. Two brokers downgraded the stock at B and down it went, almost as fast as a ship hit by a torpedo.

I do not follow many stocks that trade near a dollar a share because they are too prone to go bankrupt, be manipulated by others, or flat line like a dead animal for years. However, in a bear market, quality stocks can suffer by being sucked down with the market trend.

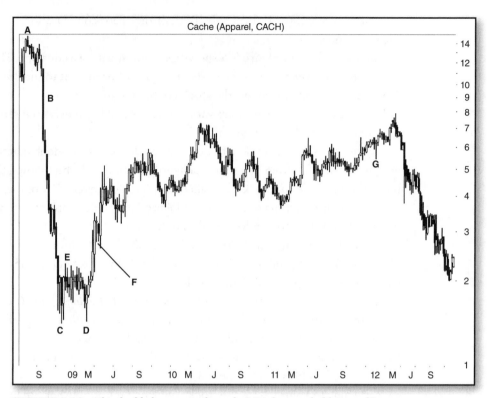

FIGURE 5.16 This double bottom trade made 86% during a hold time of 3 years.

This stock is one I had traded before, so I had been tracking it during the bear market and was comfortable with it. When it reached oversold territory, I became interested.

I looked at the fundamentals and was pleased to find that the company had almost no long-term debt. Insiders were buying since September, but the sizes were unimpressive, ranging from about 1,000 to 20,000 shares.

In early April, I bought and received a fill at 3.10. "Late to a confirmed Eve & Adam double bottom," I wrote in my trading notebook. I show the buy as point F on the weekly scale.

Eve (bottom C) is so called because it is wider than an Adam (D) bottom. Adam bottoms can be one price bar and tend to be tall and narrow, but Eve tends to have a conglomeration of price bars near the same price and gets wider fast over its height.

My targets were 8, 13, and 16. Those targets were set at valleys when the stock traded much higher. I felt that if I held long enough, the bull market recovery would carry the stock back to where it was.

I held on as the stock bobbled up and down like a cork riding the waves. I tracked the stock throughout.

In mid-January 2012, here is what I wrote about the sale. "This is trading near the yearly high and it's a good time to exit. Sell reason: Fundamentals, weakness. If the prediction is right that the market will drop in March [this stock started down as the chart shows], I am liquidating my stocks that show gains and are looking to drop. This recently peaked, but I don't like the industry (women's apparel) and a broker downgraded the stock."

I sold (G) and received a fill of 5.80 for a gain of 86%. The stock peaked at 7.88, so I sold well short of the top. In retrospect, I am glad I sold it then because the stock dropped. The last quote I have (November 2014) shows a low of 23 cents.

Application **Figure 5.17** shows the configuration that applies to this trade. The inset is from Figure 5.10. The AB move is more than 6 months long, matching the A1-B1 move (note: monthly scale). The A1-B1 cloudbank is like a block of resistance waiting above the stock.

The bear market took the stock down in a swift move, from B1 to C1, matching the BC drop. The B1-C1 move saw the stock drop from almost $14 to below $1.50 in 3 months. Ouch. It hurts just to read that. Imagine if you owned the stock and held during the decline.

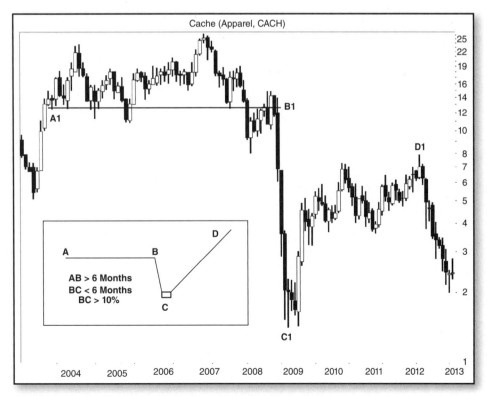

FIGURE 5.17 The monthly scale; the setup in the inset applies.

C1 is the double bottom and price climbed to D1. Notice that the inset suggests a rise above the AB resistance, but that did not happen in this case. That is the only difference I see between the predicted behavior and what happened.

■ Closing Position

Twin bottoms are easy to find, but novices assume they are double bottoms. They only become valid double bottoms when price closes above the top of the chart pattern (confirmation).

Just over half (56%) of twin bottoms will confirm as valid so that is why waiting for an upward breakout is important. Almost one in five (19%) double bottoms will bust an upward breakout, too. That is why the setups and configurations presented in this chapter are vital to trading. By knowing the likely outcome of a trade ahead of time, you can minimize the aggravation and save money.

Setup Synopsis

Figure 5.18 may help you identify the various types of trading setups. See the associated figure for an explanation.

"Occurs" in the figures means how often I found the configuration in the stocks I looked at. If two configurations apply to your situation, then the one with a more frequent occurrence (a higher percentage) is the one you should choose to follow.

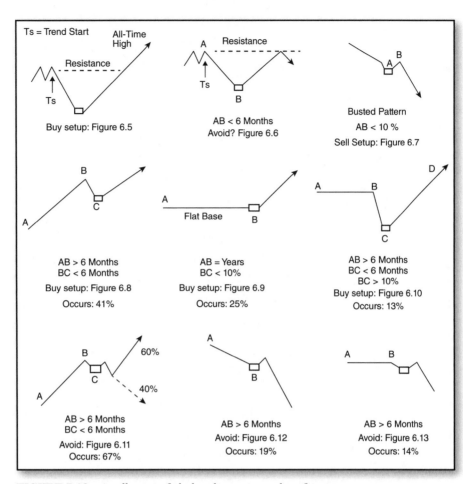

FIGURE 5.18 A collection of ideal trading setups and configurations.

CHAPTER 6

Double Tops

A double top is a twin peak pattern that has two peaks near the same price but separated by days, weeks, or even months. A confirmed double top means the stock is sinking like a freighter going down in a hurricane. Should you abandon it? Probably not, but read this chapter to understand that sometimes you will need a life preserver.

If you are a position trader or buy-and-hold investor, the decline after the double top confirms is frequently less than 20%. For swing and day traders, double tops offer an opportunity for a small profit.

Let us take a closer look.

■ Behavior at a Glance

One of the questions I ponder when buying or selling a stock is, Should I wait for confirmation? To answer that, I used 1,209 stocks and found 14,796 twin peak patterns from bull markets going back as far as January 1990. Few stocks covered the entire period.

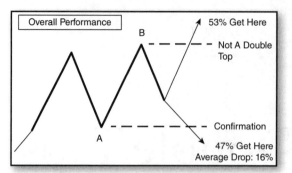

FIGURE 6.1 Fifty-three percent of twin-peak patterns have price close above the top of the chart pattern.

Figure 6.1 shows the results. Confirmation occurs when price closes below the twin peak pattern (below A). It verifies that you have a valid double top and not just squiggles on the price chart.

I discovered that 53% of the time the stock will close above the top of the chart pattern (B). That is a huge potential failure rate if you sell short before confirmation.

■ Fifty-three percent of twin peak patterns will not confirm as double tops.

Just because you see a twin peak pattern in a stock you own is no reason to sell the stock. The smart choice is to wait for price to confirm a double top.

Even after confirmation, the drop may not be significant anyway, so holding on might be the best choice for investors and position traders.

Of the 47% of twin peaks that do confirm as double tops, the average decline is 16%, with a median drop of 13%. Knowing that half of all double tops will decline 13% or less, does that make you want to sell? Of course, the actual decline could be much larger.

Pullbacks

After price confirms a double top, the stock drops. Frequently, 62% of the time in fact, the stock attempts to return to the breakout price. That retrace is called a pullback, and by definition, it must occur within a month of the breakout.

Figure 6.2 shows how often pullbacks occur in double tops and their behavior.

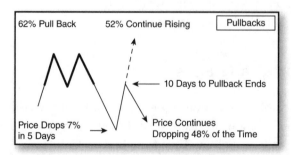

FIGURE 6.2 This is typical pullback behavior.

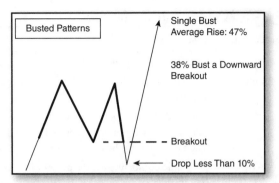

FIGURE 6.3 Performance of busted double tops.

The average pullback takes 5 days and sees price drop 7% until the stock bottoms. Then it takes another 5 days (10 days total since the breakout) to peak. From there, 52% of the time, the stock continues rising and eventually closes above the top of the double top. The other 48% of the time, the stock resumes a downward trend.

To uncover these statistics and others in this chapter, I found 2,830 double tops in 962 stocks. I discarded those from bear markets because I wanted to concentrate on bull markets in this book. The oldest pattern hails from July 1991, and the most recent was from November 2014.

■ Sixty-two percent of double tops will have pullbacks.

Busted Tops

Figure 6.3 shows what happens when the stock drops less than 10% below the breakout price and reverses. That combination, when the reversal sends price closing above the top of the chart pattern, is what I call a busted pattern. The stock is supposed to make a significant drop after the breakout but it does not.

How often does a double top bust? Answer: 38% of the time. That means 38% of the time the stock will fail to drop more than 10% below the breakout price. If you short the stock at the breakout price, can you make money before price rises?

After a double top busts, the rise can be spectacular, sending the stock soaring 47% above the top of the chart pattern (for single busted patterns only). The Buy Setup (later in this chapter) discusses this scenario.

■ Thirty-eight percent of double tops will bust a downward breakout.

■ Identification

Double tops are easy to identify, but **Table 6.1** lists the guidelines. As I discuss them, refer to **Figure 6.4**.

TABLE 6.1 **Identification Guidelines**

Characteristic	Discussion
Uptrend	Price should trend upward in the weeks leading to a double top.
Two peaks	Price forms two distinct peaks that can be any shape, from rounded turns to one-day price spikes.
Top separation	The median width between the two tops is about a month. Tops too far apart (like a year) will not be recognized as readily as those two or three months apart. The two peaks can be close together but must form two distinct minor highs.
Drop between tops	A common guideline for the height of the double top is 10%. Tops farther apart will likely have larger declines between the two peaks than tops closer together. The decline between peaks should look proportional to the size of the peaks. The drop should form a distinct minor low.
Volume	Volume trends downward about two-thirds of the time from peak to peak. That means the right peak has less volume than the left one. Do not discard a double top because volume trends upward.
Breakout	Sometimes called confirmation. Price is said to breakout when the stock closes below the lowest valley between the two peaks. When a breakout occurs, it confirms the chart pattern as a valid double top. An unconfirmed chart pattern is just squiggles on the chart.

FIGURE 6.4   This double top precedes a large drop in the stock.

Uptrend. Since we are looking for a top, price should trend upward into the first peak, beginning from the trend start. The trend start is off the chart on the left, but the rise from A to peak B shows the type of upward move I am looking for.

There is an old saying that a reversal pattern needs something to reverse. Look for double tops with a substantial uptrend such as that shown.

Two Peaks. When searching for double tops, find two peaks (BD in this example) *near* the same price. Rarely will you see two peaks stop at the same price, but it does happen. In the stocks I looked at, the average price difference between peaks was 29 cents.

The shape of the two peaks can appear vastly different, too, but will often look similar. By that, I mean both peaks will appear wide as if they do not care about the obesity problem, or both will be vegetarians, slim, perhaps just one-day price spikes.

Top Separation. The time between peaks in my database averages 38 days (calendar, not trading days) with some less than a week apart and the longest about a year apart. If the two peaks are too far apart, traders will not recognize them as a double top.

Drop between Tops. The classic guideline says that price should drop at least 10% below the highest peak. I let the chart patterns dictate their behavior. My selections showed a drop that averaged 15%. Small patterns will show a smaller drop between peaks than do those with peaks spaced farther apart.

The drop should look proportional to the height of the peaks. Be suspicious of a large drop between two small peaks or two substantial peaks with only a minor retrace between.

Volume. I dislike volume because it helps but only to a minor degree. For double tops, the volume trends downward from the first peak to the second 61% of the time. The performance difference for those trending up compared to those trending down is just one percentage point. Yawn.

The double top in Figure 6.4 has volume trending lower (E) according to linear regression. It looks like it trends upward to me, but I wear reading glasses.

Breakout. Price breaks out of the double top when it closes below the price of the valley between the two peaks (C). Price has to close below line C before the double top becomes valid.

■ Buy Setup

The only buy setup I recommend is when a double top busts. What does that mean? Look at the inset of the ideal configuration in **Figure 6.5**.

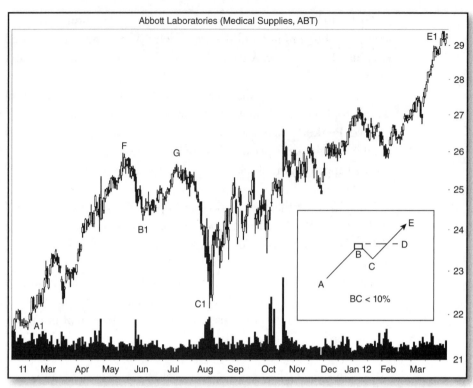

FIGURE 6.5 This is an example of a busted double top.

The stock climbs along trend AB, leading to the double top at B (represented by the box). The length of this trend and the slope is not as important as what happens.

A downward breakout sends price lower but not for long. After dropping less than 10%, the stock turns at C. The new uptrend continues, and it busts the pattern when the stock closes above the top of the double top at D. Price continues rising, E, often posting a substantial gain.

Be warned that stocks can bust more than once. If the stock reverses before rising more than 10% above D (the top of the chart pattern) and then continues more than 10% below the bottom, it double busts the pattern. Triple busts see price move up (busting a downward breakout), then down, and then up again. For more information about single, double, or triple busted patterns, consult the glossary.

The stock chart shows an example of a single-busted double top. Price climbs a hill from A1 to F, forms a second peak at G, and confirms the pattern on the decline to C1. Notice that peaks F and G are not the same price, but they are close enough for government work, as they say. The decline from the bottom of the double top (B1) to C1 measures 8.5%, just shy of the 10% cutoff for a busted pattern. The stock single busts the double top when it closes above the higher of the two peaks (F) on its way to E1 and beyond. The stock gained 99% (not shown).

Here is what to look for in this setup.

1. Qualify the double top using the identification guidelines discussed in Table 6.1, including closing below the bottom of the chart pattern (confirmation).
2. Price must drop less than 10% below the bottom of the double top.
3. Wait for the stock to turn and close above the top of the chart pattern.
4. If you wish to buy the stock, you can use a buy stop placed a penny above the top of the chart pattern, or you can trigger a conditional order to buy the stock at the open the day after price closes above the top of the chart pattern.
5. Place a stop-loss order a penny below the bottom of the double top or at a location of your choice.

Table 6.2 lists statistics related to busted double tops.

1. Double tops bust frequently, 38% of the time. That means price fails to drop more than 10% below the bottom of the chart pattern over a third of the time. For those desiring to short a double top, be careful.

2, 3. The average rise for all types of busted chart patterns (single, double, and three or more busts) is 33%. If your double top busts once, the rise averages 47%. I have not found a reliable way to determine whether the stock will single, double, or triple bust. Searching for support and resistance areas helps, though.

TABLE 6.2 Statistics for Busted Double Tops	
Description	**Result**
1. Percentage of double tops that bust	38%
2. Average rise after busting	33%
3. Average rise after single bust	47%
4. Percentage of single busts	67%
5. Percentage of double busts	14%
6. Percentage of triple+ busts	19%

4–6. Of the 38% of double tops that bust, 67% of them single bust, 14% double bust, and the remainder bust three or more times.

Table 6.2 suggests that a single bust will occur twice every three trades. Avoid trades with lots of overhead resistance that might cause the stock to reverse and double or triple bust.

■ Sell Setup

I have only one sell setup because an analysis of the statistics says that the pace of the rise from the trend start to the start of the double top is not as significant as the time to make the journey.

Look at the inset of **Figure 6.6**. It shows the ideal sell setup. Price turns at the trend start, A, and moves into the first top, B. Price recedes to D and rebounds to form a second top at C. The price of the two tops is nearly the same. The two peaks *look* like they top out near the same price. The pattern becomes a double top when price closes below D, which I show as a dashed line to E. After that, price drops to the ultimate low, F.

FIGURE 6.6   The ideal sell setup and an example.

The only thing to look for in this setup is to measure the time between the trend start (A) and the top of the first peak (B). For the best performance, that duration should be six months or less. Keep in mind that the stock needs something to reverse, so the run from A to B should be high enough to justify taking a position in the stock (assuming the stock returns to the launch price, A. It may not, but it serves as a good guideline).

The stock chart shows an example of this setup. The trend start is at A1. It is the first time looking left from the double top where price rises from a low by at least 20% (read the glossary's *Trend Start* definition if this is confusing). The duration from A1 to B1 is less than six months in this example.

B1-C1 is the double top. It confirms as a valid chart pattern when the stock closes below the price of the valley between the two peaks, D1. At G, the stock pulls back for a few days before tumbling on its way to the ultimate low, F1.

Here are the steps for using this setup:

1. Find a double top that obeys the guidelines listed in Table 6.1.
2. Find the trend start, which is the lowest valley before which the stock climbs by at least 20%.
3. Measure the time from the trend start to the first peak of the double top.
4. If the duration is more than six months, then discard the double top.
5. Look for underlying support that might block a decline.
6. If the industry and general market are trending down, then continue to the next step; otherwise, wait for better trading conditions.
7. If the distance from the breakout price (the lowest valley between the two peaks of the double top) to support (step 5) is an attractive percentage away, then consider shorting the stock or selling a long holding.
8. Cover the short when the stock encounters support.

Table 6.3 shows the performance statistics for this setup, based on perfect trades.

TABLE 6.3 Statistical Analysis of the Sell Setup		
Description	Inbound Trend ≤6 Months	Inbound Trend >6 Months
1. Occurrence, samples	68%, 1415	32%, 675
2. Post-breakout average loss	17%	13%
3. Median loss	14%	9%
4. Losses over 25%	21%	13%
5. 5% failure rate	13%	22%
6. 10% failure rate	34%	50%

1. I found plenty of examples to make the statistics solid, but they could still change, especially in a bear market. These numbers apply to bull markets only.

The majority of double tops had durations from the trend start to the first peak six months long or less. Those were the patterns that outperformed, too.

2, 3. The table shows that the short inbound trend column (middle one) outperforms the longer duration column (right). By measuring the time from the trend start to the first peak and making sure it is six months or less, you improve the chances of a profitable trade.

Conversely, a short duration inbound trend (six months or less) could mean a larger decline if you own the stock on the long side.

Half the stocks will decline less than 9% to 14%, depending on the inbound trend duration.

4. Larger declines (losses more than 25%) occur when the inbound trend is six months or less. My guess is that investors and traders have more faith that an uptrend will continue if it has been in existence for a long time (more than six months). They assume price will continue rising, so any drop is a buying opportunity (buy the dip). Their buying blunts any meaningful drop.

5, 6. The failure rates are high in both columns, but the longer duration trend is outrageous. Half of double tops (50%) will fail to see price drop at least 10% after the breakout.

■ Best Stop Locations

Table 6.4 shows how often price hits two stop locations.

1. Within the pattern. A stop-loss order placed somewhere between the highest peak and lowest valley of the double top has a 69% chance of being hit. The average loss would be 3%, but the missed trades would drop an average of 15% without a stop in place.

2. Penny above the pattern. A safer location for a stop-loss order is a penny above the highest peak in the double top. That order would trigger an average of 1% of the time, resulting in a 7% loss. The trades would go on to drop an average of 12% (below the bottom of the double top) if you decided to hold on.

■ The best stop location is a penny above the top of the highest peak in the double top.

TABLE 6.4	Stop Locations for Double Tops		
Description	Chance of Being Hit	Average Loss	Missed Trades, Losses
1. Within the pattern	69%	3%	15%
2. Penny above the pattern	1%	7%	12%

■ Configuration Trading

To trade the following configurations, begin with these guidelines:

1. Find a double top on the *daily* chart that obeys the identification guidelines listed in Table 6.1.
2. Using the *weekly* scale, match what you see on your chart to one of the configurations. Figures 6.15 and 6.16 should help.
3. Read the text before shorting or selling a long holding beause the decline may be meager. Otherwise, short (or sell a long holding) at the open the day after the breakout or place an order to short a penny below the bottom of the pattern.
4. Place a stop-loss order at a location of your choice.

I found the following configurations by looking at 165 chart patterns with large post-breakout declines (more than 25%) in bull markets.

The first happens 62% of the time, and it comes in two variations. **Figure 6.7** shows them in the insets.

Price rises over the long term, often years, but it should be at least 6 months long (AB). A double top appears at the top (B), right where you would expect it to happen. The stock reverses and price drops to D, making a decline traders wished they had participated in.

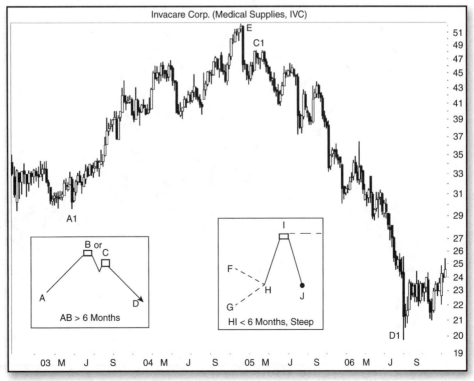

FIGURE 6.7 Price forms a double top after a long-term rise.

A variation of this setup occurs when the double top appears to the right of the peak, at C. The BC drop is quick, maybe a month or two, but the outcome follows the same trend.

The stock chart shows an example of this variation. Price climbs the slope from A1 to E. E is where the stock tops out, but the double top appears later, at C1. The delay is not much in terms of time or percentage decline from the peak in this example. The breakout from the double top confirms the pattern as a valid one and sends price skittering down the hill, to D1.

A third variation of the double top pattern happens just 8% of the time, so it is rare. Price trends up (GH) or down (FH) going into the start of the vertical move (HI). During the HI climb, the stock behaves like a fighter plane going vertical. It makes a huge climb upward. A double top appears (I), and the stock dives, arriving back at earth (J) at a price near where it started the move higher (H).

The HI climb is often just a few months long and steep. The rise may take price higher by 50% or even 100%. On the weekly chart, it looks like a straight-line run. The return trip (IJ) may not be a straight-line run down. Rather, price can meander as it drops.

Short Retrace in Downtrend

Figure 6.8 shows the last configuration that results in a large decline. This variation occurred 30% of the time in the stocks I looked at.

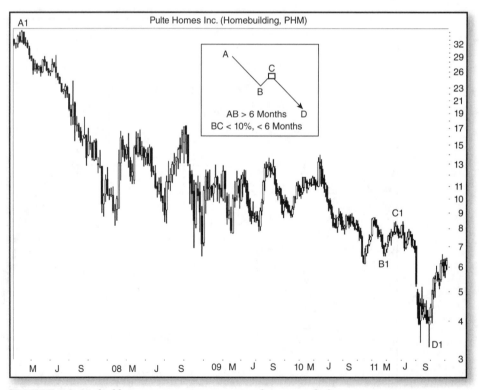

FIGURE 6.8 A double top appears as a retrace in a long-term decline.

Price descends over the long term from A to B before bottoming and retracing up to C. The retrace is quick, often taking less than a month or two to complete the journey, and the percentage change is small, too.

At C, a double top appears like storm clouds on the horizon, and the downward breakout from this pattern sends the stock dropping, eventually bottoming at D.

The key identifier in this pattern is the downward inbound trend. In effect, the double top acts as a continuation of the prevailing longer-term downtrend (A to D) and less as a reversal of the short-term retrace (the rise from B to C).

The stock chart shows an example of how this plays out. Price starts the decline from A1, taking the stock down substantially to B1. C1 is where a double top appears (weekly scale). The downward breakout sends the stock dropping to D1 where it bottoms.

The surprising behavior of this configuration is that after such a long downtrend, you would expect the stock to be near the end of the trend, which it is (on the time scale). And yet the double top sends the stock tumbling even farther.

Double Top Failures

Figure 6.9 shows an example of how double tops fail. Price forms a peak at A, and that spells overhead resistance. A double top pops up at B, right where you would

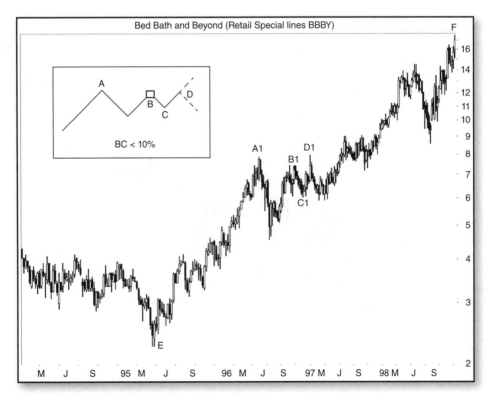

FIGURE 6.9 A double top forms at resistance, but the decline is small.

expect a reversal pattern to appear. The stock breaks out downward, but the decline is unexpectedly small, often less than 10% (C). A rise to D confirms a busted pattern. Where the stock goes after that is unknown. Some move up and some drop as the dashed lines show.

The stock chart shows an example on the weekly scale. The uptrend begins at E and rises to A1 in an exciting surge higher. A double top appears at B1, and it forms at overhead resistance setup by peak A1.

The stock drops to C1 and confirms a downward breakout (it is hard to see), but eventually price works its way higher (D1), and the uptrend resumes, to F.

What is perplexing about these types of failures is that the double top appears at overhead resistance, right where you would expect to see it. A confirmed downward breakout should drop price a meaningful amount (15% or more) and yet it does not. Buying demand halts the decline and overpowers the bears, sending price zipping upward.

This configuration occurred 50% of the time in the 196 charts I looked at. It is the most frequent failure configuration.

Busted Uptrend

Figure 6.10 shows the next failure of a double top. This one occurs in a strong uptrend. The inset shows the action.

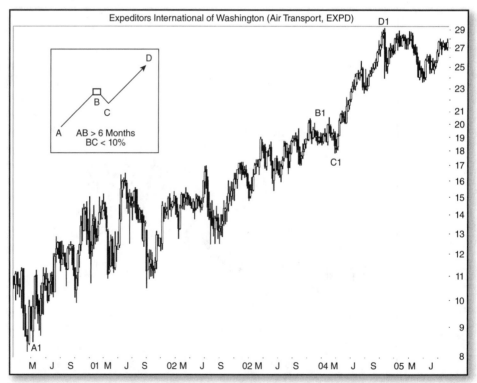

FIGURE 6.10   A double top in a strong uptrend fails.

Price rises in a long-term move from A to B. A double top forms at B, and a downward breakout not only confirms the chart pattern as a valid one but also sends price lower.

The drop to C is less than 10%. What went wrong? The stock joins the strong current from the upward push (AB), and it carries price higher, to D, busting the downward breakout.

The stock chart shows an example. Price moved up from A1 to B1 in surf so choppy it would make me want to turn my skiff around. The two peaks on either side of B1 are the double top (weekly scale). Price drops a smidge to C1 before powering higher to D1.

This configuration occurred 38% of the time. You will see this type of failure in strong uptrends with no nearby overhead resistance to block an advance.

V Bottom Failure

This last configuration happens just 12% of the time and **Figure 6.11** shows the setup.

Price falls from A to B over the long term (more than 6 months). Then the stock bounces (BC). The bounce happens quickly, a steep upward move that takes a month or two, but the recovery can be quite steep. A double top appears (C) and it signals

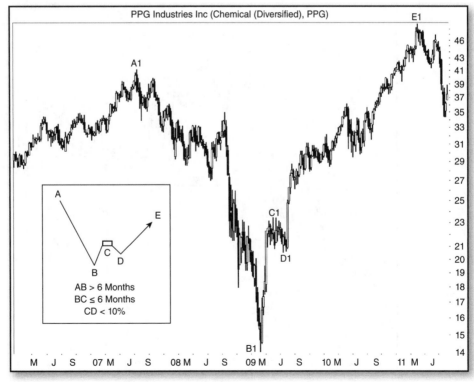

FIGURE 6.11 A double bottom appears after a V-shaped decline.

the upward retrace is over. Price drops from C to D, and yet the decline is meager, often less than 10%. The stock busts the downward breakout when it soars to E.

The stock chart shows an example of this type of double top failure on the weekly scale. Price tries digging a hole on the move from A1 down to the bear market low (B1). The recovery is both quick and steep. A double top appears at C1 and price declines to D1. The decline is small compared to the drop from A1. The stock turns and climbs to E1, joining the recovery in a new bull market.

This is the only failure configuration I found in a downward price trend, and this example had a good reason to fail: the bull market started. The strong upward trend of the market worked to defeat the bearish implications of the double top.

■ Measure Rule

The measure rule is a tool to help gauge how far price might tumble after the breakout.

Compute the height of the double top from the tallest peak to the lowest valley between the tops, and subtract the height from the breakout price. The result is a price target.

For example, **Figure 6.12** shows a double top in the inset at AB. Because peak A is taller than B, we will use A in the formula. The target price is $C - (A - C)$.

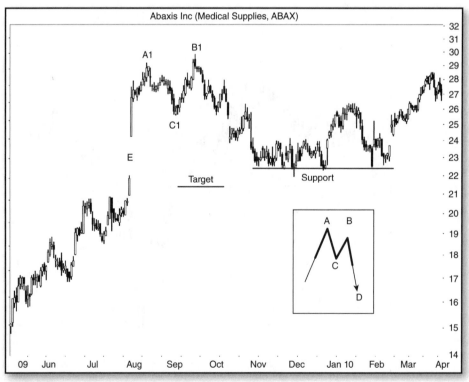

FIGURE 6.12   The measure rule applied to a double top.

Let us apply this technique to the stock chart. The taller of the two peaks is B1, which has a high price of 29.80. The low at valley C1 is 25.56, giving a height of 4.24. Subtract the height from the breakout price (C1) to get a target of 25.56 − 4.24, or 21.32. I show the approximate location of the target in the figure.

The stock eventually made it down to the target in June (not shown).

The measure rule for double tops using their full height works just 48% of the time.

For a more conservative target, use half the height: C − (A − C)/2. That would cut the height to 2.12 in this example, giving a closer target of 25.56 − 2.12, or 23.44. The half height measure rule works 75% of the time for double tops.

Once you have calculated a target, look for nearby underlying support that might stop a decline. Not shown in the chart but there was support at 23 back in March 2008, with additional support in July and September. As you can see, the stock did find support near 23 starting in November 2009.

Tests for support and resistance show that gaps (E) can act as areas of support, but they do not work well. Price stops within a gap just 20% of the time. This chart shows an example of gap supporting price when the stock moves horizontally starting in November.

- The measure rule works 48% of the time for double tops.

■ Trading

Before we discuss an example, let us discuss how the different types of traders could use double tops.

Investors, those buy-and-hold folks, will find that 29% of double tops, on average, decline at least 20%. Flipping that around, if you own a stock showing a double top, you have a 71% chance that the decline will be less than a trend change (20%).

For position traders, those that hold the stock until a trend change, be nervous if you own a stock showing a double top. It is not an automatic sell, but you will want to do your homework to determine whether the fundamentals are peachy.

Be aware that the quarterly financial numbers are just a snapshot in time and will have changed by the time you read them. That is why the stock chart represents the best real-time opinion of the stock.

Swing traders will want to do their homework as well to see whether the stock is worth shorting. Clearly, you do not want to own a stock showing a confirmed double top unless it busts the downward breakout. You also do not want to short a double top until it confirms (see Figure 6.1).

Day traders can make some money by trading double tops, but like everything else they do, traders have to be nimble. The post-breakout drop likely will be short.

Use the measure rule to help set a price target and to see whether the trade is worth taking.

Example

How do you trade a double top? Consider **Figure 6.13**.

Look at the left inset first, the better of the two configurations. Point E marks the start of a downtrend. The stock drops for a time but then retraces to form a double top at F. The double top confirms and price resumes trending toward G.

Notice that the double top is near the start of the downtrend and not the end. This configuration matches Figure 6.7 when the double top comes after the stock peaks (C).

Compare the left inset in Figure 6.13 with the right one. Price starts its downtrend from H. The stock drops and moves lower for a long time until reaching I. Price bounces and a double top appears at J. The double top confirms but price hardly drops at all before beginning an upward trend toward K. This configuration matches the one described in Figure 6.11.

The setup shown in the right inset often occurs at the transition from bear to bull markets. The bear market sees price drop from H to I before a retrace forms the

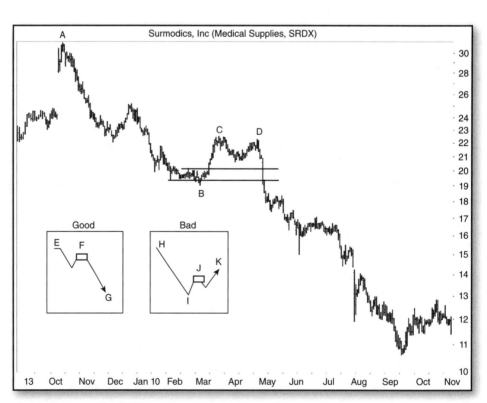

FIGURE 6.13 This double top appears in a downtrend.

double top. A bull market begins and the double top busts or has a small post-breakout decline. Then the bulls take price upward to K, starting a new long-term uptrend.

The stock chart shows an example of the left inset (daily chart). The bear market ended in March 2009 and the stock nearly doubled off its low, peaking at A. Then things went south for the stock.

Price started the downward trend at A, and it bottomed at B. B is actually the trend start for this double top because the move from B to A is a rise of more than 20%.

As the chart shows, the trend start is close, much less than 6 months. That is good news for performance. Short inbound trends (as measured from the trend start to the first peak), on average, see price drop after the breakout by 17%, but trends longer than 6 months see price drop just 13% (from Table 6.3). That may not sound like much, but the difference between those two numbers is 30%.

Having the double top (CD) floating in a downward current from A to B is a plus.

This double top confirmed when price closed below the valley between the two peaks. I would be worried that price would find support between the two horizontal lines starting from the horizontal consolidation region (B). But this stock shot right through support and kept on dropping.

The stock bottomed at 8.28 (not shown), bounced, and formed a double bottom before making a wonderful recovery.

Weak Quarter

When I studied an event pattern called a dead-cat bounce, I found that one dead-cat bounce followed another 29% of the time within 3 months and 42% of the time within 6 months. Often weak quarterly earnings caused those events. The next chapter discusses an earnings miss.

Should a double top appear in a stock having a weak quarter, the double top could represent a profit opportunity. Consider shorting the stock.

If you own the stock long, it might be wise to sell it soon after the report of weak quarterly earnings. Problems with earnings often take a long time to fix, so the weakness will persist. The drop can be breathtaking from some stocks after the report of weak earnings or even after a downward revised outlook.

Actual Trade

I looked through my trades and found one that used a double top to exit an existing position.

Figure 6.14 shows the trade (without a price scale because it split twice). I bought the stock in July 1996 at a price of 23.25 (all figures are split unadjusted) and held it until seeing the double top (AB).

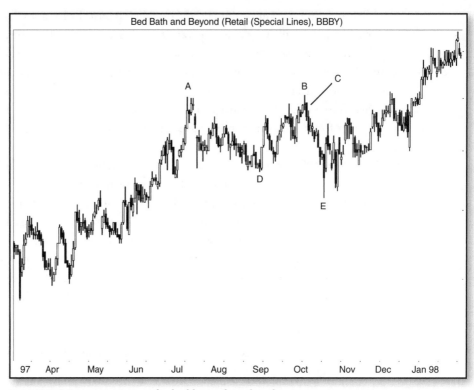

FIGURE 6.14 Appearance of a double top forced a sale.

Point A shows the first peak and B shows the second. Between those is D, the confirmation price.

At C, the day I sold, I wrote this in my notebook. "Sunday 10/4/97. I placed an order to sell half my holdings at the market tomorrow. Why? A budding double top formation. I know that you should wait for confirmation, but the decline to 30.50 from the current 35.00 is just too far to wait. If it continues to rise (fundamentally speaking, the prospects are bright), then I still have half my holdings. If it declines to the formation base, at 30.50, or continues down for another 18%, then I'll have the opportunity to buy more."

The 18% number is old, based on fewer samples from an earlier decade. The updated average decline from a double top is 16%.

The day after the stock peaked at B, I sold it at 35.50. I made 52% on the trade after holding it for 15 months.

Did I make a mistake selling? The stock declined 19% from C to E, so I avoided that profit giveback. However, the decline below confirmation (D) was a lot smaller, just 6%. This double top busted when price closed above B in December.

I still held half my position. On the second half of the trade, I made 153% in about 2.5 years.

Application Facing the same situation today, I would consult this book to find Figure 6.5 applies (buy a busted double top). Of course, I would not know it busted the downward breakout until December, well after the October sale.

Figure 6.9 shows the best match for this situation (in fact, the stock chart shows the same stock, the same time period, on the weekly scale). The inset shows a stock meeting overhead resistance (A) in the form of a second peak (B). The figure applies to short sales, not long trades, but it suggests any downturn will be small. Of course, there could be exceptions.

Figure 6.10 shows the same configuration as Figure 6.5 except that the variation looks at the stock as a sell candidate. I was not interested in selling short, so the figure does not apply. Even so, it suggests any downturn will be small, which is reassuring.

Knowing that the decline from most double tops is not significant (to me), I would do my homework to check out the stock and the company and probably hold onto the entire position. Just because I see a bearish chart pattern is no reason to sell a stock immediately. There has to be supporting evidence that the company, industry, or market are weak, too.

■ Closing Position

Double tops can fool the inexperienced. They see twin peaks that top out near the same price and label them a double top. The peaks only become a valid double top after confirmation, that is, after price closes below the valley between the two tops.

Waiting for confirmation removes 53% of losing trades, on average. The 53% number is how often a twin peak pattern will see price first close above the top of the pattern instead of below it.

Price drops an average of 16% below the breakout price, but 38% of double tops will see price fall no more than 10% below the bottom of the chart pattern. In other words, 38% will bust a downward breakout.

All of this suggests that making money trading double tops is as difficult as eating a bowling ball. Well, maybe not that hard.

The setups and configurations in this chapter should help you determine which situations are more likely to turn into big winners and which trades you should avoid.

Setup Synopsis

Figure 6.15 may help you identify the various types of trading setups. See the associated figure for an explanation.

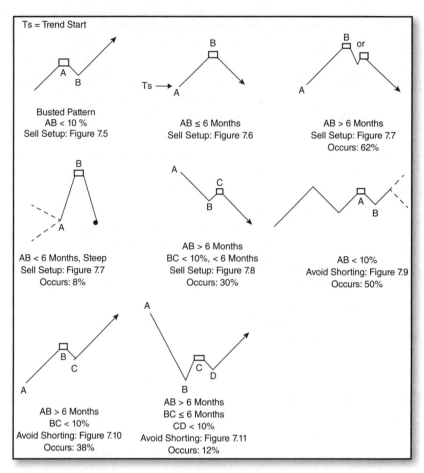

FIGURE 6.15 A collection of ideal trading setups and configurations.

"Occurs" in the figures means how often I found the configuration in the stocks I looked at. If two configurations apply to your situation, then the one with a more frequent occurrence (a higher percentage) is the one you should choose to follow.

CHAPTER 7

Earnings Miss

This chapter has a different format from the others because it is not a chart pattern but an event pattern. I want to explore what happens after a bad earnings surprise.

How many times have you asked yourself, "Should I sell before earnings come out?" This chapter answers that question and explores the behavior of stocks after a company announces poor quarterly earnings that surprise the market.

■ Behavior at a Glance

Figure 7.1 shows a model of how stocks behave after a bad earnings announcement. Because large numbers can skew averages, I show the median moves and the time it took to make those moves.

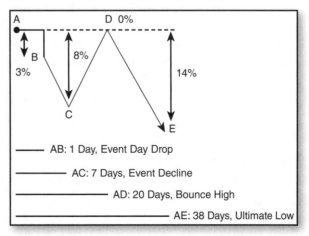

FIGURE 7.1 The median move after a bad earnings announcement.

The last close before the announcement is point A, and it is the point to which all numbers on the chart refer. Point A could be the day *before* the announcement or it could be the day *of* the announcement, depending on when the announcement came out (before the market opened or after the close).

B is the day the market reacts to the announcement. Price drops a median of 3% in 1 day. But the decline continues to C, falling 8% in a week. The A to C move is what I call the event decline because it is the market's reaction to the earnings news.

Then the stock bounces to D. The bounce takes the stock up to break even, and it takes a median of 20 days to get there (as measured from A, the last close before the announcement).

After the stock completes its bounce, it tumbles, dropping price 14% in 38 days (or almost 3 weeks after peaking at D).

The up and down movement of the stock resembles a tennis ball dropped from a roof to the driveway below. The ball drops, bounces, and then rolls down the driveway unless the dog eats it.

■ Identification

Each quarter most companies release earnings. The date they will make their announcement is publicly available on their website or at sites like Yahoo Finance a few weeks ahead of time. You can use the date of the year earlier release to get an idea of the timing.

When the market becomes aware of poor earnings, the stock tumbles because it disappoints the whisper number. The whisper number is what analysts expect from the company. In other words, the results fall short of market expectations, so traders sell the stock, forcing price down.

That is how an earnings miss is supposed to happen, but there are variations. Sometimes the price goes up for a day only to reverse the next day. Sometimes the stock does not react for several days and then tumbles.

Table 7.1 describes how I dealt with the announcement timing. This helped determine whether the breakout was upward or downward.

Before Market Open. I looked for a close outside the trading range of the day before the announcement. If the stock closed below the prior day's low, the earnings report was bad, and I logged the information. A close above the high meant an upward breakout, which I ignored. I was only interested in bad earnings surprises, not good ones.

TABLE 7.1 Breakout Guidelines	
Announcement Timing	**A Downward Breakout Occurs When**
Before market open	Price closes below the low of the prior trading day.
After market close	Price closes below the low on the announcement day.
Time not supplied	Price closes below the low of the prior trading day.

I chose this method to determine a breakout because of the wide swing the stock can take during the first trading session after the announcement (the big move day). I used to use the trading range of the big move day to gauge a breakout. Now I use the day before.

After Market Close. When a company announces earnings after the market closes (call it Day 1), the big impact happens the next day (Day 2). I looked for a close (on Day 2 or later) below the low of Day 1. If, on Day 2, the stock happened to close above the high of Day 1, then I ignored the quarterly report and the upward breakout.

Time Not Supplied. When the announcement timing is not supplied, I looked for a close below the low of the day before the announcement as the downward breakout trigger. A close above the high of that day meant an upward breakout, which I ignored.

■ Examples

Let us look at several stocks to get an idea of what an earnings miss looks like and how the stock reacts.

Example 1: FLIR Systems

Figure 7.2 shows an example on the daily scale. Look first at the inset.

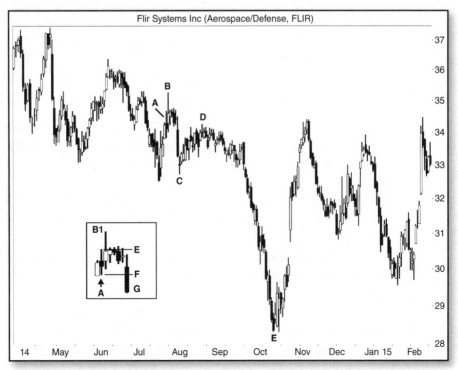

FIGURE 7.2   This example of an earnings miss takes several days before the market begins trending.

This is a zoom of the earnings announcement at B, which I show as B1. The first close outside of the large price swing (EF) of the day before B1 gives the breakout direction. That happens on bar G when the stock closes below line F.

Look at the stock chart. I labeled the turning points to match the ideal configuration in Figure 7.1.

I define the *benchmark close* as the last close *before* the earnings announcement (the close at A in this case). If the announcement is before the market opens or if the announcement time is not supplied, then the benchmark close is the prior day's close. If the announcement is after the market close, then the benchmark close occurs on the day of the announcement.

In this example, the company announced earnings at B, before the market opened. The market was supposed to react to the announcement on that day, and it did, but it did not set a trend. The stock closed higher by 1% after making a wide swing upward, but it closed well below the high. That 1% rise contrasts to the median drop of 3% from the model shown in Figure 7.1.

Over the next several days, the stock moved sideways and then broke out downward from its trading range before bottoming at C. C became the event decline low. The stock at this point took 8 days to get there and hit pavement 4% below the benchmark close.

The stock bounced to D, which was 0% below the benchmark close, matching the median bounce height for earnings misses, before rounding over and collapsing to E. The bounce to D took 26 days, slower than the 20-day median.

What looked like a promising earnings announcement at B actually turned into a 17% drop from the benchmark close (A) to E.

Example 2: Alaska Air

Figure 7.3 shows another example of a bad earnings announcement.

Before the market opened, the company announced earnings (B) that were worse than the market expected. That becomes clear when the stock closed down 9% for the day.

The repercussions of the announcement continued as the stock moved lower to bottom at the event decline, C, 16% below the benchmark close (in this case, the close at A).

Then the stock bounced, taking off and carrying the stock to D, just 3% below the benchmark close, before crashing on the way to E, 18% below the benchmark close.

Notice that if you timed the bounce right, you could have almost recovered your money. Also notice that if you sold at E, the airline stock then became a moon shot to 71, 30 points higher, leaving you watching from the ground.

FIGURE 7.3 This earnings announcement sees the stock drop 9% in one day.

Example 3: Southwest Airlines

Figure 7.4 shows another airline stock with weak earnings that showed surprising strength.

This earnings announcement occurred before the market open, so the word got out quickly. The stock dropped 2.4% on the day of the announcement (B).

The stock closed lower for two more days, bottoming at C, 7% below the close at A. From close to low, the 7% event decline was large (although slightly below the 8% average), but that was as bad as it got.

The bounce to D happened so fast that it took only 2 days before price peaked. The bounce almost made it back up to the benchmark close, A, falling less than 1% shy.

The decline after the bounce flew the stock to E, just a penny above C. After that, the airline caught the wind and soared.

The stock followed a similar profile a year earlier. It bottomed just 2% below the benchmark close before recovering.

Although it takes some work to match earnings announcements to a stock chart (some websites such as Google do it for you), it is worth doing to see how your investment might unfold during a bad earnings announcement.

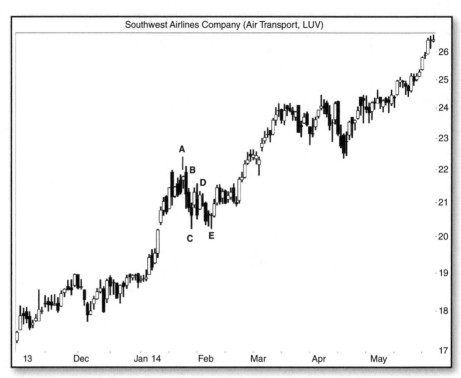

FIGURE 7.4 A good price run-up to the earnings announcement suggested the post-breakout performance would be mild.

- Consult the historical record to see how the stock last behaved after an earnings miss.

The Numbers

Now that we know how a stock reacts to a bad earnings announcement, let us examine the numbers. **Table 7.2** shows them.

I looked at 4,813 bad earnings announcement from 471 stocks in bull markets with reports coming from February 2003 to February 2015. Not all stocks covered the entire period and few had announcements going back that far.

1. Event-day drop. The event day is the day traders learn of the earnings miss. The stock reacts to the event by declining a median of 3% and an average of 4%. In Figure 7.1, the event-day drop is the AB move.

2, 3. Event decline and timing. The stock continues declining for a median of 7 days, dropping 8% below the benchmark close. The benchmark close is the last close *before* traders learn of the event. The event decline corresponds to the low at C in Figure 7.1

TABLE 7.2	Statistics for Bad Quarterly Earnings		
Description		Median	Average
1. Event-day drop		3%	4%
2. Event decline		8%	10%
3. Days to event decline ends		7	13
4. Bounce high		0%	−1%
5. Days to bounce high		20	36
6. Ultimate low		14%	18%
7. Days to ultimate low		38	77
8. Days to breakeven		28	112
9. Do large one-day drops result in bigger declines to the ultimate low? If so, how often?		Yes, 62%	
10. How many stocks do not bounce?		25%	
11. How many stocks reach breakeven during the bounce?		50%	
12. Do stocks that bounce decline farther?		Yes	
13. Do bad earnings affect stocks most near the yearly high, middle, or low?		Yearly low	
14. What are chances of bad earnings in three and six months?		24%, 43%	

4, 5. Bounce high and timing. The median bounce brings the stock back up to breakeven (0% below the benchmark close), but the average falls short of breakeven (−1%). It takes a median of almost 3 weeks for the bounce to peak. The bounce high is D in Figure 7.1.

During the bounce, half the stocks will recover more than they lost during the event and half will not.

6, 7. Ultimate low and timing. I think of the ultimate low as how bad the decline will get. It takes a median of 38 days to drop 14% before the stock moves back up at least 20% (the ultimate low is the lowest valley before a stock rises by 20%). I show the ultimate low as point E in Figure 7.1.

8. Days to breakeven. The breakeven price is the benchmark close (the last close before the announcement).

It takes a median of 28 days and an average of 112 days to reach breakeven. The wide difference between the two numbers is because some stocks took a long time (years) to recover or may not have recovered by the end of the study.

9. Do large 1-day drops result in bigger declines to the ultimate low? One-day drops larger than the 3% median suffer larger drops to the ultimate low than do those stocks with shallower 1-day drops. You have a 62% chance of having a larger decline to the ultimate low after a 1-day drop greater than the median 3%.

What does this mean? Almost two-thirds of stocks will suffer larger declines to the ultimate low if traders really dislike the earnings report.

10. How many stocks do not bounce? There is a 25% chance the stock will not bounce. Instead, the stock bottoms at the ultimate low and recovers. A *no-bounce* recovery is better than having a stock bounce and then sink farther (to the ultimate low).

11. How many stocks reach breakeven during the bounce? Answer: Half of those that bounce. If you hold onto the stock after an event decline, you can recover a good portion of your loss during the bounce, but your timing has to be exquisite and the stock has to cooperate, too.

12. Do stocks that bounce decline farther? Yes. A stock that does not bounce means it reaches the ultimate low during the event decline and then recovers. The median drop to the ultimate low when there is no bounce is 9% versus a 17% drop after a bounce occurs. The averages show the same trend, 11% versus 20%, for no-bounce/bounce stocks, respectively.

■ Stocks that bounce tend to drop almost twice as far.

13. Do bad earnings affect stocks most near the yearly high, middle, or low? A friend of mine told me that stocks near the yearly high, the ones with the highest performance relative to other stocks, fall more after an earnings miss than poorly performing stocks.

She was looking at stocks with high relative strength (performance relative to other stocks). I did not have relative strength readings for the stocks, so I used price. Stocks with high relative strength should be trading at or near the yearly high, by definition. Those stocks are outperforming all others.

I sorted the results into where the benchmark close was in the yearly trading range (lowest third, middle third, and highest third). Stocks with an earnings miss within a third of the yearly low performed worse than did those in the middle of the yearly range. Those in the middle of the yearly range performed worse than did those stocks near the yearly high. The widest difference was between the lowest and highest third, with the lowest third performing a median of 19% worse.

Is a third of the yearly high too wide a margin? I ran two tests and narrowed the margin to 5% and 1% below the yearly high. In other words, stocks within 5% or even 1% of the yearly high declined *less* after an earnings miss than stocks in the other ranges.

■ If your stock is near the yearly low and it misses earnings, the stock will get whacked harder than if it were higher in the yearly trading range.

14. What are chances of bad earnings in 3 and 6 months? I looked at the likelihood of having additional bad earnings in the next two quarters and found that they were 24% and 43%, respectively. The 43% number covers both quarters, so you have a 43% chance of having at least one bad earnings report within 6 months after a bad quarter.

■ Day Traders

Having looked at the numbers, what conclusions can we make for the four trading styles?

For day traders, the analysis is easy. The earnings report does not apply. Why? Because only a few companies report their earnings when the markets are open (I have seen it happen two or three times out of thousands).

If the announcement happens before the market opens, then the news will be factored in when trading begins. If the news comes out after the close, then it will affect the next day's trading.

However, day traders will find the model in Figure 7.1 helpful. Knowing that the stock has a downward bias for up to a week after the announcement allows day traders to position themselves on the correct side of the market. They will want to short a stock after an earnings miss then go long while it climbs during the bounce phase, and so on.

■ Swing Traders

The model in Figure 7.1 fits swing traders best.

If you own the stock and a bad earnings surprise happens, the stock is going down. It is best to cash out quickly, especially if you can catch it on the day the market reacts to the announcement.

If you are an end-of-day trader like me, then consider holding onto the stock as it bounces. Yes, you will have to ride out a drop to the event decline low. That is a median loss of 8% or an average of 10%.

You can place a limit order at breakeven and let that take you out automatically when the stock rises. Or you can ride it up using swing trading techniques to better time the exit.

Figure 7.5 shows one of my more recent disasters. I bought the stock at B, just two trading days after the stock hit a low (A).

For a few months, I was making money. The stock had its ups and downs, but it remained above my buy price most of the time.

Then the company announced earnings after the close at C.

The next day (D) the stock plummeted, closing down almost 14% below the prior close. I learned about it after the close.

I decided to sell the stock at the open the next day, thinking that this was only the beginning of the decline. As the chart shows, I sold on the day the stock bottomed (E).

That trade is why I wrote this chapter, to better understand how the market reacts to an earnings miss. Given the same situation, I would use a trendline (EF) to signal

FIGURE 7.5 This trade has good timing on the entry but bad on the exit.

the exit. A close below the trendline would tell me to sell the stock at the open the next day. That exit would have taken me back to about breakeven.

The stock recovered and them some, climbing all the way to 64.99. The drop that followed took the stock below E. It kept going down to 41.37 before bouncing and forming a double bottom.

■ Position Traders

Position traders are looking for swings of 20% or more. A 20% rise or drop in a stock is what I call a trend change. Market professionals define a bull market as a rise of 20% from a low in an index such as the Dow Jones Industrials. A bear market occurs when an index drops at least 20% from a high. I applied those numbers to stocks to signal a trend change.

Position traders try to exit before a stock changes trend. If you are a position trader, should you sell your stock after an earnings miss?

To answer that, I looked at how often the ultimate low meets or exceeds a 20% drop. I found that 32% of trades dropped at least 20% on the way to the ultimate low. That means 68% recovered before reaching a 20% decline.

Before making a decision to sell, consider these questions:

- Have the fundamentals (price to earnings, price to sales, and so on) worsened?

- How has the stock reacted to prior earnings misses?

- Is the industry suffering, too? Industry weakness may mean a larger drop in your stock.

- Is the general market trending lower? If everything is going down, then expect your stock to be weak, too.

- Have the reasons for owning the stock changed?

The answers to these questions may help you decide whether to hold onto the stock or sell. For example, if the earnings miss occurs in a bear market, it is probably a good idea to sell and sit in cash until a bull market returns.

If the market is suffering a retrace in a bull market, pulling down almost all stocks, then it is probably prudent to hold onto the stock. However, you may wish to sell the stock and buy a more promising opportunity.

■ Buy-and-Hold Investors

Much of what I wrote for position traders applies to investors that buy-and-hold. Investors are content to wait for years, sometimes decades for their stocks to achieve a good value. For example, I sold Michaels Stores for a gain of almost 5,000% after holding it for 16 years.

An earnings miss of one quarter or even several quarters sparks a yawn from buy-and-holders. They worry about a company going bankrupt. Unless the earnings miss signals a major malfunction in the company or the start of a downward spiral, then they are content to hold on.

I checked my database and looked for the number of stocks that made significant drops after an earnings miss. I found that 22% of stocks dropped at least 25%, but just 3% dropped by half (declined at least 50%).

You have a 97% chance that the decline will be less than 50%. Your stock could be one of the 3% that make a massive drop, so have Scotty in engineering tune-up the shields.

If the earnings miss concerns you, then look at the condition of the general market. If a bear market is occurring, you may want to sell a portion or all of the stock.

Bear markets can take stocks down by more than 50%. For example, the 2007 to 2009 bear market in the Dow Industrials took the average down 54%. That decline is large, but it pales to the damage many stocks suffered. Quality stocks dropped by 66% and more.

Look at the condition of the industry. If the entire industry is suffering, then maybe it is time to sell.

Visit the company's website to assess the condition of the company. Review their financials and talk to shareholder services. The Form 10-K report has a good section on problems facing the company, including any pending lawsuits. If you need food for your nightmares, Form 10-K is a good place to start.

■ Trading Examples

Example 1: Interpublic Group of Companies

Figure 7.6 shows a situation that you may run across.

The company announced earnings before the market opened at A. The stock gapped up on the news but then eased lower over the next week.

If you owned the stock, should you sell?

I drew lines B and C to mark the high and low of the day before the announcement. Because the stock closed above B, it had an upward breakout, not a downward one. Thus, you would hold onto the stock.

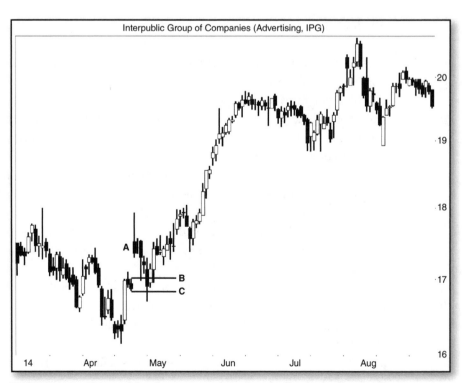

FIGURE 7.6 This stock breaks out upward, so do not sell.

An upward earnings surprise takes the form that you see here. The stock may or may not gap up on the news, but it closes substantially higher than the prior day.

If the earnings report is surprisingly good, then the stock will continue higher for a time. However, within about a week to 10 days, you will find that the stock starts to retrace those gains. If you are a swing trader, you will want to sell at the top of that bounce on or before the retrace begins.

This stock followed that profile by gapping higher at A and then retracing, giving back all of those gains before resuming the upward move.

■ Example 2: Monster Worldwide

Take a sheet of paper and cover up the chart of **Figure 7.7** to the right of the vertical line at D.

The stock suffered a bad earnings surprise at A. The event decline bottomed at B and the stock bounced to C, recovering all that it lost on the drop to B.

If you owned the stock and sold it at breakeven, you would have been blessed with good timing. After peaking at C, the stock dropped.

FIGURE 7.7 How would you trade this stock?

It is now three months later and another quarterly report is due. The stock has been moving lower since the peak in March (upper left of chart).

The company announced earnings before the market opened, at E. Notice that it gapped lower, staging a downward breakout from D.

How do you trade this stock?

Because the stock has been trending lower for five months now and this is the second quarterly earnings miss, the news is not good.

The last time it missed earnings, the stock recovered all of its losses. Will it do the same this time?

A check of the statistics provides an answer. A quarter of the stocks hit breakeven 53% of the time. That means the stock during the bounce climbs far enough to reach or exceed the benchmark close (the last close before the earnings announcement). A second quarter of bad earnings reaches breakeven 50% of the time, slightly less than the first quarter of bad earnings.

■ A second quarter of bad earnings will reach breakeven during the bounce 50% of the time compared to the prior quarter's 53% of the time.

Unfortunately, that does not help much.

If this were my trade, I would assume that I would get my money back, but I would also put a stop in place because of the long decline from the March peak and because this is the second time the company has flubbed earnings.

Slowly, move your paper to the right, and let each price bar appear. After each bar appears, ask yourself if you would sell now. I think you will find that trying to time the exit is difficult.

The stock peaked at F and then pretended to be a rollercoaster before heading lower. A worst-case stop placed below line G would limit losses. I would wait for a close below the line before selling at the open the next day.

■ Measure Rule

Because we know that the stock was weak (long downtrend, two quarters in a row of bad earnings), then a limit order to sell midway to breakeven might be a good strategy.

Here is how this works. Add the last closing price before the announcement (D) to the value of the event decline low (G) and divide by 2. This will give you the middle of the move down. Place a limit order to sell at that price. In this case, the benchmark close is 6.62, and the event decline low is 5.36 for a target price of $(6.62 + 5.36) \div 2$, or 5.99. The stock missed the target by 9 cents. However, this method works 80% of the time.

■ Closing Position

I have seen stocks I owned stumble after earnings announcements. For example, Hartford Financial Services Group, an insurance company stock I own, dropped 7% in one session after the report of earnings that surprised the market (and me). I learned of the decline after the market close.

What should I do?

To answer that, I read this chapter. The "Behavior at a Glance" section showed me how the typical stock behaves *after* the market reacts badly to the report of earnings. One of the chart examples from this chapter matched my situation, too. Now I can formulate a plan for the future.

With the information provided in this chapter, now I have the tools to trade appropriately and help rescue my wallet from the clutches of an earnings miss.

CHAPTER 8

Flags and Pennants

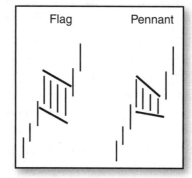

Flags and pennants are the hand tools of the swing and day trader. Sometimes the patterns identify a move midway in the trend. That is valuable information for trend traders because it allows them to predict the trend's end.

The only substantial difference between a flag and a pennant is their shape. Flags form rectangles while pennants make wedges along a strong price trend. Both patterns can slope up, down, or sideways, but you will likely see them form against the short-term trend.

The statistics in this chapter assume flags and pennants are the same chart pattern. For simplicity in this chapter, when I write "flags," I mean both flags and pennants.

■ Behavior at a Glance

The statistics in this chapter come from 662 stocks in bull and bear markets from October 1991 to November 2014. I found 1,700 flags but discarded bear market patterns, leaving 1,198 from bull markets.

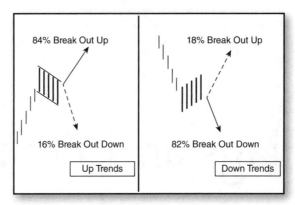

FIGURE 8.1   The breakout direction.

Figure 8.1 shows the breakout direction, sorted by the inbound price trend, either up or down. The inbound price trend is not the primary trend (which is often measured in months), but the very short-term trend (measured in days to a few weeks). I used the very short-term trend because flags are short patterns with limited influence.

The left panel shows the breakout direction in an upward price trend. The five thick black lines represent the flag. A flag in a bull market breaks out upward 84% of the time and downward 16% of the time, regardless of the slope of the flag itself (up, down, or sideways). For reference, I show the flag with a downward slope.

An up or down breakout occurs when price closes outside the flag boundary. The flag boundary is the imaginary line formed by joining the tops or bottoms of price as the flag forms. I show the boundaries as two diagonal lines hugging the top and bottom of the flag.

Alternatively, use a close above the top of the flag or flagpole, whichever is higher, as an upward breakout indicator. Similarly, some use a close below the bottom of the flag to signal a downward breakout. Using the flagpole top or flag bottom helps reduce false breakouts but also reduces profits.

The right panel shows the breakout direction for flags in a downward price trend. Again, the inbound trend is very short term, measured in days to weeks.

In a downward price trend, flags break out downward most often, 82% of the time in fact. Upward breakouts cover the other 18%. Again, the numbers ignore the slope of the flag itself.

The implication of the breakout direction is obvious. If you buy a flag before the breakout, you will be wrong 16% to 18% of the time. Even if you guess the correct breakout direction, you could still lose money when the stock reverses quickly. How often does that happen? The next section gives part of the answer by looking at throwbacks and pullbacks.

Throwbacks and Pullbacks

Throwbacks and pullbacks are land mines waiting to explode when traders stumble over them. Price reverses and moves for a time in the adverse direction, flushing out more traders, before heading off in the original breakout direction.

Figure 8.2 shows the typical behavior of price during a throwback and pullback.

A throwback occurs within a month of an upward breakout, by definition. I like to see white space between price at the top of the throwback and the chart pattern. The stock returns to the price near the top of the flag or breakout price before resuming its upward move.

The left panel of Figure 8.2 shows statistics for throwbacks. Throwbacks happen 52% of the time.

When a throwback occurs, price rises after the breakout by an average of 10% and it takes 6 days to peak. The stock returns to the breakout price in another 6 days for a total of 12 days to complete the trip.

The right panel of Figure 8.2 shows statistics for pullbacks.

A pullback is similar to a throwback except inverted. Pullbacks happen 54% of the time when price breaks out downward but returns to the bottom of the flag, or breakout price, within a month. I like to see white space between the stock and the bottom of the pullback, but this is only a guideline. If price just slides sideways along the breakout price, I do not count that as a pullback.

During the average pullback, price drops 9% in 5 days before beginning the return to the flag. It completes the journey in 11 days. After that, the downward move resumes.

Busted Flags

There is a one-liner that says, unbreakable toys are useful for breaking other toys. The broken toy in this case is a busted pattern. They are useful for making money.

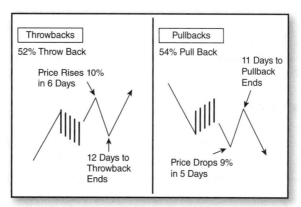

FIGURE 8.2   Typical throwback and pullback behavior.

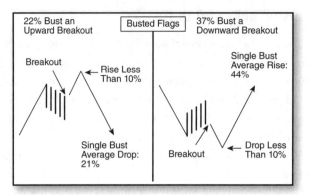

FIGURE 8.3   The ideal busted flag.

In a busted pattern, price breaks out and moves less than 10% before reversing and closing on the opposite side of the chart pattern (above the top or below the bottom of the flag). How many flags bust?

Figure 8.3 shows an upward breakout from a flag on the left side of the figure. In a busted upward breakout, price rises less than 10% above the breakout price before reversing. Then the stock drops, and for a single bust, price declines more than 10% below the bottom of the flag. The decline that follows averages 21%.

Twenty-two percent of flags will bust an upward breakout. That means if you buy the stock, you have a 22% chance of making no more than 10%.

The right half of Figure 8.3 shows the case of a busted downward breakout. Over a third (37%) will bust.

The busting process is similar for downward breakouts as it is for upward ones. Price breaks out downward and drops less than 10% before reversing and closing at least 10% above the top of the flag (for a single bust). The average rise for flags with single busted downward breakouts is 44%.

- Between 22% (upward breakouts) and 37% (downward breakouts) of flags will bust a flag or pennant.

The bust rate (22% or 37%) is high because the move after a flag is often small, leading to a quick reversal.

■ Identification

Let us look at an example of a flag, shown in **Figure 8.4**. The very short-term trend begins at A and moves upward in a straight-line run until peaking at B. Then the flag begins. Price slopes downward following two roughly parallel boundaries before bottoming at C. Most of the time the flag will slope against the trend (in this example, a downward flag slope in an uptrend), but the flag can slope in any direction.

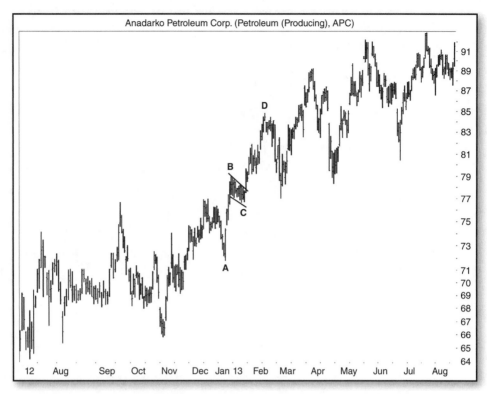

FIGURE 8.4 This flag is well shaped.

The trend ends at D after which the stock makes a large drop.

Figure 8.5 shows two examples of pennants. The first appears in an upward retrace in a longer-term downward. The retrace begins at A and rises to B where the pennant appears. In this example, price breaks out upward from the pennant and climbs to C before reversing. This pennant is an example of a single-busted pennant. Notice the slope of the pennant is downward in the upward AB move.

Pennant E shows the swift downtrend beginning at D. Here is an example of a pennant that bends toward the trend (downward). The breakout is downward at F, and price drops to G before ending the trend.

Notice that neither pennant gives much profit opportunity.

Table 8.1 lists the identification guidelines for flags and pennants.

Flagpole. I like to see price moving up (or down) at a brisk pace. This up or down move is the flagpole. Figure 8.5 shows good examples of flagpoles at AB and DE.

All flags should rest on a flagpole. If they do not, then they are normal congestion regions, places where the stock pauses for a time, and does not flag.

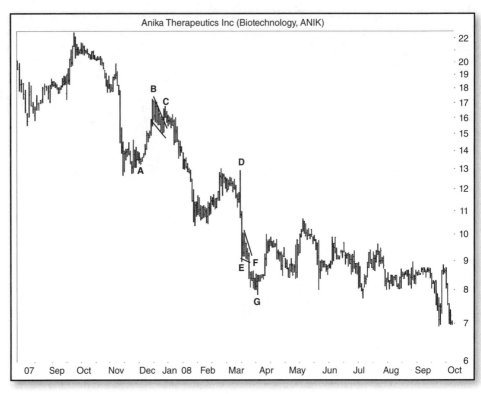

FIGURE 8.5 Two pennants appear in a stock.

Three-Week Maximum. By convention, flags and pennants are three weeks long or less; otherwise, they are classified as different chart patterns (rectangles, triangles, wedges, and so on).

TABLE 8.1	Identification Guidelines
Characteristic	**Discussion**
Flagpole	The flag or pennant must rest on a flagpole, which is a price trend of unusual vigor. In the best situations, the flagpole price shows little overlap from day to day. In the worst case, price rises at a more sedate pace.
Three-week maximum	The length of a flag is three weeks or less.
Shape	Flags look like small rectangles where price stays within two parallel (or nearly so) trendlines. They resemble a small flag on a flagpole. Pennants show a converging (narrowing) price trend.
Slope	Flags and pennants slope against the price trend most often but can slope in any direction: up, down, or sideways.
Volume Trend	Trends downward over 80% of the time.
Breakout	A breakout occurs when price closes outside the flag or pennant boundary.

Shape. Flags look rectangular, but pennants tend to take any shape. However, most pennants narrow to a point. In doing research for this book, I classified everything that was not a rectangle as a pennant. **Figure 8.6** shows an example of a pennant that broadens out.

Slope. Flags can slope in any direction: with the trend, against it, or horizontal. Most often, though, the flag will slope against the short-term trend.

Volume Trend. From the start of the flag to the end, volume slopes downward the majority of the time. Do not discard a flag because it has an unusual volume shape.

Breakout. A breakout occurs when price closes outside the flag boundary.

■ Buy Setup 1

The first setup is to buy a busted flag. **Figure 8.6** shows an example of a busted pennant in a downward price trend.

Price trends down following the AB move, often in a straight-line run. The flag appears at B, represented by the box. The breakout is downward and price drops to C.

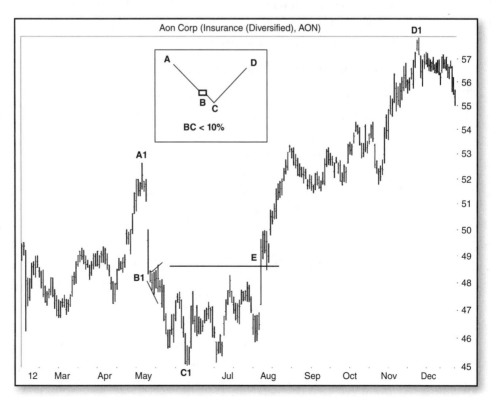

FIGURE 8.6 This busted pennant leads to a large gain.

The BC drop is less than 10%, by definition a busted pattern. The stock turns and rises above the top of the flag. When price closes above the top of the flag (or flag-pole, whichever is higher), it busts the downward breakout. The AB trend could be upward, too, but the breakout from the flag must be downward in this setup.

The stock chart shows an example of a busted pennant. The shape of this pennant (B1) is unusual because it broadens out (price forms higher highs and lower lows) instead of converging. You can think of a flag as an area where price pauses in a strong trend, so the flag can take many shapes.

The short-term trend begins at A1 and drops into the pennant at B1. The breakout from this pennant is downward, and price drops just 4% when it bottoms at C1.

Then price starts to recover in a choppy pattern that eventually sees the stock close above the top of the pennant at E. When that happens, it busts the downward breakout.

The stock continued moving up (D1) and more than doubled in price (not shown). Here is what to look for in this setup.

1. Follow the guidelines in Table 8.1 to identify a flag.
2. For the best results, look for the trend to start above the flag. Figure 8.6 shows an example of the very short-term trend beginning above the pennant (A is above B).
3. Price should drop no more than 10% below the breakout price before reversing and closing above the top of the flag.
4. Buy at the open the next day.

Table 8.2 gives more information on this setup.

1. Over a third of flags with downward breakouts will bust. If you short a stock anticipating a drop of more than 10%, you will be wrong 37% of the time.

2, 3. The average rise for all types of busts (single, double and three or more) is 26%. If you look at single busted patterns only, the average rise is a tasty 44%. Yum.

4–6. Of the 37% that bust, they split into single busts (55% of those), double busts (15%), and the remainder (30%) bust at least three times.

TABLE 8.2 Statistics for Busted Flags and Pennants	
Description	**Result**
1. Percentage of flags that bust	37%
2. Average rise after busting	26%
3. Average rise after single bust	44%
4. Percentage of single busts	55%
5. Percentage of double busts	15%
6. Percentage of triple+ busts	30%

This setup assumes you hold until the trend changes. That means buying the day after price closes above the top of the flag or flagpole and selling at the highest peak before price drops at least 20%. That is difficult or impossible to do repeatedly. Thus, your results will vary, so do not expect to make 44% trading flags in this manner, or even 26%. You may do better or worse.

■ Buy Setup 2

This setup is how swing and day traders can use flags.

Some traders call flags half-staff patterns. That means they appear in the middle of a price trend. **Figure 8.7** shows an example.

Look at the inset first. This is how a half-staff pattern is supposed to work. The short inbound trend (AB) is supposed to equal the outbound trend (CD). In words, from the start of the short trend (A) to the top of the flag or flagpole (B, whichever is higher), is supposed to equal the length from the bottom of the flag (C) to the trend end (D). This measure is also the basis for the measure rule, a guideline that helps predict a price target.

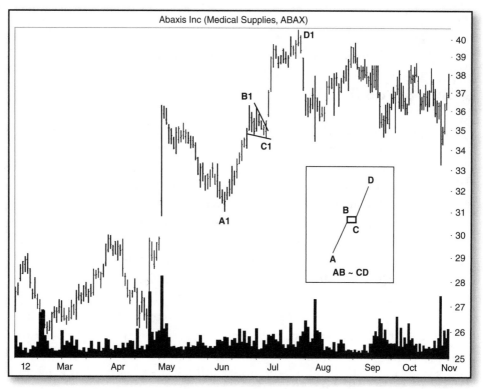

FIGURE 8.7 This pennant appears about midway along trend A1-D1.

The stock chart shows an example for the pennant at B1-C1. The trend begins at A1 and ends at B1, the top of the flagpole. The length measures $5.25. That compares to the C1-D1 length of 5.99, as measured from the bottom of the pennant (C1) to the high at D1.

How is this information useful for trading? If you calculate the AB move and assume the CD move will be as long, you will be right 53% of the time for upward breakouts and 55% of the time for downward breakouts.

Here are the guidelines for this setup.

1. Follow the guidelines in Table 8.1 to identify a flag.
2. For upward breakouts, the trend should start below the flag. For downward breakouts, the trend should begin above the flag. That is, look for flags that act as continuation patterns and not reversals.
3. Measure the move from the start of the short-term trend to the top of the flag (bottom of the flag for downward breakouts). If Figure 8.7, that is the A1-B1 move (31.04 to 36.29 or 5.25).
4. For upward breakouts, add the length in step 3 to the bottom of the flag (34.59 + 5.25 or 39.84). The result becomes the preliminary target. For downward breakouts, subtract the result from the top of the flag to get the target.
5. Using the preliminary target, look for nearby overhead resistance (upward breakouts) or underlying support (downward breakouts) where the stock may reverse. That support or resistance area becomes your final target.

You can increase the success rate of this approach by dividing the AB move in half.

■ Buy Setup 3

Figure 8.8 shows the ideal situation for this setup in the inset. The stock rises to A and makes an all-time high. Then price retraces from this high, leaving behind overhead resistance.

The stock tries to make a new all-time high and a flag appears along the way, at B. The difference of the rise from the price of B to A is not very much, meaning the stock need not climb much to enter all-time higher territory. This it does after the breakout on the way to C.

Look at the stock chart for an example. Over the past 26 years, peak A1 is the highest the stock has reached. It backpedaled after A1 until reaching D. Then the stock made a nice run up to E in a burst of energy, following a nearly straight line.

A flag appeared (B1) when the stock retraced to F. The stock broke out upward from the flag (the day before F).

Peak A1 is at 48.22 and the breakout is at 45.83 (the close on the breakout day) for a difference of 2.39, or 5%. All the stock has to do is climb more than 5% to exceed the all-time high and climb above overhead resistance.

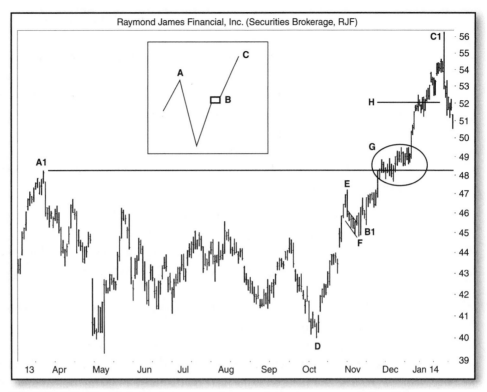

FIGURE 8.8 The ideal situation occurs when a stock breaks out to an all-time high.

How far can the stock be expected to rise? If the flag is midway in the price trend, we can estimate a target. The trend starts at D, 40.01, and rises to the high at E, 47.20, for a climb of 7.19. Add this to the low at the bottom of the flag (to the left of F, the flag low before the breakout), 44.94, to give a target of 52.13. I show the target as line H.

Once you see the stock close outside of the flag boundary, buy at the open the next day. That would get you into the stock at about 45.95 with an expectation of a rise to about 52. That is a gain of about 6 or 13% if everything works perfectly.

You can also estimate the number of days it will take to complete the trade by counting the price bars from D to E. If the stock climbs at the same velocity, it will take as many bars to reach H. This measure is a guideline only, and it does not work well in this case.

As the stock lifts off from the breakout, it stumbles in the circled area at G. This is at or near the value of the old high at A1. A pause at an old high is expected (because of resistance). If the stock broke out downward from this area, it would be an automatic sell. The old high at A1 is 48.22, near the round number 48, so I would place a conditional order to sell on a *close* below, say, 47.93 (an odd number far enough below 48 to avoid traders placing their orders at 48).

The lowest *close* is 48.06 in area G even though the stock dropped to a *low* of 47.65.

You could place an order to sell at the target, 52.13, or try to finesse a higher exit. For short-term swing trades like this, I find it useful to use a sell order at the target price. You will not catch the high, but it is often close. In this example, the stock climbed to 56.31 before making a large swing downward.

I conducted a study of flags and pennants with upward breakouts and compared those situations in which the stock pushed through overhead resistance to those that stopped. Even though I used the short-term trend leading to and exiting from the flag, I still discovered interesting results. **Table 8.3** shows them.

1. Most of the flags (67%) ran into overhead resistance after the breakout on the way to the trend high.

2. Flags that saw price rise into virgin territory (an all-time high, no resistance) showed post-breakout gains that averaged 25%. When the stock hit overhead resistance, the rise averaged just 16%.

3. The median rise is 16% for those flags breaking out to new highs compared to 13% for those mired in resistance.

4. Large gains, those over 25%, were more plentiful for flags without overhead resistance (27% of them) compared to just 18% of flags with overhead resistance.

5, 6. The 5% failure rate is just 2% for those breaking out to new all-time highs (no overhead resistance). That means just 2% of the 220 flags failed to see price rise at least 5%. This compared to a 14% failure rate for those flags with overhead resistance.

The 10% failure sees more flags and pennants fail, of course, as the table shows. How can you use this information?

1. Identify a flag using the guidelines in Table 8.1.
2. Find the price at which the stock will enter all-time-high territory.
3. Compute the percentage change from the flag's breakout price to the all-time-high price. Use: $100 \times$ (High Price − Breakout Price)/Breakout Price. For example, if the breakout price is $20 and the all-time-high price is $25, then the

TABLE 8.3	Statistical Analysis of Buy Setup 3	
Description	No Overhead Resistance	Overhead Resistance
1. Occurrence, samples	29%, 220	67%, 519
2. Post-breakout average gain	25%	16%
3. Median gain	16%	13%
4. Gains over 25%	27%	18%
5. 5% failure rate	2%	14%
6. 10% failure rate	21%	41%

stock will have to climb $100 \times (25 - 20)/20$, or 25%, before it clears overhead resistance.

4. Does the percentage gain in step 3 seem reasonable? If not, then look for another setup.

I measured the gain from the breakout price to the all-time high and found that the median rise was 5% and the average was 8%. If step 3 gives significantly higher numbers than those two, then consider looking elsewhere for a more promising trade.

5. You can place a buy order a penny above the flagpole or flag, whichever is higher, or wait for the breakout then buy at the open the next day.

■ Best Stop Locations

If you were to place a stop-loss order at the bottom of the flag after an upward breakout, price would hit the stop during a throwback 46% of the time. In other words, during a throwback the stock drops below the bottom of the flag almost half the time.

If a throwback occurs 52% of the time, and 46% of those are stopped out for a loss, how many flags result in a losing trade? Answer: 24% (46% of 52%). That is a high failure rate.

- A stop placed at the bottom of a bullish flag (upward trends, upward breakouts) will trigger 24% of the time.

For downward breakouts, if you were to place a stop-loss order at the top of the flag, you would be stopped out during a pullback 53% of the time. If 54% of flags have pullbacks in a downward price trend, and 53% of them will be stopped out, that means 29% of trades will end in failure. That is huge.

- A stop-loss order placed at the top of a bearish flag (downward trend, downward breakout) will trigger 29% of the time.

■ Measure Rule

The measure rule is actually a guideline to determine a price target after the breakout from a flag or pennant. It gives an indication of how far price might move. It is an estimate and nothing more. The stock may move considerably more or less than what the measure rule says.

I mentioned in Buy Setup 2 that flags and pennants sometimes appear midway in a price trend. You can use that idea to help determine where price will stop. That method is the traditional way to use the measure rule for flags and pennants. Calculate the height of the flag, including the flagpole, and add the height to the bottom of the flag to get a target.

Here are some unconventional variations of the measure rule.

Consider the flag shown in **Figure 8.9**. The flag is at AB. Calculate the height of the flag. Subtract the low price of B (85.08) from the high price of A (91.30) to get a height of 6.22. Add that result to the breakout price (C, 87) to get the target shown on the chart at 93.22.

Alternatively, you can add the flag's height to the top of the flagpole for a more aggressive target. Or you can use both the breakout price and flagpole top to find a range of targets where the stock might land.

Look for nearby overhead resistance (upward breakouts) or underlying support (downward breakouts) to help determine where price might reverse.

The stock will hit a target found using the flag height added to an upward breakout 91% of the time. Price reaches the downward breakout target 86% of the time.

For the traditional measure rule, refer to the discussion of Buy Setup 2.

FIGURE 8.9 The height of the flag only gives a target.

■ Trading

I do not have any good sell *setups* (I discuss sell configurations in a bit) to discuss with you. However, here are some tips I found useful when trading flags and pennants.

In looking at hundreds of flags and pennants, I found a common theme among those that outperformed and those that did not. **Figure 8.10** shows the ideal situation in panel A.

The stock price is represented by a solid line that starts out low on the left (C) and rises steadily (D), following the arrow higher. This is the long-term primary trend.

A very short-term uptrend appears (DE) that leads to the flag, E. After an upward breakout, the short-term trend continues to F. This is how well-behaved flags should act. Notice that the breakout and the slope of the primary trend are upward.

Now look at panel B. The primary trend, GH, is downward. The flag, I, appears in an upward retrace, HJ, of that downtrend. After J, the stock resumes its downward move. The rise after the flag (I to J), is short, resulting in a failed trade or reduced profit.

You will want to trade flags and pennants in a rising price trend (as shown in panel A) and avoid those situations shown by panel B (an upward retrace in a falling price trend).

- Look for flags and pennants when the primary (long-term) price trend is upward.

- Avoid buying a flag or pennant with an upward breakout as part of a retrace in a downward primary trend.

Sell Configurations

I found three configurations that work well for flags and pennants on the sell side. Look at panel A in **Figure 8.11** for the first configuration.

The primary trend, which for flags and pennants is a long-term price trend that lasts six months or more, is downward in this scenario. Price drops from D to E. Along the way, a flag appears. This is the best configuration for a flag when you intend

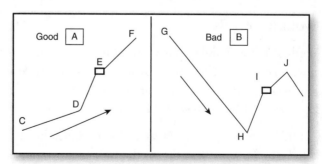

FIGURE 8.10   Two configurations to look for.

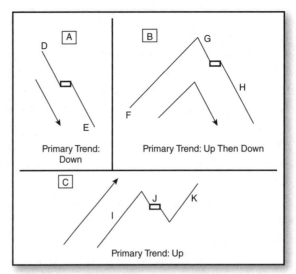

FIGURE 8.11 These three sell configurations for flags and pennants work well.

to sell a stock short. A downward breakout from the flag joins the primary downward trend and the receding tide lowers all boats.

Panel B shows a less successful scenario than panel A. Here the primary upward trend (FG) changes to downward, GH. Near the turn, a flag appears.

This is a difficult scenario to spot because you will not know when the primary trend changes from up to down until well after it completes the turn.

Imagine that the stock broke out downward from the flag (the box near G), you shorted the stock, but then price started climbing. You would be caught in a rising price trend where losses can be unlimited.

The last panel, C, shows a retrace in an upward price trend.

The primary trend is upward, IK, with a flag appearing in the retrace, J. Here a trader is trying to short the stock in an upward price trend and hoping that either the primary uptrend changes to a downward one or the retrace lasts long enough to make a tidy profit. This configuration is the worst performing of the three setups.

Avoid Reversals

Another useful trading tip is to avoid flags and pennants that act as reversals of the short-term trend. That means avoiding upward breakouts in a downward trend or downward breakouts in an upward trend. The move after a reversal averages between 33% (uptrends) and 50% (downtrends) shorter, vastly limiting profit opportunities.

- Trade flags and pennants that act as continuation patterns. Look for the breakout to be in the same direction as the very short-term trend.

■ Focus on Failures

Overhead resistance is a killer for many chart patterns, including flags. One example of this I show in **Figure 8.12**.

In February 2006, Yahoo started trending sideways (between the two horizontal lines, A) and that lasted until quarterly earnings came out in July (B). The stock dropped, bounced (a dead-cat bounce chart pattern), and formed pennant C. The pennant broke out upward, but it had a low probability of winning. Why? Mostly because companies have difficulty fixing earnings problems in one quarter but also because of overhead resistance.

The stock climbed only to D before tumbling.

■ Before trading a flag or pennant, look for overhead resistance.

■ Avoid trading a stock within three weeks of an upcoming earnings announcement.

■ A second dead-cat bounce (a 1-day decline of at least 15%) will occur within 6 months 38% of the time.

FIGURE 8.12 This stock runs into trouble with overhead resistance.

■ Actual Trade

Here is an actual trade I made using a flag. It is a special case, called an earnings flags, which is an event pattern.

When a company announces earnings that are better than expected, the stock shoots up, pauses to form a flag or pennant, and then resumes the upward trend. The trade does not always work, of course, but **Figure 8.13** shows a swing trade in which it did work.

On April 18, the company announced earnings after the market close that were better than expected. When the stock opened, it gapped higher (see Figure 8.13).

The stock climbed to C where it started to retrace. That retrace became a flag.

To get a target, I subtracted the announcement day's low (B, 12.19) from the flagpole's high (C, 13.47), giving a height of 1.28. I added the height to the flag low at E to get the target of 14.07.

I also calculated another target using the height of the flagpole from C to A added to E to get a target of 15.16. I felt this was too far for the stock to climb. Why? Because of overhead resistance (not shown) setup by a symmetrical triangle in December 2004 at 14 and up.

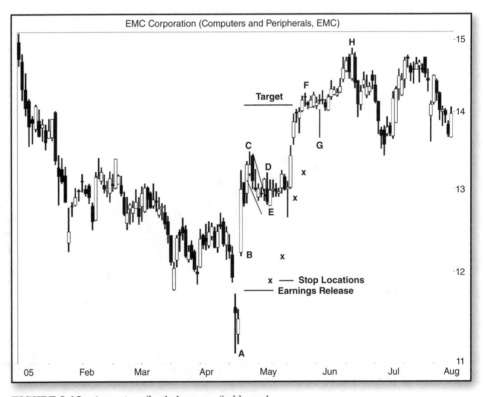

FIGURE 8.13   A earnings flag led to a profitable trade.

The stock broke through the top flag trendline (and closed above it) so I bought the stock the next day, receiving a fill at 13.13 (D).

I made note that a stop at 12.71 (below the flag low of 12.79) would be a good location, but that I never placed it with my broker. The S&P 500 Index and NASDAQ Composite hit a support area and looked to rise out of that area.

Had I placed the stop at 12.71, the downward spike to the right of E would have triggered the stop and taken me out of the trade for a loss.

Two days after buying the stock, I placed a stop at 11.94, below the 12.00 round number and below a 62% retrace of the flagpole rise from A to C. I show that on Figure 8.13 as the lowest x.

On May 8, I raised the stop to 12.17 and then raised it to 12.91 on May 13 and to 13.23 on the May 19. The 13.23 stop is 3 cents below a 62% Fibonacci retrace of the rise from E to F. I show those stop locations with x's.

On May 26, G, I wrote in my notebook, "I think this stock has peaked, short term. MACD [moving average convergence/divergence] says momentum turned lower today (5/25). The stock has fulfilled the flag measure rule and is butting up against overhead resistance coupled with a NASDAQ that's poised to tumble."

I sold and received a fill at 14.15, making 8% on the swing trade. The peak at H was the highest the stock reached until 2007.

■ Closing Position

Figure 8.1 taught us that flags and pennants break out in the direction of the prevailing price trend over 80% of the time. Throwbacks and pullbacks occurred randomly. Busted patterns happened frequently, too, from 22% for upward breakouts to 37% for downward breakouts.

Figure 8.10 showed flags that followed the trend perform better than do those that appeared in the retrace of a downtrend.

Some flags and pennants appear midway in a price trend, making it easy to predict where the trend will end.

By assessing the primary trend (the move longer than 6 months or more) leading to a flag or pennant, you can identify more profitable situations and make money trading them.

Setup Synopsis

Figure 8.14 may help you identify the various types of trading setups. See the associated figure for an explanation.

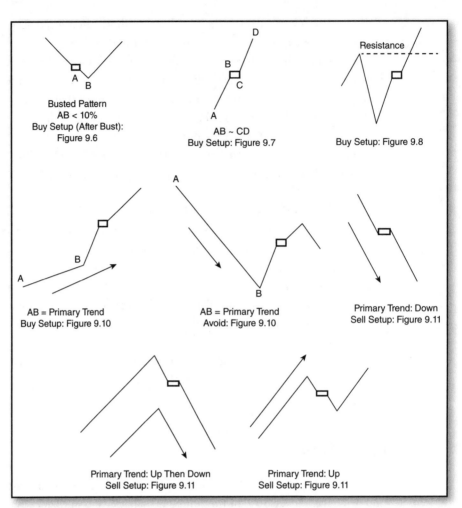

FIGURE 8.14 A collection of ideal trading setups and configurations.

CHAPTER 9

Head-and-Shoulders Bottoms

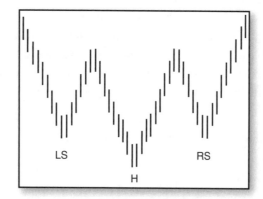

If you are new to chart patterns, the head-and-shoulders bottom can be an intimidating pattern. Many questions spring to mind about their appearance, making you wonder whether the bumps and dips you see on a screen really form a valid pattern. The pattern becomes valid only when the stock breaks out upward (confirmation).

This chapter will tell you what to look for, and more important, what the typical behavior is after the pattern breaks out.

◼ Behavior at a Glance

I used 1,002 stocks and found 2,866 head-and-shoulders bottoms from bull markets going back as far as July 1991 and as recent as January 2015. **Figure 9.1** shows the overall performance statistics of the group.

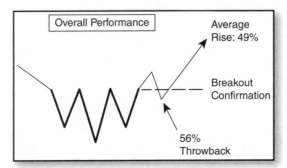

FIGURE 9.1 The average rise is 49% after a head-and-shoulders bottom.

After price breaks out of the chart pattern, it throws back (returns) to the breakout price 56% of the time.

The average rise from the breakout price to the ultimate high is 49%. The ultimate high is the highest peak before price drops at least 20%.

The median rise for head-and-shoulders bottoms is far less, 33%, so several large gains pull the average upward. Regardless, do not expect to make 33% or 49%. The numbers discussed here come from thousands of perfectly traded chart patterns. Your results could be better or worse. Do not use the numbers as a benchmark of how you might do trading them. Use them only for comparison with other chart patterns.

■ A throwback occurs 56% of the time.

Throwbacks

Figure 9.2 shows the behavior of stocks with throwbacks from head-and-shoulders bottoms.

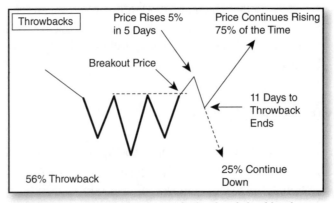

FIGURE 9.2 Throwback behavior for head-and-shoulders bottoms.

A throwback occurs when a stock breaks out upward from a chart pattern but returns to the pattern's trendline boundary or breakout price within 30 days.

During a throwback, price rises an average of 5% in 5 days. Then the stock begins the return trip that takes an additional 6 days before the stock bottoms (11 days total).

After that, if owners of the stock are lucky, price climbs to higher ground. That happens 75% of the time. The other 25% see the stock continue lower, closing below the bottom of the chart pattern and probably resulting in an argument with the spouse over market losses being too big.

If a throwback occurs and results in a loss 25% of the time, why not wait until the stock again closes above the breakout price? The disadvantage of this approach is that you will remain out of potentially winning trades 44% of the time (because 44% of head-and-shoulders bottoms do not have throwbacks). Those stocks missing throwbacks tend to outperform, too, rising an average of 57%, well above those with throwbacks (43% average rise).

By waiting, you miss the most promising trades and buy into weaker situations. That is the exact opposite of what you should do.

- After a throwback, price continues lower 25% of the time.

Busted Bottoms

Not all chart patterns work as expected. For head-and-shoulders bottoms, that means 14% will bust. A bust occurs when price breaks out of the head-and-shoulders bottom but rises less than 10% before reversing and closing below the head.

Figure 9.3 shows an example. Price breaks out upward, throws back, and then continues down. For the 14% that bust, they split into three groups: single busts (49% of them), double busts (35%), and three or more busts (15%). The loss after a single bust averages 22% below the bottom of the head.

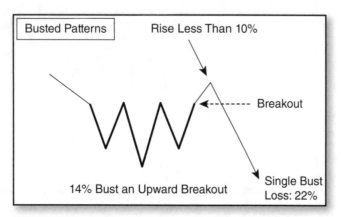

FIGURE 9.3 Performance of busted head-and-shoulders bottoms.

Double and triple busts are similar to single busts in that the up-and-down movement continues. A double bust, for example, would occur as follows: The stock breaks out upward and rises less than 10%. Then it reverses and closes below the head (first bust) but falls less than 10% before reversing and rising again. This time, the rise continues more than 10% above the top of the head-and-shoulders, busting the pattern a second time. A triple bust would see price stop before the last 10% rise and drop instead. The decline would then take price at least 10% below the bottom of the head.

In essence, when busting, the stock has to close either above the top or below the bottom of the chart pattern and reverse *before* moving more than 10% away from the pattern. If the stock moves more than 10% away from the pattern, the busting count ends.

■ Price busts a head-and-shoulders bottom pattern 14% of the time.

■ Identification

Figure 9.4 shows two examples of head-and-shoulders bottoms, one at ABC and the second at GHI. Refer to **Table 9.1** and Figure 9.4 as we discuss the identification guidelines.

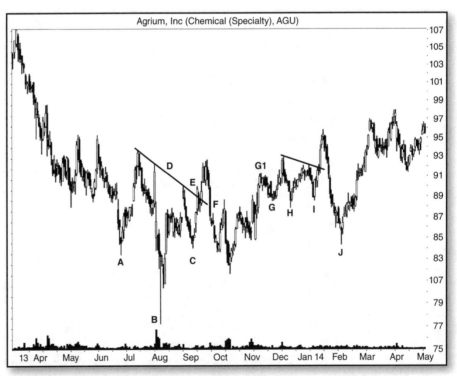

FIGURE 9.4 Two head-and-shoulders bottoms appear with varying performance success.

TABLE 9.1	Identification Guidelines
Characteristic	**Discussion**
Downtrend	Price usually trends downward into the head-and-shoulders bottom.
Shape	Look for a three-valley pattern with the middle valley below the other two.
Symmetry	The two shoulders should appear symmetrical across the head from one another (similar distance from the head) and bottom near the same price. If you were to flip the pattern upside down, it should look like a person's head and two shoulders.
Volume	Usually heaviest on the head, followed by the left shoulder.
Neckline	A line that joins the two armpits to help signal a breakout.
Breakout	Signals when price closes above the down-sloping neckline or closes above the right armpit when the neckline slopes upward. An upward breakout confirms the chart patterns as a valid head-and-shoulders bottom. Otherwise, it is just squiggles on a price chart.

Downtrend. In most cases, price trends downward into the first shoulder. In head-and-shoulders bottom ABC, price starts its downward trend at 115 (not shown). The ABC pattern acts as a reversal.

However, the GHI pattern has a trend that starts at B and moves upward leading to the head-and-shoulders. The GHI pattern acts as a continuation of the upward trend.

Shape. Look for three valleys with the middle one below the other two. Each valley should be a distinct minor low. The first valley is the left shoulder, the middle valley is the head, and the third valley is the right shoulder.

Symmetry. The two shoulders should bottom near the same price and be similar distances from the head. The head should be proportional to the two shoulders such that if this were a torso, the neck would not be too short or too long, and the shoulders should be level (or nearly so).

Volume. Statistics say that volume is highest on formation of the head 43% of the time, the left shoulder 39% of the time, and the right shoulder 18% of the time. Do not exclude a head-and-shoulders bottom because it has weird-looking volume. The ABC pattern has volume highest on the head.

Neckline. The neckline is an imaginary line that connects the two armpits and is used to help with the measure rule and the breakout signal. I show the neckline as line D.

Breakout. A breakout occurs in two ways. First, it happens when price closes above a down-sloping neckline (as in the ABC head-and-shoulders bottom). Second, when the neckline slopes upward, a close above the right armpit works best. In the ABC pattern, E is to the left of the breakout candlestick.

■ Buy Setup 1

If you have read other chapters in this book, you may find these setups similar to other chart patterns. The performance statistics show these setups work. More about the statistics in a moment. First, let us review what the setup looks like.

Figure 9.5 shows what to look for in the inset. Price rises to a peak at A. The stock had never reached that high before, so it is an all-time high. Then the stock drops going into the head-and-shoulders bottom (B) so that the chart pattern acts as a reversal and not a continuation pattern. Point A is the trend start, the highest peak before which price drops at least 20%.

After an upward breakout, the stock climbs above A to new all-time high territory on its way to the ultimate high at C.

The stock chart shows an example of this setup. The stock makes an all-time high at A1 (A1 is the trend start in this example) and then moves lower into the head-and-shoulders bottom at DEF. In this example, volume is highest surrounding the head, which is typical.

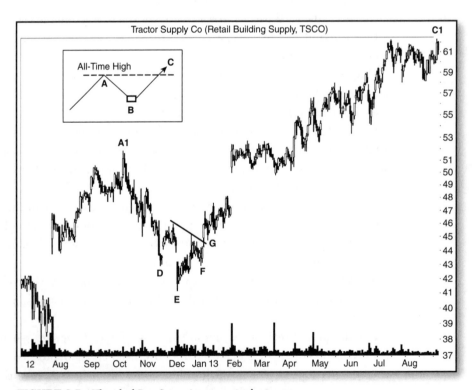

FIGURE 9.5   The ideal Buy Setup 1 appears in the inset.

Price breaks out upward but throws back to G before climbing. When the stock reaches the price of A1, it struggles to make higher highs. After a few months, the stock resumes the climb and heads up to C1 (upper right). C1 is not the ultimate high. The stock reached that a year later, 81% above the breakout price.

For best results, here are the conditions for this setup.

1. The inbound price trend, from the trend start to the left shoulder, should be less than 6 months. The trend start is the highest high or lowest low before which price drops or rises, respectively, at least 20%.
2. Look for a head-and-shoulders bottom that obeys the identification guidelines listed in Table 9.1.
3. Price should enter into the chart pattern from above, not below. In other words, the head-and-shoulders bottom should act as a reversal of the primary downtrend, not as a continuation pattern.
4. Find the price at which the stock will enter all-time high territory.
5. Compute the percentage change from the head-and-shoulders breakout price to the all-time high price. If the stock has not broken out yet, use the high at the right armpit as the breakout price.

Percentage change = 100 × (High Price − Breakout Price)/Breakout Price. Using Figure 9.5 as an example, the breakout price is 44.77 (G) and the all-time high price is 51.87, A1, then the stock will have to climb 100 × (51.87 − 44.77)/44.77, or 16%, before it clears overhead resistance.

6. Does the percentage gain found in the prior step seem reasonable? If not, then look for another situation.

For reference, the median rise from the breakout price to the all-time high was 17%, and the average was 26% for the chart patterns studied. If step 5 gives significantly higher numbers than those two, then reconsider taking the trade.

Look for thin overhead resistance. Once a stock pierces that resistance, price can rise until it trips over itself.

Table 9.2 shows the performance statistics for Buy Setup 1.

TABLE 9.2 Statistical Analysis of Buy Setup 1		
Description	Inbound Trend ≤ 6 Months	Inbound Trend > 6 Months
1. Occurrence, samples	26%, 686	7%, 185
2. Post-breakout average gain	80%	55%
3. Median gain	56%	43%
4. Gains over 25%	86%	76%
5. 5% failure rate	0%	1%
6. 10% failure rate	3%	4%

1. Inbound trends longer than six months are rare, so the better-performing short trends should be plentiful enough to find easily.

2–4. The 80% average rise from head-and-shoulders bottoms associated with short inbound trends is misleading. It is high because of several large gains. The 56% median rise gives a more accurate picture of this setup's performance.

Note that head-and-shoulders bottoms with long-term inbound trends tend to underperform.

This setup does well with most (86%) of the chart patterns showing large gains, that is, gains over 25%.

5, 6. The 5% and 10% failure rates are measures of how many head-and-shoulders bottoms fail to see price rise at least 5% or 10%, respectively, after the breakout and before price drops at least 20% or closes below the head. In both cases, the failure rate is tiny as the table shows.

This setup is an outstanding performer, but the key is to find chart patterns in a bull market at or near the all-time high that can push through overhead resistance.

■ Buy Setup 2

This setup happens most often and it results in underperformance.

Overhead resistance is like a gatekeeper. Sometimes it lets stocks through and sometimes not. The prior setup showed what the chart looks like when it lets stocks through. This setup shows what the chart looks like when overhead resistance swats the stock down.

Figure 9.6 shows the situation in the inset.

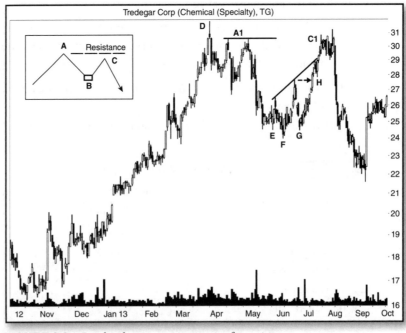

FIGURE 9.6 Overhead resistance stops price from rising.

Price rises until it reaches A. Point A need not be a peak at all. It could be any feature of overhead resistance, including minor highs and lows, round numbers, horizontal consolidation regions, and so on.

In Figure 9.6, you can consider point A as the trend start, but it need not be. The trend start is any peak before the start of the head-and-shoulders bottom before which price drops at least 20%. The trend start may or may not coincide with overhead resistance.

Price drops into the head-and-shoulders bottom, B, before breaking out upward and climbing. On the way up, the stock hits overhead resistance at C and runs away. In fact, the stock drops thereafter, moving down at least 20% or closing below the bottom of the chart pattern.

The stock chart shows an example of this setup.

Price forms a needle peak at D, marking the trend start for this head-and-shoulders bottom. Below that, the twin peaks at A1 will become resistance that later stops the advance.

Price slides down the mountain to form a head-and-shoulders bottom at EFG. Because the neckline of the head-and-shoulders bottom slopes upward, use the price of the right shoulder as the breakout price (H). The stock climbs to C1, hits overhead resistance setup by twin peaks A1, and then drops, ending the advance.

Here are the conditions for this setup:

1. The inbound price trend is less than six months long (for the best results). This measures from the trend start to the first bottom at the left shoulder.
2. Look for a head-and-shoulders bottom that obeys the identification guidelines listed in Table 9.1.
3. Price should enter the chart pattern from above, not below, so that the head-and-shoulders bottom acts as a reversal of the primary downtrend.
4. Look for overhead resistance that might stop the stock.
5. Compute the percentage change from the head-and-shoulders breakout price (your buy price) to overhead resistance. For the example shown in Figure 9.6, the percentage change would be resistance at A1 minus the breakout price, H, divided by the breakout price or $100 \times (30.53 - 27.65)/27.65$, or 10%.
6. Is the potential gain high enough to make a reasonable profit? If not, then look for another situation.

Table 9.3 shows how this setup performs.

1. Most of the samples appear for inbound trends within 6 months of the left shoulder. Fortunately, those are also the best-performing ones.
2–4. The average rise ranges between 22% and 35%, depending on the duration of the inbound price trend. The median rise is lower. Unlike the average, the median value is not swayed by large or small values.

TABLE 9.3 **Statistical Analysis of Buy Setup 2**

Description	Inbound Trend ≤ 6 Months	Inbound Trend > 6 Months
1. Occurrence, samples	55%, 1,419	11%, 285
2. Post-breakout average gain	35%	22%
3. Median gain	23%	14%
4. Gains over 25%	47%	28%
5. 5% failure rate	4%	14%
6. 10% failure rate	18%	34%

The number of head-and-shoulders bottoms that see price rise more than 25% is respectable for short inbound trends (47% of them), but the longer inbound trend suffers. Only 28% of those patterns see price rise more than 25% after a breakout.

5, 6. The 5% and 10% failure rates for short inbound price trends (4%, 18%) is substantially less than the 14% to 34% rate for the longer inbound trends. Select only head-and-shoulders bottoms with short inbound trends for the fewest failures.

■ Buy Setup 3

The prior buy setups filtered the head-and-shoulders by the move from the *trend start* to the chart pattern. Then it sorted the patterns by the appearance of overhead resistance. This setup uses the primary price trend to determine buy candidates.

I found that a downward primary price trend leading to the start of the head-and-shoulders bottom gives better post-breakout performance from the stock than does an upward price trend. In essence, this variant determines whether the stock acts as a reversal or continuation of the primary price trend. Reversals outperform continuations.

Consider the inset of **Figure 9.7**. Find the left shoulder of the head-and-shoulders bottom (B). Then look back one year (A). If price is higher a year ago, then the primary trend is downward leading to the chart pattern. If the year-ago price is below the low at the left shoulder, then the stock has trended upward going into the head-and-shoulders. As simple as this approach is, it correctly identifies the primary trend.

After the breakout, price climbs to C. Please do not assume that C will rise to the same price as A. It may or may not. Ideally, C will be at an all-time high, combining the best of this variant with Buy Setup 1.

The stock chart gives an example of this setup. The head-and-shoulders is at B1, although on the weekly scale, it does not look like one. A year ago (measured from the left shoulder), the stock was at A1. After the breakout, the stock climbed 67% to C1, the ultimate high.

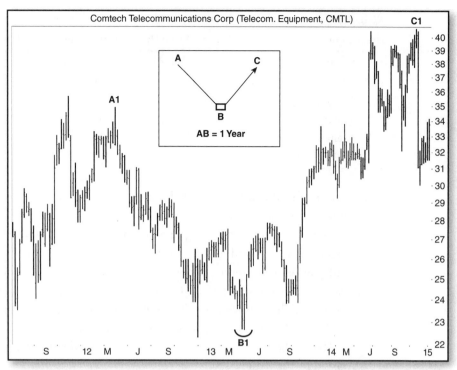

FIGURE 9.7 When the primary price trend is downward leading to the left shoulder, the stock tends to outperform after the breakout.

Here are the steps to make use of this information.

1. Use the identification guidelines listed in Table 9.1 to find a head-and-shoulders bottom.
2. Compare the low price at the left shoulder valley with a year earlier. If the year-ago price is below the left shoulder, then look elsewhere for another chart pattern. Only use flat or downward price trends going into the head-and-shoulders bottom.
3. Wait for price to close above the down-sloping neckline or above the right armpit (for an up-sloping neckline).
4. Buy at the open the next day.
5. Place a stop-loss order a penny below the head or at a location of your choice.
6. Hold until price hits your target (swing and day traders), price stalls at overhead resistance (swing traders) or is about to change trend (position traders and buy-and-hold investors).

Table 9.4 shows how this setup performs. I sorted the inbound price trend into three categories: up, down, and flat. To be flat, the year-ago stock price needed to be within 1% of the left shoulder low.

TABLE 9.4	Statistical Analysis of Primary Downward Trend		
Description	Primary Trend Up	Primary Trend Down	Primary Trend Flat
1. Occurrence, samples	53%, 1,533	41%, 1,167	3%, 72
2. Post-breakout average gain	44%	54%	55%
3. Median gain	31%	35%	42%
4. Gains over 25%	58%	62%	64%
5. 5% failure rate	6%	3%	8%
6. 10% failure rate	17%	12%	19%

1. The up and down trends had the most samples. Be cautious, depending on numbers from the flat trend because of the sample count.

   According to the statistics, in a bull market, most often the primary price trend will be upward leading to the head-and-shoulders bottom. That agrees with the historical tendency for the stock market to rise.

2–4. Flat trends show the best performance followed by down and up trends respectively. The upward primary trend vastly underperforms the other two, on average (44% average gain versus 54% and 55%).

   The median rise for upward trends is 31%, which is well below the 42% posted by the flatliners.

   The table shows the number of large gains, a count of those that see price climb at least 25% after the breakout. Almost two-thirds of head-and-shoulders bottoms with flat inbound price trends did exceedingly well.

5, 6. I show two types of failure rates, 5% and 10%. This is a count of how many head-and-shoulders bottoms fail to see price rise at least 5% or 10% after the breakout.

The downward price trend shows the lowest failure rates, with the flatliners showing the highest. This measure is why I consider the downward trend to be superior to the others. You should be able to find a downward price trend easily (enough samples); it sports a large median and average post-breakout gain, with a low failure rate. You will find it difficult to find a flat inbound price trend (72 out of 2,772 patterns, some too recent to determine the ultimate high so they are not included).

When searching for this configuration (a downward primary trend), I found that many of the head-and-shoulders bottoms appeared close to the transition from bear to bull markets.

■ Sell Setup

Because the head-and-shoulders bottom is a bullish pattern, sell indications are few. The only sell setup worth discussing depends on busted head-and-shoulders bottoms like that shown in **Figure 9.8**.

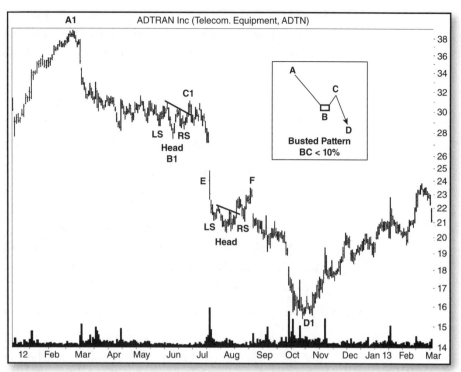

FIGURE 9.8 Two busted head-and-shoulders bottoms appear in a stock, leading to large declines.

The inset shows the configuration where price trends downward from A to the head-and-shoulders bottom at B. The stock breaks out upward from the chart pattern but rises only to C, a move less than 10%, to qualify as a busted pattern. Price drops and closes below the bottom of the head-and-shoulders bottom, busting the upward breakout.

The stock chart shows two examples of busted patterns on the daily scale. The trend start is at A1 and price drops but makes a rounded turn to the right. This gently sloping base makes it appear that the stock is poised to launch a recovery.

A head-and-shoulders bottom appears (B1) at the end of the rounded turn and price breaks out upward. Unfortunately, the stock climbs only to C1 before reversing. When the stock closes below the head, it busts the chart pattern.

After peaking at C1, the stock moves sideways for about two weeks and then news hits the wires. The company announces quarterly earnings that missed expectations. The stock gaps lower (E) and finds support at the second head-and-shoulders bottom. This one has a dual head, so it is really a complex head-and-shoulders bottom.

The stock breaks out upward from this chart pattern, too, and rises to F. Then the stock gaps down like water over a falls.

When a chart pattern fails, there is always a reason, but many times investors or traders are left scratching their heads, wondering what happened. Sometimes the reason is that traders decided to sell and that pressure overwhelmed buying demand.

In ADTRAN's case, the catalyst was disappointing earnings. If you bought into the first head-and-shoulders, you would have had two weeks to sell the stock. If you waited for a close below the head to sell, then that was too late because the next day, the stock gapped open lower.

- If a company announces disappointing earnings, swing traders should consider selling immediately.

Here is what to look for in a busted head-and-shoulders bottom.

1. Use Table 9.1 to help find a head-and-shoulders bottom.
2. Price should breakout upward and rise no more than 10% above the breakout price.
3. Price must then reverse direction and *close* below the head.
4. Sell a long holding or consider shorting at the open the next day.
5. If shorting the stock, place a stop-loss order a penny above the top of the chart pattern (usually the armpit) or at a location of your choice.

Table 9.5 lists statistics related to busted head-and-shoulders bottoms.

1. Few (14%) head-and-shoulders bottoms bust.
2, 3. The average decline after a busted head-and-shoulders bottom is 13% as measured from the low at the head to the ultimate low. The ultimate low is the lowest valley before price rises at least 20%. It represents a perfect trade.
A single busted head-and-shoulders bottom sports an average drop of 22%.
4–6. Of the 14% of head-and-shoulders bottoms that bust, they split into single busts (49%), double busts (35%), and three or more busts (15%).

If you own the stock and a busted head-and-shoulders appears, should you sell? The answer is "yes" if you are a swing or day trader. Sell immediately. If you are a position trader, one that waits for a trend change (from bullish to bearish, often a drop of 20%), then it might be prudent to wait out the decline. Why? Because only 24% of busted head-and-shoulders bottoms see declines more than 20%. If you hold onto a stock, you stand a 76% chance of seeing the stock drop less than 20%.

TABLE 9.5	Statistics for Busted Head-and-Shoulders
Description	**Result**
1. Percentage of head-and-shoulders bottoms that bust	14%
2. Average drop after busting	13%
3. Average drop after single bust	22%
4. Percentage of single busts	49%
5. Percentage of double busts	35%
6. Percentage of triple+ busts	15%

If you are an investor (buy-and-hold) then hold onto the stock unless you expect a significant shift in the profitability or viability of the company. Check recent fundamentals to be sure.

■ Best Stop Locations

A stop-loss order can protect profits or limit losses, but it can also take you out of winning trades before they have time to blossom.

If you are a seasoned trader, you probably use stops. Where is the best place in a head-and-shoulders bottom to put a stop? **Table 9.6** gives the answer.

I programmed my computer to look at each of the 2,866 head-and-shoulders bottoms and report on the lowest price as the stock moved from the breakout to the ultimate high.

1. Penny below the breakout. If you place a stop-loss order a penny below the breakout, you risk being stopped out 52% of the time. The loss will be small, amounting to commissions and anytime the stock gapped open lower. The numbers do not reflect commissions, slippage, or other fees and expenses.

The 1,486 trades you were stopped out of would have made an average of 49%.

2. Penny below the right shoulder. If you placed a stop a penny below the right shoulder, the risk of being stopped out drops to 14%. However, the average loss grows to 4%. The average gain of the 387 missed trades was 49%.

3. Penny below the lowest shoulder. If you placed a stop-loss order a penny below the lower of the two shoulders, the chance of being hit drops a smidgen, to 12%. The average loss grows to 5% and the trades you missed out on would have returned an average of 46%.

4. Penny below the head. Finally, if you placed the stop a penny below the head, price would trigger a stop just 3% of the time, but the average loss would be 6%. The trades you missed would have made 45%.

A penny below the head seems to be the best place for a stop. It only triggers 3% of the time and the loss is a manageable 6%. A look at the missing trades reveals that

TABLE 9.6 Stop Locations for Head-and-Shoulders Bottoms

Description	Chance of Being Hit	Average Loss	Missed Trades, Gains
1. Penny below the breakout	52%	0%	1,486, 49%
2. Penny below right shoulder	14%	4%	387, 49%
3. Penny below lowest shoulder	12%	5%	355, 46%
4. Penny below head	3%	6%	90, 45%

just 8 of them made over 100%, and 26 made over 50%. So you do not give up too many big winners.

- Place the stop-loss order a penny below the head unless another location offers advantages.

■ Configuration Trading

The following eight configurations are setups that you will want to avoid. If you skip a trade because it resembles one of these eight and the stock goes on to be a big winner, then that is what happens in the big leagues. However, the odds suggest that these configurations will lose money more often than not.

ABC Correction

Ralph Elliott theorized that price moves along the primary trend in five waves and against that trend in three waves. **Figure 9.9** shows the three-wave variety, which is commonly called an ABC correction.

After price moves up following the primary trend, often for several months (or years), price retraces a portion of that upward move in three waves. The first is wave A, which takes price lower, followed by a rise (B), and finally another wave down (C).

In the 230 failed head-and-shoulders bottoms I examined, I found that 31% of the time, the stock forms a head-and-shoulders bottom in wave B. The stock quickly reversed and tumbled during wave C, handing the investor or trader a loss.

The ideal buy signal in this situation is after wave C completes. Thus, if price drops from a peak in a straight-line run down and then forms a head-and-shoulders bottom, ignore it. Wait for the retrace and another drop in the stock before buying.

Wave counting is an art. It will take some practice before you can correctly identify an ABC correction of the primary uptrend. Look for a long upward move followed by a three wave (down, up, down) combination. The ABC correction should

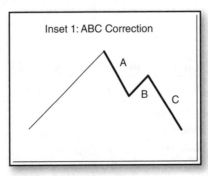

FIGURE 9.9 ABC correction.

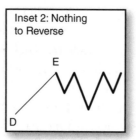

FIGURE 9.10 Nothing to reverse.

be proportional to the primary uptrend (not too short and not too long). In other words, if the length of the ABC correction is anywhere near the length of the primary trend, then you have made a mistake. If you are unsure, then just skip the trade.

Nothing to Reverse

Figure 9.10 shows the second most common failure among head-and-shoulders bottoms. Head-and-shoulders acting as reversals outperform continuation patterns. I checked my spreadsheet and found that continuation patterns suffer 5% failures almost twice as often as reversals (7% versus 4%, respectively).

The inset shows what to avoid. Price moves into the chart pattern from below the pattern, following route D to E. At E, the stock may overshoot the top of the pattern for a week or two, making it look like a reversal, but the primary trend is still like that shown, from D to E. Ignore the brief overshoot.

Figure 9.4 gives an example of this type of overshoot in the head-and-shoulders bottom at GHI. G1 is the overshoot. After bottoming at B (the trend start), price rises going into the chart pattern.

Seventeen percent of the patterns I looked at suffered this "nothing to reverse" failure.

Base Failure

Figure 9.11 shows two types of base failures. Price drops into the head-and-shoulders bottom from the top (F to G). The stock confirms the chart pattern on the move up to H but then reverses. Price drops just below the head (I) to take out any stops residing there before moving back up.

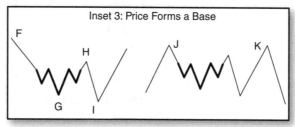

FIGURE 9.11 Price forms a base.

This is an annoying failure. After bottoming at I, the stock pushes higher, confirming that you had the right idea about buying the reversal pattern. Unfortunately, you watch from the sidelines while the stock zips upward.

This type of failure happens at bottoms after a long decline, but it also occurs on the way to building a double top. The right half of the inset shows an example. Price drops from J, forms a busted head-and-shoulders bottom, and then rises up to K where it forms a second top, stopping near the price of the first top (J).

In both cases, the drop below the head is minor. It seems the stock needs to do more work to build a firm base before moving higher.

I looked at busted head-and-shoulders bottoms and found that 37% of them stopped their decline within 5% of the head low (the lowest price in the chart pattern). Of course, that means the other 63% continued lower, and it means the drop from the breakout price to 5% below the head can be a hefty one.

I do not know how to protect against this type of failure. You might say that if this type of failure occurs, buy the stock back when price climbs back above the original breakout price.

This configuration appeared 16% of the time in the chart patterns I looked at.

Neckline Resistance

Figure 9.12 shows what happens to some unlucky trades. The left armpit, L, is above the right armpit and the stock rises after the breakout (M) to the price of the left armpit (L) before hitting a wall of overhead resistance. The stock dies and heads for the grave.

Fortunately, this type of failure is rare (8% of the patterns I looked at). However, of the head-and-shoulders bottoms suffering 5% failures, over half of them (56%) stopped between the breakout price and the taller of the two armpits.

That suggests a buy order placed above the taller of the two armpits would help protect against this type of failure.

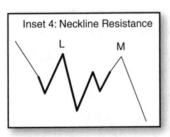

FIGURE 9.12   Neckline resistance.

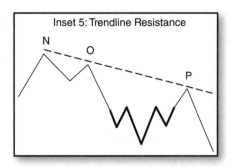

FIGURE 9.13 Trendline resistance.

Trendline Resistance

Figure 9.13 shows a trade I avoided in Southwest Airlines that had this configuration. Price trends lower following peaks N and O. A trendline drawn connecting those peaks (dashed line, in this example) represents overhead resistance that later blocks an upward move. At P, price approaches the trendline and reverses.

Often you will see the stock stop before actually touching the trendline. The key is to look for overhead resistance setup and avoid trading those situations.

This configuration occurs 7% of the time.

Long Downtrend

If you like to bottom-fish for stocks, then the failure shown in **Figure 9.14** is one we all wish to avoid. Price trends lower for months (Q), even years, and you decide the stock has bottomed after the appearance of a head-and-shoulders bottom.

You buy the stock and it climbs to R (5% above the breakout price) before reversing. The stock continues lower, much lower (S), so much lower that your bottom-fishing expedition has turned into a muddy mess.

I do not know how to avoid this type of failure. Sometimes you can have amazing timing by buying a stock when price bottoms. And sometimes it looks like the disaster shown in Figure 9.14. A stop placed below the head can limit losses.

I found this variation occurred in 6% of the patterns I looked at.

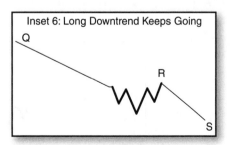

FIGURE 9.14 Long downtrend keeps going.

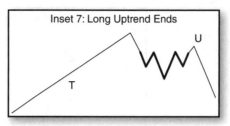

FIGURE 9.15   Long uptrend ends.

Long Uptrend Ends

If you avoid bottom-fishing, then how about a momentum play? **Figure 9.15** shows the setup that happens just 5% of the time.

In a raging bull market, every stock seems too expensive to buy, but you want to make money, not watch from the sidelines. So you go shopping for stocks and find one that looks like Figure 9.15. Price has been trending upward for months (T), maybe years. Why would it fail now, especially in a frothy bull market?

You research the stock and analysts agree. They love the company. So do you. You buy the stock.

Then what happens? Price climbs to U before turning and breaking the uptrend. Uh-oh.

No big deal. In a rising price trend, a stock will advance, retrace, and advance. But this time the stock tumbles and starts digging toward the earth's core. Without a stop in place, you are sitting on a small loss that grows into a huge one. What is worse, it could take years before the stock recovers enough to get your money back.

I had this situation with FMC Corporation. Starting in late 2008, the stock kept going up and up and up. In 2014, I could not find a better setup, so I bought the stock. Price dropped, recovered to make a new high, and then the trend changed. The stock dropped by 61%. Fortunately, I sold it quickly and took only a small loss.

Be careful when using momentum to trade. When the upward momentum ends, gravity rules, so look out below.

Range Bound

Figure 9.16 shows the last type of failure I studied and it happened just 5% of the time.

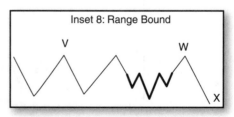

FIGURE 9.16   Range bound.

Price leading to the head-and-shoulders bottom (V) trades between a high price and a low one, essentially moving horizontally for weeks or months. Then a head-and-shoulders bottom appears. After the breakout, the stock rises up to the top of the range, W (or does not even make it that far), before reversing and busting the breakout (X).

To avoid this failure, wait for price to close above the top of the trading range.

■ Measure Rule

The measure rule is a tool to help determine how far price will rise after the breakout. It is only an estimate, not a guarantee, but some claim it can serve as a minimum target.

Figure 9.17 shows an example of how to use the measure rule. Measure the vertical distance from the low price at the head (A, 36.65 in this example) to the neckline (a line connecting the armpits) directly above (B, 40.50). In this case, the height is 3.85.

For down-sloping necklines, add the height to the breakout price to get a target. In this example, that is where the neckline crosses the stock at D, about 40, for a target of 43.85.

FIGURE 9.17 Use the measure rule to help determine a price target.

If the neckline slopes upward, use the right armpit (C) as the breakout price.

For simplicity, my spreadsheet uses the average of the right (C) and left armpits (the peak to the left of B) to get the neckline price, and the right armpit high as the breakout price.

The measure rule works 73% of the time. If you divide the height of the head-and-shoulders bottom in half and use that for the height, price hits the target 88% of the time.

- The measure rule for head-and-shoulders bottoms works 73% of the time.

■ Trading

The buy setups have common elements that help improve performance. Look for the following.

- A short inbound price trend. The inbound trend should be less than 6 months long, but less than 3 months long is even better.

Measure the time from the trend start to the bottom of the left shoulder. The trend start is the lowest valley or highest peak before which the stock climbs or drops, respectively, at least 20%.

- Reversal not continuation. Price should trend downward into the head-and-shoulders bottom, not upward. Ignore any overshoot that may appear in the week or two before the start of the head-and-shoulders bottom. In short, the head-and-shoulders bottom should act as a reversal of the primary price downtrend, not a continuation pattern.

- Avoid overhead resistance. Look for overhead resistance that is either close enough that you can expect the stock to push through it to all-time high territory, or is far enough away that you can expect to make a reasonable profit before resistance stops the advance.

Actual Trade

Figure 9.18 shows an actual trade I made using a head-and-shoulders bottom chart pattern.

Look at the inset first, which is on the weekly scale.

The stock peaked at A and made a sharp plunge to B where the head-and-shoulders hid. The stock climbed in a sort of rounded turn to C, where I sold the stock.

The stock chart on the daily scale shows the details.

The left shoulder of the head-and-shoulders bottom is at D, head at E, and right shoulder at F. The DF shoulders are uneven, so the head-and-shoulders looks like it needs medical attention. However, the two shoulders are just 3% apart.

FIGURE 9.18 A head-and-shoulders bottom was the buy signal for a profitable trade.

As the stock reached bottom at E, insiders were buying, according to one source I checked. The company warned of weakness in the coming year due to slow housing starts, and it intended to buy back shares (up to 12%). Yippee! I love when the company takes a position in their own stock.

I thought that this would be a long-term trade, maybe four or five years before the housing and construction markets recovered.

The near-term target was 50 with a potential to reach 70 (the high near A) and resistance at 40–42 that the stock would have to plow through. Support rested at 37 and 33 (on the inset, you can see how long price held in the 34 to 40 area on the way down).

I show the neckline (the diagonal line connecting the two armpits) of the head-and-shoulders bottom, but I did not buy until G. I received a fill at 39.91.

On July 11, I placed a volatility stop at 46.91, below the low on that day (I). The location was also below support in June (see Figure 9.18).

Almost a week later, I sold the stock and received a fill at 49.48.

Here is what I wrote in my notebook about the sale. "The other stocks in the industry are or have been trending lower. I expect this one to drop, maybe not far, but I don't want to give back profit if I get a downward breakout from the rising wedge (see chart). Price is near the top of resistance at 51."

I made 25% on the trade.

I am very pleased with the timing. I bought into the situation a bit late but exited before the plunge. The inset shows how much damage the drop made.

Application   Figure 9.7 is the only one that applies to this situation. A year before the stock formed the left shoulder (September 11, 2005) the stock was about 20% higher. So the primary trend was downward, just as the setup requires.

According to the chart, the stock was a buy.

■ Closing Position

The head-and-shoulders bottom is a strong performer, posting an average gain of 49% for perfect trades. However, in 25% of the cases, price reaches the ultimate high during a throwback, suggesting gains are limited. Fourteen percent of the time, the stock rises no more than 10% before reversing (busting).

By using the setups and configurations discussed in this chapter, you can improve your chances of having not only a successful trade but one that makes a lot of money.

Setup Synopsis

Figures 9.19 and **9.20** may help you identify the various types of trading setups. See the associated figure for an explanation.

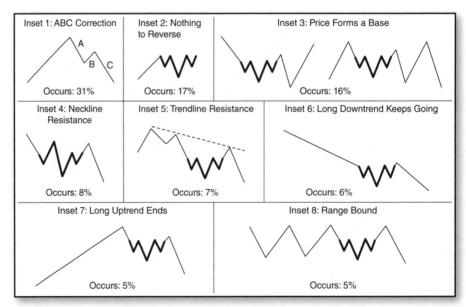

FIGURE 9.19   Configurations to avoid.

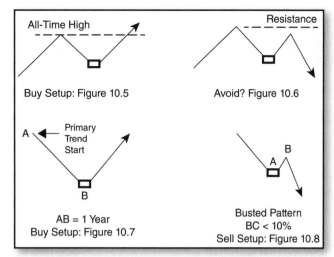

FIGURE 9.20 A collection of ideal trading setups and configurations.

"Occurs" in the figures means how often I found the configuration in the stocks I looked at. If two configurations apply to your situation, then the one with a more frequent occurrence (a higher percentage) is the one you should choose to follow.

CHAPTER 10

Head-and-Shoulders Tops

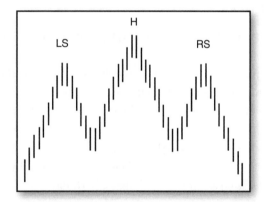

The head-and-shoulders top is perhaps the best-known chart pattern. The name matches the pattern's shape, so its appearance is intuitively obvious. But there is a catch to identification. If price does not close below the neckline, then you only have squiggles on a price chart and not a head-and-shoulders top.

To learn about the behavior of head-and-shoulders tops, I looked at almost 2,500 of them from bull markets. This chapter describes the amazing results I found.

■ Behavior at a Glance

I searched through 1,035 stocks to find 2,478 head-and-shoulders tops, all from bull markets. **Figure 10.1** shows that after the head-and-shoulders top (thick line) breaks out downward, the stock falls an average of 18% and a median of 15%.

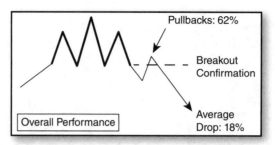

FIGURE 10.1   The average behavior of a head-and-shoulders top.

Pullbacks occur 62% of the time. That means price returns to the breakout price in almost 2 of every 3 trades, and it does so within a month of the breakout, often within a week.

Pullbacks

Figure 10.2 shows the average performance of head-and-shoulders tops with and without pullbacks.

A pullback occurs when the stock returns to the breakout price within 30 days. Often you see price drop far enough below the breakout price to leave white space. In other words, a pullback does not occur if the stock just slides along the breakout price.

The average pullback sees price drop 8% in 5 days. Then the stock begins to return to the breakout price. The average elapsed time from the breakout to the day the stock peaks during a pullback is 10 days.

In 60% of the cases, price continues rising far enough to close above the price of the head. The other 40% see price tumble like a novice skier rolling down a hill.

- Sixty-two percent of head-and-shoulders tops will have pullbacks.

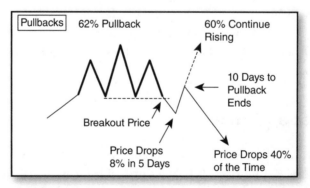

FIGURE 10.2   Pullback behavior for head-and-shoulders tops.

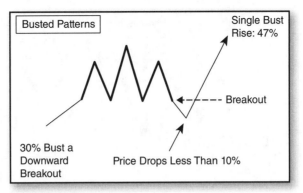

FIGURE 10.3   Performance of busted head-and-shoulders tops.

Busted Tops

Figure 10.3 shows the average busted head-and-shoulders top. Thirty percent of head-and-shoulders tops will bust. *Bust* means the stock breaks out downward but turns before closing 10% or more below the bottom of the head-and-shoulders. Then price must rise far enough to close above the head.

The stock can continue busting. In a single bust, the stock closes above the head, but it must continue rising by at least 10% to stop the bust count. If it reverses again before climbing 10% and closes below the bottom of the head-and-shoulders, it double busts. The busting continues until the stock moves more than 10% away from either the top or bottom of the head-and-shoulders pattern.

The average rise after a single bust is 47%. Such a large gain presents a buying opportunity that I will discuss later (See Buy Setup).

- Head-and-shoulders tops bust 30% of the time.

■ Identification

Figure 10.4 shows a head-and-shoulders top with a left shoulder (LS), head and right shoulder (RS) as marked. A neckline joins the armpits, BC, and signals a breakout at D.

Refer to **Table 10.1** as I discuss identification guidelines.

Uptrend. Most, 74%, of the head-and-shoulders tops will see the primary price trend climb into the left shoulder. Another 21% have the primary price trend moving down, leading to the head-and-shoulders top. The remaining patterns have a flat trend.

To determine the primary price trend, I compared the closing price at the left shoulder high to a year earlier. If the left shoulder was higher, then the primary trend

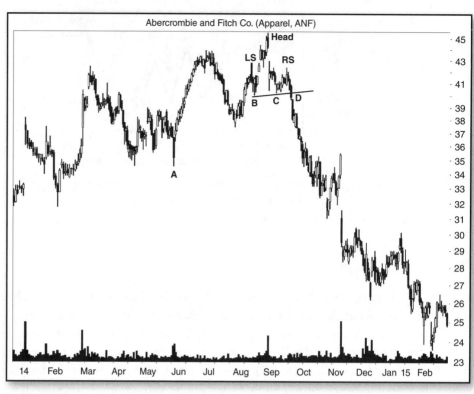

FIGURE 10.4 This head-and-shoulders top becomes part of a double top that sees price drop dramatically after the breakout.

TABLE 10.1	Identification Guidelines
Characteristic	**Discussion**
Uptrend	Price trends upward going into the left shoulder of a head-and-shoulders top most of the time.
Shape	The chart pattern should look like a person's head with adjacent shoulders. If it does not resemble a bust, then consider discarding it. Discard patterns with a neck too tall or too short, unequal shoulders, and so on.
Symmetry	The two shoulders should be opposite the head at nearly the same distance. They should top out near the same price. The entire pattern should look proportional.
Volume	Highest on the left shoulder, then the head, and then the right shoulder.
Neckline	This is an imaginary line joining the two armpits. It can help signal an early entry to a trade when price closes below an up-sloping neckline.
Breakout	A close below the right armpit works well as the breakout price (especially if the neckline slopes downward), but an up-sloping neckline can also signal an entry when price closes below it.
Confirmation	If price does not close below the neckline or right armpit, you do not have a head-and-shoulders top.

was upward. A lower close meant the trend was downward. As simple as this method is, it works well.

Shape. A head-and-shoulders top mimics its name with two shoulders on opposite sides of a head. Figure 10.4 identifies the left shoulder, head, and right shoulder. Each of those bumps is a minor high (a short-term peak).

Symmetry. The head-and-shoulders top should be symmetrical in both time and price. In the best-looking head-and-shoulders tops, the left and right shoulders should be equidistant from the head. The two shoulders should top out near the same price, too. The head should tower above the two shoulders and yet look proportional.

For guidance, the head-and-shoulders top should look like a bust of a person. The head should not be unusually tall or squat, nor should one shoulder be far below the other. No hunchbacks allowed here, please, but be flexible. Rare is the perfect looking head-and-shoulders.

Volume. Volume is highest on the left shoulder (41% of the time), head (37%), and right shoulder (22%). Do not discard a head-and-shoulders top because of an unusual volume pattern. Despite what others say, volume is not significant to performance. I checked. Honest. Cross my heart.

Neckline. The neckline is not important to identification. Rather, use it to signal a breakout. Draw a line connecting the two armpits (BC in Figure 10.4). Traditionally, when price closes below the neckline it signals a downward breakout (D).

The problem with using necklines is that steep, down-sloping ones may never trigger a breakout.

Breakout. When price closes below the neckline or right armpit, it signals a breakout. If price does not breakout, then you do not have a head-and-shoulders top. I used a close below the right armpit to signal a breakout. That made data collection easier than using a close below the neckline.

Confirmation. Price must breakout downward from the head-and-shoulders top; otherwise, you are just looking at squiggles on a price chart.

■ Buy Setup

The only well-performing buy (long) setup for a head-and-shoulders top is when it busts. I show an example of that in **Figure 10.5**.

The inset shows the setup. Price moves up from A, setting up the head-and-shoulders top as a reversal. However, price could just as easily trend down into the start of the pattern, too. The performance difference between reversals and continuations is minor. You will not find many continuation patterns and even fewer that bust, so price moving upward into the pattern is the most likely scenario.

I show the head-and-shoulders top as box B. The BC drop must not be more than 10%.

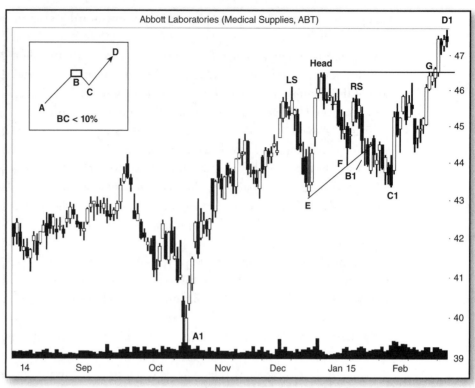

FIGURE 10.5 The ideal buy setup appears in the inset.

After C, the stock trend reverses and price closes above the top of the chart pattern, heading to D. With luck, the stock will single bust and post an average rise of 47%.

The stock chart shows an example of a head-and-shoulders top with the left shoulder (LS), right shoulder (RS), and head perched between them.

The stock price moved from below 40 at A1 to the start of the head-and-shoulders. A neckline joins the left armpit, E, to the right one, F. When price closed below the neckline (B1), it confirmed the head-and-shoulders top as a valid pattern and signaled a breakout.

This stock walked down to C1, a decline of 3% below the right armpit (I used the armpit and not the neckline to determine the breakout price).

Then the stock reversed and moved higher. It closed above the top of the pattern at G. I drew a horizontal line there to better show this. At G, the stock busted the chart pattern and continued to D1. Not shown, but it has moved 11% above the head, so this is a single busted pattern.

For best results, here are the conditions for this setup.

1. Qualify the chart pattern as a head-and-shoulders top. It should follow the iden-tification guidelines shown in Table 10.1.
2. After the breakout, price must drop by no more than 10%.

TABLE 10.2	Statistics for Busted Head-and-Shoulders	
Description		Result
1. Percentage of head-and-shoulders tops that bust		30%
2. Average rise after busting		35%
3. Average rise after single bust		47%
4. Percentage of single busts		70%
5. Percentage of double busts		12%
6. Percentage of triple+ busts		17%

3. Price reverses and closes above the top (head) of the head-and-shoulders top.
4. Buy at the open the next day.
5. Place a stop loss below the bottom of the head-and-shoulders or at a location of your choice.

Table 10.2 shows some statistics for this setup that will help with trading.

1. Head-and-shoulders tops bust frequently, if you consider 30% as frequent. The rate is more than double the 14% bust rate for head-and-shoulder bottoms.

2. After a head-and-shoulders top busts, the stock climbs an average of 35% above the top of the chart pattern.

3. For those stocks that single bust only, the average rise is a whopping 47%. Tell your neighbors.

4–6. I logged three types of busts. Single busts, double busts, and three or more busts. Of the 30% that bust, most of them (70%) will be single busts. That means the stock breaks out downward, reverses quickly (within 10% of the breakout price), and climbs more than 10% above the top of the chart pattern. Double and triple busts see the up and down ripples continue until the stock moves at least 10% away from the chart pattern.

■ Sell Setup

The statistics tell an interesting tale of behavior that many chart patterns share. A stock moving up for a long time that encounters a head-and-shoulders top will suffer less (after a downward breakout) than one moving up for a short time.

That finding surprised me. It is as if the drop is an annoyance and not a reason for panic among buy-and-hold investors.

■ Long inbound price trends suggest a milder post-breakout decline.

When we narrow the focus to trends less than six months long, we find that steep uptrends result in post-breakout losses larger than more shallow uptrends. The smart money pushes up the stock and then eases off. When price rounds over, they all sell, forcing price down farther than for stocks with less enthusiastic traders.

- Steep uptrends leading to the start of head-and-shoulders tops suggest a higher velocity post-breakout decline.

Look at the inset of **Figure 10.6** to see what is important in this setup.

The trend start is at A. The time between A and the left shoulder peak must be less than 6 months. Head-and-shoulders tops with that configuration tend to drop most. If the rise from A to B is more than 50%, that is a bonus. Steep drops tend to follow steep rises.

The stock breaks out downward from the chart pattern and price moves lower, to C.

The stock chart shows an actual example.

The trend start is at A1. Before that, the stock climbed dramatically (more than 20%, not shown). Price moved from a low at A1 of 3.45 to a high of 6.40 at the left shoulder peak. That is almost double, and it took the stock less than 4 months to make the journey. I used a minimum rise of 50% within 6 months to qualify as steep and short. Those are arbitrary settings.

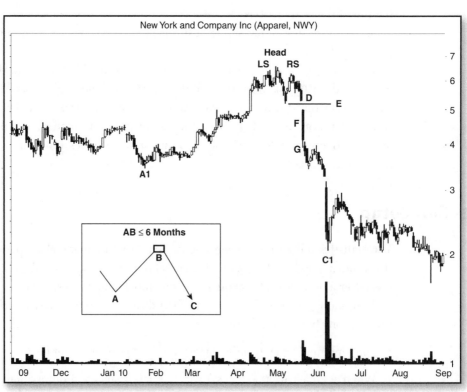

FIGURE 10.6 Stocks with short and steep uptrends will tend to suffer more after the breakout.

As I mentioned, I used a close below the right armpit to signal a valid head-and-shoulders top (a breakout). The breakout price is at line E in this example, drawn from the right armpit. Price officially broke out of the head-and-shoulders top at candle F. That day was the first close below the right armpit.

If you owned the stock and sold at the open a day after the breakout (G), you would have lost 25% (as measured from the close at D). That drop pales in comparison to the plunge from G to the ultimate low at C1. That move measured 48%. If you decided to hold onto the stock until the low in late August, the drop from the close at D totaled 68%.

Here is what to look for in this setup.

1. Use Table 10.1 to help identify a head-and-shoulders top.
2. Locate the trend start, the lowest valley before which price rises at least 20% or the highest high before which price drops at least 20%.
3. If the time from the trend start to the left shoulder peak is less than 6 months, then expect a larger drop post-breakout.
4. If the rise from the trend start to the left shoulder is more than 50%, then expect a larger drop post-breakout.
5. The day after the breakout, sell a long holding at the market open or go short with a new position.
6. If shorting a stock, place a stop-loss order a penny above the head or at a location of your choice.

Table 10.3 lists performance statistics related to the sell setup.

1. Most of the samples (66%) have short trends (6 months or less) leading to the left shoulder.
2, 3. The loss (median and average) is larger for short inbound trends than for longer ones. Measure the inbound price trend length from the trend start to the left shoulder peak. Trends six months or less tend to outperform (decline farther, post-breakout).

TABLE 10.3 Statistical Analysis of Sell Setup 1		
Description	Inbound Trend ≤6 Months	Inbound Trend >6 Months
1. Occurrence, samples	66%, 1,580	31%, 743
2. Post-breakout average loss	19%	15%
3. Median loss	16%	11%
4. Losses over 25%	25%	16%
5. 5% failure rate	7%	13%
6. 10% failure rate	26%	41%

4. Large losses, those over 25%, accompany head-and-shoulders tops with short inbound price trends. A quarter of those chart patterns will decline more than 25%.

I found that long-term inbound trends accompany meager drops after the breakout. This suggests position traders and buy-and-hold investors should not sell a stock showing a head-and-shoulders top.

5, 6. The 5% failure rate is a tad large (7%) for short inbound price trends. The 10% failure rate is much worse, up to 41%. Ouch!

The table teaches us that, if you want to swing trade head-and-shoulders tops, then look for short but steep rises leading to the start of the chart pattern. If you own a stock, then be worried if the rise leading to the start of the chart pattern is short (less than 6 months) and steep (over 50%). The stock may experience a larger drop than do those with longer and shallower inbound price trends.

■ Best Stop Locations

If you want to short a stock showing a head-and-shoulders top, where is the best location to place a stop? **Table 10.4** shows some of the locations I researched.

1. **Penny above the breakout.** A stop placed a penny above the breakout price will trigger 46% of the time, handing the trader a breakeven loss. Trades that were stopped out would have dropped an average of 18% if sold at the ultimate low.

2. **Penny above the right shoulder.** If you placed a stop a penny above the right shoulder, the stock would hit the stop 8% of the time, resulting in a loss of 4% without commissions or fees included. Had you ignored the stop, the missing trades would average losses of 18%.

3. **Penny above the highest shoulder.** Using the higher of the two shoulders lessens the risk of the stop being hit to 7%, but it increases the loss to 5%. The missed trades would average losses of 18%.

4. **Penny above the head.** Placing a stop a penny above the head is the safest place (1% risk of being hit), but it also boosts the loss to 7%. The missed trades lost 15%, but samples are few.

■ Place a stop-loss order a penny above the head for the smallest chance of being hit.

TABLE 10.4 Stop Locations for Head-and-Shoulders Tops			
Description	Chance of Being Hit	Average Loss	Missed Trades, Losses
1. Penny above the breakout	46%	0%	1,139, 18%
2. Penny above right shoulder	8%	4%	204, 18%
3. Penny above highest shoulder	7%	5%	167, 18%
4. Penny above head	1%	7%	26, 15%

■ Configuration Trading

To trade the following configurations, begin with these guidelines:

1. Find a head-and-shoulders top on the *daily* chart that obeys the identification guidelines listed in Table 10.1.
2. Using the *weekly* scale, match what you see on your chart to one of the configurations. Figure 10.15 should help.
3. Short at the open the day after the breakout or place an order to sell a penny below the bottom of the right armpit.
4. Place a stop-loss order at a location of your choice.

I sorted my database of head-and-shoulders tops by the drop to the ultimate low and visually looked at hundreds of them. The following is what I found.

Failure 1

Inset 1 of **Figure 10.7** shows the scenario that happened 54% of the time, by far the most frequent of the setups I studied.

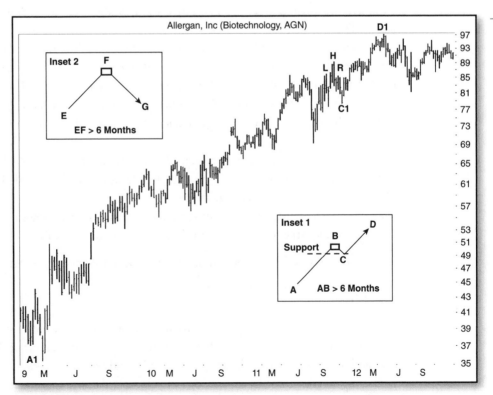

FIGURE 10.7 A long-term uptrend does not end with a head-and-shoulders top.

The ideal stock started trending higher at A and developed the head-and-shoulders top at B. The AB move was long, over 6 months, and many times it was years long.

Point A was *not* where the "trend start" began. Rather, it was where the primary trend started. Although that may sound like the difference between *toe-may-toe* and *toe-mah-toe*, the difference was significant. The trend start is the lowest (or highest) price before which the trend changes by at least 20%.

The downward breakout dropped the stock to C, often about 5% lower, before the stock found footing and resumed the upward run to D. Many times, underlying support stopped the stock from continuing down, so be sure to look for that when deciding to sell a long holding or sell short.

The stock chart on the weekly scale shows an example of this scenario. A1 begins the primary uptrend just as the bear market ended. The stock made its way higher, following a sawtooth pattern that might draw blood if you rubbed it against your skin.

The head-and-shoulders (LHR) top appeared after 2.5 years of upward move. One might think that the stock must be tired by this time, that the upward run was at an end, and a head-and-shoulders top would signal a trend change.

Wrong. What happened? Almost nothing.

After the breakout, the stock dropped to C1, just 4% below the breakout price. Then the stock resumed its upward run. This chart shows it peaking at D1, but it continued moving higher until April 2013 when another head-and-shoulders top appeared. This one bit, and the stock was hospitalized for a 29% drop.

I scratched my head trying to figure out why this stock did not drop farther. Clearly, the underlying strength in the stock kept it soaring. But the bear market helped, too. The bear market was not kind to this stock (and many others). This stock plummeted from 70 to 29, or almost 60%, during the bear market. One could expect a nice-sized bounce after such a large decline. The bounce lasted over 3 years, and it took the stock from 29 to 116.

If I had to make a list of things to check before buying, I would look at the strength of the industry. If it is doing well, then the breakout from a head-and-shoulders top is likely to be less severe than otherwise.

Of course, the market trend is also important (but research shows it is less important than the industry trend). If the market is soaring, then look for a less severe drop.

- If the industry and market are doing well, expect a shallower decline.

Quick Test

Instead of using the primary trend, I used the length of the trend start to the start of the head-and-shoulders top. **Table 10.5** shows the post-breakout performance of head-and-shoulders tops with various inbound trend lengths.

The big declines occurred after short inbound trends, those within 100 days (about 3 months). Those stocks suffered a median decline of 17%. At the bottom

TABLE 10.5 **Post-Breakout Performance versus Trend Start Length**

Trend Start Length (Days)	Median Drop	Samples
1 to 100	17%	1,215
101 to 200	15%	529
201 to 300	14%	263
301 to 400 (~1 year)	11%	133
401 to 500	12%	73
501 to 600	9%	64
601 to 700	11%	43
701 to 800 (~2 years)	11%	42
801 to 900	9%	26

of the table, we see that stocks with long inbound trends, almost three years long, dropped just 9%. However, there were only 26 samples, which I consider too few to be reliable. Even so, the results are unmistakable. As the inbound trend length from the trend start to the left shoulder increased, post-breakout performance decreased.

- Long inbound price trends (trend start to formation start) suggest a less severe post breakout drop.

Success 1

Inset 2 of Figure 10.7 matches the one I found for successful patterns. Notice that both insets 1 and 2 have inbound trends longer than 6 months.

In Inset 2, the stock moves up at a good clip until it forms a mountain peak towering above the landscape (E to F). The journey up to the summit is a long one, taking over 6 months. The drop post-breakout (F to G) is often 25% or more. This setup occurred 37% of the time in the 252 stocks I looked at. It was the most common pattern for large declines after a head-and-shoulders top.

Failure 2

Figure 10.8 shows the next failure of a stock to show a large decline after a head-and-shoulders top.

Inset 1 shows what I found in 19% of the 265 head-and-shoulders tops I looked at.

The stock begins its climb at A. Point A is *not* the trend start. It is where the primary trend begins.

The AB move is a long one, over six months in duration. Then a short-term decline sets in. That is the BC move. A quick rise to the head-and-shoulders top (D) sees the stock peak at or near the old high (B). If peak D falls short or rises slightly above the price of B, that is fine.

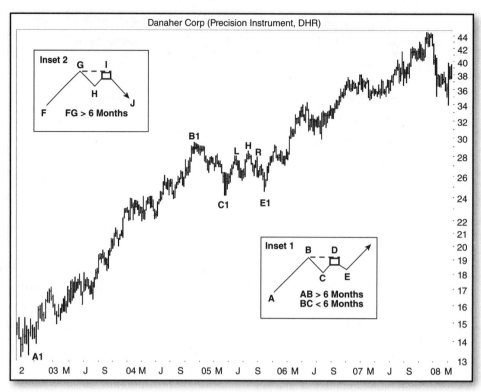

FIGURE 10.8 This retrace, followed by a head-and-shoulders top, did not make for a large decline.

After the breakout, price drops to E. The drop is small (often about 5%), and the stock recovers easily to venture back to new highs.

The stock chart shows an example (weekly scale) of this scenario. The primary trend begins at A1, and it carries the stock up to B1. Then a short retrace follows to C1 before a short rise lifts the stock up to the head-and-shoulders top. The breakout from this pattern sends the stock tumbling to E1, but the drop is a minuscule decline of just 6%.

After bottoming at E1, the stock skedaddles higher, almost doubling in about two years.

The position of the head-and-shoulders top in the BE trend is what distinguishes this failure type from Failure 3. In this configuration, the head-and-shoulders is near the price of peak B. In Failure 3, the head-and-shoulders appears well below the price of peak B.

Success 2 Inset 2 shows a similar configuration that I found in 25% of the head-and-shoulders tops with large post-breakout declines. This configuration is the third most common for stocks that made large declines.

The FG move is often a long one, over 6 months in duration, setting the stage for a tired stock. The length of the decline from the first peak (GH) and rise to the second peak (HI) varies. In some stocks, both are more than 6 months long, but in many others, the journey is a short one (less than 6 months).

If you see what looks like a double top on the weekly chart and the second peak on the daily chart is a head-and-shoulders top, then be worried if you own the stock. Price might get walloped when the head-and-shoulders breaks out downward (I to J).

Failure 3

Failure 3 is similar to Failure 2 except for the location of the head-and-shoulders top. Look at the inset of **Figure 10.9**.

Point A is where the primary trend begins. Price rises for at least six months, to B, before a retrace begins. The BC drop can be long or short term. After the stock bottoms at C, it makes a quick rise to the head-and-shoulders top, D. The trend reverses and price drops to E, but the decline is not significant, maybe 5%, maybe a bit more. Then the stock rejoins the primary uptrend and away she goes.

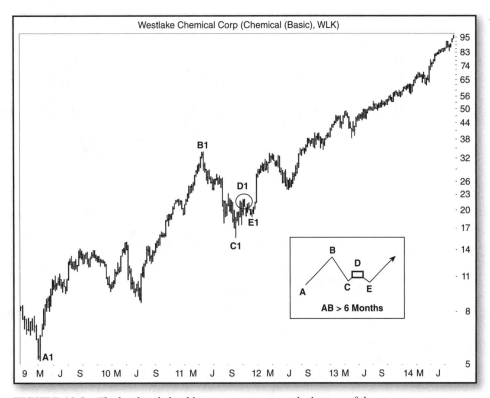

FIGURE 10.9 The head-and-shoulders top appears near the bottom of the retrace.

In Failure 2, the head-and-shoulders top forms at overhead resistance (shown by dashed line BD). In Failure 3, the chart pattern appears well below peak B.

Look at the stock chart (Figure 10.9) on the weekly scale. The primary trend begins at A1 and the stock rises to peak at B1. A short but steep decline takes price down to C1 where it reverses and rises to the head-and-shoulders top (D1). A short drop to E1 completes the drop and the stock rises from there.

This type of failure occurs 18% of the time. Because there is so little difference between this failure and the prior one, combined they represent 37% of the failures I looked at.

Failure 4

The last type of failure appears in **Figure 10.10,** and it reminds me of a cargo ship. In this failure, the stock floats between overhead resistance and underlying support.

A flat price trend begins at A. By flat, I mean that the top of the trading range tends to bump up against overhead resistance, creating a ceiling on price movement. The trading range is often a coarse affair with tall price swings that peak near the same price (on the weekly scale, please!).

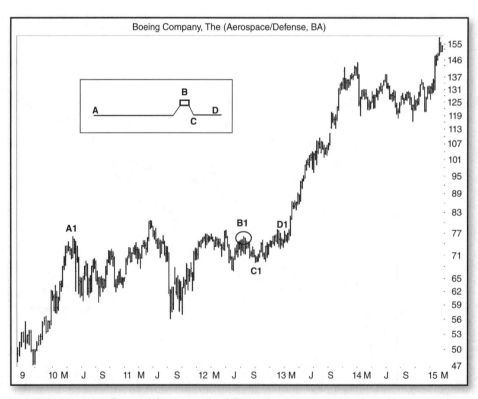

FIGURE 10.10   A flat trend dominates this failure scenario.

A head-and-shoulders top appears at B and price drops to C, a short dip below the breakout, before resuming the flat trend, to D.

The stock chart on the weekly scale shows an example of this behavior. The tall trading range starts at A1 and hits overhead resistance near 77. Although it is difficult to see on weekly charts, a head-and-shoulders top appears at B1. This chart pattern breaks out downward and price eases lower to C1. The stock rises and hits overhead resistance at D1 before pushing into new-high territory.

Those shorting the stock on the breakout of the head-and-shoulders top and holding on stood to lose a significant amount of money when the stock became a bird and soared to 155 from about 70.

This configuration occurred 9% of the time.

Success 3

Figure 10.11 shows a scenario that occurred 32% of the time in head-and-shoulders tops after which price plummeted. That occurrence placed this configuration second.

The AB decline can be long or short term, so I did not specify any time limit. What is important is that the primary trend is downward leading to B (see inset).

FIGURE 10.11 A large decline can follow stocks already in a downward primary trend.

At B, the short-term trend is up, and it leads to the head-and-shoulders top (C). Because the primary trend is downward (the AC drop), a downward breakout joins the prevailing current and carries the stock lower to D.

The stock chart shows an example of this configuration. The stock peaks at A1 as the second peak in a tall double top. The stock sinks to B1 before it rises to the head-and-shoulders top (LHR). A downward breakout sends the stock significantly lower, to D1.

Because I did not see this configuration for small declines, be worried if you own a stock showing this setup. The stock may make a small drop and recover after the breakout, but it could also act like Cree and see price plunge 43%.

■ Measure Rule

The measure rule sets a price target. Some call it a minimum move to expect, but I do not. **Figure 10.12** shows two examples of how it is used.

Two head-and-shoulders tops are cleverly labeled L (left shoulder), H (head), and R (right shoulder). Let us consider the March pattern first.

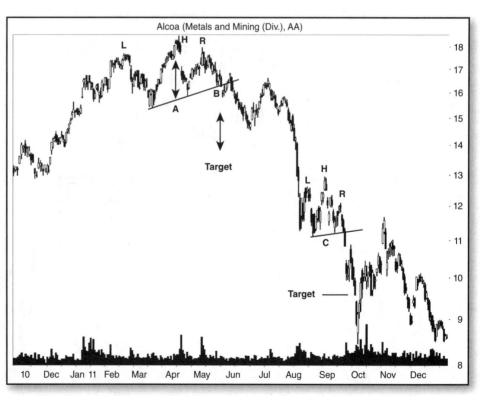

FIGURE 10.12   The measure rule can help set a target price.

Compute the height of the chart pattern from the peak at the head (H, 18.47) minus the price of the neckline directly below (A, 15.83). The neckline joins the two armpits.

Subtract the height (2.64) from the breakout price (B, 16.26) to get a target of 13.62.

My spreadsheet uses a slightly different calculation. I use the average of the two armpits and the high price on the day of breakout. In this example, that gives a target of 13.15. The full height works 58% of the time according to the spreadsheet.

If you divide the height in half and use that, it works 86% of the time.

Computation of the September head-and-shoulders top works the same way. The head is at 12.93, and the neckline below (C) is 11.16 for a height of 1.77. Subtract the height from the breakout price (11.34) to get a target of 9.57. The half height measure would give a target of 10.46.

As a check on the numbers, convert the drop into a percentage. For the first head-and-shoulders, the predicted drop is the height of the chart pattern, 2.64. Divide that number by the breakout price (16.26) and multiply by 100. That gives 16% (or 100 × 2.64 ÷ 16.26). That is near the average drop (18%) for head-and-shoulders tops.

The second pattern gives a predicted drop of 100 × 1.77 ÷ 11.34, or 16%.

If the percentages are unrealistic, then they are probably wrong, especially if they predict a negative target. Look for underlying support to help determine where the stock may stop its decline.

- The measure rule works for head-and-shoulders tops 58% of the time.

■ Trading

How do you use the information in this chapter to trade head-and-shoulders tops? To answer that, let us use the head-and-shoulders top shown in **Figure 10.13** as an example.

Inset 1 is the configuration that applies to this situation. Price rises over the long term from A to B. Peak B sets up resistance that D runs into. The head-and-shoulders top at D breaks out downward, but price does not drop far before the uptrend resumes.

Inset 2 shows the stock using the weekly scale. A1 is where the long-term uptrend begins, but it also corresponds to the trend start. That is a coincidence.

Peak B1 corresponds to B2 on the daily stock chart. From there, the stock slides down to C1, up to the head-and-shoulders at D1, and down to E1. Notice that C1 and E1 rest on support setup by the prior peaks as the horizontal line near $37 highlights.

When you look at the stock chart and ask, "How far down will price drop," Inset 2 shows the answer with the horizontal line. That line is a good guess, but price could plow through it, anyway.

In this example, the sideways move from the start of the horizontal line to January 2014 shows that overhead resistance (now support) is strong enough to hold the

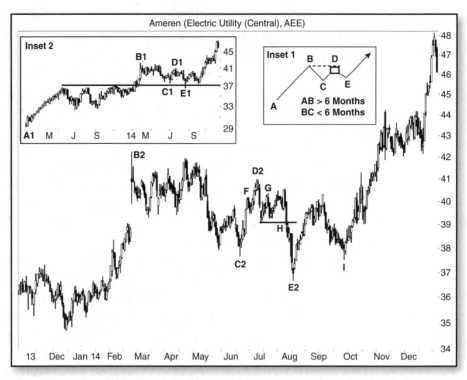

FIGURE 10.13   This head-and-shoulders top does not see price drop far after the breakout.

stock down like a wrestler pinning his opponent. Often, I allow the stock to sink into the support region, so I would expect support in the 35 to 37 area, but the stock could drop as far as 32.

The daily stock chart starting with B2 shows a closer view of the setup. The head-and-shoulders top is at F (left shoulder), D2 (head), and G (right shoulder). The pattern confirms as a valid head-and-shoulders top when the stock closes below the horizontal line at H (because the neckline, not shown, slopes downward. It connects the valleys between F and D2, and D2 and G).

Most of this discussion just describes the lay of the land. When I am considering a trade, I like to know the territory; otherwise, you could walk into a minefield.

If you owned the stock, can you tell how far the stock will decline after the breakout from the head-and-shoulders top? Consider the launch (not lunch) price.

Notice the short rise from C2 to the first shoulder (F). This is how far the chart pattern has to reverse. Thus, you can reasonably expect the stock to return to the launch price, perhaps stopping slightly above C2. In this example, though, the stock does better by declining to E2, 8% below H. Still, there was not much of a price rise to reverse.

The measure rule helps set a price target using the height of the pattern. If you do that by just looking at the D2 to H distance and visually projecting that height below H, you can see that it will bottom about midway between C2 and E2. However, this chart is on the log scale, so that is a dangerous way to proceed (because vertical distance can look compressed. Use the linear scale instead.). Using the numbers for the head to right armpit distance, the target is 37.13, very close to the bottom at E2.

Compare the size of the F-D2-G head-and-shoulders top with the size of the C2-E2-I head-and-shoulders *bottom*. The bottom is much bigger than the top and in the world of chart patterns, size means power. The taller the chart pattern, the larger the post-breakout move. The top *looks* small in this case compared to the bottom. In fact, the statistics prove that F-D2-G is a small head-and-shoulders top. As a small fry, do not expect a large decline.

Actual Trade

Figure 10.14 shows the sale of a stock I owned. Here is what I wrote for the sale. "Sell reason: Head-and-shoulders top. This [stock] has moved horizontally since March and has pierced support with a closing black marubozu candle. That suggests more down move ahead. Because this is near my 39 price target, I'm selling the earliest and higher priced shares.

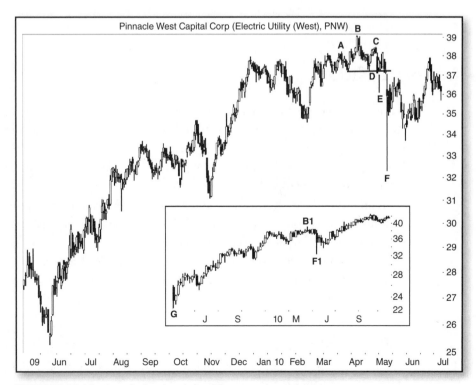

FIGURE 10.14   I used a head-and-shoulders to exit a trade.

"This is a good opportunity to reduce my utility holdings for diversification, because as a group, I'm too concentrated in them. I'm toying with selling the entire position but believe this has more upside to it. So, I'll hold onto the rest. Price has closed below the neckline of the head-and-shoulders top, too."

The inset, on the weekly scale, shows the upward move in the stock from the low at G to the head-and-shoulders top at B1. F1 is the one-day plunge in the stock.

The stock chart uses the daily scale. ABC is the head-and-shoulders top. A sell signal occurred when price closed below the neckline at D. I sold the next day (E).

As luck would have it, the stock had a sharp sell-off at F but recovered to close near the open for the day. As the inset shows, the stock recovered and moved to new highs. On the portion I sold, I made 41% (including dividends).

Application How do we apply the information in this chapter to the setup shown in Figure 10.14?

Price trends higher from G to B1 over the long term, so Figure 10.7 applies. That is the only figure that has price trending higher over the long term with the head-and-shoulders forming a peak, not sliding down a short-term trend (as it does in Figures 10.8 and 10.9).

Although I sold a portion of my holdings in a timely sale (which missed the sharp plunge at F), I held onto the remaining shares. Thus, I was given the opportunity to participate in the rise after the head-and-shoulders busted, just as Inset 1 of Figure 10.7 shows.

■ Closing Position

If there was one chart pattern people seem to know, it is the head-and-shoulders top. After the breakout, a pullback happens 62% of the time. Once a pullback completes, price actually rises more often than it falls, 60% to 40%, respectively. The 40% number suggests a few stocks got buried deep enough to pull the average decline for all head-and-shoulders tops down to 18%.

In other words, do not panic if you see a head-and-shoulders top. It could mean the end of life as you know it, but with 30% of head-and-shoulders tops busting a downward breakout, the chance of encountering a huge drop is small. Lower the risk by selecting trades from the setups and configurations discussed in this chapter, those that show small post-breakout drops (unless you want a large decline). Either way, be careful.

Setup Synopsis

The following figure may help you identify the various types of trading setups. See the associated figure for an explanation.

"Occurs" in the figure means how often I found the configuration in the stocks I looked at. If two configurations apply to your situation, then the one with a more frequent occurrence (a higher percentage) is the one you should choose to follow.

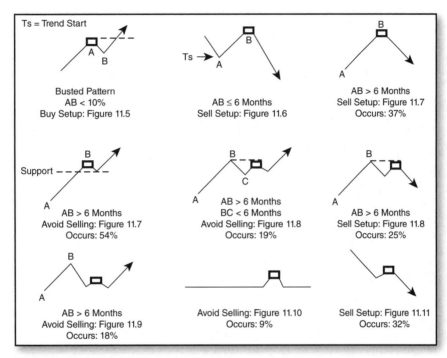

FIGURE 10.15   A collection of ideal trading setups and configurations.

CHAPTER 11

Measured Move Down

T he measured move down is an important chart pattern for two reasons. First, you can use it to predict how far price might drop as the pattern unfolds, and second, it is a wonderful tool to gauge how far price might rise after the pattern ends.

This chapter deviates from the usual format because of the nature of the chart pattern.

■ Behavior at a Glance

Figure 11.1 shows the various features of the measured move down.

The first leg sees price drop in a straight-line run until finding support. A retrace of the first leg decline forms the corrective phase. Once the retrace completes, the stock makes another strong move down, in another straight line.

The first leg, corrective phase, and second leg complete the measured move down chart pattern. However, in this chapter, I will refer to the bounce that often returns price to the corrective phase area and the move to the ultimate high or low (ultimate low is shown only).

For this chart pattern, the ultimate high or low depends on the direction of break-out. I define the breakout for this pattern as the first close above the top or below

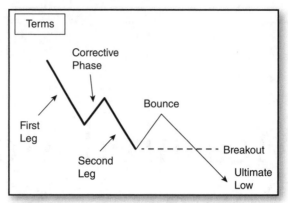

FIGURE 11.1 The various features of the measured move down.

the bottom of the measured move. In Figure 11.1, I show a downward breakout. Downward is the most common breakout direction for this chart pattern.

Measured Move Down Performance

I trimmed my database of measured move down patterns to reflect only those that obeyed the identification guidelines. For example, if the second leg was too short, I removed that pattern from my database. I also added hundreds of additional patterns from recent years. Thus, the performance numbers in this book are substantially different from the ones in my book *Encyclopedia of Chart Patterns*.

I used 1,036 measured move down patterns in bull markets found in 527 stocks with the earliest pulled from August 1991 and the most recent from January 2015.

Figure 11.2 shows the median performance of the various parts of a measured move down.

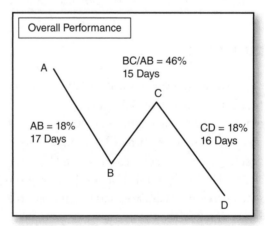

FIGURE 11.2 The median percentage change of the various parts of a measured move down.

The first leg, AB, sees price drop 18% in 17 days. The corrective phase, BC, sports a median retrace of 46% of the AB drop, and it does this in a median of 15 days. Finally, the second leg, CD, sees the stock drop the same amount as the first leg, 18%, but the decline is a day quicker, at 16 days.

- The two legs of a measured move down are about the same length.

Downward Breakouts

I separated performance into downward and upward breakouts. A downward breakout occurs when price closes below the bottom of the measured move. A downward breakout occurs 67% of the time.

That may sound confusing since price is dropping in the second leg, so where is the breakout? The bounce provides the answer. If price bounces high enough, the stock will close above the top of the measured move, creating an upward breakout. If the bounce is small and price drops, you will get a downward breakout. Because the bounce is near the bottom of the pattern, a downward breakout is more likely.

Figure 11.3 shows what I found.

The measured move down is the ABCD pattern. After the second leg (CD) completes, price bounces from D to E, retracing a median of 35% of the height of the measured move. This is the first bounce, and it carries price until it peaks at the first minor high.

Additional up and down waves carry price up to F, a median of 39% of the height of the measured move. After that, the stock slides downward and drops a median of 9% below the bottom of the measured move before a recovery begins at the ultimate low.

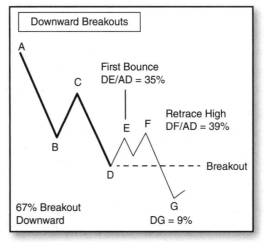

FIGURE 11.3 These performance statistics are for downward breakouts.

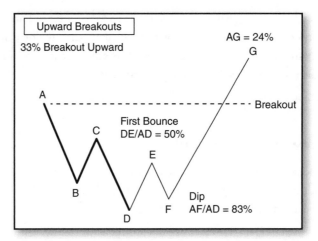

FIGURE 11.4 Upward breakouts see a higher first bounce.

- After a downward breakout from a measured move down, the stock bounces but eventually drops a median of 9% below the bottom of the pattern.

- A downward breakout occurs 67% of the time.

Upward Breakouts

Price breaks out upward from a measured move down 33% of the time.

Upward breakouts follow a different trajectory when price first closes above the top of the measured move. **Figure 11.4** shows the ideal configuration.

The first bounce (DE) retraces half of the height (50%) of the measured move. Following the bounce, a dip occurs. I measured the dip between the date of the first bounce high and the date of the breakout. Price dropped to 83% (AF) of the height of the measured move. That move almost retraced the entire drop, meaning the stock nearly reached the price of D.

After F, the stock climbed and made its way higher, to G. The AG move saw price soar a median of 24% above the top of the measured move before encountering a trend change (that is, price hit the ultimate high and reversed).

- After an upward breakout from a measured move down, price rises a median of 24% above the top of the chart pattern.

- An upward breakout occurs 33% of the time.

■ Identification

What should you look for in a measured move down? **Figure 11.5** shows an example. Refer to **Table 11.1** as I discuss identification guidelines.

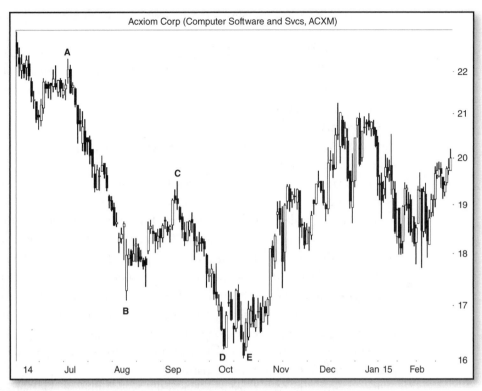

FIGURE 11.5 An example of the measured move down chart pattern.

TABLE 11.1	Identification Guidelines
Characteristic	**Discussion**
First leg	Look for an extensive straight-line run that takes price down. The leg should be mostly straight, not curved.
Corrective phase	The corrective phase retraces almost half of the first leg. Often the move will appear as a straight-line run, too, but allow exceptions. The retrace should not be extensive. Price must remain below the top of the first leg.
Second leg	The second leg appears as another straight-line run down, often mirroring the slope and extent of the first leg, offset by the corrective phase. The bottom of the second leg should be below the corrective phase. Avoid second legs that curve.
Proportional	The two legs and corrective phase should look proportional to one another. Discard any pattern that has two short legs and a long corrective phase or tall legs and a short corrective phase.
Breakout	A breakout occurs when price first closes above the top of the measure move (upward breakout) or below the bottom of it (downward breakout).

Pattern ABCD is a measured move down. Let us discuss the particulars of the pattern.

First Leg. The first leg (AB) begins the measured move down. Look for an extensive straight-line run. Often the first leg will begin from a peak, but it need not be a major high, just a turning point, perhaps after a long advance. Peak A is part of a downtrend already in progress.

Corrective Phase. The corrective phase (BC) is where the stock retraces a portion of the AB move. The retrace often, but not always, appears as a straight-line run, although at a much slower pace.

The corrective phase should not reach the top of the first leg (C should remain well below A).

Second Leg. Ideally, the second leg (CD) mirrors the length and time of the first leg. It is also a straight-line run down. A minor low often ends the second leg. The second leg should end below the corrective phase (D should be below B).

The second leg in this example is obviously shorter than the first leg.

Proportional. The first and second legs, along with the corrective phase, should appear proportional to each other. You should not see a small corrective phase with two long legs nor the reverse (long corrective phase and short legs).

Notice how leg AB looks similar to CD in both slope and length. Retrace BC looks proportional to the entire ABCD pattern.

Breakout. A breakout occurs when price closes either above the top of the measured move or below the bottom of it. This measured move breaks out downward at E.

■ Performance Details

The idea behind the measured move down is that the first leg will approximate the length and extent of the second leg. Is this true?

Table 11.2 shows the answer. The first leg averages a 20% decline in 26 days compared to a 21% decline for the second leg in 27 days. The median numbers are

TABLE 11.2 Measured Move Down Performance

Description	Average	Median
First leg decline	20%, 26 days	18%, 17 days
Second leg decline	21%, 27 days	18%, 16 days
Corrective phase retrace	48%, 21 days	46%, 15 days
Retrace <38%. Is leg 2 longer?	No. Only 37% are longer	
Retrace 38% to 62%. Is leg 2 longer?	Yes, 54% of the time	
Retrace >62%. Is leg 2 longer?	Yes, 81% of the time	

even closer. So the answer is yes, the first and second legs are about equal in both percentage decline and the time it takes to complete the drop.

The corrective phase retrace does *not* mean that the stock climbed an average of 48%. Rather, it means the stock *retraced* almost half of the first leg's decline.

The bottom half of the table compares the amount of the corrective phase retrace of the first leg (less than 38%, between 38% and 62%, and greater than 62%) with the length of the second leg.

I found that, if the corrective phase retraces greater than 62% of the length of the first leg, then there is an 81% chance the second leg will be longer than the first leg.

- If the corrective phase retraces greater than 62% of the first leg, then expect a longer second leg. Short retraces mean shorter second legs.

■ After the Measured Move Down

Once the measured move completes, what happens next? **Figure 11.6** shows a frequency distribution of measured moves.

After a measured move down completes, the stock bounces (or else the second leg would be longer). I found that 23% of the measured moves see price reverse before reaching the start (B) of the corrective phase. That represents path E, which leads to a downward breakout.

Twenty-eight percent will enter the corrective phase (BC) and turn there, following path F. Those following path F breakout downward, too.

Fifteen percent will rise above the top of the corrective phase (C) but turn before closing above the top of the measured move (A). The stock follows path G and breaks out downward, too.

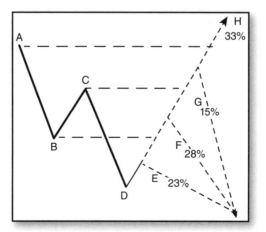

FIGURE 11.6   A frequency distribution of stocks after a measured move down completes.

The remainder of the time (33%), the stock closes above the top of the measured move and follows path H, staging an upward breakout.

The numbers are additive, so that 51% of the time (23% + 28%) the stock will reverse before closing above the top of the corrective phase. Another example says that 67% of the time, the stock will break out downward after a measured move down completes.

The trading implications of this should be obvious. You can use the percentages to determine the likelihood of price reaching various points in the measured move. Keep in mind that the percentages are just probabilities, so anything can happen in real time.

■ The Measure Rule

Use the measure rule to help predict where the second leg will bottom. **Figure 11.7** shows two examples of how the measure rule works.

For the ABCD measured move down, compute the length of the first leg from its high at A (67.62) to the low at the start of the corrective phase (B, 64). The result is 3.62. Subtract the height from the top of the corrective phase (C, 65.47) to get a

FIGURE 11.7 Use the measure rule to help predict where the stock will bottom in the second leg.

target of 61.85, as shown. Price reaches the target on bar D. However, this method of using the full height works just 54% of the time.

- The measure rule based on the full height of the first leg works 54% of the time to set a second leg target.

Notice that the first bounce, E, does not make it into the corrective phase before the stock reverses and breaks out downward at F.

Consider the measured move down GHIJ. The high at G is 64.11 and the low at H is 58.50 for a height of 5.61. For a more accurate and closer target, let us take 70% of this height and use that in the computation. I chose 70% because it works 90% of the time.

The high at I is 61.76, so subtracting the adjusted height of 5.61 × 70% or 3.93 gives a target of 57.83. I show the target on the chart, and the stock reaches it on the way to J.

Notice that the first bounce takes price back up to K, which resides within the corrective phase boundaries (HI). After K, the stock moves above G (not shown), breaking out upward.

- For a more conservative target, multiply the height of the first leg by 70% to get a second leg target. Price reaches the target 90% of the time.

■ Trading

On the basis of **Table 11.2**, we can formulate trading tactics.

If a straight-line run occurs followed by a retrace, assume you have a measured move down forming. Use the length of the first leg to determine how far down the second leg will go.

If price retraces a lot of the first leg, then look for a longer second leg. If the retrace is small (less than 38%), then look for a short second leg.

Once you have a price target for the second leg, you can wait and see where the stock actually forms a bottom (it should be the first minor low after the corrective phase). If the stock still looks like a measured move (proportional), then buy the stock and ride the recovery back up to the corrective phase or perhaps higher.

Example Trade

Say you want to use the information in this chapter to trade a stock. Although the trade I am about to discuss is easy, reality is often harder. Many variables can occur to sabotage a trade.

Consider the situation in **Figure 11.8**. A measured move down appears at ABCD. The first and second legs along with the corrective phase look proportional. The pattern obeys the identification guidelines of Table 11.1.

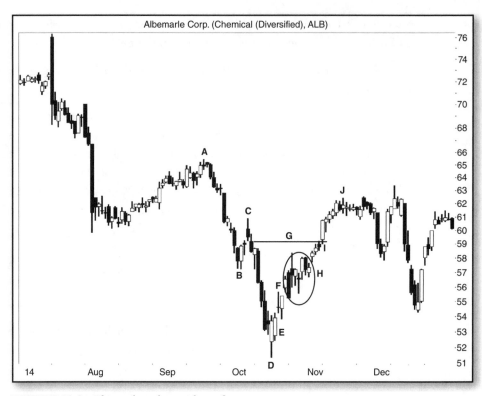

FIGURE 11.8 This trade makes a tidy profit.

As price drops in the second leg (C to D), you notice that each day the stock makes a new low. At E, the stock makes a higher low. This suggests, but does not guarantee, that the downtrend has ended, and the stock has completed the measured move down.

The next day, F, you buy the stock at the open. The trade fills at 54.63, the opening price.

The target is the corrective phase, BC. You take the average of the high at B (60.90) and the low at C (57.22) for a target of 59.06. I show the target as line G.

As price climbs, it enters a volatile stage, which I have circled on the chart. The top of this area punches into the corrective phase. That could be a sell signal, but it is below your target. You get greedy and decide to hold on, waiting for the stock to hit your target.

The stock leaves the circled area and starts trending again. Each day, the stock makes a higher low. When price touches the target price at I, the stock has made three higher lows, starting the day after H.

It has been my experience that when a stock makes three higher lows (ideally, accompanied by three higher highs, too), it is trending. Instead of selling at the target line G, you trail the stop higher. How? Each day place a stop-loss order a penny below the prior day's low, but never lower the stop.

This works great as price climbs to J. At J, the stock makes a lower low and closes out the trade at 61.43. You made more than 12% on the trade in about a month.

Before trying a trade using a measured move down, try your ideas on paper. Find a hundred (I am not kidding) measured moves down and count how often your setup works. Look at stop placement to limit losses when the setup fails. Set an exit price if the setup works.

Learn from the experience. You will find the measured move down to be a valuable tool whether you trade using it or not. I find it valuable to know that price will often retrace back to the corrective phase. I can make money with that kind of knowledge.

■ Closing Position

The measured move down is one of my favorite chart patterns. I use it most often, not to predict where the stock may reverse (at the end of the second leg) but to predict a return to the corrective phase.

To know that price bounces after the measured move ends and drops below the second leg 67% of the time is valuable. If you own a stock falling victim to a measure move, you can exit on the rise to the corrective phase knowing that selling was the right move.

CHAPTER 12

Measured Move Up

Y ou may not be familiar with the measured move, but it has been around for decades. I use the pattern to predict price is going to return to the corrective phase.

What does corrective phase mean? Let us take a closer look by first defining terms.

■ Behavior at a Glance

Figure 12.1 shows the various components of a measured move up. Ideally, the first leg will be a straight-line run up. Following that comes the corrective phase. The corrective phase sees price retrace a substantial portion of the first leg move. After the corrective phase, the second leg begins, and it completes the measured move.

I show what typically happens after the measured move ends. The stock dips before breaking out upward. I define a breakout for this pattern as when price closes above the top or below the bottom of the measured move. The chart shows an upward breakout because it occurs most often.

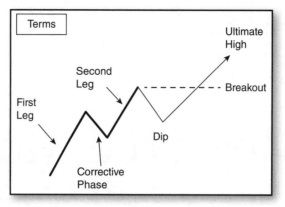

FIGURE 12.1 Various features of the measured move up.

MMU Performance

Figure 12.2 attaches numbers to the components of an ideal measured move up. The numbers are medians, not averages.

The first leg (AB) sees price rise 26% in 21 days. Then the corrective phase (BC) retraces 47% of the first leg's move up, and it takes a median of 19 days to complete the trip.

If you consider that it takes 3 weeks to rise 26% and nearly the same amount of time to retrace half that, then the retrace must be at a slower pace. Perhaps the stock is on its lunch hour.

After the pause is over, the second leg (CD) resumes the upward move and price rises 24% in 20 days.

Notice that the first and second legs have nearly the same percentage rise and take almost the same time to complete.

■ In a measured move up, the second leg nearly equals the length of the first leg.

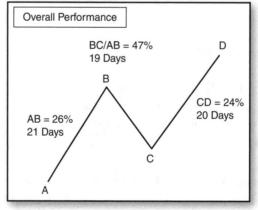

FIGURE 12.2 The median performance of each component of a measured move up.

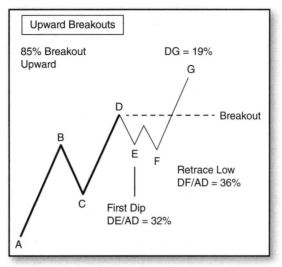

FIGURE 12.3 A detailed look at the behavior after a measured move down completes when the breakout is upward.

Upward Breakouts

Figure 12.3 shows an upward breakout from a measured move. Again, the numbers are medians. That means half the measured moves I looked at posted better numbers and half did worse.

The measured move is ABCD, shown here using a thick line. After the pattern completes (D), the stock dips. The first dip, E, retraces 32% of the height of the measured move. Additional dips may follow with the lowest one (F) bottoming out between the end of the measured move and the breakout. The dip retraces 36% of the height of the measured move.

After the upward breakout (a close above the top of the measured move, D) price continues climbing 19% (G) before the trend changes. The trend change occurs at the ultimate high after which price drops by at least 20%.

- After a measured move up completes, upward breakouts see price rise a median of 19%.

Downward Breakouts

Downward breakouts have a slightly different profile than do upward breakouts, as shown in **Figure 12.4**.

The measured move is ABCD. After the measured move completes, the stock dips (E) and retraces 47% of the height of the measured move. That is almost half. Then the stock recovers (F, the highest peak after D) but does not reach the height of

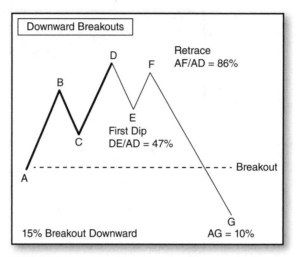

FIGURE 12.4 Downward breakouts have price closing below the bottom of the measured move.

peak D. The AF move represents 86% of the height of the measured move. Although I show only one dip (E), there can be several before the stock peaks at F.

The stock drops and eventually closes below the bottom of the measured move up (A), staging a downward breakout.

After the breakout, the stock becomes a drowning victim and price sinks until bottoming at G, 10% under the start of the measured move (A). G is the ultimate low, so expect price to rise at least 20% thereafter, by definition.

■ Downward breakouts from measured moves up see price tumble 10% below the bottom of the chart pattern.

■ Identification

Figure 12.5 shows two examples of measured move up chart patterns, ABCD and EFGH. Refer to **Table 12.1** for a discussion of identification guidelines.

First Leg. In well-formed measured moves, the first leg should be a straight-line run but allow variations. That means price should not bend much (curve) as it rises. Both the AB and EF first legs are good examples of what to look for.

Corrective Phase. Price retraces a portion of the first leg and the figure shows this. The corrective phases, BC and FG, show straight moves down. The stock does not retrace too far, meaning C remains above A, and G remains above E.

Second Leg. The second leg completes the chart pattern. The second leg is another strong move up as the chart shows in CD and GH. Notice that both legs are

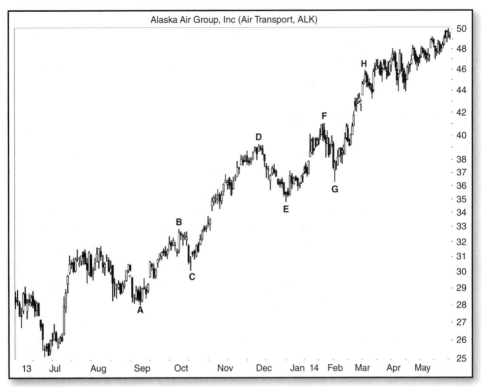

FIGURE 12.5 Two examples of measured move up patterns.

straight and rise at almost the same slope as the first legs. However, it is rare that you will see the same slope in both legs.

Avoid patterns in which the second leg does not exceed the top of the corrective phase. In Figure 12.5, for example, D must be above B, and it is.

TABLE 12.1 Identification Guidelines

Characteristic	Discussion
First leg	Price climbs in a near straight line. Avoid curving moves, but be flexible.
Corrective phase	Price retraces a good portion of the first leg advance, often in a straight-line run down. The bottom of the corrective phase must remain above the bottom of the first leg.
Second leg	A straight-line move higher takes price above the start of the corrective phase.
Proportional	The corrective phase length should look proportional to the length of the measured move. In the ideal pattern, the two legs should be similar in length.
Breakout	The first close above the top or below the bottom of the measured move determines the breakout direction.

Proportional. Notice that the entire pattern looks proportional. The corrective phase is not too long nor too short compared to the length of the legs. Although leg CD is longer than AB, it is not awkward looking.

Breakout. An upward breakout occurs in both of these examples.

■ Performance Details

I used 468 stocks to find 1,059 measured moves in bull markets, with the first pattern found in January 1991 and the most recent taken from December 2014. **Table 12.2** shows the performance results of those patterns.

I removed patterns from my database that were not proportional and added many recent patterns. The recent ones tended to be smaller and better shaped (straighter legs and similar slopes, for example). That means the performance numbers vary widely from the statistics in my other books.

The top half of the table shows the extent of the two legs and the corrective phase, both as averages and medians.

For example, the first leg rises an average of 36% in 38 days, but the median is less, 26% in 3 weeks. Compare those results to the second leg. They are not identical but are close enough for horseshoes and hand grenades (as the saying goes). Because I chose patterns that had second legs similar to the first legs, I would expect the results to be close.

The corrective phase is a measure of how far down the first leg the stock drops. The average is 48% in 27 days or a median of 47% in 19 days.

The lower half of the table uses a frequency distribution of the corrective phase retrace and maps the length of the second leg compared to the length of the first leg. I know that sounds confusing.

For example, if the retrace is short (less than 38% of the first leg), does that mean the second leg will be longer than the first one? No. A short retrace accompanies a short second leg 80% of the time.

TABLE 12.2 Measured Move Up Performance

Description	Average	Median
First leg rise	36%, 38 days	26%, 21 days
Second leg rise	31%, 33 days	24%, 20 days
Corrective phase retrace	48%, 27 days	47%, 19 days
Retrace <38%. Is leg 2 longer?	No. Only 20% are longer	
Retrace 38% to 62%. Is leg 2 longer?	No. Only 45% are longer	
Retrace >62%. Is leg 2 longer?	Yes, 64% of the time	

- A short retrace accompanies a short second leg 80% of the time.

If the retrace is between 38% and 62%, is the second leg longer than the first? Again, no, but the numbers are closer. The second leg is longer 45% of the time.

For big retraces, those when the stock corrects more than 62%, the second leg is longer almost two out of three times (64%).

- Retraces larger than 62% associate with longer second legs.

After the Measured Move Up

Figure 12.6 may look like some kind of star map, but it is easy to understand. The measured move up is ABCD. We know that price retraces after D; otherwise, the CD leg would be longer.

How far down does price retrace? A frequency distribution of the movement provides the answer. In 43% of the cases, the stock takes path E and remains above the top of corrective phase (B). Thirty-one percent of the time, the stock enters the corrective phase BC, finds support there, and turns to breakout upward. That is path F.

In 12% of the cases, the stock drops below the corrective phase (C) but remains above the bottom of the measured move (A). Again, the breakout is upward. I show that as path G.

Downward breakouts occur 15% of the time (H) with the remainder, 85%, staging upward breakouts.

As I said, these numbers are the result of a frequency distribution, a counting of how often price reaches one of the turning points. The other pictures and tables in

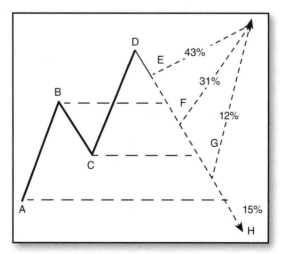

FIGURE 12.6   A frequency distribution of where the stock stops after a measured move up completes.

this chapter show the median or midrange performance. Half of the measured moves will show larger numbers and half will show smaller ones.

■ The Measure Rule

We can use the statistics to help predict a target price based on the performance of the typical measured move. Consider the measured move up ABCD in **Figure 12.7**.

Let us assume that the second leg will be as long as the first leg and make a projection based on that.

The measured move begins at A. This is the low price where the stock bottoms before its rise out of the short downtrend. The low at A is 29.36.

The stock rises to B, the top of the corrective phase, peaking at a high price of 41.47. The height is the difference between those two, namely, 12.11. Add that height to the low price made during the corrective phase C (38.26) to get a target of 50.37.

The stock at the end of the measured move, D at 50.97, almost meets the predicted target exactly.

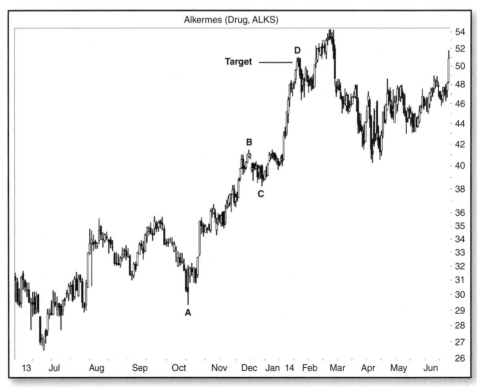

FIGURE 12.7 Use the measure rule to help predict where the second leg will reach.

That is the way the measure rule is supposed to work, but it does not always perform that well. In fact, the measure rule using the full height works only 42% of the time.

To boost the success rate of the rule to more than 90%, multiply the height by 60% and use that to project the target. In this case, 60% × 12.11 is 7.27 giving a closer target of 45.53.

- The measure rule works 42% of the time for measured moves up.

Trading

Price rises in a series of waves and those waves sometimes form a measured move.

If you see price rise in a straight-line run, where the stock climbs at a consistent pace, then expect the retrace to backtrack about half of that rise (the first leg move). That is what the numbers from Table 12.2 say. It may not unfold that way, but at least the information provides guidance.

If the retrace of the corrective phase is unusually short, then expect a short second leg. If the retrace is larger, then expect a longer second leg.

Actual Trade

Figure 12.8 shows an actual trade I made. Let me tell you about it.

FIGURE 12.8 A measured move up failed to see price return to the corrective phase.

I bought the stock on August 5, 2011, as a dividend play, filled at 22.23. The yield at the time was 5.4%, far above the near 0% that money market funds and banks were paying at the time. The day before, the Dow Jones Industrials plunged 520 points (4.6%), so this was an opportunity to buy low and ride the stock higher.

It turns out I bought two days too soon. I could have snagged the stock as low as 20.59 (with perfect timing). Sigh.

The stock climbed and hit my target of 29 a year later, but I did not feel like selling. Dividend-paying stocks, like electric utilities, are the kind I buy and hold for years while collecting the fat dividend.

Here is what I wrote about the sale on October 1, 2014: "Sell reason: measured move up with a retrace back to the corrective phase and shaky dividend. This stock has recovered nicely to give me a 15% gain. With rumors a while back of a dividend cut, and since this is on Hawaii, I'm getting out while the getting is good. It could continue up, but my guess is it'll retrace, and I want to get out while it's near the top of its yearly range. The measured move up is from the August 2014 low to September high."

I show the measured move as ABCD. I expected the stock to retrace back to the corrective phase, BC, and did not want to ride the stock back down. If they cut the dividend, the stock could drop a percentage point for each percentage point cut. That happened to three utility stocks during the 2007 to 2009 bear market.

I sold the stock and received a fill at 26.55 for a gain of 19%, but when you add in the dividends collected, I made 37%. Yum, almost better than chocolate.

As the chart shows, the stock did not retrace to the BC corrective phase. In fact, it climbed. On December 4, the stock gapped up on news that the company would spin off its bank and that NextEra Energy offered to buy the company for a deal worth about $33.50 a share.

Having sold my stake, I sat on the sidelines drooling. And eating chocolate (think comfort food).

■ Closing Position

Knowledge is money. Knowing the behavior after the appearance of a measured move can give you confidence to maintain a position in a winning trade.

After the second leg completes, 31% of the time the stock sinks into the corrective phase before powering upward again. The resulting move sees price closing above the top of the measured move 85% of the time. Wow.

You can use the length of the first leg and corrective phase to predict the top end of the second leg. Your prediction will not work every time, of course, but at least you have a clue. Combine that clue with nearby overhead resistance to refine your prediction, and then trade accordingly.

CHAPTER 13

Price Mirrors

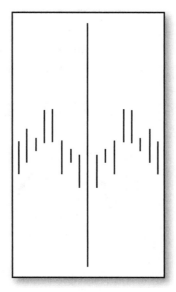

Imagine that you just bought a stock. How far up or down will it go? When will it turn? Answering those questions correctly can make you a bundle. Flub them and you could be in for a heartbreaking loss.

Price mirrors—a reflection around an invisible vertical line or point on the stock chart—can help answer those questions. Mirrors do not always work, but when you have no other way to predict where and when price will turn, price mirrors may help.

This chapter does not come with statistics on how often this technique works. Rather price mirrors are a visual skill. Use your imagination when looking at charts. Take an unfolding chart pattern and project the completed pattern into the future. The results will give you guidance and the opportunity to profit or to avoid a loss.

By becoming accustomed to using price mirrors, when you encounter a situation that calls for a guess on the future path of a stock, you will know what to do.

■ Example 1

Figure 13.1 comes from the first chart I looked at. I say that because price mirrors are not hard to find. Some even work!

This chart shows four of them, one marked with line G; all of them have small circles attached. The other three are at valleys A (reflected around the peak between the two As), E (reflected across valley H), and peaks F (reflected around the right peak D).

Starting on the far left, notice the twin bottoms at A. If you bought the stock at the first A, you could guess that price would form a second bottom near the same price. That is what happened at the second A.

Also notice how the stock made two vertical moves, the first leading to the left A and the second returning from the right A. The move between the two As is also vertical. If you imagine a vertical line positioned between the two As, the left side of the pattern mirrors the one on the right. That is how price mirrors are supposed to work.

Here is another example. I drew a thin vertical mirror line (G), centered on the May 2010 peak. Peaks B reflect across line G. The reflection is not entirely accurate because

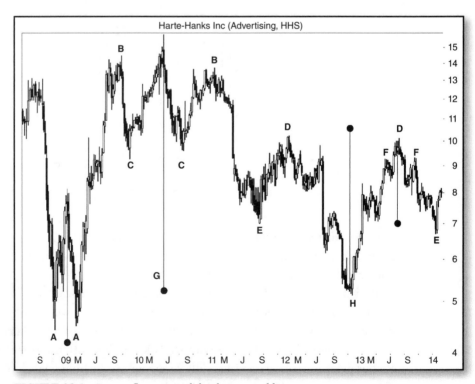

FIGURE 13.1 Price reflects around the thin vertical line.

the two Bs do not share the same price, and the right B is further from the line than the left B. But the reflection provides guidance where and when the stock might turn.

Valleys C reflect across line G, too, so price mirrors work for both peaks and valleys. Notice that line G is not centered between the two Cs, but it is close.

Ds, Es, and Fs form more reflections, peaks, or valleys that see price pausing near the same value in the future.

When I use price mirrors, I think of potential chart patterns and split them in half. For example, the A bottom becomes a double bottom. Peaks B (and F) form head-and-shoulders tops. The E bottoms have a head at H, creating a head-and-shoulders bottom.

When I see a left shoulder form then a head, I can imagine where the right shoulder will appear and how long the birth will take.

- Head-and-shoulders tops/bottoms and double tops/bottoms lend themselves to price projection using mirrors.

■ Example 2

Figure 13.2 shows a second example of price mirrors. I drew vertical line F between the two valleys at E. If you take the left half of the chart and fold it over the right, the price movement would not be an exact match, but some of it would be close.

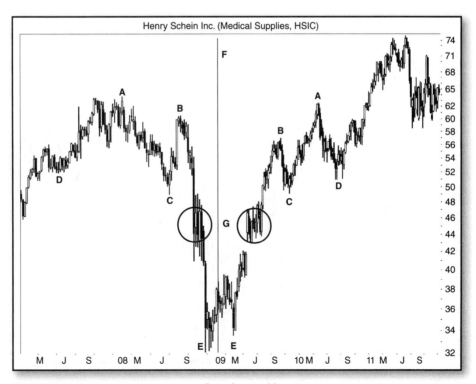

FIGURE 13.2 More price mirrors, reflected around line F.

Peak A on the left is a rounded turn, but peak A on the right is pointy. They summit near the same price and almost the same time. That is helpful when projecting a turn.

The right peak at B falls short of the left one. Notice how the left peak is closer to line F than the right one.

Points C, D, and E show similar reflections across line F. Notice how price pauses at the two circled regions, G.

The price mirror fails when the stock climbs after D on the right side, even though the left side predicted it would fall (that is, price drops to the left of D and there is no corresponding reflection).

■ Example 3

Figure 13.3 shows the last example. I did not draw a vertical line where the reflection would be, but the chart shows matching peaks and valleys.

For example, the two valleys at A bottom near the same price, but valleys B are uneven. Peak D on the right is a distinct peak, but on the left, it is part of the trend lower.

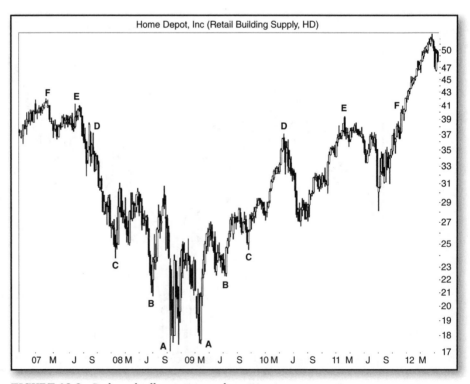

FIGURE 13.3 Peaks and valleys stop near the same price.

Notice the distance between peaks D and E on the left compared to the mirror image of D and E on the right. It seems that peaks and valleys reflected on the right take longer to form than do those on the left. That time component seems to be stock specific, because the other two charts do not show as much variation.

More examples: Peaks A in Figure 13.2 are almost the same distance from line G, but the two Bs are not. In Figure 13.1, the right C is closer to the vertical line than the left one.

What this demonstrates is that the time and price components vary. You can still use it to guess *when* price will turn and at what price, so the method adds value.

In essence, price mirrors are another method to determine where support and resistance will appear in the future. The method does not always work, of course. Few things in technical analysis do, but price mirrors give you a road map to consider when trading.

■ Closing Position

Price mirrors are the basis of many chart patterns. The head-and-shoulders pattern, for example, shows remarkable symmetry across the head. Double tops and bottoms are twin peaks and valleys reflected across a vertical line between them.

By using the past to predict how price might behave in the future, you may be surprised at how often the technique works. When it works, it can help improve your trading results. And when it fails, you can blame me.

CHAPTER 14

Price Mountains

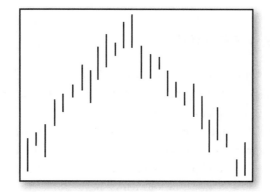

A price mountain is just as it sounds. Price forms a peak and then makes a large decline. How long will it take price to climb back up the mountain peak? Of course, the answer depends on how tall the mountain is.

During the year 2000 technology bubble, many investors became caught buying stocks as upward momentum plays and held them as they declined. They thought the stocks would recover and make new highs. Some did. Many did not. Intel, for example, peaked at nearly 76 in August 2000. It recovered to almost 38 in December 2014. Fourteen years is a long time to wait to get half your money back.

The justification for buying a stock *after* a price mountain is that the stock could reach the summit again. As this chapter explains, it could be years before that comes true.

■ Behavior at a Glance

Figure 14.1 shows the typical (median numbers) price mountain, shown as the thick line. I measured the decline from peak A to valley floor B, and the median drop was 17%. This is not a meaningful number because it depends on the parameters I used to find price mountains. For example, I excluded all drops less than 10%. If I changed that to 30%, then the median decline would be substantially longer and so would the recovery time.

The recovery time is how long it takes a stock to return to the price of peak A. In Figure 14.1, the recovery completes at C, and the median time is about three months (92 days).

When viewed on the longer-term charts (weekly, monthly), price usually begins its recovery in a V-shaped move off the low at B. After rising for a time, the stock usually retraces a portion of the rise before resuming the upward move. I show that stair-step rise in the move from B to C.

■ Recovery Statistics

To find price mountains, I used 471 stocks with data beginning in January 1990 and ending April 2015, but not all stocks covered the entire period. I found 7,388 price mountains at least 10% high.

Table 14.1 shows how tall mountains are by the decline from mountain peak (high price) to valley floor (the lowest closing price), and the average or median time price takes to climb back up to reach the peak.

Because a number of stocks have not exceeded their mountain peaks (I included them, assuming they reached the peak at the end of the study), the average recovery time is minimal. As more data becomes available, the recovery time will lengthen.

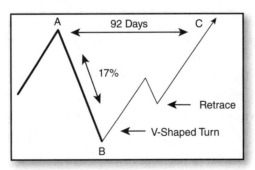

FIGURE 14.1   The typical price mountain, but the numbers are misleading.

TABLE 14.1	Frequency Distribution of Recovery Time by Mountain Height	
Peak to Valley Drop	**Average Recovery Time**	**Median Recovery Time**
Up to 20%	2.5 months	1.5 months
21% to 30%	7 months	5 months
31% to 40%	1.2 years	9.5 months
41% to 50%	1.9 years	1.4 years
51% to 60%	3.4 years	3.0 years
61% to 70%	4.8 years	4.4 years
71% to 80%	6.4 years	5.6 years
81% to 90%	9.0 years	7.9 years
More than 90%	12.0 years	13.7 years

For example, if the drop from the peak to valley is up to 20%, it takes an average of 2.5 months for the stock to recover back to the price of the peak. If the stock drops 51% to 60%, it takes an average of 3.4 years and a median of 3 years to recover.

If you are contemplating buying a stock showing a price mountain, be careful because it could be years before the stock returns to the old high. However, timing the buy after a price mountain bottoms can mean a scrumptious return.

You can think of the table as the decline the general indices suffer during a bear market. For example, if you bought at the peak in the S&P 500 Index in October 2007, the index bottomed 58% lower in March 2009. The table says to expect a recovery time of 3.4 years. The index recovered all of its losses in April 2013, for a duration of 4 years.

- The taller the price mountain, the longer the recovery time.

Example

At the start of this chapter, I mentioned Intel as one of those stocks with a price mountain. **Figure 14.2** shows it on the monthly scale. The stock reached a peak of almost 75 in August 2000 during the tech bubble. The decline from peak (A) to valley (B) measured 84%. The stock has climbed only halfway up the peak.

Recovery Behavior

After a price mountain completes, how does price behave?

Figure 14.3 shows an example of a price mountain at A. A is the highest high before price tumbled to B. B is not the lowest low. Rather, it is the lowest close. I use the close to avoid tall one-day price spikes (flash crashes).

FIGURE 14.2   Intel has not recovered from the 2000 price mountain.

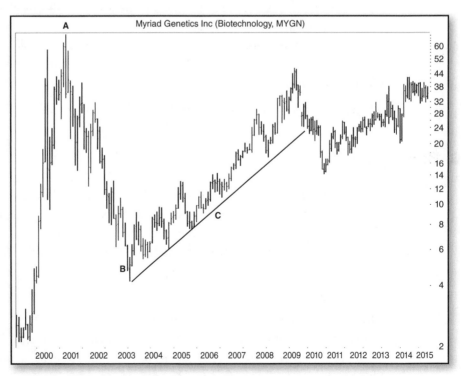

FIGURE 14.3   A price mountain leads to a straight-line run, monthly scale.

I drew trendline C to emphasize the recovery trend. In this case, the stock follows a straight-line run upward. The stock has not fully recovered from this price mountain yet (meaning the stock has not reached the price level of A).

Figure 14.4 shows three more examples of price mountains. The price mountains appear at the three peaks marked A. The following valleys (lowest close) appear at B. Trendlines C emphasize the straight-line recovery and the slope of the recovery.

■ The recovery appears V-shaped.

Recovery Time

Because the drop from a mountain peak to its recovery appears V-shaped (the vast majority of the time), I measured the time from peak to valley and from valley back up to the price of the following peak.

I found that the median drop (in Figure 14.1, this is the AB move) took 37 days (average was 115, or about 4 months) and the recovery (BC) took 42 days (average was 162, or about 5 months). The recovery is slower 60% of the time when compared to the drop from the peak to valley floor. The two values (37 and 42) do not add up to the median 92 days shown in the figure because of how the median is computed. The 92-day number is the median time for the combined drop and recovery.

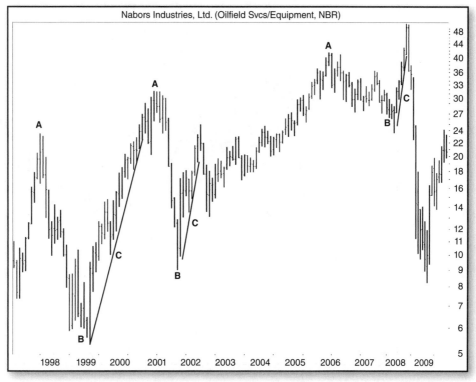

FIGURE 14.4 Three price mountains and their recovery. Monthly scale.

- Compute the time it takes price to drop from the mountain peak to the lowest close in the valley. Sixty percent of the time, the recovery will take longer than the result.

■ Trading Price Mountains

Figure 14.5 shows one of the rare exceptions to a sharp move higher (a V turn) after price reaches the valley. In this example, the price mountain is at A. Price drops to B at the lowest close and then follows trend C. Notice that the slope of the recovery is more horizontal than the other examples in this chapter.

After looking through many charts of price mountains, I noticed that the recovery is nearly always a straight-line run ... for a time. In some cases, the stock reaches about midway to the summit and then falters. The stock may retrace or it may move horizontally before beginning another push to the summit.

Figure 14.2 shows an example of this stair-step recovery. After price bottoms at B, the stock makes a strong move up (V-shaped, following the diagonal trendline). Then it goes horizontal, following trend C before resuming the uptrend. This horizontal move, of course, occurs well below the midpoint to the summit in this example.

FIGURE 14.5 A price mountain on the weekly chart with a more shallow recovery.

For trading (Figure 14.5, weekly chart), a trendline (D) drawn down from peak A, skirting the tops of price on the way down until *after* the stock bottoms (B), makes for a good entry signal. When the stock closes above the down-sloping trendline at E, buy the stock.

If you draw a trendline similar to D on the other charts in this chapter, it appears to work quite well as an entry signal. But it all depends on where the stock bottoms (B).

Figure 14.6 shows an example of how timing the entry can be difficult with price mountains.

The price mountain peaks at A and price finds the lowest close at the bar to the right of D. If you were to draw a trendline down from A, skirting price tops (monthly chart), it would cross price at about 61. The stock recovers to peak at C, about 82, for a potential gain of 34%. That gain occurs only if you trade the stock perfectly.

Look at the kind of gain you would have tasted if you bought the stock near the low at D. The stock climbed from ~34 (lowest close) to more than 190.

Tall price mountains are warnings that it could take years before a stock recovers, so do not buy a stock in anticipation of a complete recovery. Just because the stock once traded at nosebleed levels is no reason to believe it will do so again.

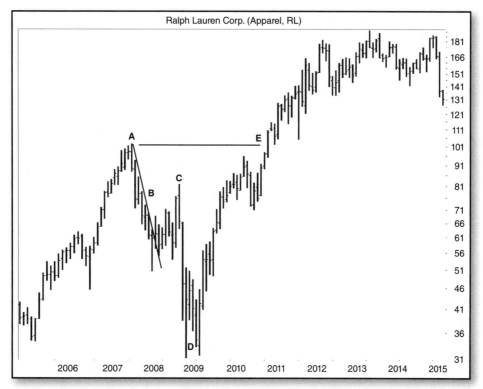

FIGURE 14.6   Down-sloping trendline B gives an entry signal, but not the ideal one.

However, there is potential for a large gain if you can time the bottom correctly. Trendlines drawn down from the mountain peak can assist in that timing. Try using the weekly scale for drawing those trendlines.

■ Closing Position

The novice investor or trader will look at a price mountain and say, "It reached that high before. I'm betting it can do it again." That prediction will likely come true, but it may not happen in your lifetime.

Use the information presented in this chapter to allow you to make an informed decision about trading a stock showing a price mountain. Otherwise, you may have parked your money in a stock that goes nowhere for years.

CHAPTER 15

Rectangles

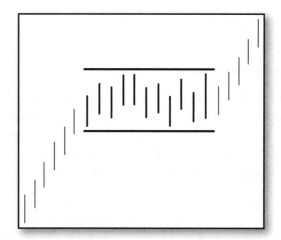

R ectangles are horizontal congestion regions that form between support and resistance. After moving sideways for a time, price eventually breaks out either upward or downward. Then what happens? This chapter answers that question.

Rectangles come in two varieties: tops and bottoms. To keep things simple and to boost the sample count (for the statistics), I stirred tops and bottoms together and just call the mixture *rectangles*.

Let us take a closer look.

Figure 15.1 shows rectangles with upward breakouts in the top half of the picture. Rectangles breakout upward almost twice as often as they breakout downward, 63% to 37%. After an upward breakout, the average rise is a massive 51%, but that is for perfect trades.

Before you reach for the paddles to restart your heart, the median rise is less, a paltry 30%. The median means half the patterns will show gains to the ultimate high greater than 30% and the other half will be wimps. Large gains can skew the average upward, so that is why there is such a large difference between the average and the median.

The bottom half of Figure 15.1 shows a rectangle with a downward breakout. Just over a third (37%) breakout downward.

The average drop from the breakout price to the ultimate low is a more sedate 16%. The median drop is 13%.

■ Rectangles break out upward 63% of the time.

Throwbacks and Pullbacks

Figure 15.2 shows a representation of two rectangles (thick lines); the top one has an upward breakout and the bottom one has a downward breakout.

When price breaks out upward, a stock showing a rectangle throws back to the breakout price 62% of the time. The stock must return to the breakout price (or come close to it) within a month; otherwise, it is just normal price movement.

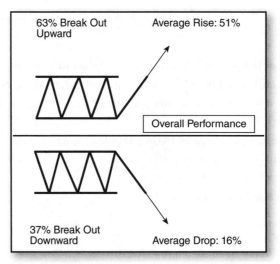

FIGURE 15.1 The overall performance of rectangles.

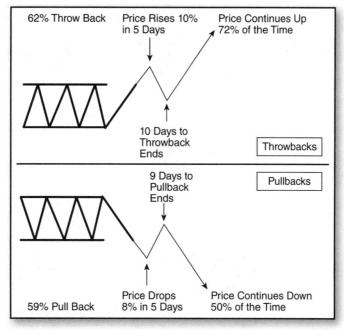

FIGURE 15.2   Throwbacks and pullbacks occur more than half the time.

Most times, however, a throwback occurs soon after the breakout. Price rises an average of 10% in 5 days immediately after the breakout. Then a retrace begins that returns price to the rectangle. The complete trip takes an average of 10 days. After a throwback completes, the stock resumes its upward march 72% of the time.

For downward breakouts, I call the price movement a pullback. Price breaks out of the rectangle by closing below the lower trendline. The move drops price an average of 8% in 5 days. Then a recovery occurs. The stock peaks in a total of 9 days after the breakout before resuming its downward run. Half (50%) will continue their downward move. Pullbacks occur 59% of the time.

■ Throwbacks occur 62% of the time and pullbacks happen 59% of the time.

Busted Tops

Sometimes price does not act as expected after a breakout. **Figure 15.3** shows the scenario.

To qualify as a busted upward breakout, price must rise less than 10% after an upward breakout and then dive to close below the bottom of the rectangle. I show this variation in the top half of the figure.

I found that 24% of rectangles bust an upward breakout. If they bust just once, the drop averages 23%. For a downward move after a chart pattern, that is a substantial

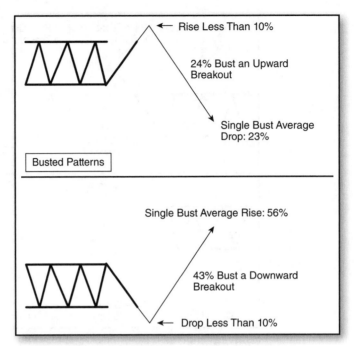

FIGURE 15.3   What happens after price busts a rectangle.

drop. In fact, a busted upward breakout sees a larger drop than if the rectangle just broke out downward (23% versus 16% drop, respectively).

Downward breakouts also bust as the lower half of the figure shows. Price breaks out downward and drops less than 10% before reversing and closing above the top of the chart pattern.

I found that a massive 43% bust a downward breakout. If you are considering shorting a downward breakout from a rectangle, then think again. The drop may not be as substantial as you hope.

Rectangles that single bust a downward breakout see price rise an average of 56%.

Rectangles can bust multiple times as price bounces from one side of the rectangle to the other before deciding on a direction of trend. I discuss single, double, and triple busted patterns later in this chapter or you can visit the glossary now for an explanation.

■ Price busts a rectangle after an upward breakout 24% of the time and busts a downward breakout 43% of the time.

■ Identification

Figure 15.4 shows an example of a rectangle on the daily scale.

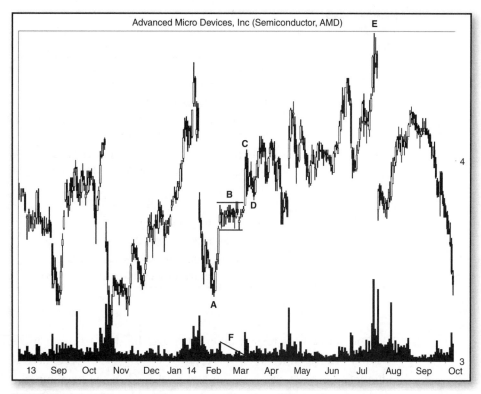

FIGURE 15.4   This rectangle has an upward breakout followed by a throwback.

Price begins its recovery at point A after a gut-retching decline from the January peak. Price moves up for about a week before the steep climb takes a rest. The stock moves sideways and forms a rectangle (B).

This rectangle is short, just over three weeks long. The stock makes its move again when it breaks out upward from the rectangle. This move mirrors the one leading to the rectangle—a straight-line advance to C.

Then the stock reverses and returns to the rectangle in a classic throwback, D. After that, the path to the ultimate high in mid July (E) is a bumpy one, but holding on until reaching the peak at E means capturing a 28% profit.

The volume trend is downward (F) as the chart shows, confirmed using linear regression from the start to the end of the rectangle. The receding volume trend is typical because it occurs 71% of the time.

The guidelines in **Table 15.1** will help with identification. Let us step through each one.

Price Trend. The rectangle shown in Figure 15.4 is a rectangle top because the inbound price trend (A to the bottom of rectangle B) is upward. If price were trending downward, the chart pattern would be a rectangle bottom.

TABLE 15.1	Identification Guidelines
Characteristic	**Discussion**
Price trend	Rectangle tops have price trending upward into the start of the chart pattern. Bottoms have price trending downward.
Horizontal movement	Price moves horizontally in rectangles, although a slight tilt is acceptable. You should be able to draw two nearly parallel trendlines bounding the tops and bottoms of the rectangle.
Touches	Look for at least five touches of the trendlines (three on one side and two on the other). Each touch should be a distinct minor high or minor low.
Length	The pattern is at least three weeks long. Shorter patterns are flags, but only if they rest on a flagpole.
Volume	Trends downward 71% of the time.
Breakout	A breakout, either up or down, occurs when price closes outside the top or bottom trendlines that confine the pattern.

Although each pattern is different, I use the short- to intermediate-term price trend to determine whether the rectangle is a top or bottom. There is a performance difference between the two, but as I explained in the beginning of this chapter, I combined the two and just called them rectangles.

Horizontal movement. Price moves horizontally, following two imaginary trendlines (shown in Figure 15.4 at B), which bound price action. Overhead resistance repulses price at the top. When the stock touches underlying support, it bounces upward. After a time, either support or resistance will give way and price will zoom off.

Touches. When looking for rectangles, I like to see at least three trendline touches of one side and two of the other, for a total of five. If you use only four touches (two of each trendline), you may be selecting bogus patterns.

The best rectangles use distinct minor highs and lows for each trendline touch.

Length. Rectangles are long, averaging 71 days (about 2.5 months). However, they can be short, too, but do not confuse them with flags. Flags sit on a flagpole and are less than 3 weeks long. Rectangles are often longer, but as you can see in Figure 15.4, they can sit on a flagpole, too (the AB move).

Volume. I used linear regression from the start of the rectangle to its end to verify that volume trends downward 71% of the time.

Breakout. Price breaks out upward when the stock closes above the top trendline. A downward breakout occurs when the stock closes below the bottom of the rectangle. Upward breakouts occur almost twice as often as downward ones.

■ Buy Setup 1

Figure 15.5 shows the first buy setup. Consider the inset first.

In this example, price rises from A to B, but the trend could be downward just as easily. The rectangle is at B, cleverly shown as a box. A downward breakout unfolds.

The decline to C is short, less than 10%. Then the trend reverses and price moves up. When it closes above the top of the rectangle at D, it busts the downward breakout. In the ideal situation, price continues to make a strong push higher.

The stock chart shows an example of how this plays out in real life. The rectangle is at B1. Price bounces between two imaginary boundaries, one on the top and the other on the bottom. Trendlines drawn connecting the peaks and valleys show that the stock touches the trendline several times each.

The stock breaks out downward by closing below the bottom of the rectangle. The drop to C1 is short, just 2% below the bottom of the pattern, before the stock reverses. Then the stock becomes a missile shot in a rapid ascent that just keeps going.

That is how this setup is supposed to work. Here is what to look for.

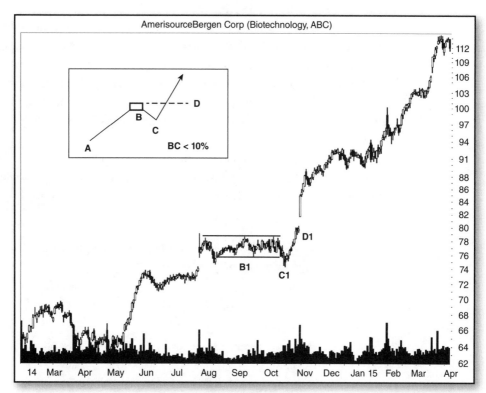

FIGURE 15.5   This rectangle busts the downward breakout and price makes a strong upward move.

1. Qualify the chart pattern using the identification guidelines shown in Table 15.1.
2. After the breakout, price should drop by no more than 10% below the bottom of the rectangle.
3. Price reverses and works its way higher to close above the top of the rectangle.
4. Buy at the open the next day or place a buy stop a penny above the top of the rectangle.

Table 15.2 shows some statistics for this setup that will help with trading.

I found 1,464 bull market rectangles in 787 stocks with the first pattern appearing in July 1991 and the most recent in April 2015. Not all stocks covered the entire period. Just 229 busted a downward breakout.

1. Of the 536 rectangles with downward breakouts, 43% of them failed to drop at least 10%. The stock then reversed direction and closed above the top of the rectangle, busting it.

2. The average rise after a stock busts a downward breakout is 38%. This includes all rectangles regardless of the number of busts (single, double, three or more).

3. If you look only at rectangles that single bust, the average rise is 56%. Do not expect your stock to rise by 56%. The number represents 150 perfect trades. The median gain is much less, 38%.

What does single, double, or triple bust mean? I counted the number of times a stock busted a rectangle. That means price moved in one direction less than 10% before reversing and closing outside the opposite side of the rectangle. If the stock then moved less than 10% and reversed to close outside the other side of the rectangle, that would be a double bust. The busting can continue in a similar manner, but I limited the count to three busts. A triple bust means it busted the rectangle at *least* three times.

For example, Figure 15.5 shows a single busted rectangle. Imagine that the stock reversed at D1 and kept going down at least 10% below B1. That would represent a double busted pattern. At D1, it would have busted the downward breakout for the

TABLE 15.2	Statistics for Busted Rectangles with Downward Breakouts
Description	**Result**
1. Percentage of rectangles that bust	43%
2. Average rise after busting	38%
3. Average rise after single bust	56%
4. Percentage of single busts	66%
5. Percentage of double busts	14%
6. Percentage of triple+ busts	20%

first time, and when it returned to below the price at B1, it would have busted the upward breakout (second bust).

This up-and-down motion can continue, as I said, until the stock determines a new trend direction and moves away from the pattern by at least 10%.

If this is still confusing, the glossary has a figure that shows the different busted variations.

4–6. Returning to Table 15.2, I did a frequency distribution of all busted rectangles to find out how many single, double, or triple busted. Most, 66%, were single busted rectangles, followed by three or more busts (20% of them) and the remainder busted twice (14%).

Let me emphasize that the frequency distribution only includes rectangles that bust. To put it another way, of the 43% of rectangles that bust, most of them are single busts. Your chance of having a double or triple bust is comparatively rare (34%).

■ Buy Setup 2

This setup is the same type of configuration that we have seen for many other chart patterns. Look at the inset of **Figure 15.6**.

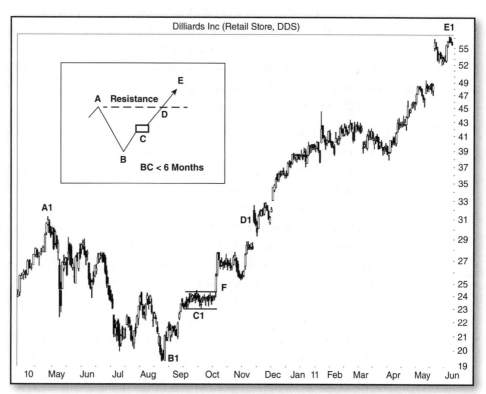

FIGURE 15.6 Price pierces overhead resistance, leading to a new high.

At A, price forms a peak. This could be a valley or some other type of overhead resistance. Avoiding overhead resistance is a key factor for good performance. If resistance is nearby and the stock pierces it without more overhead resistance getting in the way, the stock can continue higher easily. The stock may not double in price, but the numbers suggest the gain will be higher than if overhead resistance is a bully and blocks the way.

The stock drops to B where the trend starts climbing to the rectangle, C. To find the trend start, look for the lowest low before which price climbs by at least 20% or the highest high before which the stock drops by at least 20%. I only show a rise to the rectangle (BC), but it could be a drop, too.

Measure the time from the trend start to the start of the rectangle (the BC move). For the best post-breakout performance, look for a duration of less than six months.

Price breaks out upward and eventually climbs above overhead resistance (D) on the way to the ultimate high, E.

The figure shows an example of this setup on the daily stock chart. Because price enters the rectangle from the bottom, the trend start should be the lowest low before which price rises at least 20%. Price at A1 is at least 20% above the low at B1, so B1 is the trend start.

The rectangle appears at C1, which is a short-term move (about a month) from B1. Price breaks out upward from the rectangle at F. A buy stop placed a penny above the top trendline would get you into this breakout exactly on time.

E1 is not the ultimate high. The ultimate high occurred in July at 61 and change, for a gain of 156%. Also, peak A1 is not the end of overhead resistance. This stock climbed through a lot of overhead resistance and only peaked into all-time high territory when it neared the ultimate high.

Here are the steps for using this setup:

1. Qualify the rectangle using the identification guidelines from Table 15.1.
2. Find the trend start, the lowest low or highest high before which price rises or falls, respectively, at least 20%. Ignore any overshoot or undershoot price makes in the week or two before the start of the rectangle.
3. Select patterns in which the time from the trend start to the start of the rectangle is less than 6 months. This makes it more likely the rectangle appears near the start of the trend instead of near its end.
4. Look for overhead resistance. It is best if the stock is trading at or near all-time highs so it can push through any overhead resistance.
5. Place a buy order a penny above the top of the rectangle or buy at the open a day after price closes above the top trendline.
6. Once the order fills, place a stop a penny below the bottom of the rectangle or at a location of your choice.

Table 15.3 shows how two variations of this setup perform. This setup assumes price can push through overhead resistance on the way to the ultimate high. The table

TABLE 15.3	Statistical Analysis of Buy Setup 2	
Description	Inbound Trend ≤6 Months	Inbound Trend >6 Months
1. Occurrence, samples	21%, 178	8%, 69
2. Post-breakout average gain	98%	50%
3. Median gain	64%	30%
4. Gains over 25%	85%	58%
5. 5% failure rate	0%	7%
6. 10% failure rate	2%	23%

sorts performance into short and long inbound trends. The inbound trend measures from the trend start to the start of the rectangle (the B to C duration in Figure 15.6).

With additional samples, I believe the performance numbers listed in the table will come back down to earth.

1. Both short and long inbound trends have comparatively few samples (8% to 21%), but I wanted to show the large gains that result if you can find this setup.

2–4. The large move up after the breakout from this chart pattern is what caught my attention. Short inbound price trends do almost twice as well as those with trends longer than six months.

Short inbound trends show that 85% of them post gains more than 25%.

5, 6. I did not find any rectangles with gains less than 5%, and only 2% failed to climb at least 10%. Those findings are for short inbound price trends only. Failure rates are substantially higher for those with longer inbound price trends.

As good as the numbers are, they depend on price reaching all-time highs. Most of the time, overhead resistance will stop the upward move, leading to Buy Setup 3.

■ Buy Setup 3

Figure 15.7 shows Buy Setup 3 in the inset. This setup has a similar configuration to the prior setup except overhead resistance stops the advance.

Point A can be any type of overhead resistance, from peaks and valleys to round numbers to horizontal consolidation regions. Point B is the trend start. The stock, in this example, rises to the start of the chart pattern but it could have declined, too.

The rectangle appears at C. For the best performance, the time from the trend start (B) to the rectangle (C) should be less than 6 months. Short moves to the start of the rectangle suggest that the rectangle is closer to the start of a new trend than the end of it. That is the type of situation you are hoping to find.

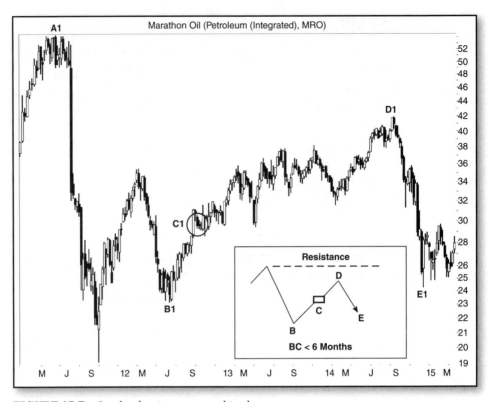

FIGURE 15.7 Overhead resistance stops this advance.

Unfortunately, the stock climbs but not very far (to D). It gets caught by overhead resistance, and the rise ends. After that, the stock drops by at least 20% below the ultimate high (E) or closes below the bottom of the rectangle.

The stock chart shows an example on the weekly scale. A knot of overhead resistance appears at A1 and downward along the winding path to B1, setup by prior price movements not shown on the chart.

B1 is the trend start leading to rectangle C1 (circled). Because we are on the weekly scale, the rectangle is impossible to see.

After the breakout, price rises to D1, the ultimate high where it bumps its head against overhead resistance. Then the stock dives off a cliff, splashing down at E1.

Here are the steps for trading this setup.

1. Qualify the rectangle using the identification guidelines listed in Table 15.1.
2. Find the trend start.
3. For best results, the time between the trend start and the start of the rectangle should be less than six months.
4. Look for overhead resistance. The farther away resistance is from the current price, the better.

TABLE 15.4   Statistical Analysis of Buy Setup 3

Description	Inbound Trend ≤6 Months	Inbound Trend >6 Months
1. Occurrence, samples	49%, 419	11%, 96
2. Post-breakout average gain	29%	18%
3. Median gain	19%	10%
4. Gains over 25%	43%	24%
5. 5% failure rate	14%	29%
6. 10% failure rate	29%	48%

5. Place a buy order a penny above the top of the rectangle.
6. Once the order fills, place a stop a penny below the bottom of the rectangle or at a location of your choice.

Table 15.4 lists the performance of this setup.

1. The short inbound trend configuration shown in Table 15.4 occurs most often of the four configurations discussed in Buy Setups 2 and 3. Almost half of the rectangles (49%) have an inbound trend less than or equal to 6 months long. They smack into overhead resistance that kills the advance.

2–4. As the table shows, performance suffers when overhead resistance gets in the way. For short inbound trends, the average post-breakout gain is just 29% with a 19% median. Gains over 25% number less than half of the trades: 43%.

The performance was worse for trades associated with longer inbound trends as the table shows.

5–6. Failure rates are high for both long and short inbound trends. They range from 14% to 48%. For inbound trends longer than 6 months, almost half (48%) will see price rise no higher than 10% before reversing or closing below the bottom of the rectangle.

■ To increase the chance of a good trade, select a rectangle with a short inbound price trend (from the trend start to the rectangle start) and avoid nearby overhead resistance.

■ Sell Setup

The first sell setup is the inverse of Buy Setup 1. Look at the inset of **Figure 15.8**.

On average, you will get better performance from a rectangle if the chart pattern acts as a reversal (using the location of the trend start to gauge the prevailing price

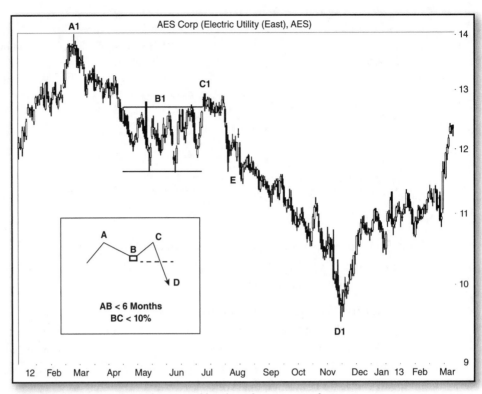

FIGURE 15.8 Price busts this upward breakout from a rectangle.

trend). In the figure, that means the AB trend (downward in this example, but it could be upward) is different from the BC trend (upward in this example).

The trend start is at A and price drops to B in less than six months for the best performance. Price forms a rectangle by traveling horizontally before breaking out upward in this configuration. The BC climb is less than 10% before the stock tumbles to close below the bottom of the rectangle. When that happens, it busts the upward breakout. The stock continues lower in the ideal case, to D, the ultimate low.

The stock chart shows an example of this configuration on the daily chart. The trend start is at peak A1 and price eases lower into the rectangle. This rectangle is not ideal because price has a difficult time touching the top trendline, but the horizontal movement is clear. The stock consolidates, as if marshaling its troops for the coming battle.

An upward breakout at C1 quickly fades, and price reverses after peaking. When the stock closes below the bottom of the rectangle at E, it busts the upward breakout. The drop from E to D1 (the ultimate low) is 18%.

Suppose you own a stock and are fearful of a massive drop. Here is what to look for in this setup.

1. A rectangle appears on your stock chart that obeys the identification guidelines outlined in Table 15.1.
2. The inbound price trend should be trending downward going into the top of the chart pattern (not entering it from the bottom). Ignore any overshoot or undershoot. The inbound trend direction means the pattern will act as a reversal and not a continuation pattern after an upward breakout. Reversals have better performance, on average.
3. The move from the trend start to the rectangle start should be less than six months. Larger post-breakout declines associate with short inbound trends.
4. Price enters the rectangle and breaks out upward but rises no more than 10%.
5. For those who wish to sell or sell short, place an order to sell a long holding a penny below the bottom of the rectangle.
6. The uptrend reverses and the stock busts the upward breakout when it closes below the bottom of the rectangle.
7. Look for underlying support where the stock might reverse. The farther below the rectangle, the larger the potential decline. Once you locate support, can you tolerate a drop to the support area? What happens if the stock punches through that support and moves to a lower support area? Can you stomach the larger loss? If you wish to tolerate such a decline, then hold onto the stock.

■ Shorting Tips

Here are some tips for shorting a stock:

- Declines will be larger, on average, if the stock acts as a reversal of the prevailing price trend, not a continuation. The busted decline averages 15% for reversals but only 10% for continuations. A reversal means the inbound price trend is downward (from trend start to rectangle start) and the breakout is upward.

- Short stocks making new lows, not those making new highs.

- Look for the industry trend to be weak also. Are other stocks in the same industry going down?

- Stocks without pullbacks tend to drop more than do those with pullbacks.

- Just 29% of rectangles with downward breakouts have declines 20% or more. That means 71% of the time, the stock will not make a big decline. These numbers are not specific to busted patterns, but to all rectangles with downward breakouts, whether they bust or not.

Table 15.5 lists performance statistics related to the sell setup.

TABLE 15.5 Statistics for Busted Rectangles with Upward Breakouts

Description	Result
1. Percentage of rectangles that bust	24%
2. Average drop after busting	13%
3. Average drop after single bust	23%
4. Percentage of single busts	44%
5. Percentage of double busts	30%
6. Percentage of triple+ busts	27%

1. I found 226 rectangles with upward breakouts that busted in bull markets. That represents 24% of the 928 rectangles I found.

2. The average decline after a stock busts is 13%. That includes all three types of busts (single, double, and three or more busts).

3. Looking at single busted stocks only, the decline from the bottom of the rectangle to the ultimate low averages 23%, which is quite good.

4–6. A frequency distribution of those stocks busting shows that 44% of them are single busts, 30% are double busts, and the remaining 27% bust at least three times.

To put it another way, if a stock busts, you have a 57% chance that it will bust multiple times. That is not reassuring. It suggests the stock has trouble trending after a rectangle breakout.

■ Best Stop Locations

Knowing where to place a stop-loss order is invaluable information. An incorrectly placed stop could take you out of a winning trade or subject you to a massive loss. **Table 15.6** shows how often price hits two stop locations for each breakout direction.

TABLE 15.6 Stop Locations for Rectangles

Description	Chance of Being Hit	Average Loss	Missed Trades, Gains/Losses
1. Penny below the pattern	4%	6%	38, 43%
2. Within the pattern	69%	3%	642, 51%
Up Breakouts Above, Down Breakouts Below			
3. Within the pattern	67%	2%	360, 16%
4. Penny above the pattern	3%	4%	17, 14%

1. Penny below the pattern. For upward breakouts, this stop location is a penny below the bottom of the rectangle. The chance of being hit is just 4%, resulting in an average loss of 6%. The trades you were stopped out of would have gone on to make a 43% average gain.

2. Within the pattern. For upward breakouts, price from the breakout to the ultimate high dipped back into the rectangle 69% of the time. A stop placed somewhere in the rectangle would take you out of 642 trades that went on to make 51%, leaving you holding a loss that averaged 3%.

3. Within the pattern. For downward breakouts, the stock bubbles back up to the rectangle and snags a stop-loss order placed there 67% of the time, saddling you with a loss of 2%. The stopped-out trades went on to make 16% (meaning they dropped 16% below the bottom of the rectangle).

4. Penny above the pattern. If you placed a stop-loss order a penny above the rectangle after a downward breakout, price would hit the stop 3% of the time. You would lose 4% and the stopped-out trades would drop 14% had you remained in them. Notice the low sample count (17 trades).

- For upward breakouts, place a stop-loss order a penny below the bottom of the rectangle. Check the potential loss from the buy price to the stop price to make sure it is not excessive.

- For downward breakouts, a stop-loss order placed above the top of the rectangle works best.

■ Configuration Trading

Many of the charts that follow have rectangles shown on the weekly scale. I found them on the daily chart, so they obey the identification guidelines from Table 15.1 even though they may not appear that way on the weekly scale.

To trade the following configurations, begin with these guidelines.

1. Find a rectangle on the *daily* chart that obeys the identification guidelines listed in Table 15.1.
2. Using the *weekly* scale, match what you see on your chart to one of the configurations. Figures 15.21 and 15.22 should help.
3. Buy at the open the day after the breakout or place an order to buy a penny above the top of the chart pattern (upward breakouts) or below the bottom of the pattern (downward breakouts).
4. Place a stop-loss order at a location of your choice.

I surveyed 76 rectangles on the weekly scale with large declines and found that 75% of them had the configuration shown in the inset of **Figure 15.9**. The results were dramatic enough to stop the survey.

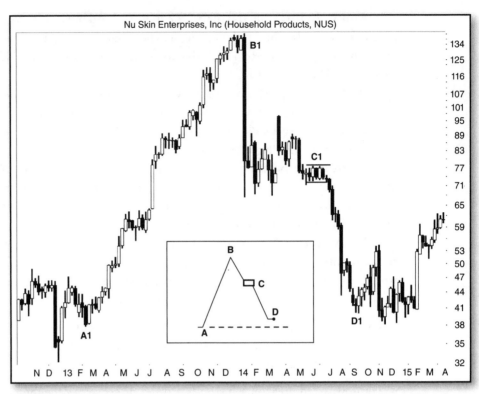

FIGURE 15.9 Price often returns to just above the launch price. Shown on the weekly scale.

The entire pattern from A to D looks like a small mountain. It may be one mountain in a range of mountains, or it can be one mountain rising from a horizontal plain. Price rises up one side of the mountain and falls back down on the other. Let us take a closer look.

Point A is what I call the launch price. It is where the price trend changes from down or horizontal to up. The move from A to B is a straight-line run, but it can pause along the way.

Price peaks at B and then the uptrend changes to down. Price falls, perhaps reluctantly, perhaps in a straight move down that reflects the move up. Along the way down, it pauses and forms a rectangle, C. The breakout from the rectangle is downward and price drops to D.

Notice that D is slightly above the launch price, A. Most of the time, the stock will remain above the launch price. I do not have a statistic to describe what "most of the time" means, but it is probably 66% or higher. In some cases, the stock pauses at or just above the launch price before dropping farther.

The stock chart shows an example on the weekly chart. The launch price is at A1 because that is where the stock changes from moving horizontally to a straight-line run up. The stock rises to B1 and then does a skydiving act. The stock lands on ledge C1, forming a rectangle there.

The breakout from this rectangle is downward and price makes another freefall to D1. D1 is where the stock bounces, eventually settling on the bottom. Notice that D1 is slightly above the launch price, A1.

On the weekly scale, at least, this straight-line move up followed by a near-return to the launch price represents how large losses occur after a downward breakout from a rectangle.

- Price often stops above the launch price after a straight-line advance and a bumpy decline.

Downward Breakout Success

Figure 15.10 shows the configuration in the inset of 21% of rectangles that lead to large declines.

The AB decline is often, but not always, extensive, both in time (years) and percentage. A long decline is a surprise for bottom-fishers who expect the rectangle to act as a reversal that stops the decline. However, in this configuration, the decline continues after a downward breakout.

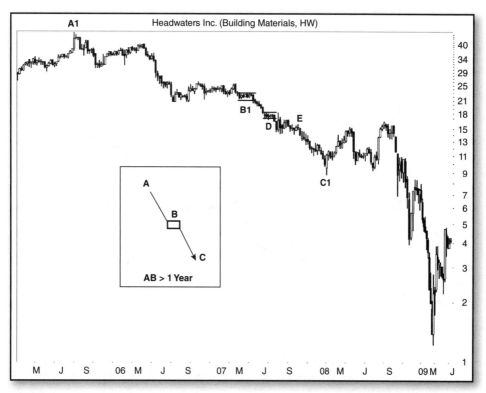

FIGURE 15.10   Price drops going into a bear market, forming two rectangles along the way.

Consider the ideal setup shown in the inset. Price drops from A to B, frequently taking at least a year to reach the rectangle. After a downward breakout, price resumes tumbling.

The stock chart shows an example. The primary trend peaks at A1 and begins its reluctant slide down to the rectangle, at B1. This one breaks out downward (weekly scale) but soon forms another rectangle, D.

A bear market begins at E, which supports the bearish move in the stock. Although the primary trend continues below $2, the ultimate low appears at C1. After C1, the stock bounces upward by at least 20%, ending the search for the ultimate low.

To trade this configuration, make sure that underlying support is far away and weak before taking a position. Of course, a slide into a bear market is helpful.

Downward Breakout Failure

Figure 15.11 shows the configuration for small losses, which is a failure of the stock to drop much after a downward breakout.

The inset shows the configuration. Price trends upward for several months, sometimes years, from A and rising into rectangle B. The breakout from the rectangle takes price down to C where it faces a stiff upwind that retards the decline. The stock turns and heads higher to D, often busting the downward breakout.

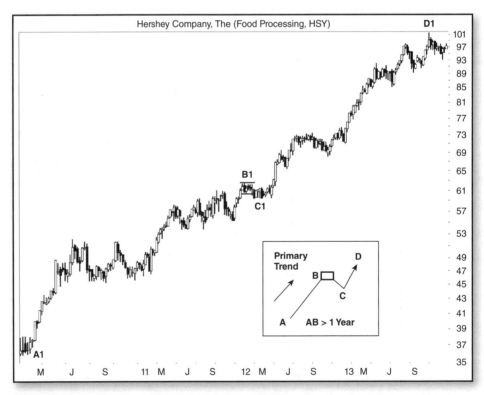

FIGURE 15.11   In an upward price trend, the stock fails to drop far after a downward breakout.

This configuration often happens in a strong move higher that can last for years. Price regroups during formation of the rectangle and its appearance may coincide with a retrace of the uptrend. But the downward breakout fails quickly and price rejoins the primary move higher.

The stock chart shows an example of this configuration. Price moves steadily higher from A1 going into the rectangle at B1 (weekly scale so the rectangle is difficult to see). The breakout is downward to C1 where the stock finds support.

The decline is meager considering the price of the stock. It is as if the stock thumbs its nose at traders, handing those that shorted the stock a loss when price rises. The rise takes the stock up to D1.

Of the 103 rectangles I looked at with small losses, 64% of them had the configuration shown in Figure 15.11.

■ Downward breakouts in strong primary uptrends lead to small losses.

Upward Breakout Success

I surveyed 110 rectangles with upward breakouts and large post-breakout gains (more than 10%) in a bull market. I found that 73% of them followed the configuration shown by the inset of **Figure 15.12**.

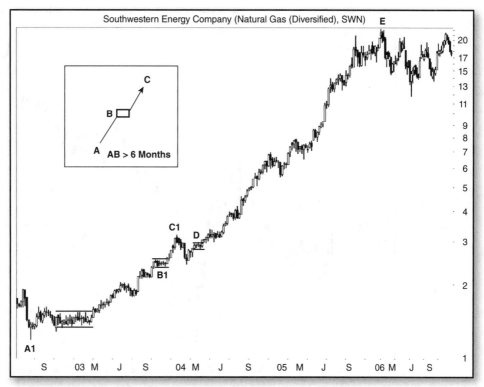

FIGURE 15.12   After upward breakouts from three rectangles, the stock soars.

The AB move is long term (over 6 months) but not always. Rectangle B appears, which has an upward breakout. That breakout sends price higher, to C.

The stock chart shows an example of this configuration at rectangles B1 and D (weekly scale).

The primary uptrend begins at A1 and rises to the rectangle at B1. The stock breaks out upward and climbs just 26% before hitting the ultimate high at C1 and running into turbulence.

The rectangle at D shares the same primary uptrend. In this case, the upward breakout from the stock sees the shares rise 600% to E. That is a nice return.

V-Shaped Success

Figure 15.13 shows a different configuration. The AB move sees price make a short run (less than 6 months) down into the top of the rectangle. Price moves horizontally (B) for a time before staging an upward breakout and climbing to C. This V-shaped turn happens 27% of the time in the rectangles with large post-breakout moves I looked at.

The stock chart shows a good example of this type of turn. Price starts to drop at A1 and creates rectangle B1 (weekly scale). The breakout from this fast drop is a

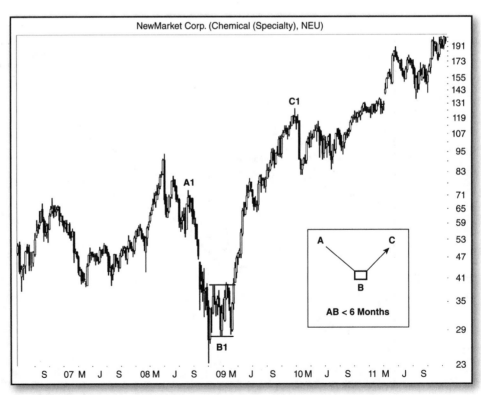

FIGURE 15.13   This V-shaped configuration results in a large move upward.

rebound just as swift. The stock returns to the price level of A1 (the launch price) and then slows its climb to C1, the ultimate high.

In this example, the rectangle broke out upward just as the 2007 to 2009 bear market ended. Buying enthusiasm helped push the stock higher.

If you can determine when a bear market ended (you can use a 20% rise from a low price in the indices), even if you are late, buy stocks. You can make an obscene amount of money when the tide changes.

Upward Breakout Failure

I surveyed 143 rectangles with upward breakouts and small gains (less than 10%). The three configurations I found split almost evenly for occurrence. The first one, shown in **Figure 15.14**, happened most often, 36% of the time.

The inset shows the setup. The AB move represents the primary trend and is often long term (more than six months) as price rises to form rectangle B. The primary trend is strong enough that the rectangle breaks out upward, but that is when the uptrend dies. The move above the top of the rectangle (C) is small, often 5% to 10%, before the stock reverses.

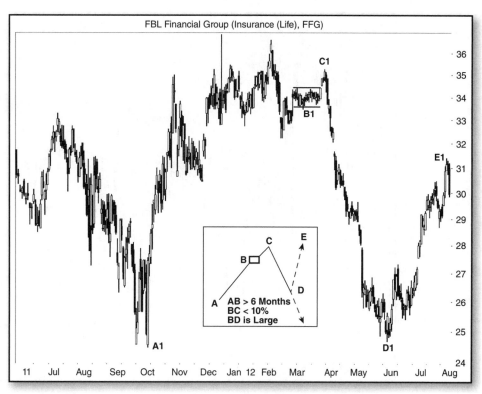

FIGURE 15.14   The upward breakout from this rectangle is short-lived.

About half the time, the stock continues down to D and beyond, leaving behind a rectangle that marks the end of an uphill run. The other half of the time, the stock after C makes a substantial decline before recovering and resuming the primary trend (E).

The daily stock chart shows an example. The primary trend begins at A1 by moving higher. At B1, a small rectangle forms with uneven tops and bottoms. Price breaks out upward and rises a smidgen (2%) to C1 before reversing. The uptrend ends and sees price drop 26% below the bottom of the rectangle before landing on solid ground at D1.

Those buying the stock long on the upward breakout likely suffered a loss when their stops triggered on the way to D1. Those who expected a large decline and shorted the stock were in for a fun ride as the stock plummeted.

Notice how the stock returned (D1) to the launch price (A1). The launch price can be a handy target.

Continuation Pattern

Figure 15.15 is similar to the prior configuration except for the BD drop. The BD drop measures the decline below the bottom of the rectangle.

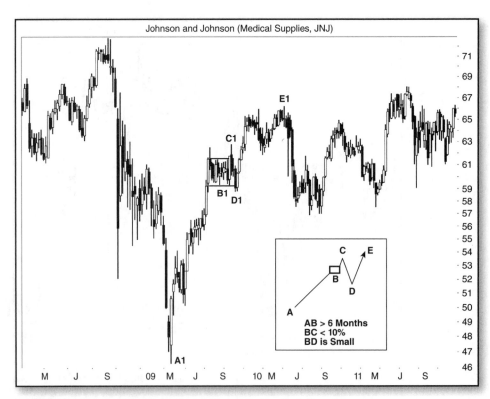

FIGURE 15.15   A double busted rectangle sees price climb for a time.

In Figure 15.14 (the prior figure), the BD drop is large, but in this configuration, it is small. Small in this case often means 5% to 10%.

In the prior setup, the rectangle often appeared at the top of an uptrend, signaling an end to the upward run (or shortly after the rectangle appeared). In the inset shown in Figure 15.15, price recovers after the short decline to D.

This configuration appeared 31% of the time in the stocks I looked at.

The weekly stock chart shows an example of this situation. Price rises from A1 to B1 where the rectangle forms. Price breaks out upward from the rectangle and advances to C1, but quickly reverses. When the stock closes below the bottom of the rectangle (D1), it busts the upward breakout (although all of these whips may be hard to see on the weekly chart).

In this example, the stock zips up to E1, busting the downward move, too, for a double bust. Since the rise to peak E1 is less than 10% above the top of the stock, the security is not finished busting the rectangle. Price drops and closes below the bottom of the rectangle, busting it for the third time.

Notice how the rectangle is part of the trend from A1 to E1. In the prior setup, the rectangle ended the primary uptrend. Whether the rectangle acts as a continuation or reversal of the primary uptrend is the major difference between this configuration and the prior one.

Downtrend Retrace

Figure 15.16 shows the last of the three small upward breakout variations. This configuration occurred 32% of the time.

In this variation, the stock trends downward from A to B, often in a short-term move. Be flexible with the duration of the inbound trend, but it is often less than six months long.

Rectangle B has an upward breakout and price rises to C before the primary trends' current pulls the stock down. It busts the upward breakout and price drops to D, often making a substantial decline.

The stock chart shows an example of this setup. Price peaks at A1 and drops quickly before moving horizontally and forming a rectangle (weekly scale) at B1. The breakout (not shown on the weekly chart) is upward when the stock closes above the top of the rectangle and moves higher to C1. Then the stock reverses and eventually makes its way down to D1.

This is another example of a triple busted rectangle. The upward breakout busts when price closes below the bottom of the rectangle on the way to F, then busts again on the rise to E, followed by the last bust on the way to D1. Imagine a trading trying to play each of those directions and being stopped out for a loss. Wow.

This stock chart also shows price bottoming at D1 just above the launch price in March 2009 (the valley on the left side of the chart). Of course, the stock makes a new low near 14 but not before a significant retrace (the move up to about 24 after D1).

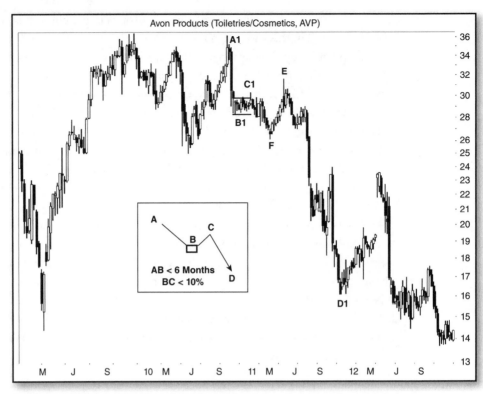

FIGURE 15.16 A rectangle with an upward breakout appears in a downtrend.

■ Measure Rule

The measure rule for rectangles follows the same theme as it does for other chart patterns. Use it to help predict a price target.

Figure 15.17 gives an example. The rectangle appears as the two horizontal lines AB. The top of the rectangle (B) is at 44.22 and the bottom (A) is at 41.89. That gives a height of 2.33 (the difference between the two numbers). Add the height to the top of the rectangle (B) for upward breakouts and subtract it from the bottom of the rectangle (A) for downward breakouts.

For example, the upward target would be 44.22 + 2.33, or 46.55. Upward breakouts in a bull market reach their target 83% of the time. If you divide the height in half and use that in the computation, it creates a closer target that the stock reaches an average of 96% of the time.

Similarly, the downward breakout target would be 41.89 − 2.33, or 39.56, based on the full height of the rectangle. This method works 61% of the time for downward breakouts. Using half the height works better, 89% of the time.

As the numbers suggest, price will not reach the target every time, but it does give an indication of how well the method works. To help improve the accuracy,

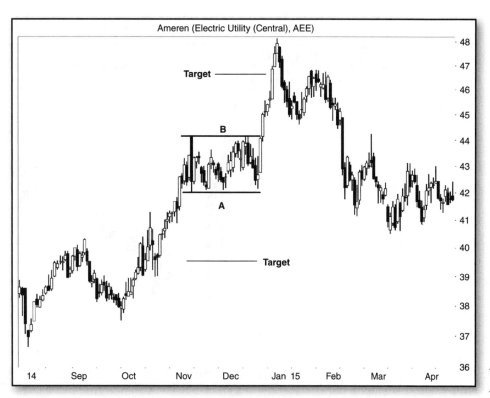

FIGURE 15.17 Use the height of a rectangle to predict price targets.

look for nearby overhead resistance or underlying support where the stock might reverse.

■ The measure rule works 83% of the time for upward breakouts and 61% of the time for downward breakouts.

■ Trading

How would you trade a rectangle? Besides "carefully," the answer depends on what type of trader you are.

Consider **Figure 15.18**, shown on the monthly chart. Ameren is an electric utility that pays a dividend of 3.7% at the breakout price of $44.22 (the top of the rectangle at C).

Buy and Hold

If you are looking for income instead of capital gains, then a utility stock might be a winning lottery ticket. However, if you are looking for utility stocks to outperform

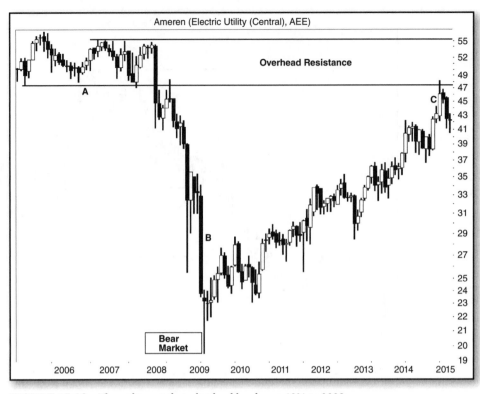

FIGURE 15.18 The utility cut their dividend by almost 40% in 2009.

most other issues, then reconsider. Often utility stocks are stodgy plodders that pay a nice dividend but are not moon shots.

You can make money in utility stocks, of course. In 2014, the Dow utilities were the best-performing index, gaining 26% for the year. That handily beat the Dow Industrials (7.5%), S&P 500 Index (11.4%), and NASDAQ Composite (13.4%).

I buy and hold electric utility stocks. When price drops far enough to give me a 5% dividend, I check the fundamentals to make sure the dividend is safe and buy the stock, often holding it for years. I just let the stock move up and down while I collect the dividend. If I need money, I sell those near the top of the chart, taking advantage of capital appreciation and the dividend, with the belief that the stock is more likely to decline than rise much farther.

Let us return to the monthly chart shown in Figure 15.18. As the bear market of 2007 to 2009 unfolded, many stocks took a hit, including electric utility stocks like Ameren. This one dropped more than half from 48 to below 20 in just over a year.

At B, the company cut its dividend by almost 40%, which helped power the stock into the ground.

Fundamentals are a better way to determine the health of a utility stock than depending on a rectangle for guidance. The effect of most rectangles is short term. The average downward breakout takes 43 days (about 1.5 months) before price bottoms, but the median drop is just 18 days. The average decline is just 16%, which is nothing for a buy-and-hold person to worry about, unless, of course, you need the money.

Position Trading

Position traders (by my definition) are people who buy and hold a stock until the trend changes. A trend change is a 20% swing in the stock. I use that gauge as applied to stocks just as the professionals use it to gauge the market swing from bull to bear and bear to bull.

A 20% drop from a peak is a bear market. Similarly, a 20% rise off a low means the bear market has ended and a bull market has begun.

How can rectangles help position traders? A look at the statistics provides a clue. If a 20% drop represents bad news for position traders, then about 1 in 4 (29%) rectangle trades will run into trouble. The 29% number is a count of how many stocks drop at least 20% after a downward breakout from a rectangle.

The appearance of a bearish rectangle is a cause for concern. Look for underlying support to help determine how far price will drop. Use the measure rule for the rectangle as I already discussed. Take the height of the rectangle and turn it into a percentage.

For the example in Figure 15.17, the height of the rectangle is 2.33 and the bottom of it is 41.89 (the breakout price) for a potential decline of 2.33 ÷ 41.89, or 6%. Even if the stock were to drop twice or even three times as much, it would still not represent a trend change. But anything can happen. Conduct any additional checks (like look at the fundamentals, search for underlying support, and so on) to determine whether a downward breakout is a cause for concern or not.

Swing Traders

Swing traders buy a stock when it is low and sell when it is high, or the reverse, catching the high to low swing.

Rectangles are made for swingers.

Let us use Ameren as a trading example. Look first at the monthly chart, Figure 15.18. The stock moved sideways in a tall trading range for years (until 2008) before the bear market knocked it down. The sharp drop took about a year, but look at how long the recovery took. Six years. Wow.

At C, a rectangle appears, although you cannot see it on this chart. After an upward breakout from the rectangle, how far would you expect the stock to climb?

My answer: Not far. I think the stock would hit overhead resistance near 48 (A) and struggle from there. If you were lucky, you might see price boil to the top end of the range, about 55.

Let us flip to the daily chart, **Figure 15.19**, which is the same chart as Figure 15.17.

The chart shows a rectangle (C) that breaks out upward. But what if it had a downward breakout? How far could price drop?

FIGURE 15.19 An upward breakout from a rectangle takes price up to overhead resistance where the stock reverses.

Using the measure rule for rectangles, we already calculated that the target would be 39.56 (the height of the rectangle subtracted from the bottom of it). I show the approximate location on the chart.

Notice that it is close to the congestion area B. B also represents a launch price, where a straight-line run up to the rectangle begins. So 39.50 represents a good downward breakout target.

If the stock continues lower, I would expect it to reach A, another launch price. Point A is where a small measured move up begins. The first leg is A to B1. B1 to B represents the corrective phase. The second leg kicks the stock up to the rectangle, C.

Because price often retraces after the measured move ends, that means a retrace back to the corrective phase B1-B.

For a downward target, B would be my first choice followed by A.

What about an upward target?

The appearance of rectangle C, after the nearly straight-line run up from A, looks like a larger measured move up. AC would be the first leg and rectangle C is the corrective phase. An upward breakout could carry the stock a distance similar to the AC rise.

The AC rise starts with the low at A (37.53) to the top of the rectangle (C, 44.22), or 6.69. If the stock rises the same amount after an upward breakout, it would mean a target of 48.84 (the bottom of the rectangle, 42.15, plus 6.69). The calculation follows the measure rule for measured moves up.

However, we know that measured moves work just 42% of the time when using the full height. Let us use 60% of the height to boost the prediction's success rate to over 90%. That would give a closer target of 60% × 6.69 + 42.15, or 46.16.

We already used the measure rule for rectangles to get a price target of 46.55. I show the two targets on the chart. Notice how close together they are. Because we also know that 48 begins overhead resistance (from Figure 15.18), that could be our upper target. Price could rise further, of course.

Because I dislike shorting a stock, I would place a buy stop a penny above the top of the rectangle to get into the swing trade as soon as price broke out upward.

That would get me into the stock at 44.23.

At D, I would see that three days have elapsed since the stock started climbing end over end. The vertical run up suggests a strong move upward. As a swing trader, one easy way to capture a vertical run is to place a stop-loss order a penny below the prior day's low as price climbs. Then trail the stop upward.

I show the initial stop location on the chart. As price made a higher low each day, I would raise the stop to a penny below the prior day's low, never lowering it, until the stop triggered.

At E, when the stock retraced, it would take me out at 47.51 for a gain of 3.28, or 7%, in 8 trading days.

After the stock peaked at E, it threw back to F and later formed a symmetrical triangle at G.

Day Traders

All of the setups and variations I looked at used daily price data. Intraday setups are difficult to find because of the lack of historical intraday data and the tedious nature of finding chart patterns. I like to trade using the daily charts, not day trade.

As such, the findings in this chapter may or may not work intraday, or they may work on some time scales and not others (for example, there may be too much noise on the 1-minute scale, which is why I prefer the 5-minute scale for day trading).

Clearly, pullbacks and throwbacks still occur on the intraday charts, as do busted patterns. What can take months on the daily charts can play out in a single afternoon for day traders.

My advice to day traders is to use the ideas presented here and tailor them to your trading style. My belief is that doing so will make you a better, more profitable, trader.

Actual Trade

Figure 15.20 shows an actual trade I made using a rectangle top. I show the rectangle on the daily chart between two horizontal lines at A.

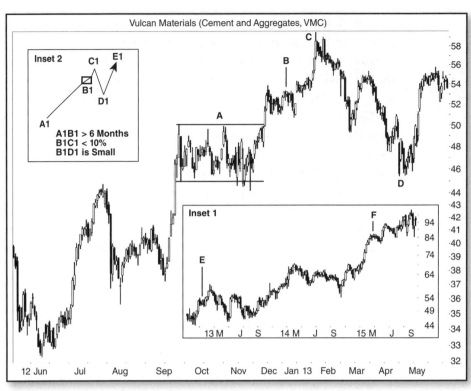

FIGURE 15.20 A throwback to a rectangle triggers a trade just before the stock drops.

I expected the throwback (because of general market weakness) to reach the top of the stock, so I waited for that to happen. When it became clear that it would not happen, I bought the stock and received a fill at 52.71 (B).

The stock reached the ultimate high at C and dropped more than 20%, to D.

My target was 66 and then 80. I thought it was clear to 66 but a longer-term chart (not shown) also shows that 60 (C) began overhead resistance that I did not see.

I placed a stop-loss order at 44, below the bottom of the rectangle. That order did not trigger since the stock never dropped that far (it came close at D).

Inset 1 shows a weekly chart. E is where I bought and F is where I sold the stock.

Here is what I wrote about the sale: "3/1/15. I placed a stop order to sell at 81. This is above my 80 target and the stock has been going vertical. The last time this happened, it dropped from 69 to 54, and this is more vertical. S&P rates this a 1 (strong sell) saying that it is overvalued."

The next day, I raised the stop to 82 and trailed it higher over the next few days to 83 and 84. On March 10, the stop at 84 triggered and filled at 83.31: "Had a tight trailing stop in place to get me out at 84, but this gapped open lower and took me out. Ouch. Talk about slippage. This has gone vertical for too long and it is overbought. Time to take profit and walk away."

I made 59% on the trade with a hold time of just over 2 years.

As the chart shows, the stock continued higher, reaching almost 107 (so far) but with increased volatility.

Application   I bought after the throwback and sold well above the ultimate high, but the following analysis assumes I bought a penny above the top of the rectangle (50) and sold at the ultimate high (C in Figure 15.20, 59.48).

Starting from the bull market peak in April 2007 at 128.62, the stock dropped to a low of 25.06 in October 2011, well after the bear market of 2007 to 2009 ended. The rectangle appeared a year later in the high 40s.

The V-shaped turn resembles Figure 15.7 with overhead resistance sitting above the stock. In this case, however, the move up from the low at 25 was a long-term one (taking over a year), but the figure shows it should be less than 6 months. Thus, the figure was not an ideal fit with this situation.

Figure 15.12 shows the stock making a long-term upward run leading to the start of the rectangle with a large move post-breakout. With overhead resistance sitting at 66—or so I thought—and the rectangle top at 50, the potential gain from the trade was 32% if I traded it perfectly. This figure applies to my situation, and it occurs 73% of the time.

Figures 15.14 and 15.15 warned of a potential failed trade. Both have long-term rises leading to the start of the rectangle with an upward breakout. Not shown in those figures is overhead resistance, but that is the cause of their short advance after the breakout. Both configurations occur about a third of the time.

If I bought the stock a penny above the rectangle's top (50) and sold it at the actual ultimate high (59.48), I would make 19%. That rise is more than the maximum 10% rise shown in Figures 15.14 and 15.15 but less than Figure 15.12 implies.

Inset 2 in Figure 15.20 shows the model (from Figure 15.15) that applies to this trade, but the fit was not perfect. After reaching the ultimate high (C1), the stock dropped (to D1) but not as far as the inset shows. The stock actually remained just above the bottom of the rectangle before recovering (that is, D1 remained above B1). I rode the recovery from D1 to E1 and turned a potential small win into a 59% victory.

■ Closing Position

It is rare that price lines sideways, caught between support and resistance. That sideways move, if it lasts long enough, is called a rectangle.

Almost two-thirds of the rectangles will break out upward and post an outstanding gain averaging 51% (for perfect trades without commissions or fees deducted). In 62% of the cases, price will throwback. A throwback could send price closing below the bottom of the rectangle. That happens 28% of the time.

Use the setups and configurations to help determine how price will move after the breakout. My guess is that they can help you improve your trading results. If so, alert the media and tell them Tom sent you.

Setup Synopsis

Figure 15.21 may help you identify the various types of trading setups. See the associated figure for an explanation.

"Occurs" in the figures means how often I found the configuration in the stocks I looked at. If two configurations apply to your situation, then the one with a more frequent occurrence (a higher percentage) is the one you should choose to follow.

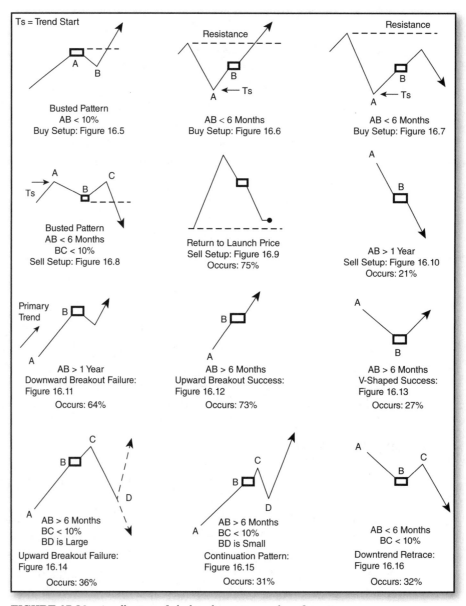

FIGURE 15.21 A collection of ideal trading setups and configurations.

CHAPTER 16

Reversals and Continuations

Here is a simple quiz. Which type of chart pattern performs better after an upward breakout, one that acts as a reversal of the trend or one that acts as a continuation?

My guess is that most people knowledgeable with technical analysis will say continuations outperform reversals. If price is rising into a chart pattern that breaks out upward, the stock stands a better chance of outperforming a chart pattern in which price trends downward into the chart pattern and breaks out upward. It is as if price is flowing *with* the existing current in a continuation, not against it as in a reversal.

Answer: Reversals outperform continuation patterns. How can this be?

Let me ask the first question in a different way. How many of you have trading setups with a rule that says something like, "If the stock is above its 200-day moving average, then buy"?

The thinking here is that if price is trending higher, you stand a better chance of making money. When I tested the same scenario with the 50-day and 200-day moving averages (by themselves, not in combination), I find that post-breakout performance is best if price is *below* the moving average the day before the breakout, not above it. Go figure.

Let me explain.

■ Behavior at a Glance

Figure 16.1 shows a picture of the four variations of upward and downward breakouts for chart patterns that act as reversals and continuations. The little box represents the chart pattern (the patterns studied in this book).

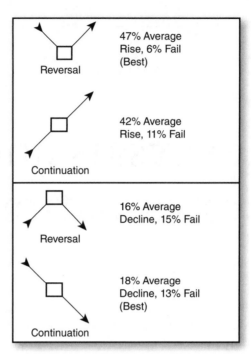

FIGURE 16.1 The average performance of chart patterns that act as reversals and continuations, for up and down breakouts.

For example, the top pattern is a reversal because price is trending downward going into the chart pattern (from a year ago) and exits out the top. Chart patterns with a downward to upward reversal configuration showed post-breakout gains averaging 47%.

The second pattern from the top shows what a continuation pattern looks like. Price rises into the chart pattern (from a year ago) and breaks out upward. Patterns with that combination showed gains that averaged 42%.

Downward breakouts show the opposite results. Patterns that act as continuations of the primary trend see price drop an average of 18% compared to 16% for reversals.

■ The Numbers

Table 16.1 shows the performance of the various combinations of primary trend and breakout direction shown in Figure 16.1. The primary trend measures from the start of the chart pattern to one year before.

TABLE 16.1	Performance of Reversal and Continuation Patterns	
Characteristic	Reversals	Continuations
1. Samples	4,006	5,049
2. Average rise	47%	42%
3. 5% failures	6%	11%
4. 10% failures	18%	26%
Upward breakouts above, downward breakouts below		
5. Samples	5,319	1,977
6. Average decline	16%	18%
7. 5% failures	15%	13%
8. 10% failures	38%	34%

1. I looked at 1,253 stocks and found 4,006 reversals and 5,049 continuation patterns with upward breakouts in bull markets. Not all stocks covered the range from May 1988 to July 2015 that I used in the test.

2. The average rise measures from the low price on the day of the breakout (to minimize any breakout day gap) to the ultimate high, which is the highest high before a trend change or before the stock closes below the bottom of the chart pattern (where it would be stopped out).

As the table shows, patterns with upward breakouts that act as reversals of the primary trend outperform continuations.

3, 4. Just 6% of reversals have chart patterns that fail to see price rise more than 5%. However, the 10% failure rate is double to triple the 5% rate.

5. This shows the number of samples for downward breakouts in bull markets.

6. As the table shows, the results are not as startling as for upward breakouts. The average decline was similar, 16% to 18% for reversal and continuation patterns, respectively. Notice that this time, continuations outperformed reversals.

7, 8. The failure rates for downward breakouts were high, from 13% to 38% with the worst performance coming from reversals.

Variations

Figure 16.1 shows four variations based on the primary trend and the breakout direction. The following variations add a third measure, the price trend from the trend start. Let me explain.

The primary trend is a simple measure. Find the first touch of a trendline in the chart pattern, often at a minor high or minor low (that is, find the start of the chart pattern). Compare the closing price of that touch with the close a year earlier. If the year-ago price is higher, then the primary trend is downward. A lower year-ago price means the primary trend is upward leading to the start of the chart pattern. Yes, this definition is important.

Compare that definition to the price trend from the trend start. From the start of the chart pattern, find the highest high or lowest low before which price drops or rises by at least 20%, respectively. Once you have that point, you can determine the price trend that leads to the start of the chart pattern. Often it is a shorter-term trend.

The following variations use the definitions for the trend start and primary trend.

The top half of **Figure 16.2** shows variations for upward breakouts. The upper left image has price trending higher for a year leading to the start of the chart pattern (P, the primary trend is upward). With an upward breakout, the pattern acts as a continuation of the primary trend.

However, the shorter-term trend (Ts, the trend start) is downward, meaning the chart pattern (box) acts as a reversal after an upward breakout. This mix of trend continuation and reversal shows a 43% average rise for chart patterns with that combination.

The best-performing variation (second illustration from the upper left) for upward breakouts shows both the primary trend and trend from the trend start falling into the start of the chart pattern. The chart pattern acts as a reversal of both downtrends, sending price upward an average of 48% after the breakout.

The worst-performing pattern is when the primary trend and trend start head upward leading to the start of the chart pattern. Patterns following that behavior act as continuations and they see an average rise of 40%.

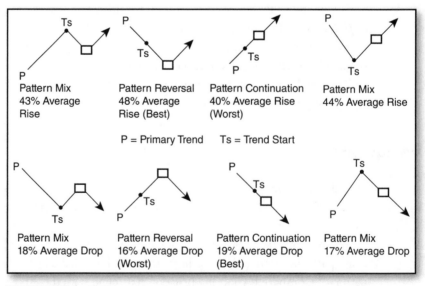

FIGURE 16.2   Eight variations based on the primary trend and trend start.

The top right illustration shows the performance of chart patterns when the trends are mixed: the primary trend is a reversal but the trend start is a continuation. The resulting average gain is 44% (second best).

Downward breakouts (the bottom four variations) show performance statistics that are closer to one another. The best variation occurs when price trends downward (primary trend and trend from the trend start) into the chart pattern. Price drops an average of 19% after the downward breakout.

The worst-performing pattern occurs when both the primary trend and trend start are climbing into the chart pattern. The chart pattern acts as a reversal, sending price lower an average of 16% before encountering a trend change.

■ Trading

Before I discuss trading, the trends displayed in Figures 16.1 and 16.2 agree. In other words, upward breakouts show reversals outperforming; downward breakouts show continuations doing best, in both figures. The numbers are different because they measure different components, but the conclusions are the same.

Figure 16.1 is like saying you have a headache. Figure 16.2 looks closer, determining whether a hammer or a migraine caused the headache.

For trading upward breakouts from chart patterns, look for chart patterns that act as a reversal of the declining primary (from a year ago) and secondary (find the trend start) price trends. That combination of inbound price trends leads to the best-performing chart patterns.

For downward breakouts, the results flip with the primary and secondary trends both moving lower for the best performance.

Table 16.2 shows results you may find helpful. The information is the same as that shown in Figure 16.2.

TABLE 16.2 Combinations of Primary and Secondary Trends versus Performance

Breakout Direction	Primary Trend	Trend from Trend Start	Performance	5% Failures	10% Failures	Rank
Up	Up	Up	40%	14%	30%	4 Worst
Up	Up	Down	43%	8%	22%	3
Up	Down	Up	44%	7%	19%	2
Up	Down	Down	48%	6%	17%	1 Best
Down	Up	Up	16%	15%	38%	4 Worst
Down	Up	Down	17%	15%	39%	3
Down	Down	Up	18%	13%	35%	2
Down	Down	Down	19%	12%	32%	1 Best

The failure rate is a count of how often chart patterns fail to see price move more than 5% or 10% in the direction of the breakout.

For example, the worst-performing configuration with downward breakouts (bottom half of table, first row) shows that 15% of chart patterns fail to see price drop more than 5%, and 38% fail to see price drop more than 10% after the breakout.

Trading Example

Figure 16.3 shows an example of a double bottom at CD. Price confirms the chart pattern as valid when it closes above the top of the double bottom, at E. Suppose that after the throwback finishes at F, you become interested in buying the stock.

Does this double bottom represent the best buying configuration or should you look elsewhere?

The start of the pattern is at C, the first bottom. A year ago, the stock was at A, on the far left, the first price bar on the chart. Back then, the stock closed at 38.81, but at C, it was a dollar less, 37.81. That means the primary trend is downward leading to the chart pattern, although it may not look like it.

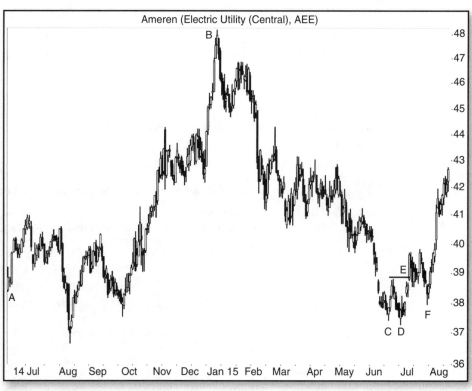

FIGURE 16.3 A double bottom appears, but does it have the best profit potential?

The trend start is at B. Why? Because that is the highest price before which price tumbles at least 20%. B begins a downward price trend leading to the double bottom.

We now have the three pieces of information to use in Table 16.2. (1) The breakout is upward, (2) the primary trend is downward, and (3) the trend from the trend start is downward. That combination results in the best ranking for performance.

The stock could fail to live up to expectations, of course, but at least you have an edge. And sometimes having an edge in the trading business is all you need.

In this example, price has not found the ultimate high yet. So far, it has reached almost 45.

■ Closing Position

One of the things that mystifies me is people saying things that they do not know to be true. For example, how many times have you heard that 90% of people trading options lose money? I have never heard of a study proving that true. Another is that patterns acting as continuations outperform reversals. The truth about that one is not as clear. Sometimes reversals work better than continuations (after upward breakouts, for example) and sometimes not (continuations after downward breakouts work better).

Do me a favor. If you have a rule that says, "only buy if price is above the x-day moving average," check to see if your setup works better if price is *below* the moving average, not above it.

CHAPTER 17

Straight-Line Run Down

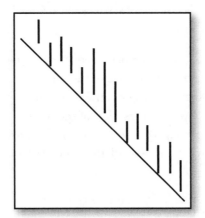

In working on this chapter, my hope was that I could learn how often price resumes a downward move. I nailed that statistic.

But the straight-line run down also occurs as a retrace in an upward trend. That confuses things. Let me explain. Have popcorn ready.

■ Behavior at a Glance

Figure 17.1 shows the average retrace after a straight-line run down ends. Line AB represents the straight-line run down pattern. Once the pattern completes, price bounces. In 18% of the cases (path C), price climbs less than 38% of the AB move before closing below B.

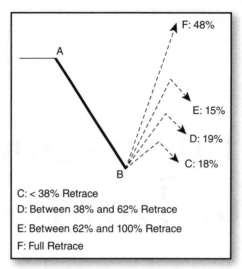

C: < 38% Retrace
D: Between 38% and 62% Retrace
E: Between 62% and 100% Retrace
F: Full Retrace

FIGURE 17.1 The average behavior of a straight-line run down pattern.

Path D occurs when price retraces between 38% and 62% of the AB move. Price takes that retrace path 19% of the time.

Path E shows a higher retrace over 62% of the time but less than a full retrace. That retrace path occurs 15% of the time.

The remaining 48% retrace the full AB drop. That means the stock makes a complete recovery almost half the time. The other 52% of the time the stock closes below B.

- After a straight-line run down completes, price bounces up but continues down 52% of the time.

■ Identification

Figure 17.2 shows an example of a straight-line run down from A to B. Price drops following a nearly straight line.

What should you look for when searching for or trying to identify straight-line runs? Price should drop at a steady pace, just like the AB move in Figure 17.2. The trend often follows a line drawn along the valleys of the pattern. In some cases, you may have a slight bend or bow along the length of the pattern. The peaks may appear irregularly shaped. That is not important because the bottom of the pattern produces the straight line.

Look at the figures in the vertical run down chapter to distinguish a straight-line run from a vertical run. Vertical runs are like dropping a stone off a cliff. Straight-line runs are like rolling the stone downhill.

FIGURE 17.2 The straight-line run down is the AB move.

That is all there is to it.

In this example, price makes a slightly higher low at C before making a full retrace of the AB run down. A full retrace occurs at D when the stock *first closes* above the price at A. If the stock were to first close below B, then the stock would have made a partial retrace of the AB move.

■ Performance Statistics

For the following statistics, I used 99 stocks to find 1,611 straight-line runs down. The earliest was from August 1996, and the most recent began in April 2015.

How do you measure the performance of straight-line runs?

I compared the height of those straight-line runs with full and partial retraces. I wanted to know whether there was a way to detect which straight-line runs would retrace their entire height (the BD retrace of the AB drop in Figure 17.2, for example).

Table 17.1 shows what I found.

TABLE 17.1   **Statistical Analysis of Straight-Line Run Down**

Description	Average	Median
1. Height (days)	37	28
2. Percentage height	26%	21%
3. Height (days) of runs with full retrace	33	26
4. Height (days) of runs with partial retrace	41	29
5. Height of runs with full retrace	20%	18%
6. Height of runs with partial retrace	30%	26%
7. Uptrend, full retrace	52%	N/A
8. Downtrend, full retrace	44%	N/A

1, 2. The height of the pattern averages 37 days. This is the average time it takes price to reach the bottom of the straight-line run down. The decline represents an average drop of 26%, which is considerable. The median drop is smaller, 21%, but that still represents a large decline. Half the patterns will see price drop more, and half will see price drop less than the median.

3, 4. These two items say that straight-line runs in which price retraces the entire drop tend to be shorter than are those with only partial retraces. That makes intuitive sense.

5, 6. This shows the extent of the drop measured as a percentage of the pattern's high price. Again, patterns with full retraces tend to be substantially shorter than are those with partial retraces.

7, 8. I sorted straight-line runs into those with a trend start below the start of the straight-line run (uptrend) and those with the trend start above the top of the pattern (downtrend). I wanted to know whether the inbound trend influenced how often price completed a full retrace of the straight-line run.

When price trended down going into the straight-line run, it completed a full retrace less often than did those in which price climbed going into the run. This makes sense because price is following the current downward, and during a retrace, it fights against that current.

The median measure does not apply to this situation.

Table 17.2 shows a frequency distribution of the retrace amount. If you ignore the whopping 48% of runs that retrace the entire decline, the most frequent retrace

TABLE 17.2   **Frequency Distribution of Retraces**

Bin	10%	20%	30%	40%	50%	
Count	0%	2%	7%	10%	10%	
Bin	60%	70%	80%	90%	100%	>100%
Count	7%	5%	4%	4%	3%	48%

is between 40% and 60% (which includes the 40% and 50% bins). Those two bins each represent 10% of the straight-line runs, the highest in the table.

■ Configuration Trading: Uptrend Variations

Straight-line runs are difficult to trade because no one knows when they will end and what will happen after they end. Instead, I offer a number of variations I spotted while cataloging them. The first batch all have the trend start below the straight-line run so that price rises into the run. I call these the uptrend variations.

Figure 17.3 shows the first two types.

Inset ABC shows price climbing in a series of upward steps. The straight-line run down occurs during B and C in this example. It does not always occur on each downward retrace (meaning you may see a straight-line run down at B but not at C or at C but not B).

The stock chart shows this stair-step move higher. Straight-line runs B1, C1, and D, are examples of the ABC variation. Pattern ABC occurs 39% of the time, the most frequent of the 218 patterns I looked at.

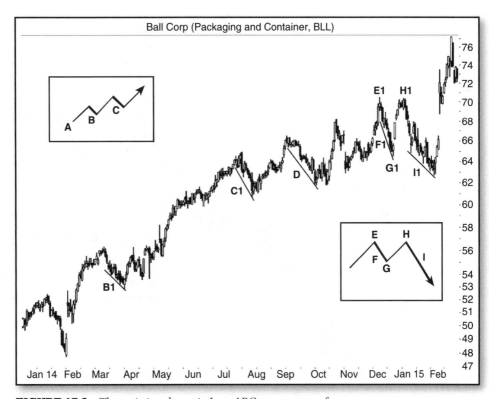

FIGURE 17.3   The variation shown in Inset ABC occurs most often.

The E-I inset shows a different variation. Price climbs and forms peak E. Then we see a straight-line run down that drops price to G. The stock recovers and climbs to form peak H. The peak may be slightly below E or slightly above it, but it looks like a double top in the making. This double top confirms when price closes below the price of valley G, which happens following path I.

A portion of the HI run can be a straight-line run down, but need not be.

The stock chart shows this configuration starting at E1. E1 corresponds to peak E in the inset. The straight-line run down is F1, but I1 is another run down, too. E1-H1 makes a double top when price confirms the pattern (closes below the low at G1) on the way to the low near I1.

In this example, the stock rebounded to make a new high. The E–I variation occurs 11% of the time (it is rare).

Double Top Variation

Figure 17.4 shows the next variation. The stock chart is on the weekly scale only for your viewing pleasure. Look at the inset first.

Price climbs upward following path A leading to the first top at B. Then the straight-line run (C) takes price down to the valley. Following that, the stock makes

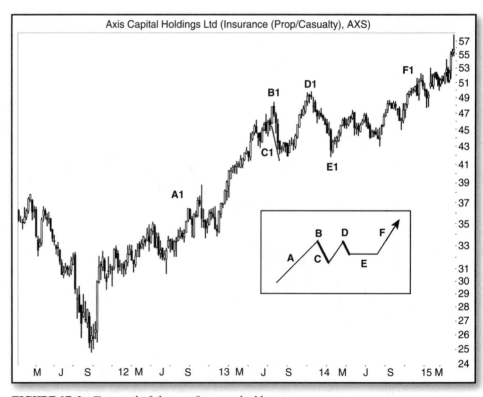

FIGURE 17.4   Twin peaks fail to confirm as a double top.

another upward push to a new high (D) but stalls at or near the price level of B, the first top.

The retrace that follows drops price to E where it remains above the valley at C. This drop (D to E) may or may not be another straight-line run down. Twin peaks BD do not confirm as a valid double top. The stock trades sideways but eventually moves higher, F.

The stock chart shows an example of this variation. The twin peaks are at B1 and D1. The straight-line run down occurs at C1, although it does not look like much on the weekly scale (I found all variations on the daily charts.). The *close* at E1 remains above the low near C1, so it does not confirm the twin peak pattern. Price moves sideways but eventually makes its way higher to F1.

This variation occurs 23% of the time in the patterns I looked at.

Mountain Variation

The last variation when the trend start is below the beginning of the straight-line run is what I call the mountain variation. Why? Because the chart just looks like a mountain range. **Figure 17.5** shows an example.

The inset shows an irregular-shaped move, starting at A. I did not attach any significance to the number of peaks or valleys on the way to peak B nor on the way

FIGURE 17.5 Price at the peak tops the other hills before a straight-line run takes price down.

down. I just show a few here to give you an idea of how irregular the terrain appears.

Price peaks at B and the straight-line run down occurs at C, on the way to D.

The stock chart shows an example (daily chart). Price peaks at B1, and the straight-line run is at C1. The stock continues lower to D1.

This variation occurs 17% of the time. There are other variations, but they rarely occur, so are not worth mentioning.

■ Downtrend Variations

I looked at almost a hundred straight-line runs in a downward price trend and found two main themes. Before the run down started, price either made a dip (74% of the time) or it did not (26% of the time).

That seemed too easy, so I concentrated on how price behaved after the straight-line run down. I found 6 types among the nearly 300 straight-line runs I looked at, 5 of which are shown below. The last one happened only 4% of the time, and I consider that odd. Why? Because the straight-line run down leads to a double bottom.

Figure 17.6 shows the first variant, which occurs 35% of the time. That is the most frequent of the six types.

FIGURE 17.6 This scenario occurs most often: 35% of the time.

Look at the inset. It shows a stock in a downward price trend that leads to a dip at A. The stock recovers and then forms a straight-line run down, B. After the straight-line run ends (C), the stock recovers and makes a substantial recovery, D. *Substantial* means a rise of at least 20%, but I did not measure this. I just looked for a big move.

The stock chart shows an example. The straight-line run down is at B1 (which corresponds to B in the inset). The dip before the run down is A1, and the recovery is D1.

Although the CD move looks straight, it can be any shape as the stock chart shows (that is, price rises from C1 to D1 before going off the chart).

Sawtooth Down

Figure 17.7 shows the next two variants. Inset ABC shows the same pattern as in Figure 17.6 only price continues down in this example, following trend C.

A is a dip in a downward price trend. The straight-line run down is B. That precedes an up and down wave, C. Wave C represents a large decline.

The stock chart shows an example. The straight-line run down is B1, corresponding to B. The dip is A1 that occurs just before the straight-line run down begins. C1 completes the variation when the stock makes a large drop.

FIGURE 17.7   These two straight-line runs are similar.

The A2-B2-D pattern is almost the same as ABC except the D leg is shorter than C. D completes and leg E begins, taking the stock upward in a large move higher. If you were to imagine a shorter leg C1 on the stock chart, it would be a good example of the A2-E variant.

The ABC variant occurs 20% of the time. The A2-E pattern happens 10% of the time.

The V-Turn

Figure 17.8 shows the last two variants. In these two examples, notice that there is no dip preceding the start of the straight-line run down. Price at A drops into the straight-line run down, B, and ends when price makes a strong recovery, to C.

The stock chart shows an example with leg B1 forming the straight-line run down. Notice how price at A1 just slides into a straight-line run down without a significant dip. Although leg C1 is not long on the time scale, price does make a substantial move higher.

This variant occurs 18% of the time.

The remaining variant is A2-E. Price moves lower in leg A2 and then a straight-line run down begins (B2). Leg D sees the stock recover but not to a large extent

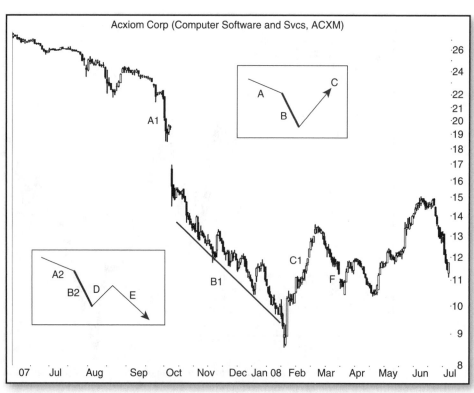

FIGURE 17.8 After these two straight-line runs end, price either recovers or it keeps dropping.

before another downward move begins. Leg E takes the stock substantially lower. This variant occurs 13% of the time.

The stock chart would show an example of this variant if leg C1 were shorter and leg F were longer.

My intention of showing these variants is that they may help you prepare for a straight-line run down that occurs in a stock you own. You may be able to tell which variant applies and trade, or not trade, accordingly.

■ Trading

Suppose you face the situation shown by **Figure 17.9**. You own the stock but are getting nervous. Price has been trending higher as the arrow at A highlights. The stock is at an all-time high (C) when price starts dropping in a straight-line run that bottoms at D. What will happen next?

To answer that question, turn to Figure 17.10, which shows the various configurations for straight-line runs down.

FIGURE 17.9   At point D, how worried should you be with the straight-line run down at CD?

We know that the primary trend is upward (A), so the bottom five configurations do not apply (they appear in downtrends).

The bullish uptrend of Figure 17.3 resembles what appears in Figure 17.9. Price is rising in a sawtooth pattern before sliding down in a straight-line run. Because the configuration is bullish, it suggests the uphill run will continue.

The bearish version of Figure 17.3 has not happened yet. I would be worried if the stock stalled at E (Figure 17.9) or showed signs of reversing.

The bullish version of Figure 17.4 does not apply for the same reason. We do not have a twin peak pattern. Yet.

Figure 17.5 is a possibility until you realize that price has to make lower lows, not higher ones. If you look at Figure 17.5, run C ends at the same price where the rise to B began. That is not the case in our situation, at least not yet.

So, the bullish uptrend in Figure 17.3 is the only configuration that applies. I show that in the inset of Figure 17.9. It suggests the upward move still has more to go.

If price were to rise and stall at E, then I would be worried and would reevaluate the situation then, but as the chart shows, that did not happen.

■ Closing Position

I have wondered what happens after a straight-line run down. Having written this chapter, I know the answer. Price bounces. Duh, right?

Figure 17.1 shows the dance moves. Less than half the time (48%) the stock will make a full recovery. The other 52% of the time, the stock turns into a stinker and digs a hole. If you are unfortunate and get caught in the slide, you could lose not only your shirt but also some body parts.

Use the information in this chapter to help better understand the significance of a straight-line run down and what to do if you encounter one along the trading highway.

Setup Synopsis

Figure 17.10 may help you identify the various types of trading setups. See the associated figure for an explanation.

"Occurs" in the figure means how often I found the configuration in the stocks I looked at. If two configurations apply to your situation, then the one with a more frequent occurrence (a higher percentage) is the one you should choose to follow.

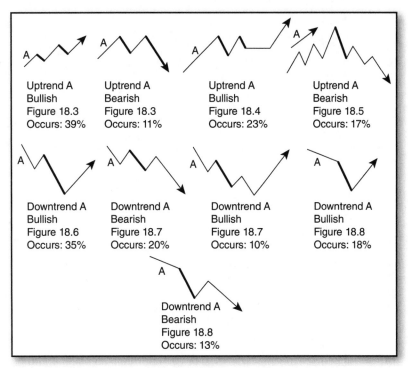

FIGURE 17.10 A collection of ideal trading setups and configurations.

CHAPTER 18

Straight-Line Run Up

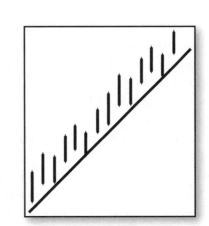

When I see a stock making a steady climb higher, I wonder how it will end. Does the stock tumble and give back all of its gains, or does it just retrace a smidgen before resuming the upward move?

To answer those questions, I cataloged over a thousand straight-line runs and then analyzed how they behaved. This chapter describes what I found.

■ Behavior at a Glance

Figure 18.1 shows a frequency distribution of how a stock typically behaves after a straight-line run up completes.

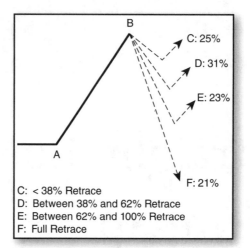

FIGURE 18.1 The average behavior after a straight-line run up.

Diagonal line AB is the straight-line run up. Path C shows price retracing less than 38% of the straight-line run. Price follows that path an average of 25% of the time, eventually closing above B.

Path D captures the retrace between 38% and 62% of the time. Price takes that route 31% of the time.

Route E shows price retracing between 62% and 100%. That happens an average of 23% of the time.

The remainder of the time, 21%, the stock makes a full retrace of the AB move. The stock closes below the price of A and heads lower.

Not shown, but I counted how often a trend change occurs after a straight-line run up. A trend change is a drop of 20% measured from the high price at B to the following low. I found that a trend change occurred 38% of the time. In other words, you have a 38% chance of losing a substantial amount of money.

- A trend change occurs 38% of the time after a straight-line run up.

■ Identification

Figure 18.2 shows an example of a straight-line run at BC. This is a particularly good example because the stock does not pause along the way and it hugs a trendline higher.

After the stock peaks at C, it retraces 51% of the BC move (in this example) by tumbling to D. Then the stock recovers by climbing 12% (measured from D to F as a percentage of D) to form the higher peak at F.

FIGURE 18.2   The straight-line run up is the BC move.

There is no need to show a table of identification guidelines. Rather, just look for price moving up in a mostly straight line. The move up at A is another example of a straight-line run up but shorter than BC.

If the stock curves some, that is fine. An upward curve happens sometimes at the very end of the move. It is as if traders are eating up the stock like hungry children until they become full. Then they stop buying and the stock tumbles.

In Figure 18.2, the EF move is also a straight-line run, but I prefer to call this a vertical run. I discuss vertical runs in a later chapter. Vertical runs see price zip higher with little overlap from price bar to bar, so the move tends to have a steeper slope than straight-line runs. Vertical runs are special cases of straight-line runs.

■ Performance Statistics

I looked through 138 stocks to catalog 1,462 straight-line runs from April 1996 to March 2015 before I threw up my hands and had enough. I did not worry about separating the patterns into bull and bear markets. I just lumped them all together. It is possible that upward runs in bear markets work differently than do those in bull markets.

Table 18.1 shows statistics related to the straight-line run up pattern.

TABLE 18.1	Statistical Analysis of Straight-Line Run Up		
Description		Average	Median
1. Height (days)		74	52
2. Percentage height		51%	32%
3. Height (days) of runs with full retrace		55	44
4. Height (days) of runs with partial retrace		78	54
5. Height of runs with full retrace		29%	24%
6. Height of runs with partial retrace		57%	35%

1, 2. The average length of a straight-line run up is 74 days with a median of 52 days. The stock climbs an average of 51% (median 32%) of the low price during the run (using the formula: (high price − low price) ÷ low price).

3, 4. As one might expect, short runs were more likely to retrace their entire length than were tall ones. I compared the length of the run (in calendar days) for runs with a full retrace of their height to runs with only a partial retrace. Those runs with a partial retrace were substantially longer than were those with a full retrace (78 days versus 55 days, respectively).

5, 6. Straight-line runs that completed a full retrace were an average of 29% higher, substantially shorter than were the ones with partial retraces (57% average height).

Table 18.2 shows a frequency distribution of how often a particular retrace occurs. It gives you an idea of how far price will drop after a straight-line run ends. For example, the 30% bin shows that only 10% of the straight-line runs will retrace 30%.

Ignoring the full retrace bin (>100%), the most popular are bins 30% to 70% with 40% reining king (or queen).

After a straight-line run up completes, price retraces. Price has a 79% chance of moving above the top of the straight-line run after the retrace completes.

- There is a 79% chance that price will make a new high after the retrace from a straight-line run ends.

TABLE 18.2	Frequency Distribution of Retraces					
Bin	**10%**	**20%**	**30%**	**40%**	**50%**	
Count	0%	2%	10%	16%	14%	
Bin	**60%**	**70%**	**80%**	**90%**	**100%**	**>100%**
Count	12%	10%	6%	6%	4%	21%

◼ Configuration Trading

I looked at 150 charts of straight-line runs up in a downward price trend and found two variations that predominated. The first occurred 77% of the time.

Figure 18.3 shows price dropping in a downtrend that starts at A and ends at B. Often B marks the transition from bear to bull market, but this configuration also occurs in bull markets.

Price rises in a straight-line run up from B to C before a retrace takes the stock back down to D. The vast majority of the time, this is not a full retrace (meaning the stock does not return to the price of B). After the CD retrace completes, the stock resumes its recovery (to E).

The stock chart shows an example of this scenario on the weekly scale. The 2007 to 2009 bear market saw price drop from (before) A1 to B1 in a steep decline that many stocks suffered at the end of the bear market. At B1, the bear market ended both in this stock and in the general market. A straight-line run up carries the stock from B1 to C1.

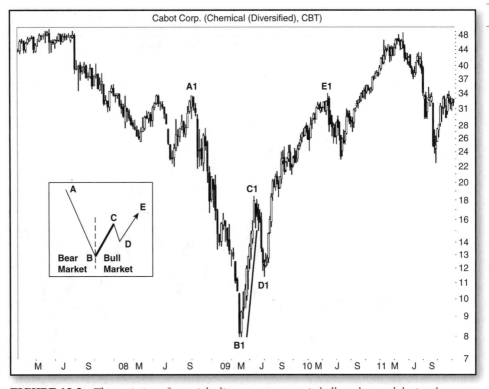

FIGURE 18.3   This variation of a straight-line run up occurs in bull markets and during the transition from bear to bull markets.

After such a swift recovery, the stock retraced a portion of that gain by backtracking to D1. After that, the stock zipped higher, carried along by the new bull market, to E1.

If you see a straight-line run up appear at the end of a long bear market, then it could be a sign of the start of the bull market.

You can buy during the straight-line run up or wait for the retrace. Depending on the strength of the new bull market, the downward retrace (CD) may be short, so you can place an order to buy the stock at the top of the straight-line run up (above the price of C on the way to E). That way, you know the retrace is over.

Alternatively, you can split the straight-line run into three Fibonacci segments of 38%, 50%, and 62%. In other words, expect the CD retrace to stop near one of those locations and then buy.

I have used a 62% retrace in some of my trades as an entry signal, but it is rare that a stock will retrace that far. Waiting for a 62% retrace means missing winning trades that retrace less.

Measured Move Down

Figure 18.4 shows the last configuration for downtrends. This one happened just 13% of the time in the stocks I looked at, so it is rare. I did not see this configuration in the bear to bull market transition. This is a bull market pattern only.

FIGURE 18.4   Price continues down in this configuration.

Price trends downward from A to B. At B, a straight-line run up begins and lasts to C. This is a partial retrace of the downward move from A. Once the run ends, the stock resumes its downward move, to D. The CD move takes the stock well below B (which is what differentiates this configuration from the last one).

The A to D move resembles a measured move down pattern, so you can read that chapter on how to trade it.

The stock chart shows an example of this configuration on the weekly scale. Price forms peak A1, and then the rosy picture turns black for owners of the stock. Price drops to B1. At B1, an upward retrace of the A1-B1 drop begins. It takes the stock higher to C1 in a straight-line advance. Once the run ends, the stock drops again, going lower to D1.

After bottoming at D1, the stock makes an unusually strong move higher, taking the stock from below 8 to 113 (not shown) in the overheated tech market bubble. After the bubble exploded, the stock deflated to just over $1.

Many of the stocks that followed this configuration just kept sinking, so the rise after D1 is unusual.

Uptrends

I sorted my database according to straight-line runs in an uptrend and found two configurations that happened. **Figure 18.5** shows the first one. This one occurred 78% of the time in the 156 charts I looked at, so you are most likely to face this configuration.

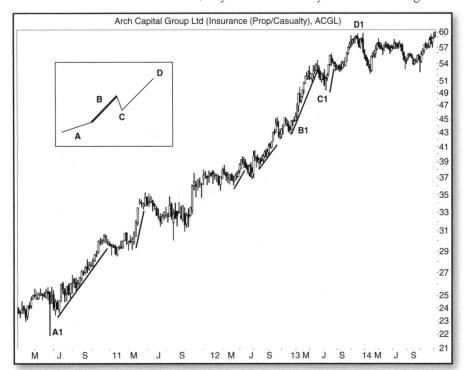

FIGURE 18.5 After a straight-line run up, the stock retraces before resuming the upward move.

Price rises (A) going into the start of the straight-line run (B). After the straight-line run completes, the stock retraces a portion of the B move, to C. The retrace may be small, or it could bottom at the start of the straight-line run. Price does not drop below the bottom of the straight-line run.

After the retrace is complete at C, the stock recovers and moves higher to D.

The stock chart on the weekly scale shows several diagonal trendlines along straight-line runs that are examples of this configuration. Let us focus on the B1 run.

Price rises from A1 to B1 over the long term. The straight-line run up begins at B1. At C1, the stock retraces only a portion of the B1 run. When the retrace completes, the stock rises to D1.

If you own the stock and see a straight-line run up like that described here, then hold onto the stock. You will experience a retrace at the end of the run up, but the majority of the time, the stock will resume the uptrend and the retrace will be shallow enough to avoid cardiac arrest.

The one exception is if the stock closes below the start (bottom) of the straight-line run. That would be a sell signal, and I describe that configuration next.

Excessive Retrace

Figure 18.6 shows the setup for this configuration in the inset. Price rises (A) until a straight-line run takes price up (B) further. Then a retrace begins. Price drops and

FIGURE 18.6   After a straight-line run up, price retraces and keeps dropping.

drops and continues down until the stock drops below the start of the straight-line run (F). When that happens, it could be time to sell.

I found that the stock continues lower following path E 59% of the time. The other 41% of the time, the stock follows path D.

The stock chart shows an example on the weekly scale of this configuration. The uptrend begins at A1 and a straight-line run up is at B1. After the run ends, the stock drops, moving lower to C1. The drop to C1 in this example is a 37% decline from the high at the end of the straight-line run (H to C1) and a drop of 21% below the start of the run (G to C1).

After price bottoms at C1, the stock rises to D1 (in this example).

From the charts I have looked at, if the stock *closes* below the bottom of the straight-line run up (F), then consider selling. The stock will likely sink to C, which could entail a significant drop, and 59% of the time the stock will continue down to E.

Look for underlying support that would stop the decline. Check the fundamentals and other measures to assure you that the stock is worth holding or selling.

■ Trading

Figure 18.7 shows (daily scale) how easy trading straight-line runs can be in some situations. If you bought the stock and then saw it begin to trend higher, almost every day, you might consider taking profit. But when?

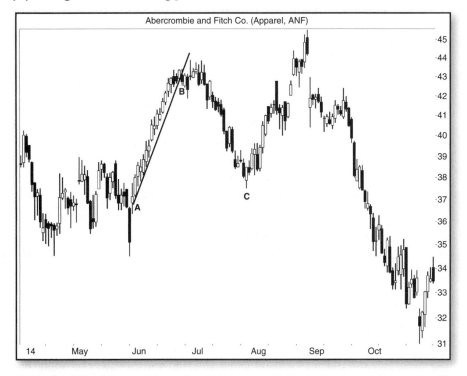

FIGURE 18.7 Swing and day traders will want to sell when price closes below the trendline.

A trendline signals the answer. You will not sell at the very peak of the straight-line run, but you can get out near the top using a trendline cross. This technique is best for swing and day traders, people who want to make money on the short swings as price moves up and down.

Here is how to use a trendline. In this example, the straight-line run is the AB move. Draw an up-sloping trendline along price bottoms like that shown and extend it as price rises. Notice that price hugs the trendline. When the stock *closes* below the trendline (B), sell at the open the next day.

As the chart shows, this technique works well in this case. Price collapses to C, a retrace of 68% of the AB move. Because the rise from A to B is a move of 27%, selling near B captures a good amount of that move.

For buy-and-hold investors and position traders, the end of a straight-line run turns into a trend change 38% of the time (see "Behavior at a Glance"). Any retrace equal to or more than 20% represents a trend change.

My advice for position traders is to look for underlying support that may stop a large retrace. Then calculate the possible loss if the stock tumbles to support. Always keep in mind that the stock can tumble farther. If the market or industry is weak, then consider selling. If both are strong, then look for any company weakness (technicals, fundamentals).

Use Figure 18.5 as the template for upward trends. That figure shows price continuing to move higher after a straight-line run/retrace pair. In a bull market, in an industry that is also bullish, holding on will be the correct move most often unless the company has flubbed up (like botched quarterly earnings or bad same-store sales).

For buy-and-hold investors, 62% of the time you will be correct holding onto a position after a straight-line run (since 38% change trend). Check the fundamentals and recognize that even though a stock may retrace more than 20%, there is a 79% probability the stock will recover to make a higher high. That happened in August (Figure 18.7) after losing 15% during the retrace. The 79% number comes from Figure 18.1 that shows 21% closing below the start of the straight-line run (so the other 79% must recover).

Figure 18.8 shows (daily chart) a variation of the trendline-sell theme. A straight-line run appears at BD. The stock signals a sell at D when price closes below the trendline. Sell at the open the next day.

This trendline-sell technique seems straightforward, right? Now look at the inset. This is the same stock chart as the AD move but zoomed in to show BC. I drew a trendline (B1-C1) that hugs price better in the early stages of development of the straight-line run.

The stock closes below the trendline at C1, issuing a sell signal, but this signal gets swing and day traders out of the stock prematurely. The sell day is near C on the longer stock chart. Notice how much profit you give away by selling near C instead of D.

FIGURE 18.8 Trading this straight-line run is not as simple as it appears.

Figure 18.9 shows another variation that you will encounter. Straight-line run BC stops at overhead resistance setup by peak A. A trader may think that a double top is forming, especially when the stock begins to retrace the BC move (by dropping to D).

Then look what happens. After D, another straight-line run begins, climbing to E. Notice that the slope of the two runs is the same, offset only by the CD move. The straight-line run has turned into a measured move up chart pattern.

Straight-line runs can be short or long. After a straight-line run ends, the stock will retrace a portion of the upward run (otherwise, the straight-line run has not ended). The vast majority of the time, 79%, the stock will continue to make another new high.

If you look at the stock on the weekly scale (shown in the inset), the straight-line run begins at B1. The run is in the midst of a longer-term uptrend in a bull market. Thus, Figures 18.5 or 18.6 apply. Because the stock did not close below the bottom of B1 during the retrace (meaning use Figure 18.5 and *not* Figure 18.6 as the template), investors and position traders would hold onto this stock. Swing and day traders would want to sell after the straight-line run up ends as soon as they can recognize that the retrace has begun.

FIGURE 18.9   This straight-line run has two parts: BC and DE.

■ Closing Position

I remember trading a stock in which I more than doubled my money. Yippee! Then I watched as the trend reversed. I not only gave back all of my gains, but I took a big loss after the stock dropped by more than half. I still cannot believe that happened. I know better, but even the professionals make mistakes.

Seeing a straight-line run up is a lot like fearing what will happen next. Fortunately, you have this chapter to refer to. Price retraces the entire run just 21% of the time, leaving 79% of the stocks to push higher.

The setups and configurations in this chapter illustrate how to tame the straight-line run up or at least to know what to expect.

Here is a tip: The next time you *more* than double your money, consider selling when it drops to twice what you paid. You never go broke taking a profit.

Setup Synopsis

Figure 18.10 may help you identify the various types of trading setups. See the associated figure for an explanation.

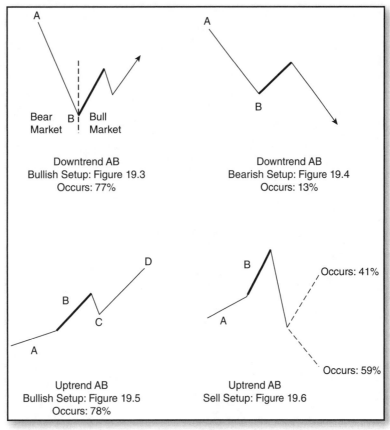

FIGURE 18.10 A collection of ideal trading setups and configurations.

"Occurs" in the figure means how often I found the configuration in the stocks I looked at. If two configurations apply to your situation, then the one with a more frequent occurrence (a higher percentage) is the one you should choose to follow.

CHAPTER 19

Tops and Bottoms

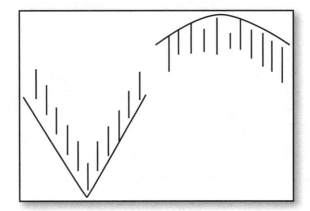

I asked a friend to look at charts of rectangles and tell me what struck her as odd. After she gave me her insight, I remarked that when price bottomed, the valleys were often V-shaped. She said that bottoms are usually V-shaped and tops are rounded.

That information surprised me, so I decided to see if I could prove it. This chapter discusses what I found.

■ Behavior at a Glance

Figure 19.1 shows the difference between narrow turns and wide ones. Both can occur at peaks and valleys.

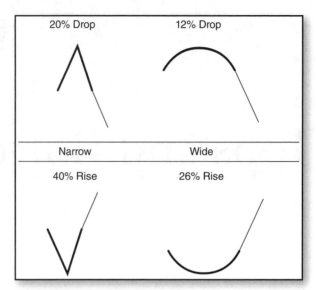

FIGURE 19.1   Wide, rounded-looking turns perform less well than narrow, V-shaped turns.

I found that narrow tops (upper left of the figure) had median declines that measured 20% below the peak. Wide turns (upper right) performed less well after price declined a median of 12%.

Bottoms followed a similar trend. Narrow bottoms showed price rise a median of 40%, but wide turns gained a median of 26%.

■ Narrow tops and bottoms perform better than wide ones.

■ Methodology

How did I uncover the results in this chapter? I looked at bull markets only, starting from March 2000. I found the highest peak and lowest valley within 15 days (substantial turns). I chose 15 days because it was wide enough to allow rounded turns to appear.

Once I had those peaks and valleys, I looked to either side and found the first price that closed down more than 5% (for peaks) or closed above 5% (for bottoms). Then I counted the price bars between those two points. The study used 51,548 samples, split almost evenly between peaks and valleys.

Figure 19.2 helps the explanation. After finding peaks A and D (the highest peak for 15 days), I looked for the first *close* 5% below each side of the peak. Then I measured the width of the peak at that point (the BC distance for peak A and the EF distance for peak D).

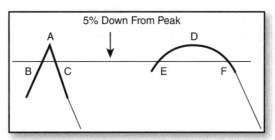

FIGURE 19.2 After finding a peak, measure the width of it by looking 5% below the peak.

Five percent down from the peak was far enough away to distinguish narrow peaks from wide ones but not too far away that both would widen out after the peak ended (in the plain between the two peaks).

I used the same technique for valleys except that I looked for the first close on either side of the valley at least 5% up from the bottom. Then I counted the price bars between the two points.

Figure 19.3 shows examples of wide and narrow peaks and valleys. The January peak (A) may look narrow, but it straddles the median nine price bars separating narrow and wide peaks. Ties are considered narrow.

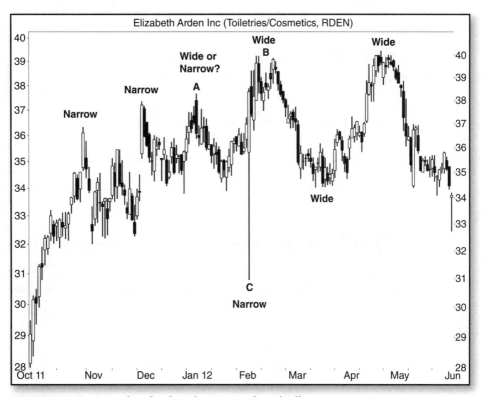

FIGURE 19.3 Examples of wide and narrow peaks and valleys.

The twin peaks at B are considered one peak because the second peak is within the 15-day window, and it is slightly below the first peak.

The long price bar at C is a narrow valley by itself.

■ Findings

I made some interesting discoveries along the way, and **Table 19.1** lists them.

1. Are peaks wider than valleys? Yes, but not that you would notice. The median width of a peak was 9 price bars (average of 12) and valleys were a median of 7 bars wide (average of 10). Thus, peaks are slightly more rounded looking than are valleys by just two price bars. Remember that I measured the width 5% below a peak and 5% above a valley.

2. Do narrow peaks perform better than wide ones? Yes. This is one of the big surprises. **Table 19.2** illustrates this in the row with 9 bars. Peaks wider than 9 bars saw median declines of 12% compared to narrower peaks that declined 20%. That is a substantial difference.

I measured performance from the peak to the lowest low before a trend change or before the stock closed above the peak. A trend change is a close 20% or more above the lowest low.

TABLE 19.1   **Statistics for Wide and Narrow Peaks and Valleys**

Description	Result
1. Are peaks wider than valleys?	Yes
2. Do narrow peaks perform better than wide ones?	Yes
3. Do narrow valleys perform better than wide ones?	Yes
4. As peaks/valleys get narrower, do they perform better?	Yes
5. As peaks/valleys get wider, do they perform better?	No

TABLE 19.2   **Median Performance of Wide and Narrow Peaks and Valleys**

	Peaks			Valleys	
Width (Bars)	Narrow (Drop)	Wide (Drop)	Width (Bars)	Narrow (Rise)	Wide (Rise)
9	20%	12%	7	40%	26%
18		11%	14		21%
27		11%	21		20%
4	23%		4	43%	
3	24%		3	44%	

3. Do narrow valleys perform better than wide ones? Yes. Table 19.2 shows this on the right half of the table, in the bar width of 7 row. Narrow valleys see price rise a median of 40% compared to wide valleys (those wider than 7 price bars) that climbed 26%.

For the rise, I looked for the ultimate high above the valley. The ultimate high is the highest peak before price drops at least 20% (high to close) or the highest peak before the stock closes below the bottom of the valley.

4. As peaks/valleys get narrower, do they perform better? Yes.

Table 19.2 shows that as the width of peaks drop from the median 9 bars (20% drop) to 4 bars (23% drop) to 3 bars (24% drop), the median decline increases.

Valleys shows the same trend beginning with 7 bars (40% rise), then 4 bars wide (43% rise) and 3 bars (44% rise).

■ The narrower the peak or valley the better the performance.

5. As peaks/valleys get wider, do they perform better? No. This is the opposite of the prior finding. I increased the width of the peak or valley by doubling and tripling the median width and comparing the median performance of peaks and valleys. The results are not as startling.

Peaks that get wider see performance drop from 12% (9 bars wide) to 11% (18 and 27 bars wide). Valleys show median rises of 26% at 7 bars wide but that drops to 20% at 21 bars wide.

■ Variations

I added the primary trend to my statistics and looked at the resulting performance. To gauge whether the primary price trend was up or down, I compared the closing price a year ago to the high or low at the peak or valley, respectively. As simple as this method sounds, it works well.

If you ignore the shape of peaks and valleys (rounded or V-shaped), I found that performance varies, depending on the inbound price trend. See **Table 19.3**.

For example, peaks with a rising primary trend saw the stock decline a median of 16% below the peak. Those peaks acted as reversals of the primary uptrend.

Peaks in a declining primary trend (think of an upward retrace in a downtrend), the stock declined a median of 18% below the peak before changing trend. Those peaks acted as continuations of the downward primary price trend.

TABLE 19.3	Performance of Peaks or Valleys Regardless of Shape	
	Trend Up	**Trend Down**
Peak	−16%	−18%
Valley	31%	37%

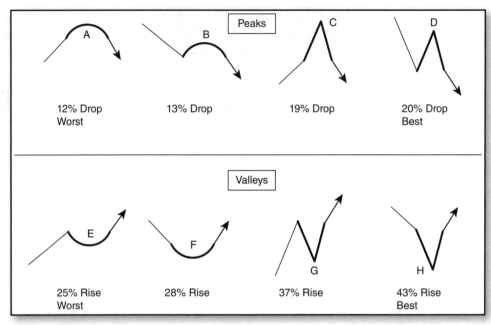

FIGURE 19.4   Performance for the various combinations of peaks and valleys.

Valleys showed the opposite behavior with reversals (primary trend down going into a valley) posting gains of 37%, but continuations (primary trend up so that the valley acted as a retrace of the upward price trend) gained a median of 31%.

When you include the shape of peaks and valleys in the analysis, you get the performance variations shown in **Figure 19.4**.

Starting from the upper left (A), I found that wide peaks (peaks wider than the median 9 price bars measured 5% below the peak) that acted as reversals of the upward price trend were the worst performing. They saw price decline a median of 12%.

Wide peaks acting as continuations (B) showed marginally better performance by seeing price drop 13% before a trend change.

Narrow peaks performed better. Reversal configuration C saw price decline a median of 19% below the peak compared to continuation D that had a median decline of 20%. Variation D was the best-performing combination of inbound primary trend and peak width.

Valley Performance

The performance of valleys was substantially better than peaks.

No surprise there.

I used the median width of 7 price bars measured 5% above the valley floor to determine narrow or wide. Variation E (Figure 19.4) showed that the worst performance came from wide valleys acting as continuations of the upward primary price trend. They showed median gains above the valley low of 25% before the trend changed.

Variation F did better by seeing price climb a median of 28% before a trend change. This variation saw the valley acting as a reversal (downward inbound primary price trend and upward outbound trend).

Narrow valleys performed better still. Variation G (continuation) saw price rise 37% compared to the best-performing combination, H, with a 43% gain. Variation H saw the valley acting as a reversal of the primary downward trend.

■ Trading

Consider **Figure 19.5**. Suppose you own the stock at D. Price has formed a peak. How do you know if the peak is wide or narrow?

The peak at A is 111.68. Five percent below this is 106.10. I drew the horizontal line B at that price. In my tests, I looked for the first and last *closing* price below that

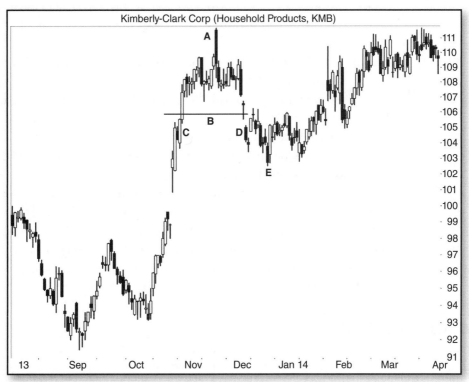

FIGURE 19.5 Wide peaks often have a rounded appearance.

5% line. I show those two price bars as C and D. Then I counted the number of price bars between C and D.

Since this is a peak, we want to know if there are more than nine bars between C and D (for valleys, you would use seven bars). Clearly there are. So this peak is wide. That suggests a smaller decline than if this peak were narrower.

In fact, all of the substantial peaks and valleys on this chart are wide ones.

If I had to make rules about the shape of peaks and valleys, they would be:

- Hold onto stocks showing wide, rounded-looking peaks (expect small declines) and sell ones making narrow, V-shaped peaks (expect large declines).

- For valleys, buy stocks making V-shaped bottoms because price will climb higher, on average, than will those making more rounded turns.

- Use the variations in Figure 19.4 to help decide how your combination of primary price trend and peak/valley width will perform.

Primary Trend

We now know that Peak A is a wide one (Figure 19.5). Let us consider the direction of the inbound primary price trend.

The high price at peak A is 111.68 on November 15, 2013. A year before, the stock closed at 83.83 (not shown). This peak acts as a reversal of the upward primary price trend. That means the stock climbs over the past year going into the peak and price drops after it.

Looking at Figure 19.4, we see that a wide peak acting as a reversal is variation A, the worst performing of the peaks.

After the peak, price declined 8% (to E) before the stock closed above the top of the peak (not shown).

If you shorted the stock, it was a stinker of a trade (a perfect trade would make 8%). If you sold a long holding expecting a large decline, you would be surprised it was so meager. The stock climbed to a high of 126 about two years later (December 2015, so far). If you held onto the stock, the gain from the peak at A to 126 is 13% for a hold time of two years. That is a meager gain in a bull market.

The best decision about this stock is to avoid trading or owning it. Shorting the stock expecting a big decline would be a mistake. Holding onto the stock saw the stock make a small decline in the near term but not recover much over the longer term. You could do better (or worse) owning a different stock.

■ Closing Position

Looking at the shape of tops and bottoms can give you a trading edge. Narrow tops and narrow valleys forecast better performance (bigger drops and bigger rises, respectively). Perhaps you can incorporate that information into your favorite trading setup.

Combine the shapes with the inbound price trend to squeeze out every ounce of performance. Narrow bottoms do best as reversals. Narrow tops outperform as continuations.

If you own stock and see a rounded top forming, the stock may plunge, of course, but the median decline should be less than from a narrow peak. A visual test can help you decide to hold onto a stock or sell it immediately, just by looking at it.

For any type of trader (day, swing, position, buy-and-hold), this kind of information can be used to improve your trading results. Preserving capital and even making money is what trading and investing is all about.

CHAPTER 20

Trends and Countertrends

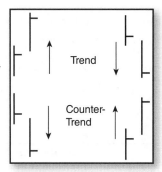

Years ago, I remember researching a stock that I wanted to buy. At the end of the day when I got a quote, it had closed lower even though the Dow Jones Industrials soared by more than 100 points. I thought, *That cannot be good for the stock.*

I did not buy the stock but was that the right decision? Research on trend and countertrend behavior in this chapter gives us the answer, but I also made some interesting discoveries along the way. I will share them with you.

■ Behavior at a Glance

Trend followers are stocks that close in the same direction as an index on a given day. They follow the trend. Countertrend stocks close in the direction opposite the index. If the index closes higher, for example, trend followers will also close higher, but countertrend stocks will close lower.

Figure 20.1 shows the median performance of trend followers and countertrend stocks. Notice that the bearish trend followers and the bearish countertrend stocks drop in the early days (circled, at A), but eventually, the bull market pulls them into positive territory after about a month. Those two categories represent stocks that drop when the market rises (bearish countertrend stocks) or when the market falls (bearish trend followers). Because they begin life as bearish in a bull market, their underperformance is expected.

The bullish trend followers perform best at the start (B), but bullish countertrend stocks overtake them at six months.

For hold times of six months to a year, the bullish countertrend stocks (C) outperform the other varieties. For shorter duration hold times, the bullish trend followers do best. The bearish trend followers are the stinkers. They underperform from the start and continue to do lousy for at least a year (D).

The chart suggests that if you want to make more money over the long term, look for bullish countertrend stocks followed by bullish trend followers.

■ Bullish trend followers perform best for up to six months, but bullish countertrend stocks outperform after that.

We will explore this behavior in the coming sections.

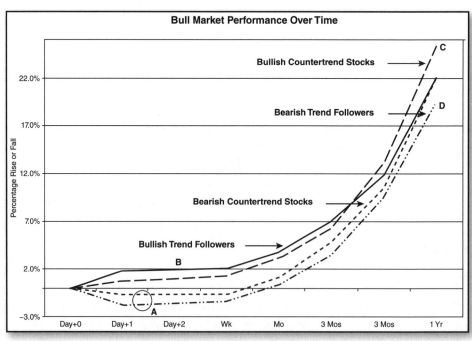

FIGURE 20.1   The performance of trend and countertrend stocks over time.

■ Trend and Countertrend Setup

To investigate trends and countertrends, I sampled three indices: Dow Jones Industrial Average, S&P 500 Index, and NASDAQ Composite. I looked at three minimum daily close-to-close moves in the indices: 0.25%, 1%, and 2%. The 1% results in the S&P 500 Index were midrange, meaning those at 0.25% performed a bit worse but were plentiful, and the 2% results were better but fewer. In this discussion, I chose the S&P Index with 1% moves to represent all of the results. The S&P Index follows more companies than the Dow but not as many as the NASDAQ Composite, so it is midrange, too.

In the sections that follow, I will refer to a *big rise* or *big drop* in the S&P (the "index"). That is the one-day move the index closed higher or lower, respectively, at least 1%.

I used the bull market from October 11, 2002 (the day after the bear market ended), to October 10, 2007 (the day before the next bear market began).

I measured the close-to-close difference in the S&P 500 Index from one trading day to the next, looking for price swings of at least 1%. For each move, I compared the move of 362 stocks (that is, as many as would fit on my spreadsheet). Some of those stocks closed in the same direction as the S&P (the *trend followers*), and others closed in the opposite direction (*countertrend stocks*).

Those stocks are from the database I use on a daily basis. They are an eclectic bunch, ranging from relative newborns (Facebook) to old timers (3M), small cap to large cap, selected from about 55 industries.

Dividends, interest, commissions, and other fees were not included in any results in this chapter (or in any of the other chapters, come to think of it).

Bearish Countertrends

When the index closes higher on the day of a big rise, but a stock closes lower, I call that a *bearish countertrend* move in the stock. **Figure 20.2** shows this graphically.

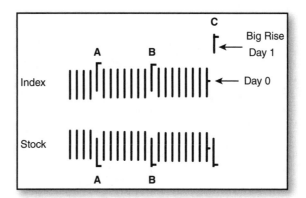

FIGURE 20.2 The stock makes two countertrend moves in the month before a big rise in the index.

The top lines represent the 21 trading days in a month before an index makes a big rise. The bottom series of vertical lines represent trading in a stock during the same days. Let us assume that the closing price of each day for both the index and stock is unchanged unless otherwise noted.

Notice that at A, the index closes higher, but the stock closes lower. That is the first bearish countertrend move by the stock. A second bearish countertrend move occurs at B when the index closes higher and the stock closes lower.

At C, the index closes substantially higher than the close on Day 0, whereas the stock closes lower. The stock is making a third bearish countertrend move by closing lower when the index makes a big rise.

In the analysis that follows, I will refer to countertrend moves like those at A and B, Day 0, and the big rise, so refer to Figure 20.2 for clarity.

Testing Bearish Countertrends

I measured the *median* performance of bearish countertrend moves over arbitrarily chosen periods, and **Table 20.1** shows the results.

For example, when the index closed at *least* 1% higher, the index actually climbed a median of 1.4% (at Day 1). The trend followers (stocks that also closed higher) did better, closing 1.8% higher. The countertrend stocks closed 0.7% *lower*.

The difference between the 1.4% gain in the index and the 1.8% gain for the trend followers is because I populated my database with volatile stocks (high beta).

The next day, the index and trend followers added 0.1 percentage points, each, and the countertrend stocks remained flat.

You can see what happened over time. At months, the countertrend stocks were outperforming the index (gains of 10.5% versus 8.5%, respectively) but still had far to go to catch the trend followers (11.9%). At year's end, the trend followers and countertrend stocks remained atop the pile (22.1% versus 22.1% and 14.7%).

■ For hold times of up to one year, avoid buying bearish countertrend stocks.

TABLE 20.1	Median Upward Moves in Index of at Least 1%: 2002–2007 Bull Market						
	Day 1	Day 2	Week	Month	3 Months	6 Months	1 Year
S&P 500 Index	1.4%	1.5%	1.6%	3.0%	5.5%	8.5%	14.7%
Trend follower stocks	1.8%	1.9%	2.1%	3.8%	7.1%	11.9%	22.1%
Countertrend stocks	−0.7%	−0.7%	−0.6%	1.1%	4.9%	10.5%	22.1%

Bearish Countertrend Stock Selection

These results uncover a valuable rule of stock selection: Avoid buying stocks that drop when the index makes a big rise. If a stock makes such a bearish countertrend move, can we use that as a rule to detect and avoid underperforming stocks? Yes.

I investigated this rule and made a startling discovery. Then I found a mistake in my spreadsheet. Forget the startling discovery.

My idea was to look at the performance of stocks in the month before the index made a big rise. If the stocks also dropped as the index climbed during those days (bearish countertrend moves) and the stocks later underperformed, then we can use those countertrend moves as a warning of future underperformance. **Table 20.2** shows my results.

I used the same test as before but included more bull market data (from March 7, 2009, to November 21, 2013, in 297 stocks). This time, I also counted the number of countertrend moves in the month before the big rise in the S&P Index.

The trend followers' row is the exception in this table. I pulled it from Table 20.4, so it includes only the 2002 to 2007 bull market. It shows how stocks that followed a bearish move in the index (a big drop) performed over time.

Let us talk about the "From-To" columns. The columns determine a range of how many countertrend moves appeared in stocks in the month *before* the big rise. The rest of the table shows the median performance that resulted in the months *after* the big rise.

For example, the 0 to 0 row counted only stocks that had *no* bearish countertrend moves (bullish countertrend moves were ignored) in the month before a big rise. The last row shows the performance over time of stocks having between 8 and 21 bearish countertrend moves. Twenty-one is the number of trading days in one month. The sample count is too small after eight.

Stocks with no bearish countertrend moves (0 to 0 row) were up 0.2% one month *after* the big rise. On the day of the big rise, those stocks closed lower by 0.8% (not shown in the table). After a week, they were down less, 0.3%. Sometime within a month, the stocks turned and were making money, closing 0.2% higher.

TABLE 20.2 Median Bearish Countertrend Stock Moves over Time

From	To	1 Month	3 Months	6 Months	1 Year	Samples
(Down) Trend followers		0.3%	3.5%	9.6%	19.5%	26,367
0	0	0.2%	4.3%	11.4%	21.2%	557
2	21	0.8%	4.8%	9.9%	18.8%	18,793
4	21	0.9%	5.2%	9.5%	18.1%	10,637
6	21	0.5%	5.5%	9.3%	17.6%	3,638
8	21	−0.1%	5.7%	9.1%	16.8%	756

The countertrend rows (2 to 8) show the performance as the number of bearish countertrends increases in the month before a big rise. At three months in the future, looking down the columns, performance improves, which I consider odd. For longer periods, though, the trend reverts to the expected, with performance deteriorating when the number of countertrend moves increases. The 1-year median shows the trend. For 0 to 0 (no countertrend moves), countertrend stocks gained 21.2%. Those with 8 to 21 countertrend moves gained just 16.8% after a year.

- As more countertrend moves in a stock occur in the month before the index rises by at least 1% (in one session), stock performance suffers.

- Avoid buying stocks that drop when the index closes at least 1% higher.

I did not investigate the reasons for this underperformance. Clearly, one bad day in the market should not stunt the enthusiasm of investors. My guess is this underperformance is a symptom of a company in trouble.

■ Size of the Drop

So far, I have not discussed the size of the drop suffered by the countertrend stocks on the day of the big rise. Let us do that now.

The median close-to-close drop was 13 cents in the countertrend stocks when the index made its big rise. Countertrend stocks with smaller drops showed year-ahead gains that averaged 35.3%. Those stocks that dropped more than 13 cents showed gains averaging 26.2%. This makes sense. The larger the countertrend decline, the worse the performance. Note that those numbers are averages.

Table 20.3 shows the median gain, not the average. The median drop was a loss of 13 cents suffered in the countertrend stocks on the day the index climbed 1%. Stocks that dropped a multiple of 13 cents suffered progressively worse performance a year later.

TABLE 20.3	Median Year Ahead Gains from Countertrend Stocks as Drop Increases	
Loss	**1 Year Gain**	**Samples**
>$0.13	18.8%	2,952
0.26	17.4%	1,720
0.39	16.0%	1,112
0.52	14.2%	735
0.65	13.7%	522
0.78	14.6%	406
0.91	14.3%	308
1.04	14.6%	250
1.17	15.6%	201

For example, stocks that dropped more than 13 cents showed median gains a year later of 18.8%. Stocks that dropped nine times as far ($1.17) gained 15.6% a year later.

■ The larger the countertrend drop in a stock the worse the year-ahead performance.

Shorting Countertrend Stocks

If you find a bearish countertrend stock, should you short it? Maybe.

Look back at Table 20.1. Bearish countertrend stocks in my database lost 0.7% on the days the S&P closed 1.4% higher. A month later, the countertrend stocks had moved into positive territory and showed gains for the remainder of the intervals up to a year.

Since countertrend stocks recover quickly, it is not enough to find bearish countertrend stocks and short them. You have to consider other factors. But searching for bearish countertrend stocks does highlight weaker securities. That is an important ingredient in a short sale candidate.

■ Consider bearish countertrend stocks as one ingredient in stocks suitable for shorting.

■ Trading Example

Here is an example of how I used the lessons we have learned so far in this chapter.

In late November 2013, I had a sizable amount in cash waiting for investment, earning almost nothing in my brokerage account. So I started shopping around for a stock to buy and found J. C. Penney, shown in **Figure 20.3**.

New management can turn around a company and when they succeed, the stock can soar. If they fail, then the stock can find itself in the morgue. For J. C. Penney, new management arrived and tried a turnaround strategy that did not work. The stock tanked, peaking at more than 43 in early February 2012 (not shown) and dropping to a low near 6 in October 2013 (shown).

In April 2013, the company brought back Myron (Mike) Ullman, who served as chairman and CEO from 2004 to 2011, to attempt another turnaround.

I became interested in the stock in late November 2013 when I saw the V-shaped bottom (trend A in Figure 20.3). I guessed that the stock might make a double bottom (dropping back to 6 from the current 10), but it was more likely to continue rising.

I understood the dangers involved in buying this stock, so I cut my position size by two-thirds and placed a limit order to buy the stock at 9.51. That figure comes

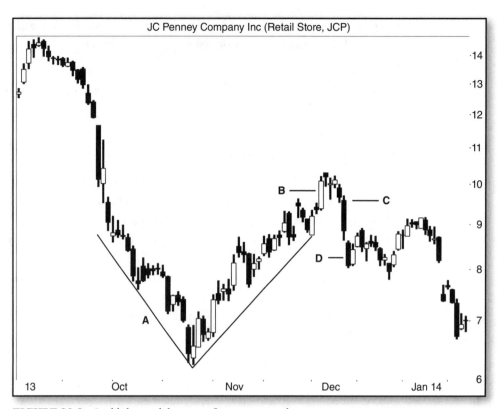

FIGURE 20.3 I sold the stock because of a countertrend move.

from B. I expected the stock to retrace its large one-day move up (nearly 8%), so I cut the move in half and a bit more to set the 9.51 number, a penny above the round number 9.50.

On the day I bought (C), the company made news. A hedge fund sold its 5.2% stake in the company. I only heard of that sale after the close. However, I checked on the stock the next day. It was down again (D) even as the Dow was up almost 200 points, or 1.3% (the S&P climbed 1.1%, too, a big rise).

When I saw the bearish countertrend move in the stock, I decided to sell my position and received a fill at 8.30. Even though I lost 13% on the trade, the dollar value was small because I bought only one-third of the normal position size.

After I sold, the stock moved sideways for about a month before tumbling again. The stock bottomed at 4.90 (not shown), down 41% below the price at which I sold.

- Use countertrend performance as a gauge of how well a company may perform in the future.

■ Bullish Countertrends

Bullish countertrend stocks are those that climb on the day the index makes a big drop. The results are exciting (for me, anyway).

Table 20.4 shows the performance over time of the S&P 500 Index trend followers and countertrend stocks after a drop of at least 1% in the index. This uses the same periods and the same methodology as Table 20.1 except that I was looking for a drop in the index instead of a rise.

For example, the S&P 500 Index closed lower by a median of 1.3% in the "Day 1" column. Stocks that also closed lower—the trend followers—dropped a median of 1.7%. The countertrend stocks climbed 0.8%. This is as it should be because I separated the trend followers from the countertrend players.

Look at the far right column. A year after the index dropped at least 1% (in one session) in a bull market it closed 13.0% higher (the median move). The trend followers posted a median rise of 19.6%, probably due to their high beta values (more volatile than the index). But the countertrend stocks were the moon shots with median gains of 25.4%. That is 30% better than the trend followers and almost double the performance of the index. Yes, you heard it here first. Countertrend stocks are the ones that closed higher (by any amount) on the day the index closed at least 1% lower.

Here is a setup based on this idea:

- Wait for the S&P 500 Index to drop at least 1%, close-to-close, on the daily chart. Let us call the first close Day 0.

- Find a stock that closes higher on the same day as the big drop in the index.

- Buy the stock at the open the next day. Alternatively, wait a week. If the stock is still higher than the close on Day 0, then buy.

- Sell it one year later.

TABLE 20.4	Median Downward Moves in Index of at Least 1%: 2002–2007 Bull Market						
	Day 1	Day 2	Week	Month	3 Months	6 Months	1 Year
S&P 500 Index	−1.3%	−1.1%	−1.0%	0.5%	2.9%	7.7%	13.0%
Trend followers (stocks)	−1.7%	−1.7%	−1.4%	0.3%	3.5%	9.6%	19.6%
Countertrend (stocks)	0.8%	1.1%	1.4%	3.1%	6.4%	13.3%	25.4%

Note that you ignore the stock for a year (with no stop in place), so this setup is more of an academic exercise than a realistic trading setup.

How often does this work? I compared the performance of the countertrend stocks with the index and found that 67% of them beat the median 13.0% rise in the index after one year. Sixteen percent lost money, so you do have to be selective and diversify to help minimize the risk of loss.

Look at the other columns in Table 20.4. In each column, the countertrend stocks beat the performance of the trend followers and the index, sometimes substantially.

Do you want to boost performance? Hold off buying the countertrend stock for a week. If it is down, then (compared to Day 0) avoid the stock. If it is still higher, then buy. The 5% failure rate (a count of how many stocks failed to rise at least 5% before dropping significantly) drops modestly from 22% to 19% and the median rise climbs from 25.4% to 27.8% if you hold for the remainder of a year. Risk drops and reward increases. What is not to like? I am in love.

- Boost returns from potential countertrend buy candidates by delaying purchase a week and reexamining the situation.

Bullish Countertrend Stock Selection

Table 20.5 is the same as Table 20.2 except applied to bullish countertrends. Again, that is when the index closes down at least 1% in one session, but the countertrend stocks close higher. Let us call the first close Day 0.

The trend followers row is from Table 20.1. It shows the median performance over time of stocks that closed higher on the day of a big rise in the index. Use it as a comparison to the countertrend moves.

The 0 to 0 row shows countertrend stocks with no bullish countertrend moves in the month before Day 0. Those stocks gained a median of 18.9% a year later.

TABLE 20.5	Median Bullish Countertrend Stock Moves over Time					
From	To	1 Month	3 Months	6 Months	1 Year	Samples
(Up) Trend followers		3.8%	7.1%	11.9%	22.1%	27,921
0	0	3.4%	8.1%	11.4%	18.9%	741
2	21	3.1%	6.5%	12.8%	23.2%	15,454
4	21	2.7%	6.1%	13.2%	24.4%	7,562
6	21	2.1%	5.0%	14.0%	27.1%	1,880
8	21	1.4%	5.1%	18.3%	35.3%	229

Stocks that made at least two bullish countertrend moves in the month leading to Day 0 did better with median gains of 23.2% at the end of a year. Samples, at more than 15,000, are plentiful, too. Read the remainder of the table in the same manner. As the number of bullish countertrend moves increases in the month before Day 0, performance generally improves, from 22.1% for the trend followers to 35.3% for the 8 to 21 row.

Here is a setup based on the idea of bullish countertrend moves:

1. Wait for the S&P 500 Index to close down at least 1%.
2. Find a stock that closes up on that day.
3. Look at the prior month and count the number of bullish countertrend moves (the index drops, but the stock rises). The more you find, the better the potential year-ahead performance.
4. Buy and hold the stock for a year.

Again, this setup is not for cardiac patients. It does not use a stop loss and it ignores the stock for an entire year.

Preliminary testing of this setup shows it works well. Comparing the median performance of stocks having at least two bullish countertrend moves against the S&P 500 Index (not shown in the table, but the index rises a median 12.8% after holding for a year), we find that 64% of the stocks beat the index after holding for a year.

The number of stocks closing down (losing trades) after a year was 19%. Sixty-five percent of the stocks were higher after holding for a month, but that also means 35% were lower. That shows the value of a buy-and-hold approach, at least for holding a year in a bull market.

- Find bullish countertrend stocks with at least two bullish countertrend moves in the month leading to a 1% or greater drop in the index. Hold the stocks for a year.

As with bearish countertrend stocks, presumably the bullish variety have something fueling their performance. One exceptional day is no reason to believe the performance will continue, and yet it does. Consider it as a tip that you have found a winner.

Size of the Rise Is the size of the rise important that bullish countertrend stocks make when the index drops on the day of the big fall? Surprisingly, no.

Table 20.6 shows the median year-ahead gains of bullish countertrend stocks sorted by the size of the one-day rise they made when the index closed at least 1% lower.

TABLE 20.6	Median Year Ahead Gains from Bullish Countertrend Stocks as Rise Increases	
Rise	**1 Year Gain**	**Samples**
>$0.15	23.5%	2611
0.30	21.4%	1427
0.45	21.4%	875
0.60	22.7%	546
0.75	23.5%	386
0.90	23.8%	276
1.05	23.8%	202
1.20	23.9%	161
1.35	23.7%	120

The median rise was 15 cents on the day the index made a big drop. A year later, those stocks rising more than 15 cents posted median gains of 23.5%. Despite varying the size of the rise in the bullish countertrend stocks, the gains after holding for a year maintained a narrow range from 21% to 24%.

■ Year-ahead performance does not change much regardless of the size of the rise bullish countertrend stocks make when the index drops at least 1%.

This chapter shows that trend and countertrend stocks can be valuable additions to a diversified portfolio. Look for them at finer shops everywhere.

■ Closing Position

As soon as I finish writing this book, I am going to finish a trading setup I have been working on. The setup uses bullish countertrends to select stocks for out performance. It is based on this chapter's results.

I am hoping to develop a mechanical system to identify bullish countertrend stocks to buy and use a count of countertrends in the prior month to signal a sale (if the number of bullish countertrends during any 30-day period drops below a threshold, then sell).

For me, the system would be a new way to momentum trade. If the system proves itself, I may add it to my toolbox.

CHAPTER 21

Triangle Apex and Turning Points

Sometimes you run across an unusual idea that is hard to believe, and yet it works. The triangle apex and price turning is one of those ideas. Let us call it the apex turn.

There are three types of triangles: ascending, descending, and symmetrical. Each of those triangles has trendlines that join sometime in the future, at the triangle's apex. If you draw the triangle trendlines carefully, you may notice that price will turn when it reaches the date of the apex.

Sometimes the turn is dramatic, such that the trend changes. Sometimes the turn lasts only for a few days before the trend resumes. But, in both cases, a turn happens within a few days of the triangle's apex.

Let us take a closer look at this behavior.

■ Behavior at a Glance

Figure 21.1 shows two symmetrical triangles. Let us take the case of the top triangle with an upward breakout.

Price bounces from side to side until the upward breakout sends price cascading through the top trendline. In the ideal case, when price reaches the date when the top and bottom triangle trendlines merge (the apex), the price trend changes (leaving a minor high or low behind).

Downward breakouts show the same behavior. Price forms a peak or valley coinciding with the date the triangle forms its apex.

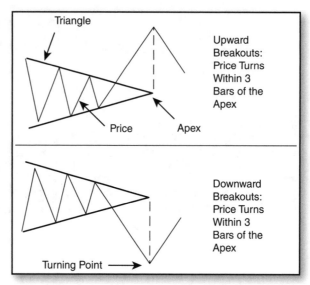

FIGURE 21.1 Price turns within three days of the triangle's apex.

I found that for both upward and downward breakouts, the median distance from the nearest peak or valley to the date of the apex is three price bars. In other words, half of the triangles form a peak or valley (price turns) closer than three bars and half turn farther away than three price bars.

■ Identification

Table 21.1 shows guidelines for using the triangle apex.

Valid Triangle. The apex turn works for all three types of triangles: ascending, descending, and symmetrical. Consult the associated chapters for identification guidelines for the triangle of your choice.

TABLE 21.1 **Triangle Apex and Turning Point Guidelines**

Characteristic	Discussion
Valid triangle	Look for a valid ascending, descending, or symmetrical triangle. Those triangles see price cross the pattern from side to side with at least five touches, total, of the two trendlines.
Apex	Carefully draw two converging trendlines and join them at the triangle's apex.
Turn	Expect price to form a minor high or low at or near the date of the triangle's apex.

Essentially, look for a price series that narrows, bounded by two trendlines. The stock should cross the triangle from side to side, touching the two trendlines with at least five minor highs or lows. The breakout can be either up or down.

Apex. Draw the two converging trendlines so that they just touch the peaks and valleys of the triangle. Join the two trendlines at the apex.

Turn. The date the triangle forms the apex, look for price to change direction. It may form a peak or a valley a few days before to a few days after the date of the apex. The turn may not last long, but at least you have some idea of when the turn may appear.

■ Examples

Before we discuss numbers, let me show you three examples of the apex turn.

Example 1: AFLAC

Figure 21.2 shows the first case. A symmetrical triangle appears at A. Notice that price crosses the chart pattern from side to side, leaving little room for white space (which is good). The stock touches the trendlines several times, just as one would expect from a valid triangle. And yet this stock poops out after an upward breakout.

FIGURE 21.2 A symmetrical triangle with an upward breakout sees price climb to C and reverse trend.

The stock rises to C, right above apex B. This is an example of the way the apex turn should work, but often the dramatic turn is not as violent or as extensive as the one shown here.

After C, the stock plummets, pretending to be a novice cliff diver that bounces off a ledge in August before plunging into the sea in October.

Example 2: Aon

Figure 21.3 shows a descending triangle in the center of the chart. If you draw the bottom trendline to skirt the lows of the triangle (line A), the stock reaches the apex at E. Directly above E is valley F, right where it is supposed to be. Price turns and moves higher.

If you wish to use an internal trendline, I show that variation, too, using line B. This trendline cuts through price but is a better fit, meaning it is closer to the valleys, giving more distinct trendline touches. I like this line best.

The apex of the triangle using line B is D. Directly above D is the peak at C. For short-term traders (swing traders using the daily scale, or day traders if this chart were intraday), this is a timely turn.

FIGURE 21.3   Price turns at the triangle apex.

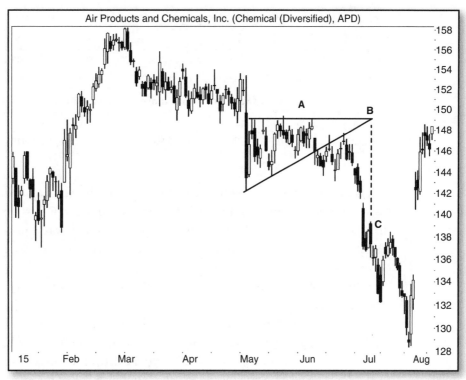

FIGURE 21.4 The stock is supposed to turn when price, C, reaches the apex, B.

Example 3: Air Products

Figure 21.4 shows what an apex turn failure looks like. Ascending triangle A is well formed and valid. Price breaks out downward and struggles for a time by moving sideways, but then someone lets the air out of the stock. Price drops.

When price reaches the apex, B, the stock is supposed to turn, either at a peak or a valley. One could argue that C is a small peak and therefore the technique works in this case, too. Or one could argue that the downward trend is unaffected.

I do not consider C to be a peak, and price continues lower. This is a failure of the apex turn method.

How often does the apex turn work?

■ The Numbers

Proving that this technique works is not as easy as it sounds. I used a visual test of 388 stocks and found 221 triangles with data from October 2006 to January 2008.

I found that the technique worked 75% of the time. That means the apex aligned with a peak or valley within a few days.

TABLE 21.2	Frequency Distribution of Distance from Apex to Nearest Peak or Valley										
Price Bars	0	1	2	3	4	5	6	7	8	9	>9
Frequency	24%	13%	11%	9%	8%	7%	8%	7%	4%	2%	8%
Cumulative	24%	37%	48%	57%	65%	72%	80%	86%	90%	92%	100%
Upward Breakouts Above, Downward Below											
Frequency	22%	14%	12%	9%	7%	8%	8%	7%	4%	2%	7%
Cumulative	22%	35%	47%	57%	64%	72%	80%	87%	91%	93%	100%

In another test, I matched the date of the apex to the nearest peak or valley using my computer (automated). I used 1,231 stocks and found 6,804 triangles. I found that the median distance from the nearest peak or valley was 3 price bars, regardless of the breakout direction. That is where the 3-bar statistic shown in Figure 21.1 comes from.

Table 21.2 shows a frequency distribution of the apex distance to the nearest peak or valley.

For example, 24% of the triangles showed the apex directly under a peak or above a valley on the same day. Price turned after that day, in other words. Another 13% showed a peak or valley just 1 day away from the date of the apex. If you combine the two, 37% showed a turn (a peak or a valley) within a day of the apex's date.

The lower half of the table shows the numbers for downward breakouts from triangles.

Use this table to help give you an idea of how well the apex turn works for stocks. If you draw the triangle trendlines carefully, price should turn near the triangle apex. The turn may not last long, so do not expect a trend change (a 20% swing from high to low or low to high). It happens, but that is rare.

■ Trading

This technique is best suited for day and swing traders. Because they are short-term traders, knowing when to sell is invaluable.

If you see a triangle forming, carefully draw the two trendlines along the tops of the peaks and below the bottoms of the valleys that form the triangle.

Expect the stock to turn near the date or time of the triangle's apex.

The apex turn is especially useful for day traders, traders that hold a stock for one trading session.

For position traders and buy-and-hold investors, the technique is only useful if you are already planning to sell an existing position or maybe buy into a new one. Why? Because the trends that often appear after the apex turn are short term, often just a few days long. These trends are like the waves washing up on a beach. Swing and day traders can make money trading those waves. But position traders and investors try to profit from the tide, not the waves. They look for the trend changes that accompany the tidal flows. The apex turn may time the turn in the tide, but that is rare.

■ Closing Position

By carefully connecting triangle peaks with a trendline and valleys with another trendline, the merging of those two trendlines can predict where price is going to turn. The turn may not last long, and the triangle's apex may be a few days early or a few days late, but you can use the forecast to plan your trade.

Having a trading plan you follow puts you far ahead of others that do not use such tools and suffer as a result.

CHAPTER 22

Triangles, Ascending

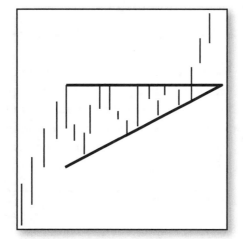

I once thought that ascending triangles were the answer to making a lot of money in the stock market. Then I started trading them and faced loss after loss. The 5% failure rate, which is a measure of how often price fails to rise at least 5% above the breakout price, is 16%. Compared to other chart patterns that sport failure rates in the low to mid single digits, 16% is huge.

The high failure rate underscores the difficulty of making money trading ascending triangles. For many of you, leave this chart pattern to the professionals.

However, there are techniques that help improve the odds of success and when you do win, there is a better potential for a large gain.

This chapter explores the chart pattern and its behavior.

■ Behavior at a Glance

Figure 22.1 shows the overall performance of ascending triangles. One of the delights of ascending triangles is that they point to an upward breakout 64% of the time. The average rise is a tasty 43%, but the median rise is less, 22%. That means half the triangles will rise more and half will rise less than 22%. Those numbers are for perfect trades, too, without commissions or fees deducted, so do not even dream of making 43%.

Downward breakouts occur 36% of the time and when they do occur, price drops an average of 15%. The median drop is just 11%, so you do have to take care if you intend to short a stock showing an ascending triangle.

- Price breaks out upward 64% of the time.

Throwbacks and Pullbacks

Figure 22.2 shows the behavior of stocks after the breakout from an ascending triangle.

Throwbacks occur after an upward breakout. Price rises an average of 7% in 5 days. Then price begins its retrace to the top of the pattern (the breakout). It completes the trip in 5 more days (10 total since the breakout).

Following that, the stock resumes its upward move 70% of the time. That means the stock will close below the bottom of the triangle 30% of the time. If you own a

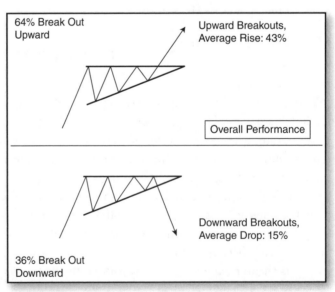

FIGURE 22.1 The overall performance of ascending triangles for both breakout directions.

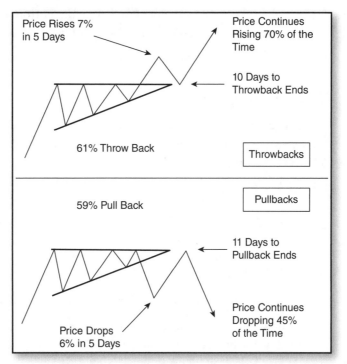

FIGURE 22.2 Ascending triangles have both throwbacks and pullbacks.

stock showing an ascending triangle, the 70% number is comforting but not a guarantee of a continued move higher.

Almost two out of three (61%) ascending triangles will have a throwback. One of the more interesting bones I dug up is that triangles that do *not* have throwbacks vastly outperform those that do. It is as if a throwback robs the stock of upward momentum and blunts the average rise. That degraded performance appears to be true for most chart patterns, not just ascending triangles.

Ascending triangles without throwbacks are like helium balloons released from the clutches of a child. They just soar and soar until a jetliner sucks them into an engine, of course. If you are not wearing a parachute, then look for the Hudson River and hope that "Sully" Sullenberger is driving. Maybe you can get out of the trade in one piece.

■ Price continues rising 70% of the time after a throwback from an ascending triangle.

Downward breakouts have pullbacks, and they happen 59% of the time in ascending triangles. The average profile of a pullback is price drops and bottoms in 5 days and 6% below the breakout. Then it recovers. That recovery takes another 6 days (11 total since the breakout) before the stock resumes its downward move. On average,

45% of the time the stock will close below the bottom of the triangle, and 55% of the time the stock will close above the top of it.

- Price continues dropping 45% of the time after a pullback from an ascending triangle.

Busted Triangles

Figure 22.3 shows the performance statistics for busted triangles. For upward breakouts, the triangle busts when price rises less than 10% before reversing and closing below the bottom of the chart pattern.

I found that 28% of ascending triangles with upward breakouts bust at least once. Instead of making money on the long side, the cleaners suck the money from your wallet or purse when the triangle busts. Busting is one reason why ascending triangles are difficult to trade.

If the bust occurs once (a single bust), price drops an average of 25% before a trend change happens.

- Price busts an upward breakout from an ascending triangle 28% of the time.

For downward breakouts, price busts the pattern when the stock drops less than 10% below the breakout price and rises to close above the top trendline. Almost *half* (44%) bust a downward breakout. The single bust rise averages 49%.

- Price busts a downward breakout from an ascending triangle 44% of the time.

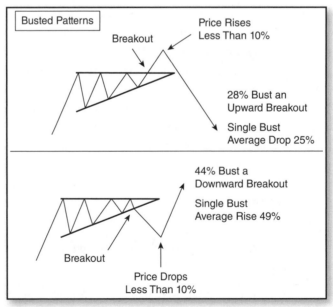

FIGURE 22.3 Price busts a triangle after the breakout when price fails to move more than 10% in the breakout direction before reversing and then closing outside the top or bottom of the chart pattern.

■ Identification

Even for experts, ascending triangles can pose a problem for identification. To solve this, I now use the guidelines shown in **Table 22.1**. Consider **Figure 22.4** as I discuss the guidelines.

TABLE 22.1	Identification Guidelines
Characteristic	**Discussion**
Horizontal top trendline	The top of the ascending triangle is flat or mostly flat. A trendline connecting them should be also.
Up-sloping bottom trendline	The bottom of the triangle slopes upward so that it joins with the top trendline sometime in the future.
Trendline touches	Price should touch the two trendlines at least five times, total, three on one side and two on the other.
White space	Price should cross the pattern plenty of times to fill the white space with price action.
Volume	Typically slopes downward and can become very low a day or two before the breakout. Do not discard a pattern because it has an unusual volume trend.
Breakout	Upward breakouts occur when price closes above the top trendline. Downward breakouts happen when price closes below the up-sloping trendline.

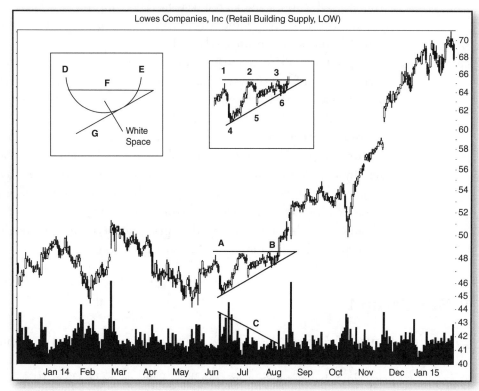

FIGURE 22.4 This ascending triangle leads to a good rise.

Horizontal Top Trendline. Price along the top of the triangle should appear flat or nearly so. The figure shows the triangle top as line AB.

Up-Sloping Bottom Trendline. Price along the bottom of the triangle follows an up-sloping trendline like that shown in the figure.

Trendline Touches. Many of the bogus ascending triangles I see novice traders select occur when they cut off a major valley. They draw a flat line from one side of the valley to the other, slap on an up-sloping bottom, and then hold up their hands and yell, "Done!"

Not so fast. Price must touch each trendline at least twice with one trendline having three or more touches. Each touch should reside on a minor high or minor low. Do not cut through price at the start or end of the pattern and count that as a touch.

Look at the inset. I drew semicircle DE as if this were a rounding turn or major low. Then I drew a horizontal line F and an up-sloping line G to resemble triangle FG. The straight FG lines do not make an ascending triangle. Why? Because this triangle only touches price once in a minor high or minor low. Line F slices through curve DE, so those are not minor highs or lows. They do not count. The bottom trendline touches curved line DE only once, along the southeast edge of the circle.

Compare that to the numbered triangle. Three distinct touches occur on the top of the triangle and three on the bottom. Sometimes price does not touch the trendline, but it comes close enough. That is fine.

White Space. Price should cross the pattern from side to side, filling the triangle with movement. The FG pattern has a huge blob of white space in the middle of it. Compare that to the 1-6 triangle. The 1-6 triangle has price crossing from side to side, covering the white space with ink (or pixels).

Volume. Depending on the breakout direction, volume trends lower over 75% of the time. Figure 22.4 shows an example of this at C. When volume slopes upward, ironically, the triangle tends to perform better (49% versus 42% average rise for up- and down-sloping volume trends, respectively). Thus, never discard an ascending triangle because the volume trend is wrong.

Breakout. A breakout occurs when price closes outside the trendline boundaries. An upward breakout in Figure 22.4 occurs at B.

■ Buy Setup 1

Figure 22.5 shows the first buy setup, and it uses a busted ascending triangle. A busted triangle for this setup depends on a downward breakout. That occurs when price closes below the bottom trendline. Price drops less than 10% before reversing and closing above the top of the chart pattern.

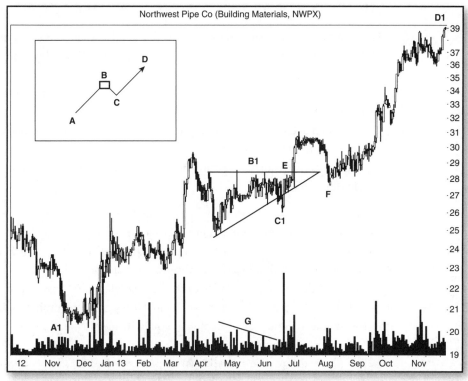

FIGURE 22.5 A busted ascending triangle leads to a large rise.

The inset shows the configuration for this setup. Price can enter the ascending triangle from any direction, but I show it rising (A) going into the triangle (B). A downward breakout occurs and sees price drop to C. The BC move must be less than 10%. Then the stock rises and closes above the top of B, on the way to D, busting the downward breakout.

The stock shows an example of this behavior on the daily chart. A1 begins the upward run at the trend start. Price rises to the triangle at B1. A downward breakout from the triangle occurs at C1, forming a nubbin that looks like something your shaver missed.

The downward breakout lasted just the day before price zipped back up into the triangle. The stock moved sideways for about a week and then broke out upward at E. Then a throwback brought the stock back down to F before recovering and moving up to D1.

Although the chart shows the stock peaking at D1, the stock goes on to post a 45% gain.

The figure shows what a well-performing single busted triangle looks like. Not all busted patterns will act this way, of course. Scanning over the busted performance numbers shows that many of the ascending triangles bust multiple times. I will discuss that in a moment.

Here are the steps for trading a single (or triple) busted pattern:

1. Qualify the chart pattern using the identification guidelines shown in Table 22.1.
2. Price breaks out downward and drops less than 10% below the bottom trendline.
3. The stock reverses and closes above the top trendline, busting the triangle for the first time.
4. You can place a buy order a penny above the top trendline or buy at the open the day after it busts the triangle.
5. Place a stop-loss order a penny below the bottom of the triangle or at a location of your choice.

Table 22.2 shows a few performance statistics for this setup.

I found 1,312 ascending triangles that I am proud to call my friends. I looked for them using 772 stocks with data starting in July 1991 and ending May 2015, using bull markets only. Not all stocks covered the entire period.

1. I found that almost half (44%) of the triangles with downward breakouts will bust. That means price will drop less than 10% before reversing and closing above the top of the triangle. It also means you will have a target rich environment to search for busted triangles.

2, 3. The average rise for all busted patterns is 34%. That measures from the top trendline until price reaches the ultimate high. Because it includes double and triple busts, the rise is smaller than the average rise of a single busted pattern (49%).

4–6. A single busted pattern has price drop less than 10% before reversing and trending in the new direction (rising more than 10% above the top of the triangle). A single bust happens 67% of the time from the pool of patterns that bust.

Double busted patterns occur after a single bust. Instead of a new trend developing, price fails to move more than 10% away from the new breakout price before reversing again and closing on the opposite side of the pattern. If a trend then develops

TABLE 22.2 Statistics for Busted Triangles with Downward Breakouts	
Description	Result
1. Percentage of triangles that bust	44%
2. Average rise after busting	34%
3. Average rise after single bust	49%
4. Percentage of single busts	67%
5. Percentage of double busts	15%
6. Percentage of triple+ busts	18%

and price moves more than 10% away from the trendline, then the busting count stops at two.

If the stock reverses again before reaching the magic 10% number, a third bust happens. Double busts happen 15% of the time, and three or more busts (which I lump together and call triple busts) happen 18% of the time. The glossary shows an example of the three types of busts.

How can you tell if a triangle will single, double, or triple bust? I have no idea. However, I check for support and resistance to help eliminate situations where overhead resistance could stop an advance. You will also want to see that the industry is doing well along with the general market.

■ Buy Setup 2

Figure 22.6 shows a setup based on the absence of overhead resistance, or the ability of the stock to pierce that resistance, and break out to all-time high territory.

Look at the inset. At A, price peaks and forms overhead resistance (but resistance can form in other ways besides a peak. I just show a peak for convenience). That resistance can be a month away or a decade away.

FIGURE 22.6 A stock can make big gains when price pierces overhead resistance.

Price drops to the trend start (or it could rise to the trend start), B. A triangle forms (C) below that resistance and an upward breakout takes price higher. On the way to all-time high territory (D), price could struggle when it hits overhead resistance, but if it pushes through, the gain can be exciting.

For best results, the triangle should appear near the start of a trend. I used six months as the separator between a long trend and a short one. Measured from the trend start (B) to the start of the chart pattern (C, the first trendline touch), if that time is less than six months, you are more likely nearer the start of the trend than the end.

When the time from the trend start to the pattern start was more than 6 months, the stocks gained an average of 33% after the breakout. Those shorter than 6 months gained an average of 44%. That is a startling difference, so pay attention to the time from the trend start to the ascending triangle.

The stock chart shows an example of this setup on the daily scale. I highlighted A1 (far left) because you may think this is near where overhead resistance is. Yes, a peak forms near A1 (not shown), and it is priced right at the top of the triangle. However, in 2006, the stock peaks much higher than the triangle (55% higher, at 47.35). So the stock had to push upward through all of that resistance before actually breaking out to all-time highs. Once it cleared resistance, the stock was free to climb farther, which it did (to 57.99). The gain from the top of the triangle to the ultimate high was 90%.

In this example, the trend start is at B1, the triangle is at C1, and price climbs to D1 (D1 is *not* the ultimate high).

Here are the steps for using this setup:

1. Qualify the ascending triangle using the identification guidelines from Table 22.1.
2. Find the trend start, the lowest low or highest high before which price rises or falls, respectively, at least 20%. Ignore any overshoot or undershoot price makes in the week or two before the start of the triangle.
3. Select patterns in which the time from the trend start to the start of the triangle is less than six months.
4. Look for overhead resistance. Select stocks trading at or near all-time highs so price can push through any overhead resistance easily.
5. Place a buy order a penny above the top of the triangle or buy at the open a day after price closes above the top of the triangle.
6. Once the order fills, place a stop-loss order a penny below the bottom of the triangle or at a location of your choice.

Table 22.3 shows performance statistics for inbound price trends six months or less and more than six months. The inbound price trend is the time from the trend start to the start of the ascending triangle.

TABLE 22.3	Statistical Analysis of Buy Setup 2	
Description	Inbound Trend ≤ 6 Months	Inbound Trend > 6 Months
1. Occurrence, samples	21%, 152	9%, 62
2. Post-breakout average gain	87%	51%
3. Median gain	64%	36%
4. Gains over 25%	79%	65%
5. 5% failure rate	1%	2%
6. 10% failure rate	4%	13%

1. Samples were few for both trends, representing only 30% of the patterns I found, so this is a rare setup.

2–4. When overhead resistance is missing or the stock pushes through it, the gains can be amazing as the table shows. If you can capture a good portion of that gain, you will be doing well. The gains are for perfect trades and likely to come down to earth with more samples.

5, 6. Failures are small but notice how the longer inbound trends fail more often (up to 13% of the time). That makes sense if you think that the chart pattern is closer to the end of the trend than the start.

To help you determine whether your chart pattern can break out to new all-time highs, **Table 22.4** shows a frequency distribution of the distance until the stock clears overhead resistance.

For example, I found 29% of ascending triangles that plowed through overhead resistance broke out to new all-time highs after rising up to 5%. Another 17% saw price rise between 5% and 10% before setting an all-time high.

You can measure the distance between the historical all-time high and the top of your ascending triangle then use Table 22.4 to see how your result compares with the historical record. Just knowing how much resistance the stock has to plow through to reach an all-time high is worth the effort of checking.

If the stock can plow through overhead resistance, and not by just a little, then you stand a good shot at having a stock trend for a long time. If a trend develops, then that is when you can make the big bucks. The trend is your friend, until it ends. Then we are talking palimony. Yuck.

TABLE 22.4	Frequency Distribution of Distance to Overhead Resistance										
Bin	5%	10%	15%	20%	25%	30%	35%	40%	45%	50%	>50%
Frequency	29%	17%	14%	8%	7%	3%	4%	2%	3%	1%	11%
Cumulative	29%	46%	60%	68%	76%	79%	83%	85%	88%	89%	100%

■ Buy Setup 3

What happens if you cannot determine whether overhead resistance will stop the stock or if you know that the stock is buried under a mound of resistance and will be unable to dig its way out? **Figure 22.7** shows an example of this scenario.

The inset shows the template for this setup. At A, overhead resistance presents a formidable challenge to making a new high. The breakout from the ascending triangle (B) sends price higher until it bumps up against resistance and the trend reverses. The stock gives up and dies by heading down to C.

In theory, if overhead resistance is far enough away, you can make money on the difference between the buy price and where you expect resistance.

The stock chart shows an example. Price peaks and forms overhead resistance at A1. An upward breakout from the triangle happens at B1 but soon, the stock hits a ceiling of resistance at D. Notice that the stock did not climb to match A1's price, so be conservative when estimating where resistance will occur.

Price tumbles and heads lower until the high thirties where it finds support (C1).

If you were to buy this stock on the breakout from the triangle, most likely the trade would have ended in a loss. The distance from the buy price to where it bumped up against resistance was not worth the risk of a failed trade.

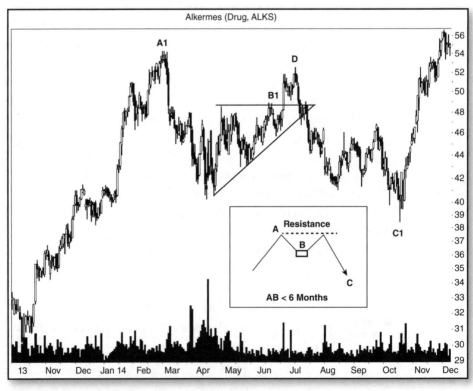

FIGURE 22.7 Overhead resistance stops the advance.

For that reason, this setup is a tricky one, but you can say that about many setups. Resistance to a further advance will appear when it wants and threaten a trade. If you are lucky, price will push through that resistance and reach all-time high territory. If not, then the trade will look like the inset in Figure 22.7.

Incidentally, triangle B1 is an example of a double-busted triangle. When price closes below the bottom of the triangle (and it does near C1, but it is difficult to see), it busts the pattern for the first time. The second bust happens when price closes above the top of the triangle. The busting process stops when price climbs more than 10% above the top of the triangle, which it does.

Here are the steps for using this setup.

1. Qualify the ascending triangle using the identification guidelines from Table 22.1.
2. Find the trend start, the lowest low or highest high before which price rises or falls, respectively, at least 20%. Ignore any overshoot or undershoot price makes in the week or two before the start of the triangle.

    In Figure 22.24 at the end of this chapter, I show the trend start at the price level of overhead resistance. That may or may not be the case, so do not depend on the trend start being the same price as the start of overhead resistance.
3. Select patterns in which the time from the trend start to the start of the triangle is less than six months.
4. Look for overhead resistance. The farther away resistance is to the current price, the better. Because this setup depends on how far resistance is above the buy price, measure that distance and decide if the trade is worth taking. If not, then look elsewhere for a more promising trade.
5. Place a buy order a penny above the top of the triangle or buy at the open a day after price closes above the top of the triangle.
6. Once the order fills, place a stop-loss order a penny below the bottom of the triangle or at a location of your choice.
7. Sell when price stalls or reverses at overhead resistance.

Table 22.5 shows performance statistics for this setup.

TABLE 22.5	Statistical Analysis of Buy Setup 3	
Description	Inbound Trend ≤6 Months	Inbound Trend >6 Months
1. Occurrence, samples	44%, 322	14%, 105
2. Post-breakout average gain	24%	17%
3. Median gain	14%	10%
4. Gains over 25%	30%	19%
5. 5% failure rate	20%	29%
6. 10% failure rate	40%	49%

1. When you trade triangles, this setup occurs most often (58% of the time).

2–4. The average gain is 24% for triangles with inbound trends (from the trend start to the triangle's start) less than or equal to 6 months long. Those greater than 6 months perform less well, 17%.

Gains over 25%, the kind I like to see, were few, ranging between 19% for long inbound trends and 30% for short trends.

5, 6. Five percent and 10% failure rates were high. Most triangles hit overhead resistance and reversed quickly.

Recall the discussion of Figure 22.2 that says 30% of throwbacks see price continuing to drop, eventually closing below the bottom of the triangle. No doubt, the results of Table 22.5 reflect (partly) the behavior of price after a throwback.

■ Best Stop Locations

Suppose you bought a stock showing an upward breakout from an ascending triangle. Where is the best location to place a stop-loss order?

A stop can protect you from a devastating loss but not always. I have owned stocks that gapped open 60% or 70% below the prior day's close, so a stop would not protect in those situations. A stop fills at the current market price, locking you into a massive drop.

To determine whether a stop would trigger, I measured how far *down* price dropped between the breakout price and the ultimate high (upward breakouts) and how far up price *climbed* from the breakout price to the ultimate low (downward breakouts). **Table 22.6** shows what I found.

1. **Penny below the pattern.** For an upward breakout, you have a 4% chance of having the stop triggered during a trade if you place it a penny below the bottom of the triangle. That would mean an average potential loss of 7% and the trades that were stopped out prematurely would have made 33%. That gain is mediocre because the average rise is 43%.

2. **Within the pattern.** If you place a stop between the top and bottom of the triangle, price will hit it 72% of the time, giving you an average loss of 4% and taking you out of trades that would have made 43%.

TABLE 22.6 **Stop Locations for Triangles**

Description	Chance of Being Hit	Average Loss	Missed Trades, Gains/Losses
1. Penny below the pattern	4%	7%	33%
2. Within the pattern	72%	4%	43%
Up Breakouts Above, Down Breakouts Below			
3. Penny above the pattern	6%	2%	13%

3. **Penny above the pattern.** I only show the results for placing a stop a penny above the triangle because the *downward* breakout price is used as the entry price and that price is already within the high-low range of the triangle. So it does not make sense for downward breakouts.

If you have a downward breakout and place a stop above the top of the triangle, the stop will trigger 6% of the time. Because the buy-in price is often close to the top of the triangle, the average loss from being stopped out is just 2%, taking you out of trades that would have seen price drop an average of 13%.

■ The best stop location is a penny either above the top (downward breakouts) or below the bottom (upward breakouts) of an ascending triangle.

■ Configuration Trading

To trade the following configurations, begin with these guidelines:

1. Find a triangle on the *daily* chart that obeys the identification guidelines listed in Table 22.1.
2. Look for the configuration that matches what you see on your *weekly* chart.
3. Buy at the open the day after the breakout or place an order to trade a penny above the top of the chart pattern (upward breakouts) or below the bottom of the pattern (downward breakouts).
4. Place a stop-loss order at a location of your choice.

The following charts use the weekly scale. I chose that scale to better place the chart pattern into the surrounding landscape. The ascending triangles and breakout direction will be difficult to see since I found them on the daily chart, not the weekly.

Here are four configurations for upward breakouts from ascending triangles that led to large gains.

Figure 22.8 shows the most common configuration. This configuration occurred in 29% of the patterns I looked at. I only used the top 143 performing triangles because the gain after that for other triangles was too small.

The AB run is downward, often over the long term (more than six months) but not always. The V-shaped turn (ABC) powers the stock upward. This configuration works best as a buy setup. Take a position in the stock on or after the upward breakout from the triangle once it becomes clear that the stock is on the road to recovery.

The stock chart shows an example of this configuration. The move down began at A1. The stock bottomed at B1 and formed an ascending triangle. The triangle looks weird here, but on the daily chart, it looks fine.

After the breakout from the triangle, the stock climbed and climbed and bumped into Matt Kowalski still floating somewhere near the International Space Station at C1.

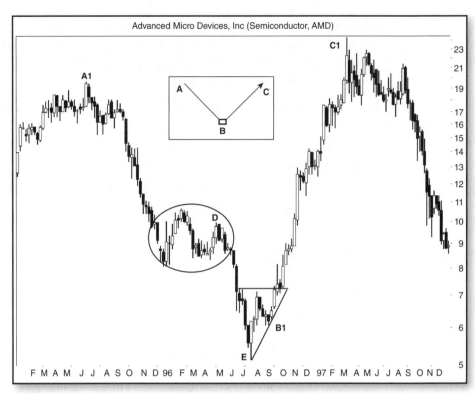

FIGURE 22.8 V-shaped turns often result in large gains.

When trading this configuration, look for a long straight-line run down to the start of the chart pattern (D to E or A1 to E). You may see pauses along the way, like that shown on the stock chart (circled), but the fewer of those, the better the likely outcome. You are looking for a V shape to the turn, but that shape will not be clear until well after the breakout.

Steady Move Up

The second most common configuration in stocks with upward breakouts and big gains is the one shown in **Figure 22.9**. It occurred 24% of the time.

The AB move (before the formation of the triangle at B) is a long one, often more than six months. An upward breakout from the triangle nudges the stock to resume its upward move, to C.

The stock chart (weekly scale) shows an example of this long climb higher. The hill begins at A1, rises to the triangle at B1, and continues to C1, after which (not shown) the price movement becomes choppy. In fact, a bear market began in mid-October 2007, near C1. The stock formed a triple top and crashed to 35 less than two years later.

FIGURE 22.9 This stock continues to rise after an upward breakout from an ascending triangle.

This setup makes me nervous because you will be buying well after the trend began. Although momentum trading has its benefits, I worry that the uptrend will end as soon as I buy. That happened with three of my trades recently when the uptrend turned horizontal/down with the general market.

With this configuration, faith in upward momentum rules. Buy after the upward breakout from the triangle and pray that the tail winds push the stock higher, far enough to make a tidy profit.

Twin Peak Failure

Figure 22.10 (weekly scale) shows a configuration I was surprised to see. Price forms a peak at A, retraces a bit, and moves to B where an ascending triangle appears. Notice that A and B are near the same price. B can be slightly above A or slightly below it. The point is that A acts as overhead resistance, but the stock does not care. After an upward breakout, the stock resumes its upward move to C.

This configuration occurred 23% of the time in the triangles I looked at.

The stock chart shows an example when price peaked at A1. The rounded turn that led to B1 looks like a cup with a handle, where triangle B1 is the handle (but valid cups are usually less than a year long). The move to C1 extends the gain for the stock.

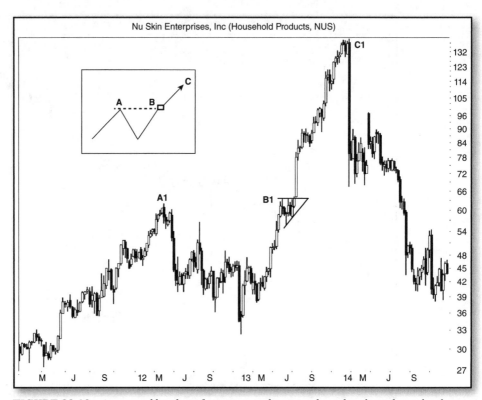

FIGURE 22.10 An upward breakout from an ascending triangle pushes through overhead resistance.

Compare the inset of Figures 22.10 and 22.6. The difference between the two is that the triangle in Figure 22.6 forms below resistance. In Figure 22.10, the triangle forms right at or very near resistance.

If the stock can break through resistance, then the reward can be a meal in itself. However, the stock could run into problems like those highlighted in Figure 22.7. In that figure, overhead resistance (A1) blocks the upward run (D).

Also, if you buy on or soon after the breakout, remember that throwbacks occur 61% of the time. You may wish to buy *after* the throwback completes and when price is heading higher.

To trade a throwback, should price drop below the top of the triangle (which is common during a throwback), then place a buy order a penny above the top of the triangle. When price completes the throwback and starts rising again, the buy order will trigger and put you into the stock in a timely manner.

Delayed Appearance

Figure 22.11 shows the ideal configuration in the inset, but the stock chart (weekly scale) is less thrilling.

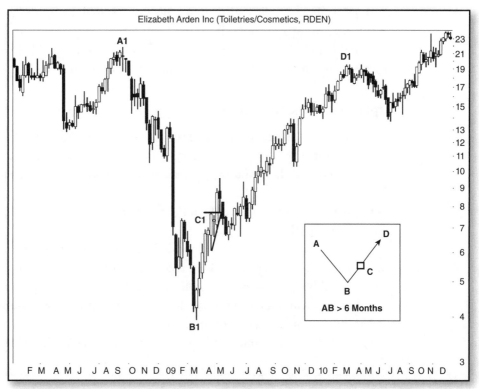

FIGURE 22.11 The V-shaped turn with a delayed appearance of an ascending triangle occurs 20% of the time.

The AB drop is often more than six months long. The stock bottoms and moves up to C where an ascending triangle is born. The upward breakout from this chart pattern sends the stock climbing to D.

This configuration appears 20% of the time.

The stock chart shows how this configuration played out for one stock. Price began an extensive decline in October 2007 (the start of a bear market, not shown), but I highlight a portion of that drop starting at A1. The drop from the bull market peak in 2007 (*not* A1) to the bottom at B1 was more than 6 months.

The stock turned and climbed to the ascending triangle at C1. Yes, this is a valid triangle on the daily chart but is difficult to see on the weekly.

An upward breakout from the ascending triangle pointed the way higher to D1.

V-shaped turns can be wonderful recovery vehicles if you can time the entry properly. That is especially true after a bear market ends, which it did at B1. Take a position in the stock after the breakout from the triangle and ride price out of intensive care.

Again, a long straight-line drop to the bottom of the V (the AB move) is best.

From the low in 2009, many stocks doubled quickly but then retraced and gave back most of those gains. If you double your money in a stock after a bear market ends, think about selling it all, selling a portion, or looking for the turn that will try to take it all away, and then sell.

Few things hurt more than watching a stock you own double in price and then head back toward zero. Avoid the pain and consider selling when the stock doubles.

Upward Breakout Failures

I searched through ascending triangles with upward breakouts and sorted the list by the smallest upward moves to find configurations that repeated. Of the 138 patterns I studied (beyond those and the upward move was too large), I found four pattern variations.

Figure 22.12 shows the configuration that appears most often, 45% of the time. This is a twin peak failure.

Price rises to a peak (A) or some other form of overhead resistance. Then it drops back only to advance again, to B. An ascending triangle forms, and it has an upward breakout. Although this sounds promising, overhead resistance acts as a whack-a-mole hammer and pounds the stock down, C, soon after an upward breakout.

The stock chart shows an example of this behavior. Price forms a peak of resistance at A1. The stock drops, attempts to make a new high at B1 where an ascending

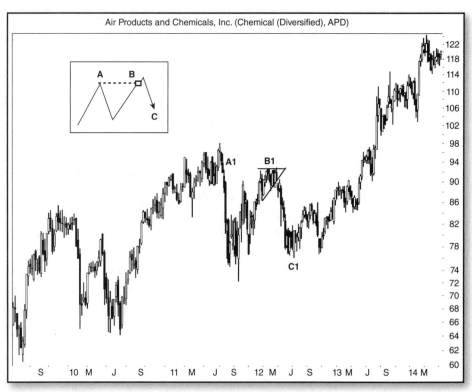

FIGURE 22.12 Price reaches overhead resistance and reverses.

triangle forms. Because this is on the weekly scale, the triangle is difficult to see, but it breaks out upward. Price rises only for a short time before reversing and heading down to C1.

The arrangement shown in (the earlier) Figure 22.10 has price making a strong push higher after the upward breakout. Figure 22.12 shows weakness, the stock trying to move up but failing. I do not know the cause for these reversals, only that they happen.

The configuration shown in Figure 22.7 has the triangle forming well below overhead resistance. With that setup, you buy on the triangle breakout, ride price up to overhead resistance, and then sell for a profit.

With the situation shown in Figure 22.12, the triangle forms at overhead resistance. A buy now often leads to a loss when price reverses unexpectedly, frequently busting the upward breakout.

This type of reversal is common at price peaks. If it happens, sell quickly instead of riding price down.

New High Dud Figure 22.13 shows what I call a new high dud. Price makes a steady push higher from A to B over the long term (most of the time, but be

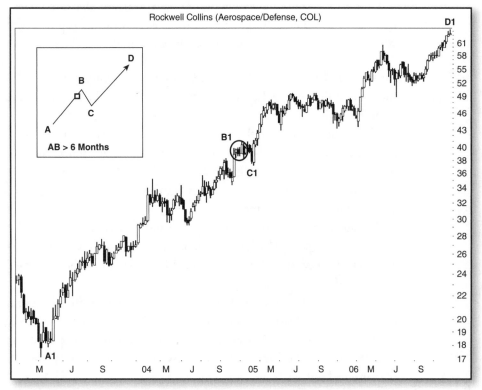

FIGURE 22.13 Price fails to continue making new highs, for a time.

flexible). The rise need not be a straight-line either. I just show it that way for convenience.

Along the way, an ascending triangle forms and has an upward breakout. Price rises to B, not much above the top of the pattern, before price collapses. The stock drops to C, just far enough to stop out traders, give them the finger, and then run away to D. The stock double busts the upward breakout.

The stock chart shows an example. The stock begins its climb at A1. Buried at B1 (somewhere in the circle) is an ascending triangle, but because this treasure hunt is on the weekly scale, you have to guess where it is.

The upward breakout fails and price drops to C1 before recovering and making a strong push higher, to D1.

Investors buying the triangle had the right idea, but those selling on the reversal missed an opportunity to almost double their money.

If you compare this figure to Figure 22.9, you will see a similar pattern unfold. In the earlier chart, the stock continues to make new highs. In this later configuration, the stock also makes new highs, but not before encountering a failed ascending triangle.

This configuration happened 29% of the time in stocks with ascending triangles that failed to make strong moves higher.

One way to trade this configuration is to wait for the throwback or downward reversal to complete. When price again closes above the top of the triangle, buy. It would be similar to trading a double-busted triangle.

Retrace in Downtrend **Figure 22.14** shows a configuration that happens 14% of the time in the failures I looked at. You can think of this configuration as a bottom-fishing disaster.

The stock is often in a short-term downtrend (AB), but be flexible with the timing. An ascending triangle appears at B and you might think that the downtrend is over. You bite in a bottom-fishing trade. Indeed, the stock makes an upward breakout, signaling that the worst is over, only to see price rise a smidgen to C before your boat begins taking on water.

The stock chart shows an example of this arrangement. Price drops from peak A1 to the triangle at B1 (the upward breakout of which is hard to see on the weekly scale, but it occurs at C1). The upward breakout from the triangle fails and price tumbles to D1.

If you owned the stock and hoped it would return to the price of peak A1, abandon that hope, at least for the short-term. Sell when price closes below the bottom of the triangle to avoid a large loss. The downward move signals a busted chart pattern that makes the bears rub their paws with glee. Avoid giving them any more pleasure and sell.

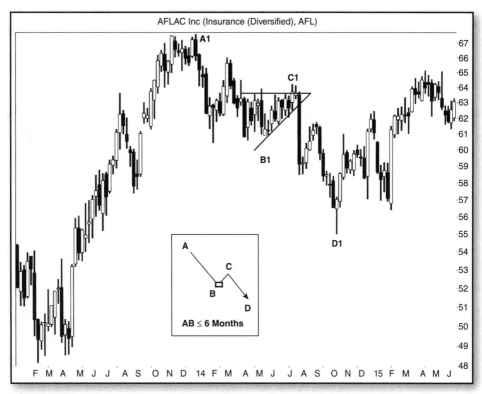

FIGURE 22.14 Price attempts to move higher in a downtrend but fails.

Bottom Reversal Failure The last failure pattern of an upward breakout appears in **Figure 22.15**. This configuration happens 12% of the time.

The stock makes a long-term decline from A to B as if the stock has caught pneumonia. The stock bounces and an ascending triangle appears. The triangle sports an upward breakout, and it looks like the stock is going to recover. Sadly, it does not. Price peaks soon after the breakout (C) before dropping to make another bottom (D). After the second bottom, the stock begins its true recovery, E, and does well until it finds out their HMO will not cover the hospital charges.

This configuration is similar to that shown in Figure 22.11. In the earlier figure, the stock continued rising (to D) instead of making a second bottom.

Unfortunately, the layout pictured in Figure 22.15 is what can happen. The stock chart (weekly scale) shows the damage that can occur with this bottom reversal failure.

Price starts its decline from the peak at A1 and loses altitude like an airplane with engine failure. It bottoms at B1 and bounces to C1 where an ascending triangle appears. The breakout from this triangle is upward but soon falters. The stock drops and touches down again at D1. Only then is the stock cleared for higher altitude. It ascends to E1, forming a big W pattern (A1-E1).

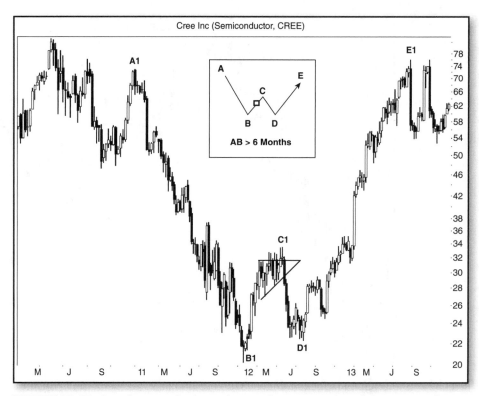

FIGURE 22.15   Price bounces after hitting bottom, but a sustained rise fails to appear after an upward breakout from an ascending triangle.

You see this type of double bounce after bear markets end. After the stock bottoms at D1, buy it. This configuration does especially well for utility stocks. You can pick up high-quality but safe dividend-paying stocks on the cheap and ride them higher.

In this situation, when the stock busts the upward breakout (by closing below the triangle's bottom), assume the stock will drop to just above the launch price (B1). Sell immediately on the adverse breakout. You can always buy back in after it makes the turn at D1, or you can wait for the stock to close above the top of the triangle again.

Downward Breakouts

I found two configurations that made large drops after a downward breakout from an ascending triangle.

Figure 22.16 shows the setup in the inset. Price begins the rise at A and reaches a peak where the ascending triangle forms, B. You might think that a downward breakout from this peak would mean a retrace of most of the prior advance. Whether that is right or not is unknown for your situation, but in the patterns I looked at, the stock dropped to C, returning to the launch price (or nearly so).

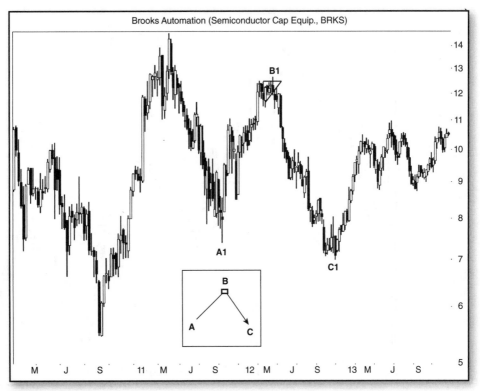

FIGURE 22.16   A downward breakout when the triangle acts as a reversal leads to a large decline.

The stock chart shows an actual example on the weekly scale. Price starts the upward run at A1. The ascending triangle forms at B1, but instead of breaking out upward, the breakout is downward. Price plummets to C1, mirroring the launch price of A1.

This configuration happens most often: 62% of the time. That is how often this up-down-large drop configuration appeared, not how often the stock made it back to the launch price.

I do not recommend shorting a stock because the most you can make doing so is 100%. That might sound like a lot, and it is, but compare that with upward breakouts where gains can be unlimited.

The configuration shown in Figure 22.16 could be one of those situations where you will want to sell a long holding. Before doing so, there are a number of things to consider. Is underlying support far away? Is the industry weak and so is the market? Why would the stock make a substantial drop? Are company and industry fundamentals under pressure? And so on. Answering those questions will go a long way to determining if the decline will be short or long.

Continuation   Figure 22.17 shows the second and last configuration of downward breakouts from ascending triangles. This configuration happens 38% of the time.

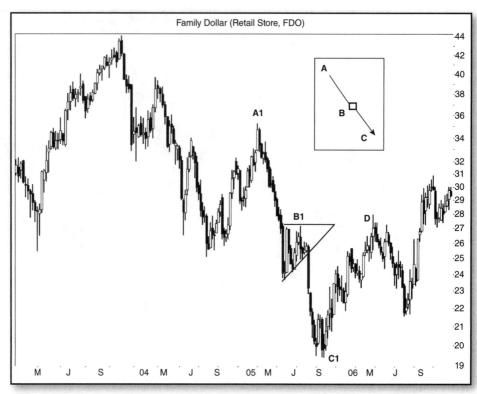

FIGURE 22.17 This triangle acts as a continuation pattern.

Inset ABC shows a downward trend with the ascending triangle appearing near the middle of the run, B. I just drew it that way, so do not place any significance on the straightness of the run or its position in the AC move.

The stock chart shows an example of this configuration on the weekly scale. The stock peaks at A1 and drops in a straight-line run until finding support at B1, where the ascending triangle appears. Because this appears on the weekly chart, the triangle is not clear. But the downward breakout takes the stock lower in another straight-line run, to C1 where the downhill run ends.

This example reminds me of a measured move-down pattern. In theory, the second leg, B1-C1, mirrors the extent and duration of the first leg, A1-B1. After the pattern completes, price often returns to the corrective phase (the horizontal movement at B1 where the triangle resides). The chart shows an example of this, where the stock stops at D, near the corrective phase B1.

When I try to determine how far price might drop, I consider the measured move-down pattern. I measure the decline posted by the first leg and assume a similar drop will occur after the breakout. If support is nearby the target, then that helps reassure me that the target is correct.

What you want to avoid is riding price down from A1 and selling right near the bottom, C1. This configuration may help you avoid that scenario.

Downward Breakout Failures

The following three configurations appear on the weekly scale for ascending triangles found on the daily charts. The weekly chart better shows the context.

In the study, I used 122 triangles with downward breakouts that dropped less than 10%. Three configurations appeared most often.

I show the first configuration in **Figure 22.18**. A triangle (B) appears in an upward price trend, AC. The breakout from this triangle is downward, but price does not drop far. Rather, it drops far enough to stop long positions out of the trade and then resumes the upward move.

The stock chart shows an example of this behavior. The uptrend begins at A1 and rises to B1. Because I am using the weekly chart, you cannot see the downward breakout, but the resumption of the uptrend to C1 is clear.

This configuration occurs most often, 58% of the time.

One way to trade this configuration is to wait for the busted pattern to close above the top of the triangle. When that occurs, buy the stock. The stock could double or triple bust, and there is a good chance of a throwback, so keep that in mind.

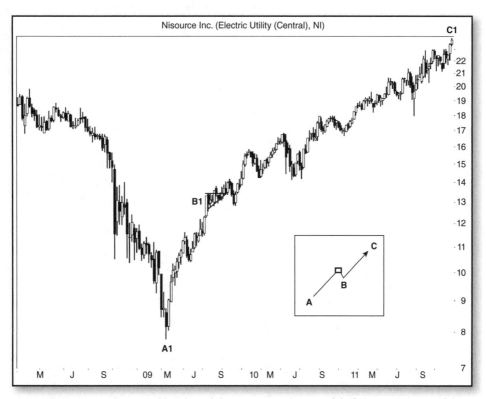

FIGURE 22.18 A downward breakout fails to see price drop much before a resumption of the up trend.

In this example, the stock makes such a startling climb because the bear market ended in March 2009. Back then, the stock was cut in half (more, actually) in about 6 months. A bullish rebound after such a decline is what traders love about bear markets.

Downtrend Reversal   **Figure 22.19** shows the next configuration. This setup is somewhat unusual because it happens just 24% of the time.

Price trends downward from A to B where an ascending triangle appears. The breakout from the triangle takes the stock lower but only for a short time. The stock rebounds and moves up to C.

The stock chart on the weekly scale shows how this scenario plays out in real life. Price peaks at A1 and begins retracing a portion of the move up from the March 2003 low. A triangle appears at B1 and price breaks out downward from it.

The downward breakout inset shows the triangle on the daily scale to make the breakout direction clearer. Price breaks out downward from the triangle at D and then turns up, rising to C1.

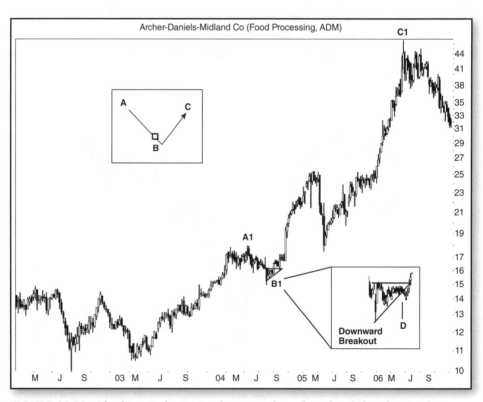

FIGURE 22.19   The downward price trend reverses after a short drop below the triangle.

In a downward price trend, wait for the ascending triangle to act as a reversal. If it does not, as in this case of a downward breakout, wait for price to recover. When the stock closes above the top of the triangle, consider buying.

Gauge how far price might rise. Assume that the stock will rise back to the launch price (the price where the decline to the triangle started). If it does, is that move a risk worth taking?

If, instead, the stock stops at overhead resistance that is close to the top of the triangle, is it still worth the price of a trade? If so, then buy.

Uptrend Variation **Figure 22.20** shows a complicated variation of Figure 22.18. In this case, the upward trend rises from A to B near where an ascending triangle occurs. A downward breakout takes price down for a time, but then it moves above the top of the triangle, to C. This move is short in both time and distance. The stock reverses and closes below the bottom of the triangle, busting it for the second time. Eventually, the decline takes the stock to D.

The stock chart shows an example of this complicated maneuver on the weekly scale. This variation occurs 18% of the time in the charts I looked at.

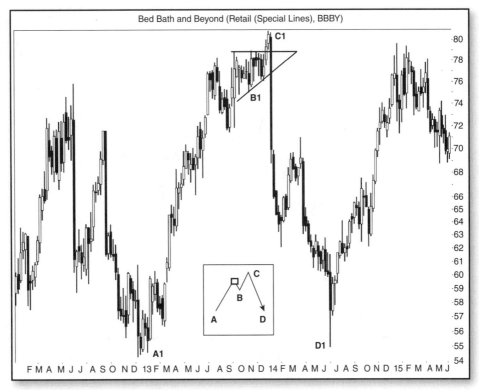

FIGURE 22.20 A double busted triangle sees price tumble.

The stock starts the run up at A1 and the triangle forms at B1. Not shown, but the triangle has a downward breakout. Price rebounds and closes above the top of the triangle, busting the downward breakout, and coasting up to C1. Then the trend reverses again, eventually busting the triangle for the second time and sending price down to D1.

A downward breakout from an ascending triangle busts 44% of the time. The discussion of Table 22.2 went through the numbers, so you can look at those. Although a double or triple bust is rare, they do occur as the chart shows.

My only advice is to exit the trade quickly when it becomes clear the stock is doing the unexpected.

■ Measure Rule

Use the measure rule to help set a minimum price target for the breakout direction you are trading. For example, consider the ascending triangle shown in **Figure 22.21**.

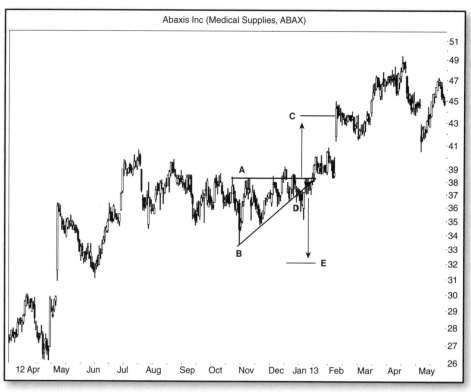

FIGURE 22.21 The measure rule works for both breakout directions.

The price at the top of the triangle is 38.44 (A) and the lowest low (B) is at 33.28 for a height of 5.16. For upward breakouts, add the height to the top of the triangle to get a target of 38.44 + 5.16, or 43.60 (C). For downward breakouts, subtract the height *from the breakout price* (where the stock crosses the up-sloping trendline). In this example, the breakout price is 37.14 (near D), giving a target of 37.14 − 5.16, or 31.98. I show that target at E.

How often does this method work?

Let me check. Hold on.

My spreadsheet says it works 70% of the time for upward breakouts but just 55% of the time for downward breakouts.

■ The measure rule for ascending triangles works 70% of the time for upward breakouts and 55% of the time for downward breakouts.

If you take the height (5.16 in this case) and cut it in half and then add or subtract it from the breakout price (depending on the breakout direction), the half-height measure rule works 85% of the time for upward breakouts and 84% of the time for downward breakouts.

Once you have calculated a price target, then look for nearby support or resistance to help gauge where the stock may reverse.

The measure rule does not say price will reach the target. Nor does it say price will exceed the target. Rather, it is just a tool to help guide traders when swing or day trading. Some call the measure rule a tool to set a *minimum* price objective, not a maximum one.

■ Trading

Let us consider **Figure 22.22** as a sample trade, shown on the daily chart.

The trend start for the stock is not shown because it began in mid-April 2014, to the left of A. The rise to the start of the chart is longer than 6 months, so that could be a warning signal that the upward trend is closer to the end than the beginning. That means the risk of a failed trade increases.

You place a buy stop a penny above the top of the triangle ahead of the breakout. When the stock zips to B, the order triggers and you buy the stock right when you should. The next day regret sets in when price returns to the triangle.

Oops.

Like unruly children, bad behavior from a stock happens from time to time. It is the cost of doing business. But when the stock closes below the bottom trendline or

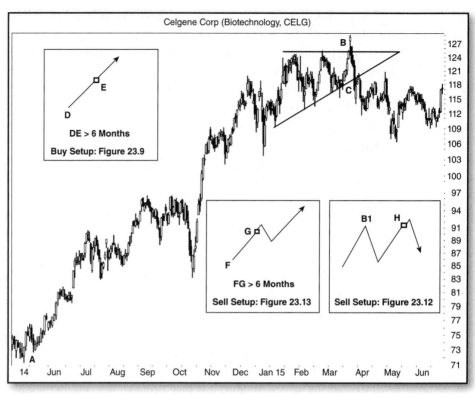

FIGURE 22.22 The stock breaks out upward from an ascending triangle to all-time highs but busts.

even below the bottom of the chart pattern (where a stop should be), then it is time to exit. You sell at the open the next day for a quick loss of just over 8%.

The stock drifts lower and you feel good about the sale. You could have ridden the stock down to 106 for a loss of 15%.

Look at the upper left inset, DE. The three insets are on the weekly scale, so keep that in mind. The DE inset is the configuration you hoped to trade. Move DE is long term, trending upward. The stock is making all-time highs and a buy looks promising.

Instead, the setup turned into the one shown as FG. The stock broke out upward and coasted just above G before reversing. If this configuration holds true, then buy when the stock closes above the top trendline and be sure to carry bottled oxygen for the climb to the summit.

However, the configuration could also morph into the lower right inset, B1. Peak B on the stock chart would correspond to peak B1 on the inset. Another triangle might form at H or it could be another type of chart pattern. More likely, though, the stock will just rise to H and drop.

The three configurations shown by the inset can help you prepare for a trade and help you manage it once it is under way. Use the probability of a configuration occurring to help determine how likely the stock will take a given path.

Figure 22.9 has a probability of occurring 24% of the time. Figure 22.12 tops the charts at 45% of the time, and Figure 22.13 peaks at 29% of the time. Although you wish to trade Figure 22.9, Figure 22.12 is almost twice as likely to occur. You might wish to rethink trading this example.

Aftermath: The stock peaked in July at almost 141 and then dropped to 92.98 a month later. Since the July peak, the stock has been trending lower.

Actual Trade

Figure 22.23 shows a trade I made in an ascending triangle. Look at the stock chart first, drawn on the daily scale. The trend start is at A2, almost eight months before the start of the triangle. The triangle appears below C, where price breaks out upward.

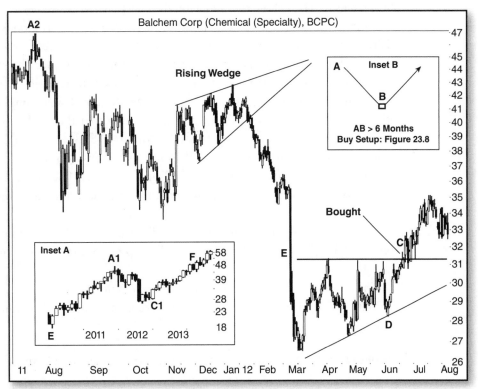

FIGURE 22.23 This ascending triangle trade resulted in a gain of 43%.

I placed an order to buy the stock at 31.25, 2 cents above the May high. The stock filled two trading days before the breakout when price pierced the top trendline but closed below it.

Here is what I wrote about the buy: "Buy reason: Ascending triangle. I like the dead-cat bounce type dip because I expect a zip back up when they get back into gear. That probably will not happen. I do not like the insider sales, either. Wait for breakout to buy."

I show the dead-cat bounce drop at E. An earnings disappointment caused this decline. Sometimes missed earnings can happen quarter after quarter, taking the stock down from 15% to 70% in one session. This stock dropped 25% from the close before the announcement to the March bottom. I usually avoid taking a position in a stock suffering a dead-cat bounce but not this time.

Insiders sold many shares in late November 2011 to January 2012. When insiders sell, it is a warning sign, but they can sell for any number of reasons (pay for bail, that kind of thing). It is not a deal breaker when they sell. It is more important when they buy, because they have fewer reasons to buy than to sell.

I placed a stop-loss order at 28.13, below the minor low at D. Upside was a target of 40, which matched the December 2011 to January 2012 congestion area formed by a rising wedge. I show the wedge on the chart.

Inset A shows the sale on the monthly chart. Point A1 corresponds to A2 on the daily chart, C1 to C. F is when I sold. Notice the stock continued climbing. Sigh.

Why did I sell? Here is what I wrote: "Sell reason: 2B top. The stock is down $5 from the high and it looks to be going lower. Insiders have been selling, especially as it peaked in the 48 region. One seller (Dana somebody) is leaving the company on the 30th. I think short term that this will go lower, maybe as low as 41, so I do not want to stick around. I think the reversal is firmly in hand. Fundamentals, however, still look great. I just do not trust what I see. The first peak is back in July 2011 [A2 on the chart]. The last 2 days, the Dow Industrials have been up 250 points and this is down today and it was down over $1 yesterday."

A 2B pattern occurs when the stock stalls at the price level of a prior peak. It is often a short-term reversal. The stock will drop but not far nor stay down for long. Usually.

The monthly chart shows that F is about level with A1.

With dividends included, I sold at an average price of 44.46 and made 43% in a year.

Application How do we apply to this trade the information in this chapter?

To clear overhead resistance (by climbing from C to A2) meant a rise of 50%. Above A2, the stock would resume making all-time highs. Instead, it reversed and headed lower for about a month, so I sold.

Expecting a 50% climb to clear resistance is too much to ask, so Figure 22.6 is out. Figure 22.7 shows a similar situation except the AB move was 8 months, not 6, and the stock did not drop far as the chart predicts (the move down after hitting resistance. See point C in Figure 22.7). A long-term inbound price trend is not ideal for that setup.

Figure 22.8 is a match. I show that in Inset B. Price drops into the ascending triangle over the long term (AB), reverses, and climbs. My worries about the trade reversing ended the move higher. The ultimate high for the trade was at 66.34 (March 2014), well above the 44.46 where I sold and 9 months later.

■ Closing Position

Perhaps the best thing you can say about ascending triangles is that the shape of them predicts an upward breakout. An upward breakout occurs 64% of the time, and then price throws back to the breakout price or trendline boundary 61% of the time. Thereafter, in 70% of the cases, the stock will resume its upward move.

That paragraph contains numbers. Too many numbers. Time for a different approach.

I like to trade busted ascending triangles. Those triangles breakout downward but reverse quickly. Busting can lead to large gains, gains that are better than from traditional upward breakouts.

By using the setups and configurations in this chapter, you can refine your trading setups to focus on those combinations that lead to the best results. Because we are dealing with probabilities here, anything can happen, but putting the edge in your favor certainly helps.

Setup Synopsis

Figure 22.24 may help you identify the various types of trading setups. See the associated figure for an explanation.

"Occurs" in the figures means how often I found the configuration in the stocks I looked at. If two configurations apply to your situation, then the one with a more frequent occurrence (a higher percentage) is the one you should choose to follow.

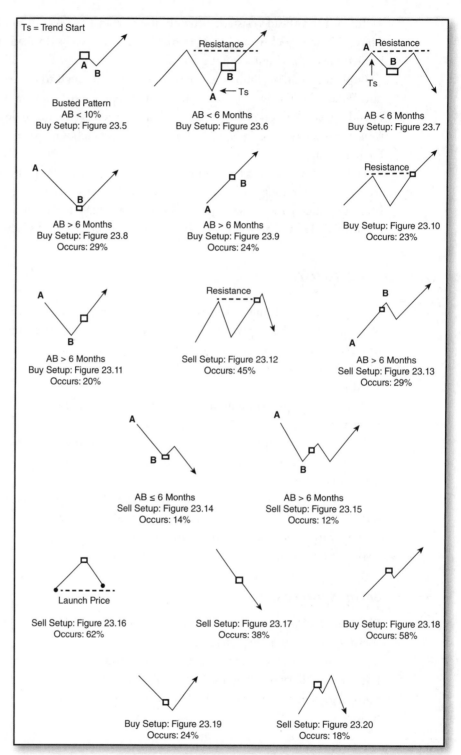

FIGURE 22.24 A collection of ideal trading setups and configurations.

CHAPTER 23

Triangles, Descending

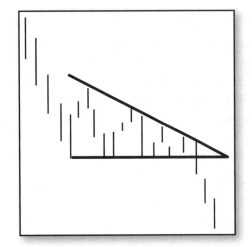

Descending triangles are an odd choice for bullish trades, but upward is the direction they work best. They beat the performance of ascending triangles in both breakout directions by one percentage point. In actual trading, you may not notice the difference.

My favorite is to wait for a busted descending triangle (after a downward breakout). Then buy it on the rebound. If it single busts, the gain can make for a worthwhile trade. I will explain the busting process later in this chapter.

■ Behavior at a Glance

Figure 23.1 shows the general performance of stocks showing descending triangles. In an earlier study of descending triangles in both bull and bear markets, I found that 64% of them broke out downward. This time, with almost 500 more samples, the numbers are closer: 47% of them break out downward. Perhaps with additional samples, a true breakout direction will emerge.

For this chapter, however, I concentrated on bull markets only. Those show upward breakouts occurring 53% of the time with an average rise of 44%. I measured the average rise from the low price on the breakout day (to minimize any gap) to the ultimate high, the highest high before the trend changes. In other words, the 44% gain is for 674 perfect trades, something no trader can duplicate.

Downward breakouts occur 47% of the time and the average decline measures 16%.

■ Price breaks out downward from a descending triangle 47% of the time.

Throwbacks and Pullbacks

Figure 23.2 shows what often happens after a breakout. For upward breakouts, price throws back 53% of the time. That means the stock returns to the trendline boundary or breakout price within a month. Drilling down, we find that price rises 8% in 5 days before peaking. In another 5 days, the stock returns to the breakout price or trendline boundary before resuming the upward move.

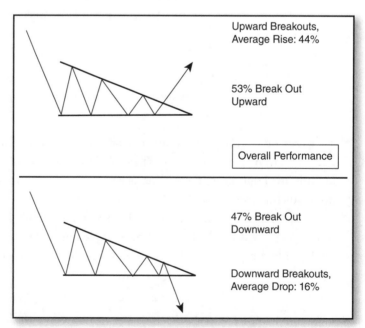

FIGURE 23.1   Price breaks out upward most often.

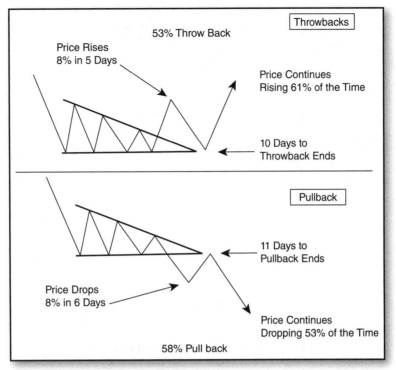

FIGURE 23.2 Performance statistics describing throwback and pullback behavior.

In 61% of the cases, the stock continues upward. The other 39% of the time the stock reaches the ultimate high during the throwback before heading south, below the bottom of the triangle.

Downward breakouts show a similar pattern only reflected downward in what I call a pullback. Price drops 8% in 6 days before bottoming. It takes another 5 days to return to the bottom of the triangle (11 days total). After that, the stock continues lower most often, 53% of the time. Of the patterns I looked at, 58% of them showed some type of pullback.

- Throwbacks to descending triangles occur 53% of the time and pullbacks occur 58% of the time.

Busted Triangles

Busted descending triangles happen when price breaks out in one direction but quickly reverses and breaks out in the new direction. **Figure 23.3** shows examples, one for each breakout direction.

Upward breakouts bust when price rises less than 10% before reversing and closing below the bottom of the triangle. I found that 25% of the descending

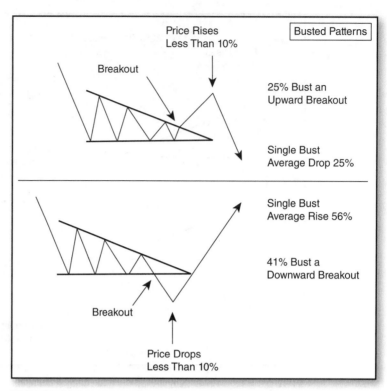

FIGURE 23.3   Price can bust a descending triangle two ways.

triangles I looked at busted an upward breakout. Those that single bust drop an average of 25%.

Downward breakouts bust when price drops less than 10% before reversing and closing above the top of the triangle (not above the top trendline). That scenario happens 41% of the time, and when price single busts, the stock rises an average of 56% above the top of the triangle. Remember, those numbers are based on perfect trades.

■ Price busts an upward breakout 25% of the time and busts a downward breakout 41% of the time in descending triangles.

■ Identification

Figure 23.4 shows an example of a descending triangle with an upward breakout. Consult **Table 23.1** as we go through the identification guidelines.

Down-Sloping Top Trendline. If you draw a trendline across the peaks (minor highs) in a descending triangle, the line should slope downward. Figure 23.4 shows the top trendline joining peaks 1 and 2, and extending down to C, the triangle's apex.

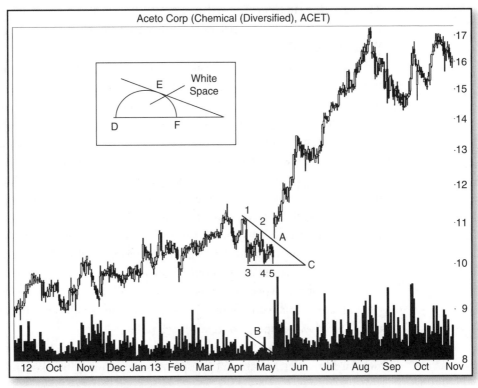

FIGURE 23.4 Traders wish all descending triangles behaved like this.

TABLE 23.1	**Identification Guidelines**
Characteristic	**Discussion**
Down-sloping top trendline	A trendline drawn along minor highs must slope downward and join with the bottom trendline sometime in the future.
Horizontal bottom trendline	Minor lows, when connected, form a horizontal or nearly horizontal bottom trendline. The two trendlines converge at the triangle apex.
Trendline touches	There must be at least five distinct trendline touches (minor highs or minor lows, three on one trendline and two on the other) to correctly describe a descending triangle.
White space	Price should cross the triangle from top to bottom often enough to cover most of the pattern until the breakout. Avoid triangles with a large block of white space in the middle of the pattern.
Volume	Volume trends downward 78% of the time and can become quite low a day or two before the breakout.
Breakout	Price can break out either upward or downward. A breakout occurs when price closes outside the trendline boundaries.

Horizontal Bottom Trendline. Another trendline drawn along the bottoms of minor lows should be horizontal or nearly so. I show the bottom trendline as line 345, extended to C.

Trendline Touches. I used to allow four touches of the two trendlines but now require five. Each touch should connect to a minor high (peak) or minor low (valley). That means at least three touches of one trendline and two or more touches of the other trendline. Figure 23.4 shows two touches along the top trendline and three along the bottom. Do not count price bar A as a trendline touch simply because it crosses the trendline. The trendline cross is neither at a minor high nor at a minor low.

White Space. Price should cross the pattern plenty of times, filling the triangle with price movement. The descending triangle in Figure 23.4 shows a good example of price crossing the pattern until after the breakout (A).

A common mistake is to cut off a rounded turn like that shown in the inset, and call it a descending triangle. The middle of triangle DEF shows too much white space, and there are not enough minor high and minor low trendline touches.

Volume. Volume typically slopes downward but do not discard a descending triangle with an unusual volume trend. The performance difference between triangles with up- and down-sloping volume is negligible.

Breakout. A breakout occurs when price *closes* below the bottom of the triangle (downward breakout) or above the top trendline (upward breakout).

■ Buy Setup 1

I like to begin by showing how busted patterns perform because they can make for terrific buying opportunities.

Figure 23.5 illustrates a descending triangle that busts. Before we discuss the stock chart, look at the inset. Point A represents a downward breakout from a descending triangle. Point B is where price bottoms. By convention, the stock must bottom less than 10% below the bottom of the triangle. Then price reverses. When the stock closes above the top of the triangle (C), it busts the downward breakout. A large rise often (but not always) follows.

The stock chart shows an example. I show the descending triangle within the two trendlines with a downward breakout to the right of A1. Price drops 8% to B1 before beginning a climb. At D, the stock closes above the top of the triangle, signaling a busted pattern.

A buy stop placed at that price would get you into the trade at the optimum time for trading a busted triangle. Setting a closer buy stop, such as when price closes above the top trendline, risks a failed trade when price hits the buy stop during a pullback only to see the stock head back down (which it does 53% of the time).

Here are the steps for trading a single (or triple) busted pattern.

FIGURE 23.5   A busted descending triangle leads to a large rise.

1. Use the identification guidelines from Table 23.1 to qualify the descending triangle as a valid chart pattern.
2. Wait for a downward breakout.
3. Price should drop less than 10% below the bottom of the triangle. Ten percent is an arbitrary limit, but it works well.
4. Price must reverse and close above the top of the triangle (not above the top trendline).
5. Either buy at the close or buy the next day at the open.
6. Place a stop-loss order a penny below the bottom of the chart pattern or place a stop at the location of your choice.

Table 23.2 shows a few performance statistics for this setup.

I found 1,642 triangles but used only 594 from bull markets with downward breakouts from July 1991 to June 2015. Not all stocks covered the entire period. Of those, 244 busted a downward breakout.

1. Almost half (41%) of triangles with downward breakouts bust. Wow. Film at 11:00.

2. The average rise from the top of the triangle to the ultimate high measures 42%. This is for perfect trades, so do not expect to duplicate the results.

TABLE 23.2	Statistics for Busted Triangles with Downward Breakouts	
Description		**Result**
1. Percentage of triangles that bust		41%
2. Average rise after busting		42%
3. Average rise after single bust		56%
4. Percentage of single busts		73%
5. Percentage of double busts		14%
6. Percentage of triple+ busts		14%

3. When a descending triangle busts once, the average rise is an astounding 56%. Very nice!

4–6. I separated busted descending triangles into three types: single, double, and three or more busts (triple busts). Single busts are the most common. They occur 73% of the time. Double and triple busts happen 14% of the time, each.

The difference between the three types is how often price crosses the triangle without moving more than 10% away from the chart pattern's top or bottom. See Glossary Figure G1 for a better description.

■ Buy Setup 2

Figure 23.6 shows the next setup that is common to many of the chart patterns in this book. Large gains can result from descending triangles which break out upward and which see the stock rise to all-time high territory.

The inset illustrates the ideal setup. Peak A marks overhead resistance. A triangle forms at B, shown here by a box. After an upward breakout (and it could be a busted downward breakout), the stock hits overhead resistance at C. The stock pushes through that resistance and breaks out to all-time high territory. Once the stock clears overhead resistance, there is nothing but unmanned drones flying above.

The stock chart shows an example on the weekly scale. Peak A1 is the highest price the stock has ever reached to that time. The triangle appears buried in the circle at B1. An upward breakout sends the stock to D where it struggles to pierce overhead resistance. Once it does, the stock moves higher to the ultimate high at C1, 222% above the breakout.

Here are the steps for using this setup.

1. Use the identification guidelines from Table 23.1 to qualify the descending triangle as a valid chart pattern.
2. Find where the trend starts. The trend start should be a peak before which price drops at least 20% or a valley before which price rises at least 20%, located before the start of the triangle.

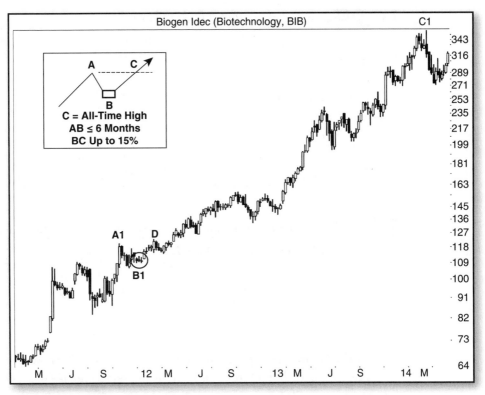

FIGURE 23.6 A descending triangle appears in the circled area, and once the stock pierces overhead resistance, a large rise follows.

3. The distance from the trend start to the start of the descending triangle should be less than or equal to six months for the best performance.
4. Measure the distance from the anticipated breakout price (estimate it) to the all-time high price. The closer to 0% that value is, the better. See Table 23.4 and the discussion for more information.
5. Buy the stock a day after it breaks out upward from the triangle.
6. Place a stop-loss order a penny below the bottom of the chart pattern or at a location of your choice.

Table 23.3 shows how this setup performs for short inbound trends (less than or equal to six months) and longer trends (the right column).

1. Samples are few for both columns, so keep that in mind. The performance is likely to deteriorate as more samples become available.

2–4. The performance numbers are exceptionally good, but your best bet is to find descending triangles with short inbound trends and avoid trading those with long inbound trends. Again, measure the time from the trend start to the start of the chart pattern. You want to find patterns that appear near the start of a trend, not at the end of one.

TABLE 23.3	Statistical Analysis of Buy Setup 2	
Description	Inbound Trend ≤6 Months	Inbound Trend >6 Months
1. Occurrence, samples	19%, 119	11%, 70
2. Post-breakout average gain	87%	46%
3. Median gain	59%	33%
4. Gains over 25%	83%	57%
5. 5% failure rate	2%	6%
6. 10% failure rate	3%	13%

TABLE 23.4	Frequency Distribution of Distance to Overhead Resistance										
Bin	5%	10%	15%	20%	25%	30%	35%	40%	45%	50%	>50%
Frequency	31%	14%	13%	8%	5%	6%	4%	1%	1%	3%	13%
Cumulative	31%	46%	59%	67%	72%	78%	82%	83%	84%	87%	100%

5, 6. The failure rates appear in the table, and three of them are reasonable. The 13% rate for long inbound trends is high. Again, select shorter inbound price trends for patterns to trade.

Table 23.4 shows a frequency distribution of the distance from the top of the descending triangle to the price at which the stock would enter new all-time high territory.

For example, 31% of the descending triangles I looked at broke out to all-time highs by rising no more than 5% above the top of the triangle.

Most of the samples (59% of them) occur within 15% of the top of the triangle. The closer the all-time high is to the triangle, the better the chance of a trade you will be happy to brag about to your mother.

■ Buy Setup 3

Buy Setup 3 happens when the all-time high is likely unreachable. *Avoid trading this setup* unless the rise to overhead resistance is worth the risk of a failed trade.

In this setup, price rises to overhead resistance and tumbles thereafter.

The inset of **Figure 23.7** shows what happens in the ideal case. At A, overhead resistance looms like storm clouds on the horizon on picnic morning. A descending triangle with an upward breakout appears at B. The stock rises to C, where it hits overhead resistance, and then price drops at least 20%.

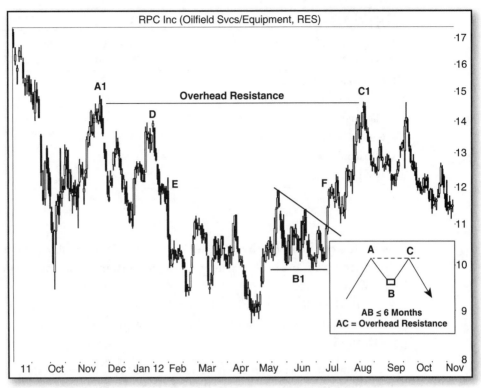

FIGURE 23.7 Price rises for a time, but overhead resistance stops a further advance.

The stock chart on the daily scale shows an example of this behavior. At A1, D, and E, overhead resistance gathers, waiting for the stock like bullies in a parking lot at a football game.

The descending triangle appears (B1) and price rises after the breakout. It hits overhead resistance at F, set up by the knot of resistance at E. The stock throws back for a time but recovers and pushes higher to C1. There, the two peaks at D and A1 combine to form resistance that stops a further upward move. The stock drops, but still posts a 44% gain on the trade (assuming you bought at the breakout price and sold at peak C1).

Here are the steps for using this setup.

1. Use the identification guidelines from Table 23.1 to qualify the descending triangle as a valid chart pattern.
2. Find where the trend starts. The time from the trend start to the start of the descending triangle should be less than or equal to six months for the best performance.
3. Measure the distance from the anticipated breakout price (estimate it) to overhead resistance. If the stock stops at overhead resistance, will the potential profit be worth the risk of a trade?

TABLE 23.5

Description	Inbound Trend ≤6 Months	Inbound Trend >6 Months
1. Occurrence, samples	52%, 326	14%, 88
2. Post-breakout average gain	31%	17%
3. Median gain	21%	8%
4. Gains over 25%	43%	22%
5. 5% failure rate	11%	32%
6. 10% failure rate	27%	58%

TABLE 23.5 Statistical Analysis of Buy Setup 3

4. If yes to step 3, then buy the stock a day after it closes above the top trendline.

5. Place a stop-loss order a penny below the bottom of the triangle or at a location of your choice.

6. Sell when the stock approaches (stalls at or reverses near) overhead resistance. If you are lucky, this setup will push through overhead resistance to form Buy Setup 2.

For descending triangles in which price reversed at overhead resistance, **Table 23.5** shows the performance split into short and long inbound price trends.

1. This setup is where most (76%) of your trades will come from if your trading matches the results of my historical study.

2–4. If traded perfectly, the average gain is 31% for short inbound trends (the middle column, which is preferred). The median rise is 21%, meaning half the trades will make more and half will make less. Almost half (43%) will make a substantial move, but that also means 57% will be flubs and duds.

5, 6. When you compare the failure rates of this setup with the prior one, these numbers are as scary as telling your dog it is time for a bath.

The numbers shown in Table 23.5 include more than 400 perfect trades, so do not expect to match or exceed those results. Depending on your skill and market conditions, you could do better or worse.

■ Sell Setup

I wish I could say, "If you see these conditions, it means price is going to drop far enough that you wished you had sold." Instead, I have to tell you about the probability of something happening.

Figure 23.8 shows the ideal setup in the inset. Point A is one year before the start of the chart pattern. It represents the primary trend. The largest declines occurred when the primary trend is downward, leading to the start of the triangle, not upward.

FIGURE 23.8 Three conditions suggest a larger decline: (1) when the primary trend is down, (2) when the trend from the trend start is also down, and (3) when the pattern appears near the start of the downtrend.

Point B represents the trend start. When the trend start is above the top of the chart pattern (meaning price trends downward), the post-breakout decline is higher than for rising price trends.

Finally, when the descending triangle appears near the start of a trend (within six months of the trend start), then there is more opportunity for the stock to drop farther.

The stock chart shows an imperfect example of these three conditions on the daily scale.

I found that using the closing price a year before the triangle begins works well as a gauge of the primary trend. If the primary trend is downward leading to the start of the triangle, the average post-breakout decline measures 18% compared to a 14% post-breakout drop associated with upward-tilting primary trends.

To use the primary trend, look for the closing price at the first minor high or minor low when the triangle begins. In this case, that is at C1. Then look a year earlier and compare the closing price with the triangle's close at C1.

In this example, the trend is upward leading to the start of the triangle. I know it looks like price trends downward, but the full year is not shown. For the best performance, look for a downward-sloping primary trend, not an upward trend as in this case. That is why this example is imperfect.

Find the trend start. The trend start is the highest high or lowest low before which price drops or rises, respectively, at least 20%. In this example, the trend start is at B1. The trend from B1 to C1 is downward. Downward trends suggest larger post-breakout declines (18% versus 15%).

Finally, look for the triangle near the start of a downtrend. Near means within 6 months in this case. The time from B1 to C1 is about a month, well within the 6-month guideline. Short inbound price trends see the stock decline an average of 17% versus 13% for longer inbound trends.

This triangle has met two out of three of the criteria for large post-breakout declines. The stock dropped 36%, from D1 to E.

For reference, here are the three guidelines that suggest larger post-breakout declines from triangles.

1. Find the primary trend, which is the closing price a year before the triangle begins (a year before the first trendline touch). The best declines show a downward primary trend (the year ago close is above the start of the triangle).
2. Find the trend start. The best declines happen in a downward price trend. That means the trend start should be above the start of the triangle.
3. Measure from the trend start to the triangle's start. Trends shorter than six months tend to see larger declines post-breakout.

■ Best Stop Locations

Where is the best location to place a stop? The answer should depend on where underlying support or overhead resistance is located. Those two are the overriding factors. However, as a general guideline, we can use the results shown in **Table 23.6** to help us with initial stop placement and adjust it for our risk tolerance.

1. Penny below the pattern. For upward breakouts, if you place a stop-loss order a penny below the bottom of the descending triangle, the stock will hit it 8%

TABLE 23.6 **Stop Locations for Triangles**

Description	Chance of Being Hit	Average Loss	Missed Trades, Gains/Losses
1. Penny below the pattern	8%	9%	33%
Up Breakouts Above, Down Breakouts Below			
2. Within the pattern	67%	3%	15%
3. Penny above the pattern	2%	7%	12%

of the time, on average. The loss from the breakout price to the stop price measures 9%. If you had stayed in those trades, they would have made an average of 33%.

Because the top of the triangle slopes downward, placing a stop within the top to bottom of the triangle does not make sense (according to my computer since the breakout will likely be within the top-to-bottom range of the triangle and it will appear as if the trade is stopped out immediately). Thus, I do not show that stop location.

2. Within the pattern. For downward breakouts, a stop placed somewhere within the top to bottom of the triangle would trigger 67% of the time. The average loss is small, at 3%, and the average drop from those missing trades would be 15%.

The high "chance of being hit" (67%) is one reason why I recommend a stop placed above the top of the triangle, not within it.

3. Penny above the pattern. If you place a stop a penny above the top of the triangle (not above the top trendline), it will trigger just 2% of the time, on average. The loss will be higher, 7%, and the missing trades will go on to drop an average of 12%.

The low chance of being hit coupled with a modest potential loss suggests the top of the triangle is a good place for a stop. Because each case is different, measure the potential size of the loss in your situation and adjust the stop location accordingly.

- The best location for a stop-loss order is a penny above the top (downward breakouts) or a penny below the bottom (upward breakouts) of a descending triangle.

■ Configuration Trading

To trade the following configurations, begin with these guidelines.

1. Find a triangle on the *daily* chart that obeys the identification guidelines listed in Table 23.1.
2. Look for the configuration that matches what you see on your *weekly* chart.
3. Buy at the open the day after the breakout or place an order to buy a penny above the top trendline (upward breakouts) or below the bottom trendline (downward breakouts).
4. Place a stop-loss order at a location of your choice.

I sorted my database of triangles according to the largest post-breakout gain and looked for common elements. Compare your situation with these scenarios to help you decide how to trade the chart pattern and what the post-breakout trend may look like.

All of the charts are shown on the weekly scale unless otherwise noted.

Figure 23.9 shows the first example. Price rises from A to B over the long term. At B, the trend changes and price drops to C, but this does not take long, frequently a few weeks to a few months.

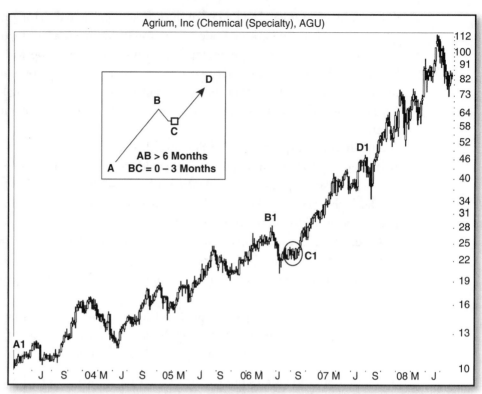

FIGURE 23.9 This configuration occurs most often.

The descending triangle appears at C, and it has an upward breakout that takes price up to D, the ultimate high.

The stock chart shows an example of this configuration. The uptrend actually begins to the left of A1, but you get the idea. Price makes a long-term climb up to B1 where the stock plummets like water over a falls. The descending triangle is buried somewhere at C1. The upward breakout drives price upward to D1. Although it looks like the uptrend continues, and it does, for statistical purposes, it ends at D1, the ultimate high. After D1, the stock drops at least 20%.

Of the 125 patterns I looked at (sorted by the post-breakout rise, which included all patterns with upward breakouts and gains of more than 35%), this configuration was the most common, happening 47% of the time.

This configuration is a variation of the one discussed in Figure 23.6. The earlier setup shows price breaking out to an all-time high. This configuration ignores that element.

Bear to Bull

Figure 23.10 shows the next configuration in the inset. The stock drops from A to C, along with the general market, entering a bear market (B) along the way. At C,

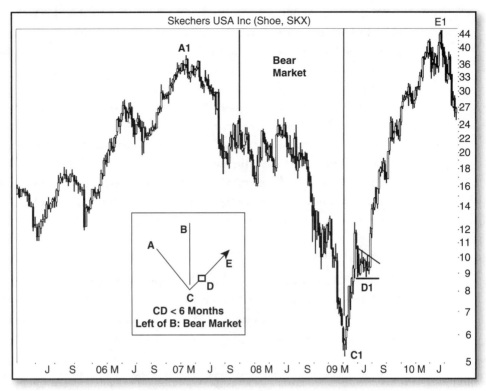

FIGURE 23.10   A bear market turns bullish, launching price upward.

the bear market ends. The turn at C in the *stock* does not have to be the exact end of the *bear market*. When I write, "bear market," I mean the general market is bearish. The individual stock may turn earlier or later than the switch from bear to bull in the general market.

Price rises in a short-term move (often less than 6 months) upward to the descending triangle, D. The chart pattern appears when the stock pauses in its bullish run. Many types of chart patterns, including descending triangles, will appear during this pause. The upward breakout from the chart pattern is a bullish omen.

If there is one time when I put every penny into the market, it is during the transition from bear to bull. I may be early or I may be late, but I am never sorry.

How do you tell a bear market has ended? I define the switch from bear to bull as when the Dow Jones Industrials close at least 20% above a low. If the low is at C, and the Dow closes at least 20% above that low, then a bull market has begun. Saddle up.

During the transition from bear to bull, most chart patterns and most stocks, really, have been waiting for a bull market to begin. When it arrives, the stocks soar like the move from D to E. It might be turbulent and short (price can double in a few months), but the move can be dramatic, highly profitable, and risky. The bear market might not be over, and should the stock double, it could give back all of its gains quickly.

Watch for a double bottom to appear, too. Price may double on the rise between the two bottoms, then return to the price level of the first bottom, only to start a slower and longer recovery (upward). That longer run is worth investing in, too.

The stock chart shows an example of the ACE configuration.

A1 begins a long drop that enters a bear market (weekly scale). The bear market ends at C1 (and this stock happens to bottom at the same time as the Dow), and price recovers to E1. A descending triangle appears with an upward breakout. Notice that the C1-D1 move is quick, often taking just a few months. The upward breakout sends price up to E1, the ultimate high.

This configuration happens 31% of the time. I excluded descending triangles that occurred in a bear market, so the 31% represents bull market patterns only, like the one shown on the stock chart.

Lazy Bottom

Figure 23.11 shows two variations that happen infrequently. Look at the left inset. The AB decline is a long one, but it represents a shallow decline. *Shallow* is difficult to define but use common sense. If I had to give a distinguishing characteristic, I would say the AB slope is not flat.

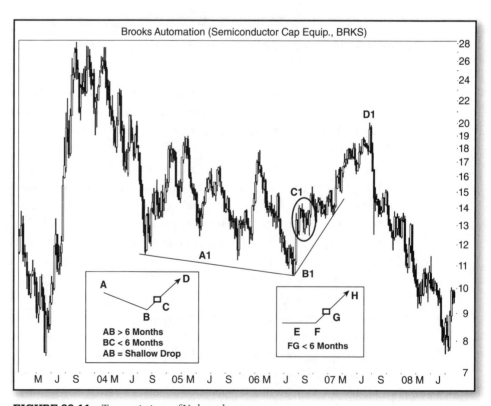

FIGURE 23.11   Two variations of V-shaped turns.

At B, the stock moves higher and forms a descending triangle at C. The triangle breaks out upward and price rises to the ultimate high at D.

This configuration occurs just 10% of the time.

The stock chart gives an example on the weekly scale. Line A1 shows the gentle slope. The stock turns at B1 and rises to C1, where the descending triangle lies buried. Upon a breakout, the stock climbs to D1.

The right inset shows a variation. In this example, the slanted AB move is now essentially flat from E to F. Yes, price can slope up or down a bit, but the move mirrors a flat base. I hesitate to put a time on the EF move, but most often it is a long-term trend (over 6 months), found using the weekly scale (which can make it appear flatter).

The rise from F to G is short term, though. In other words, the breakout from a flat base sends price higher but then pauses. The pause is when the descending triangle appears like a gopher looking out of its hole. The remainder of the pattern unfolds like the CD move described earlier.

This configuration appears 9% of the time.

Upward Breakout Failures

The prior section discussed descending triangles that had upward breakouts that lead to large gains. This section discusses the disasters, those triangles with upward breakouts and upward runs that poop out.

I found only 107 bull market patterns with upward breakouts before the "small rise" turned into a large one (up to 10%), forcing me to stop.

Figure 23.12 shows an example in the upper left inset. Price begins a long-term upward trend from A to B. B is where the descending triangle appears. It has an upward breakout, but price does not rise much before it reverses.

The reversal kicks the stock below the bottom of the pattern, busting the upward breakout. The stock drops less than 10% below the bottom of the pattern (C) before it reverses again. This time, a trend appears, and the stock is on its way upward, to D. When it closes above the top of the triangle, it busts the triangle for the second time.

The stock chart shows an example of this configuration. Price begins the uptrend at A1. A descending triangle appears at B1, and it has an upward breakout, but because the chart is on the weekly scale, you cannot see the breakout.

Price reverses and drops to C1 where it reverses again. The second reversal pushes the stocks upward, eventually climbing to D1, the ultimate high.

This configuration occurred most often, 29% of the time.

The lower right inset shows a similar configuration. The difference between this inset and the one on the upper left is the retrace from F to H. Price moves lower from peak F, reaches G where a descending triangle appears, breaks out upward, and then quickly drops to H. The stock double busts the upward breakout (the first bust occurs at H then busts the second time when price closes above the pattern on the way to I).

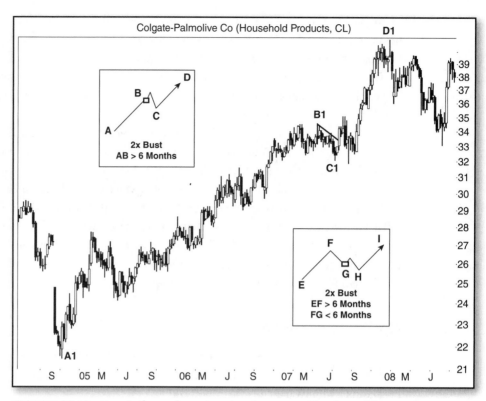

FIGURE 23.12 Two similar configurations show how upward breakouts fail most often.

This scenario occurs 19% of the time, so the two configurations represent almost half (48%) of all patterns.

The Reversal

Figure 23.13 shows what every investor fears: a significant reversal of the uptrend. The inset shows the simplicity of this horrific event.

Price rises over the long term from A to B. The upward breakout from the descending triangle brings hope to investors that the upward trend will continue. And it does, but only for a short time.

Soon, bears push price out the lighthouse window and the stock begins falling, taking the stock down to the rocks at C and below.

The stock chart shows the carnage. The uptrend begins at A1, rises to B1 where the descending triangle lies hidden. An upward breakout busts when the stock reverses and drops to C1.

When you look at the stock chart, notice that the reversal appears at the end of the trend up from A1. Buying into an existing trend late in the game is a dangerous play, as this configuration shows.

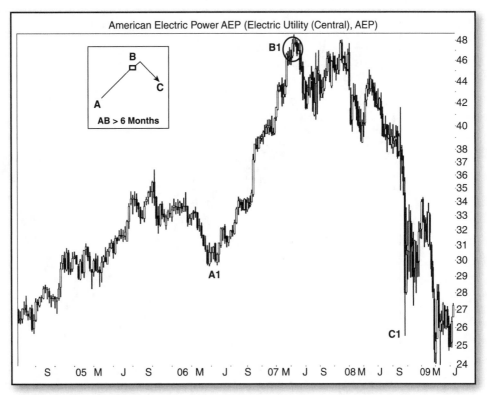

FIGURE 23.13 A reversal of the long-term trend occurs after an upward breakout.

This configuration occurs 17% of the time in the descending triangles I looked at.

Bottom-Fishing

Figure 23.14 shows the difficulty of trying to bottom-fish, that is, trying to time the purchase in a downward price trend.

The stock follows the current downward, dropping from A, and investors or traders may think that the stock cannot drop any farther at B. It has already dropped so far. It *has* to be near its end. Some investors view the price as an exceptional value. And it *is* a tasty treat, but after the upward breakout fails from the descending triangle (B) and the stock drops to C, it becomes an even better value, not a tasty treat but a bone investors choke on.

The stock chart shows an example of this bottom-fishing expedition. Price tumbles from A1 to B1. A descending triangle with an upward breakout occurs at B1 (weekly scale so it is hard to see), and traders and investors pile into the stock. But the downward move is not finished. The stock plummets to C1, drowning those that bought the upward breakout.

This scenario occurs 14% of the time.

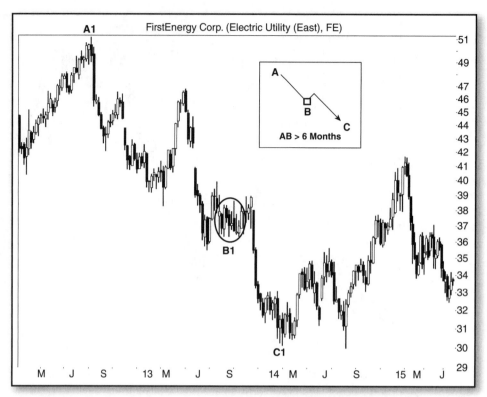

FIGURE 23.14 Trying to bottom-fish in this configuration leads to drowning.

Downward Breakouts

Preservation of capital. Perhaps you have heard that phrase. I have not taken a poll, but my guess is that professional traders would prefer to preserve their money instead of taking an outsized risk on a winning trade.

If you own a stock, should you sell after a downward breakout from a descending triangle and preserve capital? Perhaps these configurations can help answer that question. Match your situation with one of these four. Your trade may follow what appears here, so you will know ahead of time how to react.

If you have read this book from the start instead of using it as a reference, this half-staff pattern will be old news. **Figure 23.15** shows the setup that happens 31% of the time in the patterns I looked at. The sample size (51) is small, but I wanted to focus on downward breakouts with big drops (more than 20%) in bull markets. Those are rare.

Price trends downward from A to the descending triangle at B. A downward breakout sends price even lower, to C. The lengths of the AB and BC moves are approximately equal. Be flexible. In my trading, I use this half-staff measure only as a prediction of how far price might drop. If the prediction suggests price

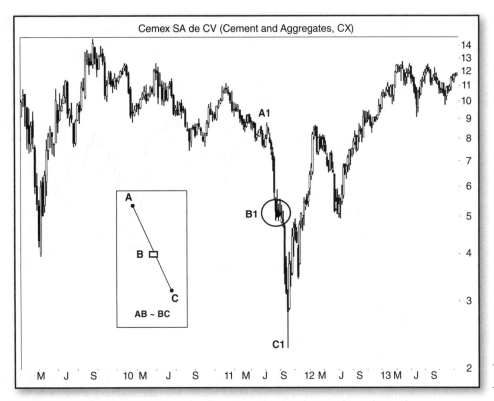

FIGURE 23.15 The descending triangle appears about midway in the price trend.

will go below zero, then I use another method. Let common sense prevail. If the projected decline means another huge loss, then the prediction is likely wrong.

The stock chart shows an example with the stock making a determined attempt to reach absolute zero, starting at A1. At B1, the descending triangle appears. The triangle has a downward breakout and tunnels down to C1.

The A1-B1 move is about four points, but the B1-C1 move is less than three. On a percentage basis, both are huge drops.

Notice how the plunge turns into a V-shaped recovery. Thus, if you want to buy the stock (bottom-fishing), wait for the turn at C1 and then hope you get lucky. Hold as the stock returns to near the price of A1.

The danger with this method is buying too soon and watching the stock head to zero, and the company goes bankrupt.

Twin Peaks

The twin peak pattern shown in **Figure 23.16** happens 31% of the time in the patterns I looked at. That ties with the prior configuration.

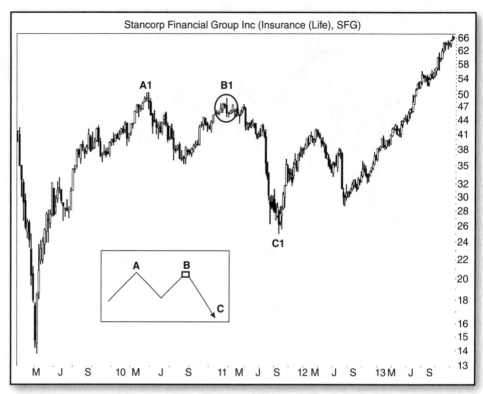

FIGURE 23.16 A second peak shows a descending triangle with a downward breakout.

The inset shows how this configuration typically unfolds. Price forms a peak at A and another at B. Somewhere at or near peak B, a descending triangle appears. The triangle has a downward breakout. The move to C often confirms the twin peaks as a valid double top (meaning price closes below the valley between peaks AB) but not always. An unusually deep valley means price can make a substantial decline without confirming the pattern as a double top.

The stock chart shows how this pattern appears on the street. Price peaks at A1 (weekly scale), retraces to form a valley, and then attempts a new high at B1. A descending triangle appears in the circle (trust me on this), which breaks out downward. Climbers seeing an approaching storm scramble back to base camp as fast as possible. Those left on the mountain get scraped off anyway, to splatter on the valley floor at C1.

As I said, the descending triangle need not appear at the exact peak, but you will find that it is close. The next configuration is a variation of the theme of overhead resistance blocking an upward advance.

Overhead Resistance

The configuration shown in **Figure 23.17** is complicated, so it appears only 20% of the time in the 51 samples I looked at.

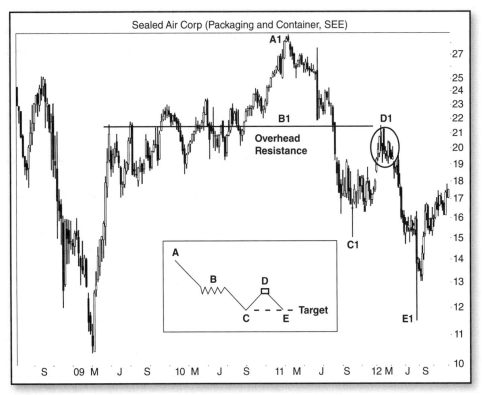

FIGURE 23.17 Overhead resistance, coupled with a downward breakout from a descending triangle, sends price lower.

Typically, price drops from A to B where support/resistance forms. The AB move need not be a decline. The AB move in this chart becomes peak A in the prior configuration. For argument's sake, let us assume that AB is a drop.

Price continues lower to C where it bounces. This bounce will be a retrace of the AC move. Price rises to overhead resistance and forms a descending triangle at D. The triangle breaks out downward (but it could also bust an upward breakout) and price drops to E.

The important phases of this configuration are a long decline (AC) and a partial retrace of that decline (CD). Once the stock bounces as high as it can to D, the downtrend resumes, taking the stock lower, sometimes substantially.

A good target (shown as a dashed line at E) is to expect a decline to the price level of C, the end of the trend before the retrace begins. My review of the patterns shows that price reaches or exceeds the target about half the time. So be conservative when estimating how much of a decline the stock will suffer.

The stock chart shows how life treats this configuration. The downward move begins at A1, mirroring the start at A, bottoming at C1 (compared to C). The horizontal line (B1) represents overhead resistance (similar to B) blocking a bounce higher than D1 (corresponds to D). Within that circle rests a descending triangle with a downward breakout. Price drops to E1, well below the bottom at C1. Such a substantial drop is unusual, so do not depend on it happening in your trade.

Launch Price

Figure 23.18 shows the last configuration for large declines from descending triangles with downward breakouts.

I have discussed the launch price before, but here is another example that I found 18% of the time.

A is the launch price, the location where the straight-line run begins that climbs to the descending triangle.

Because we are on the weekly scale, the *quick* part can be measured in weeks to months. On the daily chart, it will look choppier, of course.

At B, a descending triangle appears and stops the advance when it breaks out downward. The stock plunges to C. Frequently, the stock will stop declining just above the launch price (A), so that is why I have drawn C above A. Sometimes, though, the decline is severe enough to not only hit the launch price but crater below it.

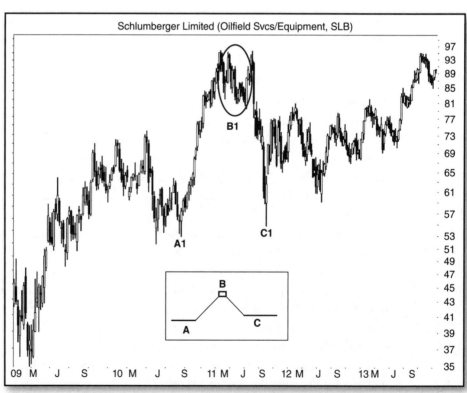

FIGURE 23.18 After a quick rise, price can return to just above the launch price.

The stock chart shows an example of this attempt. Price begins its upward move at the launch price, A1. Within the triple top at B1, a descending triangle appears. This one breaks out downward, but price struggles for a time at the high altitude before being blown off the price mountain. The decline is swift in this case, but it need not be, and the stock bottoms at C1, slightly above the launch price.

Whenever I see a quick rise (such as the move starting at A1), I worry about a quick decline after a reversal pattern. It will not unfold as often as I expect (as I said, this configuration appears just 18% of the time), but keep it in mind. It could save you a bundle.

Downward Breakout Failures

If you expect a large decline after a descending triangle, the chances are you will be wrong. The median decline is 13%. To some, that will be a large decline (day and swing traders), but to position traders and investors (buy and hold), it represents a speed bump. Annoying, sure, but not alarming, unless you are riding a bicycle.

Figure 23.19 shows the configuration that occurs 26% of the time in the 99 stocks I looked at with downward breakouts and declines less than 10% in bull markets.

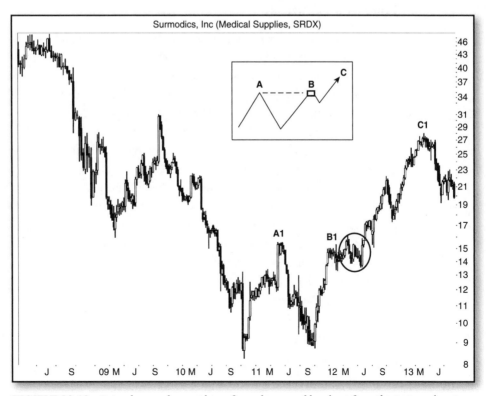

FIGURE 23.19 Price drops only a smidgen after a downward breakout from this twin peak pattern.

Compare the inset with that of Figure 23.16. The images are similar. The earlier figure shows a large post-breakout decline. Figure 23.19 shows a shallow dive before a rebound.

Peak A (Figure 23.19) represents any type of overhead resistance, often it is from a peak like that shown. The stock at B bumps its head on a ceiling of resistance. But the drop after the breakout does not last long nor does price drop much before rebounding and climbing to C.

The stock chart shows an unusual example of this configuration. Here, the long-term trend is downward, starting at the upper left of the chart. Price forms a double bottom with peak A1 in the middle. The price at A1 is where resistance later forms.

The move up to B1 hits that resistance and price slides sideways as if doing laps in a pond, waiting to decide on a new trend direction. After a few months (weekly scale), a descending triangle appears in the circle. It has a downward breakout, but lifeguards arrive just in time to keep the stock from drowning. Price climbs out of the pond and up the beach, to C1.

You can explain the large decline shown in Figure 23.16 by saying the stock more than tripled from the 2009 bear market low. It needed to retrace some of those gains, so the stock dropped. But the stock in Figure 23.19 almost doubled in price from the first low (of the double bottom).

The Tired Climb

Figure 23.20 shows two configurations in the insets. In the left one, price rises from A to B, but the duration can be any term (long or short). Price peaks at B, retraces, and a descending triangle appears at C. The triangle has a downward breakout, and it fools traders into thinking a large decline is unfolding. Instead, the stock reverses and makes its way upward to D. Peak D may be above peak B or below it.

The right inset shows a long-term trend (over 6 months long), EF, leading to the descending triangle, F. The triangle has a downward breakout and price retraces for a time (less than 10%, FG) before recovering.

The stock chart shows an example in the left inset. Price makes a terrific moon shot from A1 to B1. Price retraces some of those gains on the way to the triangle at C1. The triangle breaks out downward before price recovers to D1, forming a double top that later confirms as a valid chart pattern.

The left inset occurred 21% of the time in the triangles I looked at, and the right inset happened 16% of the time. Together they represent over a third of the downward breakout failures.

The Bounce Pause

Figure 23.21 shows two variations of the next configuration. Together they happen 21% of the time.

Price at ABC makes a stair-step drop (called a measured move down or a simple ABC correction). Price recovers from C to D and stalls near or at the price level of B. After

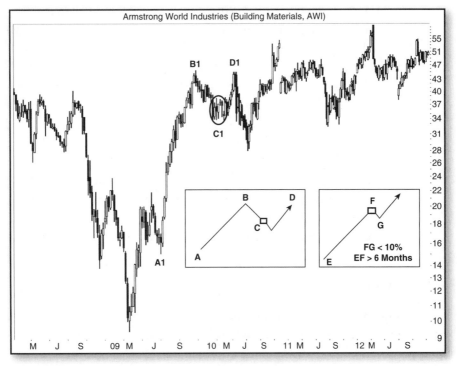

FIGURE 23.20 The two configurations differ only by the location of the descending triangle.

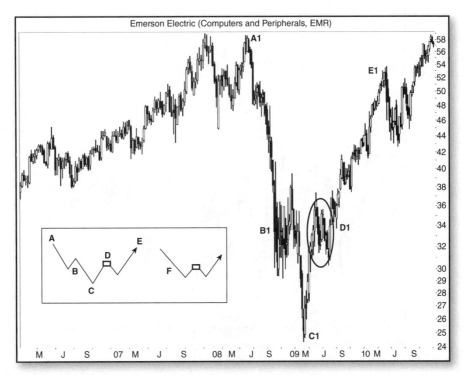

FIGURE 23.21 Price bounces after a sharp bear market decline.

a downward breakout from the descending triangle (D), bullish enthusiasm overcomes bearish selling pressure and the stock rises to E. The variation occurs 13% of the time.

In the right variation, the stare-step decline is missing (during the F move). Price rebounds, hits the triangle, and drops for a short distance before busting the downward breakout. This variation occurs 8% of the time, so it is very rare.

The stock chart shows an example of the left variation on the weekly scale. Price is a meteor entering the atmosphere at A1, heading toward zero. At B1, the stock pauses for a few months and moves sideways before impacting the earth at C1.

After C1, price returns to the corrective phase of a measured move down (B1, corresponding to B). A descending triangle appears somewhere in the price jungle at D1. A downward breakout happens, pushing price down for a time, before a recovery takes the stock up to E1.

If you look at the B1-C1-D1 pattern, it is a head-and-shoulders bottom on the weekly scale.

Flat Base

Figure 23.22 shows an unusual flat base on the stock chart. The price trend is choppier than a hacksaw blade and just as unfriendly to one's skin.

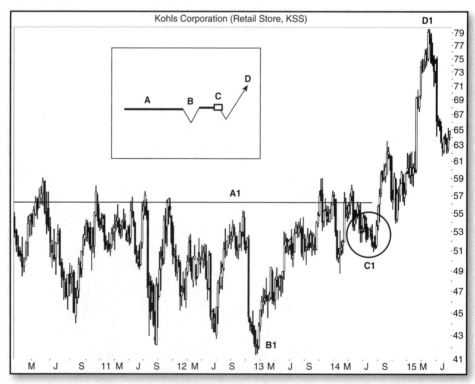

FIGURE 23.22   This unusual flat base leads to a descending triangle with a downward breakout that fails to see the stock drop much.

Consider the inset. This shows price moving horizontally at A, driving in and out of potholes (B) before reaching the descending triangle at C. The triangle has a downward breakout, dropping a tad before zipping upward to D. This variation occurs 15% of the time.

The stock chart is an attempt to show an example of this configuration. The stock hits overhead resistance at A1, making the top of the trading range appear irregular but flat overall. The bottom of the range shows many large valleys (B1). In the circle (weekly scale) appears the triangle with a downward breakout. The stock launches and climbs to D1 before the pilot suffers oxygen depletion and falls back to earth.

My experience with flat bases is that chart patterns will appear just below the top of a flat base. The flat base is like a roadway where the chart pattern becomes a pothole. Price hits the pothole and sinks into it before driving back out. Then the stock makes a nice upward climb.

■ Measure Rule

The measure rule helps set a price target. The target is not a concrete boundary that all triangles strive for. Rather, I like to think of the measure rule as a minimum expected move.

Figure 23.23 shows an example of how the measure rule works. Compute the height of the triangle. The top of the triangle is the first minor high touch at A, at 21.25. The bottom of the triangle is the horizontal line at B, 18.62 for a height of 2.63 (the difference between the two values). For upward breakouts, add the height to the breakout price and for downward breakouts, subtract it.

Because this triangle breaks out downward, we subtract the height from the bottom of the triangle to get a target of 15.99. Price touches the target at D.

For upward breakouts, let us assume that the breakout price is 20 at C. The upward target would be 20 + 2.63 or 22.63 (not shown).

How often does the measure rule work? For upward breakouts, price reaches or exceeds the target 73% of the time. For downward breakouts, it works 49% of the time.

If you take half the height and use that in the computation instead of the full height (use 1.32 instead of 2.63), then the rule works 89% of the time for upward breakouts and 74% of the time for downward breakouts.

Once you have a target, look for nearby overhead resistance or underlying support and assume price will turn there.

■ Price reaches the measure rule target 73% of the time for upward breakouts and 49% of the time for downward breakouts.

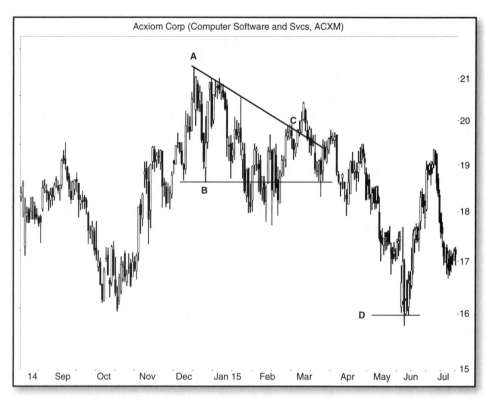

FIGURE 23.23 Use the measure rule to help predict a price target.

■ Trading

Suppose you are shopping for a descending triangle to buy and see the one shown in **Figure 23.24** (at C1). Assume you spotted the triangle before the upward breakout at D1. Should you buy this triangle, just ignore it, or short the stock?

Look at the upper right inset, shown on the weekly scale. Notice that the primary trend is downward. That should be obvious from the chart, but let us check anyway.

By definition, the primary trend begins a year before the start of the triangle. The triangle begins in May 2015, and the dip at A1 is in May 2014. Because A1 is above the start of the triangle, the primary trend is down.

If you were to look back even further, the downtrend started in August 2013. Because price is falling, what makes you believe the downtrend will end soon?

I looked through the configurations and setups in this chapter and found that Figure 23.8 matches this situation. I show the inset from Figure 23.8 on the lower left.

The decline from A to C represents the primary trend, and it is down. We have already discussed the primary trend for this stock (A1 to C1). The BC trend is also down. Looking at the stock chart, price drops from B1 to C1, following the BC blueprint.

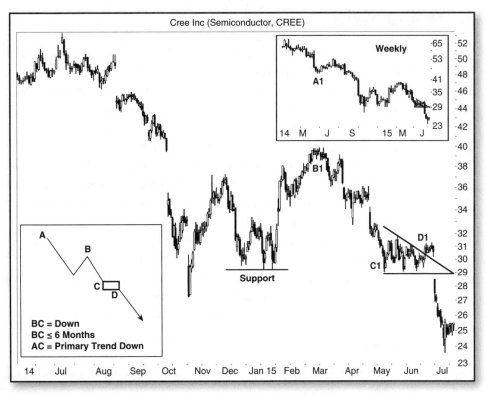

FIGURE 23.24 A busted descending triangle leads to a swift decline.

BC is six months or less. The B1-C1 drop is about two months long. In other words, everything shown in the left inset is the same as what we see on the stock chart except for one important detail. Do you know what it is?

The answer is the breakout direction. The inset shows a downward breakout, but this stock chart breaks out upward (at D1).

If you flip back to Figure 23.8, you will see an almost identical stock chart. Notice in that figure that the price of C1-D1 rests on support formed in May and even the slide into February.

On Figure 23.24, we see support during December to January. If Cree behaves similarly to Monster Worldwide, then the stock will make a dramatic move down.

Despite the upward breakout (D1) at a support area (December to January), I would be worried about both the primary trend and short-term trend being down. A check of similar stocks might also show a weak industry.

For those reasons, I would avoid going long on this trade.

If you look at the monthly chart (not shown), Cree is near support setup by a trendline drawn along the bottoms of price starting in 2002. It suggests the downtrend is close to ending. Again, a closer look at company fundamentals and the competition would help determine whether this stock will be a bottom-fishing candidate or just a loser.

Many chart patterns are best suited to day and swing traders because the move is quick (time) and short (distance).

However, if you are a position trader looking for a trend change or a buy-and-hold investor, should you be worried when seeing a descending triangle in a stock you own?

To answer that, I looked at my spreadsheet and found how often a rise or decline of 20% occurred. A 20% move in the Dow Jones Industrials signals a switch for bull to bear or bear to bull. I just applied that thinking to individual stocks.

I found that 30% of the 594 descending triangles with downward breakouts in a bull market had price decline at least 20%. That also means a stock will not suffer a large decline 70% of the time.

For upward breakouts, the 674 descending triangles that qualified showed 59% of them had price rise at least 20% after the breakout.

In other words, if you own a stock and a descending triangle breaks out downward, check the fundamentals, but most likely, you can ignore the triangle.

For upward breakouts, there is a decent chance of the stock posting a good gain.

Actual Trade

Figure 23.25 shows an actual trade I made using a descending triangle to exit a position.

In early October, when the stock plunged at A, I placed an order to buy the stock and received a fill at 55.12. That price is approximately where A is on the chart.

Here is what I wrote in my notebook: "This is a steal at 57.58, where it closed today [the day before I bought]. Has a small dividend, about 3.2%. This is a value play, long term holding. Half position [half as many shares as normal since it was a bear market]."

A weird looking symmetrical triangle appears at B, and I made note of it for the second buy at C: "12/13/08. I placed a limit order to buy at 55.85. This is at the apex of a small symmetrical triangle in November 2008 [B]. Price appears to be executing a throwback to the apex. Based on fundamentals, this is a screaming value play with a 3+% dividend, to boot. Of course, the stock has to turn around and go up. . . . This would make a full position in the stock.

"If it were to drop to 50.25, then sell. That would represent a 10% loss. Upside target is 70+. If it hits 70, that would be a 27% gain, not including the dividend."

About a month later, I was writing in my notebook again: "Sell reason: This looks to be falling through a descending triangle, so I know it is going lower. No sense holding on especially with a lawsuit against them for marketing their drugs for off-label uses."

I sold the stock and received a fill at 54.97, less than either of my two buys, and yet I made a small profit because of two dividend payments.

Notice that the bottom of the descending triangle (line E) is not flat. That bothers me now, but, apparently, it did not then. I think this is better classified as a symmetrical triangle and not a descending one.

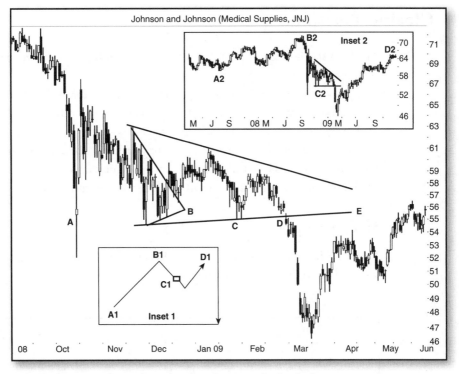

FIGURE 23.25 This trade made money because of a dividend payment.

Application What does the information from this chapter say about the descending triangle in Figure 23.25?

First, I was bottom-fishing, going long just before the end of the 2007 to 2009 bear market. That market turned bullish in March 2009, just as the stock bottomed.

Look at Inset 2. This is the stock on the weekly scale. Price over the long term rises from A2 to B2, drops to the descending triangle at C2, recovers, and climbs to D2.

The configuration shown in Figure 23.20 fits the chart perfectly (except for the extended drop to the March low in Figure 23.25). I show the inset to that figure as Inset 1. Notice how the A1 to D1 points match A2 to D2.

If I wanted to trade this as a busted pattern (which Figure 23.20 shows), the drop to the March low was 17%, too far for a busted pattern (the limit is 10%). Still, it would have been a decent (but not great) buying opportunity because the stock climbed to 109.49 in 2014 from an entry price of 64.50 (the top of the triangle). That is a 70% gain in 4 years if traded perfectly. Good but not great.

None of the other configurations apply as closely as Figure 23.20. What is clear from this chart is that the stock was not a buy candidate. The bear market had yet to end (so Figure 23.10 did not apply), the stock was trending down, and it had a downward breakout from the triangle.

Of course, I did not buy the stock because of the descending triangle. I sold on a downward breakout, which in this case was the right play. Imagine if I held on and sold it at the March low. Yuck.

■ Closing Position

The big surprise from descending triangles is that they break out upward more often than downward.

Throwbacks and pullbacks happen randomly, but that behavior is something traders need to be aware of. You do not want to be stopped out of a trade during a throwback only to watch from the sidelines as price doubles.

There are a number of setups and configurations that apply to most situations you will come across. Hopefully, they will provide guidance for your trading. Use them to help predict which setups result in better moves and which trades to avoid.

Setup Synopsis

Figure 23.26 may help you identify the various types of trading setups. See the associated figure for an explanation.

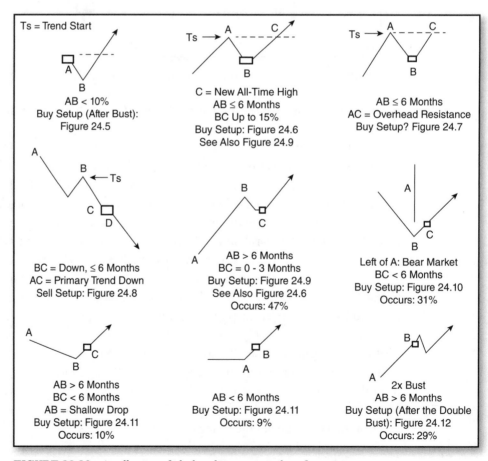

FIGURE 23.26 A collection of ideal trading setups and configurations.

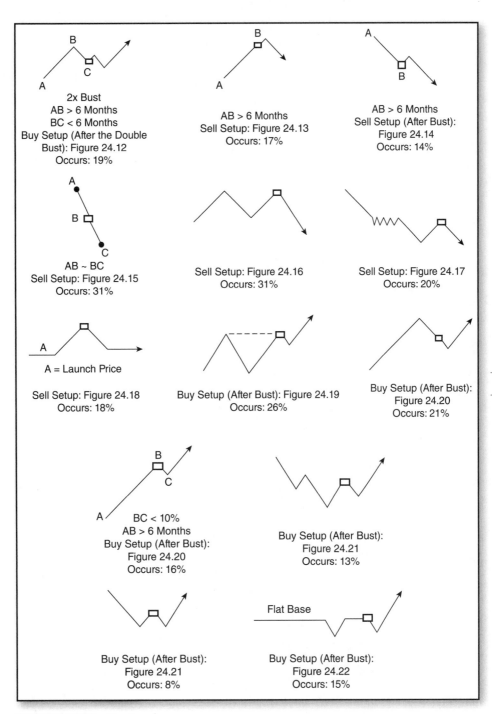

FIGURE 23.26 Continued

"Occurs" in the figures means how often I found the configuration in the stocks I looked at. If two configurations apply to your situation, then the one with a more frequent occurrence (a higher percentage) is the one you should choose to follow.

CHAPTER 24

Triangles, Symmetrical

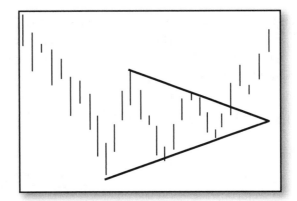

Symmetrical triangles are one of the more common patterns that you will see on the charts. Price bounces between two converging trendlines until the breakout. The breakout sends price shooting upward in a bull market and downward in a bear market. That makes sense, given the market influence pulling on the stock.

One of my friends fears symmetrical triangles because she lost a lot of money when one appeared in a stock she owned. The adverse breakout took the stock down, and instead of selling, and she became a deer caught in the headlights. Then road kill.

Do not let that happen to you.

To help prevent such tragedies, let us take a closer look at this unique pattern.

■ Behavior at a Glance

Figure 24.1 shows the overall performance of symmetrical triangles. In bull markets, upward breakouts occur an average of 61% of the time. When they do occur, the rise averages 40%.

Downward breakouts happen 39% of the time, and price drops an average of 14%.

For both upward and downward breakouts, the numbers refer to over 2,700 perfect trades. That means the stock is bought at the breakout price and sold at the ultimate high or ultimate low, before the trend changes. Do not expect your trade to perform as well. You could do better . . . or worse.

■ *Price breakouts out upward 61% of the time.*

Throwbacks and Pullbacks

Figure 24.2 shows a complicated-looking figure. The top half shows the typical behavior after an upward breakout from a symmetrical triangle.

I found that 57% of the time the stock will throw back to the breakout price. It does this by breaking out upward, coasting 8% higher in 5 days before returning to the breakout price or trendline boundary. The complete trip takes 10 days. By convention, a throwback must occur within a month.

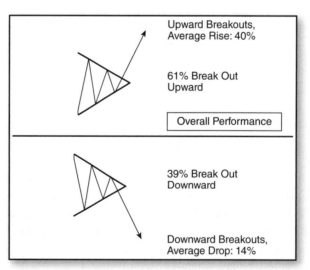

FIGURE 24.1   Upward breakouts occur most often in bull markets.

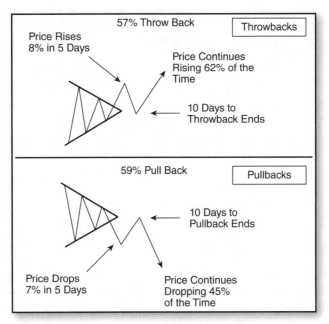

FIGURE 24.2 Throwbacks and pullbacks occur over half the time after breakouts from symmetrical triangles.

After that, the stock recovers 62% of the time, leaving the other 38% to see price continue dropping below the bottom of the triangle.

Pullbacks are similar to throwbacks except that the breakout is downward.

Price drops an average of 7% in 5 days before returning to the breakout price or trendline boundary. The complete trip takes 10 days. After the pullback completes, price drops 45% of the time. That means the majority of the time (55%) price continues rising above the top of the triangle.

I found that 59% of symmetrical triangles have pullbacks.

- A throwback occurs 57% of the time and pullbacks happen 59% of the time in symmetrical triangles.

Busted Triangles

Of the three types of triangles, ascending, descending, and symmetrical, the symmetrical triangle busts the most, for both breakout directions.

Figure 24.3 shows the numbers for symmetricals. Upward breakouts bust when the stock rises less than 10% before dropping and closing below the bottom of the triangle (not below the bottom trendline). The average decline for single busted symmetricals measures 14% below the bottom of the triangle.

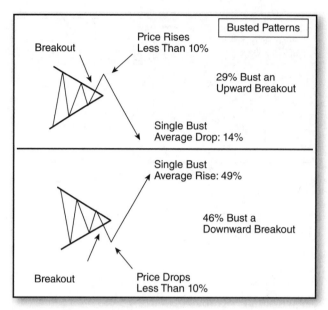

FIGURE 24.3 Symmetrical triangles bust frequently, especially downward breakouts.

I found that 29% of symmetrical triangles with upward breakouts bust the breakout.

Downward breakouts see price drop less than 10% before reversing and closing above the top of the triangle. The rise averages 49% for triangles that bust only once.

Almost half (46%) of all symmetrical triangles bust a downward breakout. I consider that statistic ding-ding-ding (alarming) for those of you that like to short a stock. Be very sure of your facts before you short a symmetrical triangle showing a downward breakout. At the very least, place an order to close out the trade if price closes above the top of the triangle (that is, if it busts the downward breakout).

- Price busts an upward breakout 29% of the time and a downward breakout 46% of the time in a symmetrical triangle.

■ Identification

Figure 24.4 shows a symmetrical triangle at A. Point B shows where a pullback bottoms and C shows where it completes. Refer to **Table 24.1** as I discuss identification guidelines.

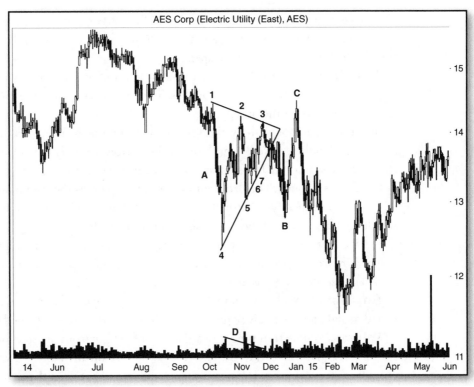

FIGURE 24.4 An example of a symmetrical triangle with a pullback.

TABLE 24.1	**Identification Guidelines**
Characteristic	**Discussion**
Converging trendlines	Two trendlines bound price movement. The top trendline slopes downward, and the bottom trendline slopes upward so that they converge at the triangle's apex.
Trendline touches	There must be at least five trendline touches, three of one trendline and two of the other. Each trendline touch should be at a minor high or minor low. Price cutting through a trendline (such as during a breakout) does not count as a trendline touch.
White space	Price should cross the pattern from side to side filling the white space with movement.
Duration	Triangles should be longer than three weeks.
Volume	Volume trends downward 83% of the time from triangle start to the day before the breakout.
Breakout	Price can breakout either upward or downward and it does so when the stock closes outside of the trendline boundary.

Converging Trendlines. Price should follow two converging trendlines. The top trendline slopes downward, and the bottom one slopes upward. They join sometime in the future at the triangle apex.

Trendline Touches. Price must touch each trendline at least twice, but I now require at total of five or more touches. That means at least three touches of one trendline and two of the other.

In the Figure **24.4**, I show the touches with numbers. There are three touches of the top trendline (1 to 3) and four on the bottom (4 to 7). Each trendline touch should be at a minor high or minor low. Price that shoots through the trendline does not qualify as a touch. The breakout (where price pierces the trendline to the right of 7), does not qualify as a touch. However, if a minor high or low is close to the trendline, but does not touch it, it can count as a touch.

White Space. Price must cross the triangle from side to side, filling the white space with price movement. If there is too much white space, then you have likely made an identification mistake.

Duration. Triangle length varies, but most are longer than three weeks. Shorter than that and they are likely pennants, providing the pennant is attached to a flagpole.

Volume. Volume trends downward 83% of the time from the start of the triangle (the first trendline touch) to the end (the day before the breakout). If volume trends upward, that is fine, too. The performance difference between the two is minor.

Breakout. A breakout occurs when price closes outside the trendline boundary. The breakout can be either up or down. Sometimes, it squeezes out the triangle's apex, but that is rare.

■ Buy Setup 1

For many of the statistics in this chapter, I used 1,069 symmetrical triangles with downward breakouts and 1,624 with upward ones, with data from May 1988 through July 2015. Not all stocks covered the entire period, and I only included data from bull markets.

The first buy setup is one of my favorites. It happens when price breaks out downward from a symmetrical triangle only to reverse and break out the top. **Figure 24.5** shows the situation, but first look at the inset.

The black box (B) represents the triangle. Price at A begins an uptrend, but the trend could just as well be downward, leading to the start of the triangle, B.

The breakout is downward from the triangle and price drops, but not far (less than 10%). The stock reverses and closes above the top of the triangle, busting the downward breakout. The stock rises to D (in the ideal situation).

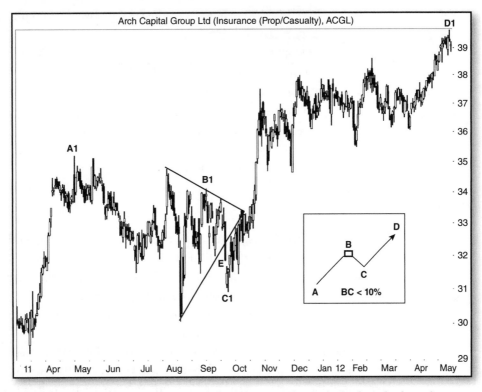

FIGURE 24.5 A downward breakout from a symmetrical triangle that busts leads to a large rise.

The stock chart shows an example on the daily chart. Price trends downward from the trend start (A1) to the chart pattern at B1. The downward breakout occurs at E and soon price bottoms (C1). The stock reverses and climbs, busting the downward breakout when it closes above the top of the chart pattern, eventually climbing higher, to D1 and beyond, posting a gain of 107% (not shown).

Here are the steps for trading a single (or triple) busted pattern.

1. Use Table 24.1 to identify a symmetrical triangle.
2. Price must breakout downward and drop less than 10% below the breakout.
3. The stock reverses direction. When it closes above the top of the chart pattern (not above the top trendline), buy at the close or buy at the open the next day.
4. Place a stop a penny below the bottom of the chart pattern or at a location better suited to your situation.

Table 24.2 shows a few performance statistics for this setup.

| TABLE 24.2 | Statistics for Busted Triangles with Downward Breakouts |

Description	Result
1. Percentage of triangles that bust	46%
2. Average rise after busting	36%
3. Average rise after single bust	49%
4. Percentage of single busts	71%
5. Percentage of double busts	15%
6. Percentage of triple+ busts	14%

1. Downward breakouts from symmetrical triangles bust frequently, almost half the time, so trades should be plentiful.

2. The average rise is 36% for all types of busts (single, double, triple).

3. For single busted patterns only, the average rise is 49%.

4–6. I split the busting process into three types of busts: single, double, and triple. The triple includes three or more busts.

A bust occurs when price breaks out in one direction, moves less than 10% before reversing. To stop the bust, price must move beyond 10% from either the top or bottom of the chart pattern. If it does not and crosses the pattern again, another bust occurs. This process continues until price moves at least 10% away from the pattern's top or bottom.

The Table 24.2 shows that single busts occur most often, followed by double and triple busts. If you see a busted symmetrical triangle, there is a 71% chance of it busting just once.

■ Buy Setup 2

This setup is rare, but if you can find it and it works as expected, riches can be yours. All you have to do is trade it properly.

Figure 24.6 shows the setup in the inset. The ABC move I show as forming a peak at B, but it need not. Peak B represents overhead resistance, the highest price the stock has ever reached. Once the stock can move above the price of B, the stock is clear of most overhead resistance (the only exception is round number resistance).

The piercing of overhead resistance is critical to this setup. The stock has to clear overhead resistance. If it does not, it turns into Buy Setup 3, a worse performing scenario.

The BC move is short, less than or equal to six months. C represents the symmetrical triangle. The triangle has an upward breakout that takes price to D. The

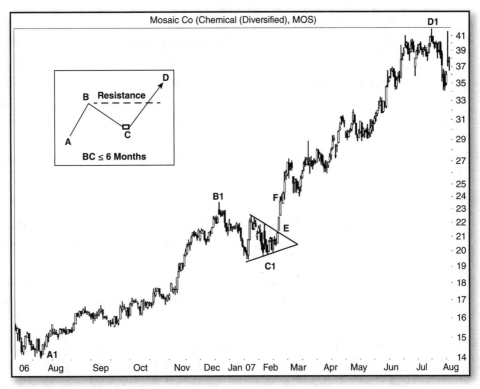

FIGURE 24.6   The stock pushes through overhead resistance to set an all-time high.

price of D shows that the stock has pierced overhead resistance and is now making all-time highs.

The stock chart shows an example on the daily scale. B1 is the highest price the stock has ever made (in this example). An upward breakout from the symmetrical triangle happens at E and price rises to F. There it moves sideways for only a few days as it burns through overhead resistance setup by peak B1. After that, the sky is the limit. The stock reaches the ultimate high just over 110 in January 2008 (not shown), after the start of a bear market, and continues to coast to over 160 in June before bears maul it.

Here are the steps for using this setup.

1. Use the identification guidelines from Table 24.1 to qualify the symmetrical triangle as a valid chart pattern.
2. Find where the trend starts. The trend start should be a peak before which price drops at least 20%, or a valley before which price rises at least 20%. The distance from the trend start to the start of the symmetrical triangle should be less than or equal to six months for the best performance.

TABLE 24.3 **Statistical Analysis of Buy Setup 2**

Description	Inbound Trend ≤6 Months	Inbound Trend >6 Months
1. Occurrence, samples	16%, 244	10%, 147
2. Post-breakout average gain	74%	61%
3. Median gain	57%	37%
4. Gains over 25%	79%	62%
5. 5% failure rate	1%	3%
6. 10% failure rate	5%	14%

3. Measure the distance from the anticipated breakout price (estimate it) to the all-time high price. The closer to 0% that value is, the better. See Table 24.4 and the discussion for more information.
4. Buy the stock at the open a day after it breaks out upward from the triangle.
5. Place a stop-loss order a penny below the bottom of the chart pattern or at a location of your choice.

Table 24.3 shows the performance statistics for this setup.

1. As I mentioned, this setup is rare, happening 26% of the time (16% + 10%). The performance numbers are for perfect trades, buying at the low price on the breakout day and selling at the high price at the ultimate high. Use the results for comparison purposes only, not as an indicator of how your trade might perform.

2–4. The short term (less than or equal to six months) inbound trend outperforms the longer term substantially. That has been the case for other chart patterns as well.

I find it gratifying that the short inbound trend setup has many (79%) of the trades seeing post-breakout rises of at least 25%.

5, 6. With such large gains, failure rates are small. Only the long-term inbound trend, at 14%, has a high failure rate.

Table 24.4 shows a frequency distribution of the distance from the breakout price to overhead resistance. The intent of the table is to give you some idea of how far price needs to rise before it clears overhead resistance for the statistics used in Table 24.3.

TABLE 24.4 **Frequency Distribution of Distance to Overhead Resistance**

Bin	5%	10%	15%	20%	25%	30%	35%	40%	45%	50%	>50%
Frequency	28%	13%	14%	9%	9%	4%	2%	4%	2%	3%	12%
Cumulative	28%	41%	55%	64%	73%	77%	79%	83%	85%	88%	100%

Over half (55%) of the chart patterns rise just 15% before clearing overhead resistance and venturing into all-time high territory. The closer overhead resistance is to the breakout price, the easier it will be for the stock to rise and pierce it.

■ Buy Setup 3

If you acquire a stock qualifying for Buy Setup 2, there is a 71% chance that it will turn into this setup. In this setup, price tangles with overhead resistance and gets electrocuted.

The stock chart in **Figure 24.7** shows an example of this setup, but look at the inset. The stock climbs to A and forms overhead resistance. Resistance can appear in many forms, such as peaks, valleys, horizontal consolidation regions, and so on.

Price returns to the symmetrical triangle, shown as box B. The stock can rise or fall going into the pattern, but the trend from A (the trend start) to B lasts six months or less for the best performance.

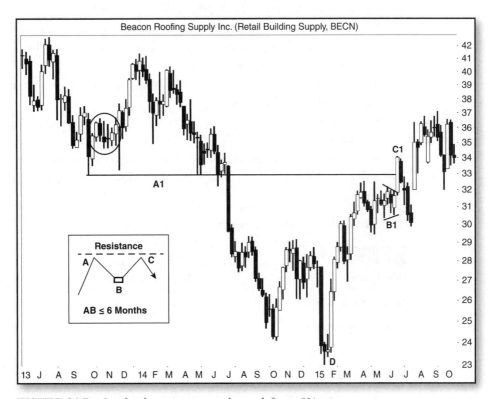

FIGURE 24.7 Overhead resistance stops the stock for an 8% gain.

After an upward breakout, the stock climbs back to overhead resistance and then stops moving up. Price tumbles, dropping at least 20% (C) or closing below the bottom of the triangle.

The stock chart shows an example on the weekly scale. A1 marks overhead resistance to an upward move setup by valleys in 2013 and 2014. The resistance area extends above the horizontal line. I would expect the stock to stop near the price of the circled area (about 35) because the congestion area looks particularly intimidating.

The triangle appears at B1. Notice that price trends upward going into B1 but downward going into B. What is important is the location of overhead resistance, A1, not the approaching trend, which can be up or down.

Price breaks out upward from the triangle and almost immediately hits overhead resistance at C1. Price reverses and tumbles below the triangle, busting the upward breakout.

Here are the steps for using this setup.

1. Use the identification guidelines from Table 24.1 to qualify the symmetrical triangle as a valid chart pattern.
2. Find where the trend starts. The distance from the trend start to the start of the descending triangle should be less than or equal to six months for the best performance. In Figure 24.20, the trend start is at D.
3. Measure the distance from the anticipated breakout price (estimate it) to overhead resistance. If the stock stops at overhead resistance, will the potential profit be worth the risk of a trade?
4. If yes to step 3, then buy the stock at the close or at the open a day after it breaks out upward from the triangle.
5. Place a stop-loss order a penny below the bottom of the chart pattern or at a location of your choice.
6. Sell when the stock approaches (stalls at or reverses near) overhead resistance. If you are lucky, this setup will push through overhead resistance and morph into Buy Setup 2.

Table 24.5 shows how this setup performs.

TABLE 24.5	Statistical Analysis of Buy Setup 3	
Description	Inbound Trend ≤6 Months	Inbound Trend >6 Months
1. Occurrence, samples	56%, 838	15%, 220
2. Post-breakout average gain	26%	17%
3. Median gain	15%	8%
4. Gains over 25%	34%	21%
5. 5% failure rate	15%	28%
6. 10% failure rate	35%	54%

1. This setup is where most of your trades will come from or evolve into (when you try for Buy Setup 2). I found that 71% (56% + 15%) of the trades fell into the category of having their run shortened by overhead resistance (the other 3% are for rare setups not worth discussing).

2–4. Compare the remarkable difference between a 74% gain from the prior set-up with the 17% or even 26% gain from this setup.

Best case, 34% of the trades made gains over 25% and that is for symmetrical triangles with short inbound trends.

5, 6. Failure rates are high, too. The 15% rate is the smallest of the four and it is three to four times higher than I like to see. More than half of all trades (54%) using this setup with long inbound price trends will see price fail to rise at least 10%. Ouch.

The key to using this setup is to know where overhead resistance is. If you can determine that with accuracy, making money in the stock market becomes a lot easier.

■ Sell Setup

What conditions predict a large downward move? Numbers from the spreadsheet provide clues that I would like to share with you. I do not have a sell setup, per se, but these tips may help you decide to keep or dispose of a stock showing a symmetrical triangle.

The average decline is 14% from the 1,069 symmetrical triangles with downward breakouts in a bull market I looked at.

■ Avoid shorting symmetrical triangles within a third of the yearly high. Stocks performing well tend to continue performing well. To put it another way, stocks with downward breakouts within a third of the yearly low saw price drop an average of 16%. Those near the yearly high decline 13%.

■ One of the best predictors of performance is pattern height. The combination of tall and narrow symmetrical triangles show declines averaging 18%, well above the worst-performing short and wide combination (11% average decline). Tall means a percentage higher than 11.55% of height divided by the breakout price. Narrow means shorter than the median width of 34 calendar days.

■ Measure the time from the trend start to the pattern start. The shorter the inbound trend, the larger the post-breakout decline. For example, inbound trends shorter than 3 months showed declines averaging 18%. Inbound trends longer than 6 months saw declines of 12%.

■ I used the closing price one year before the start of the symmetrical triangle to determine the primary trend. If the primary trend is downward heading to a symmetrical triangle with a downward breakout, you can expect a larger decline than

TABLE 24.6	Stop Locations for Triangles		
Description	Chance of Being Hit	Average Loss	Missed Trades, Gains/Losses
1. Penny below the pattern	5%	9%	40%
Up Breakouts Above, Down Breakouts Below			
2. Penny above the pattern	5%	4%	16%

an upward primary trend and downward breakout. The losses average 16% for the downward trend and 13% for the upward trend.

■ Best Stop Locations

If you were to buy or short a stock showing a symmetrical triangle, where would you place your stop?

Table 24.6 shows the best stop locations but only two make sense for symmetrical triangles: either above the top or below the bottom of the triangle.

1. Penny below the pattern. Suppose the breakout is upward. If you place a stop-loss order a penny below the bottom of the triangle, the chance of it being hit is just 5%. The average loss would be about 9%, and those missed trades would have made an average of 40%.

2. Penny above the pattern. If you were to short the stock, then placing a stop above the top of the triangle (not above the top of the trendline) would trigger 5% of the time. The average loss would be 4%, and the trades you missed would go on to drop an average of 16%.

- Place a stop-loss order a penny above the top (downward breakout) or below the bottom (upward breakout) of a symmetrical triangle.

■ Configuration Trading

To trade the following configurations, begin with these guidelines:

1. Find a triangle on the *daily* chart that obeys the identification guidelines listed in Table 24.1.
2. Look for the configuration that matches what you see on your *weekly* chart.
3. Buy at the open the day after the breakout or place an order to buy a penny above the top trendline (upward breakouts) or below the bottom trendline (downward breakouts).
4. Place a stop-loss order at a location of your choice.

If you shove aside the spreadsheets and look at charts, lots of charts, you can find patterns that repeat. The best-performing symmetrical triangles with upward break-outs sift into two basic configurations. Let us discuss them.

Figure 24.8 shows the first variation in the inset. In a good number of cases, the price trend at A is flat (or reasonably so). That means price along the bottom, top, or both tends to look flat (weekly or monthly scale is best). Sometimes you can draw a near-horizontal trendline connecting the peaks or valleys.

I did not see a consensus in the 152 charts I looked at regarding the length of the rise (B) to the symmetrical triangle, C. Many times, the stock will climb just above the top of the triangle, and the triangle will act as an upward reversal in a short downward trend. (The stock chart shows an example of this. The peak to the left of C1 is above the top of the triangle, and yet the triangle breaks out upward.)

After an upward breakout, price rises to D, the ultimate high.

The stock chart on the weekly scale shows an example. The flat base starts at A1 and ends at B1. It is irregular looking, but overall, one could say price moves horizontally along the bottom as the horizontal line shows.

FIGURE 24.8   A flat base launches price upward before a symmetrical triangle forms.

After B1, the stock starts its rise and peaks just above the symmetrical triangle (to the left of C1). The triangle appears at C1, although it is difficult to see on the weekly scale.

An upward breakout sends price climbing to the ultimate high at D1.

This configuration appeared most often, 56% of the time. A variation of this configuration showed the triangle at C appear at or very near the turn at B. That variation happened 7% of the time, giving a combined total of 63%.

V Bottom

Figure 24.9 shows the next configuration in the inset. The stock moves lower from A to B, often in a steep correction or bear market decline. At B, the stock bottoms and turns. The triangle can appear here (at or near B) or price can recover for a time (to C) before the triangle forms. After the upward breakout from the triangle (C), price rises to the ultimate high at D.

The stock chart shows an example of this behavior on the weekly scale.

The downtrend begins at A1 and takes price down to B1 in a violent bear market drop. The rise from B1 to C1 mirrors the decline in this example but need not. A

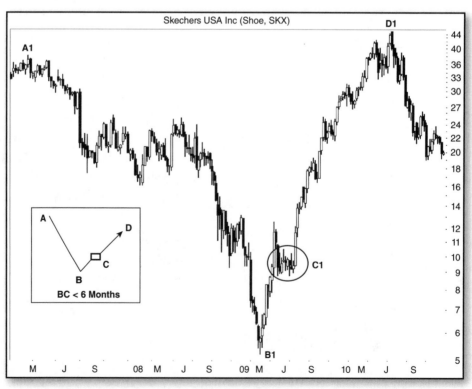

FIGURE 24.9 Price forms a symmetrical triangle after price reverses in a V bottom.

symmetrical triangle may appear at C1 or it may appear closer to the turn at B1, as I said.

After an upward breakout from the triangle, price rises until reaching the ultimate high months later (D1).

If you have read many chapters in this book and studied the figures, you may come to the opinion that V-shaped turns represent a terrific buying opportunity. This chart shows such an example. It helps that a bear market ended, powering the stock higher when the bulls stampeded. But if you can buy a stock near the bottom of a V-shaped turn, you can do well.

This configuration happened 36% of the time in the stocks I looked at.

Upward Breakout Failures

What configurations do we see when the stock rises less than, say, 10% after an upward breakout? This section looks at the variations.

Figure 24.10 shows a configuration that happened 48% of the time in the 166 patterns I looked at.

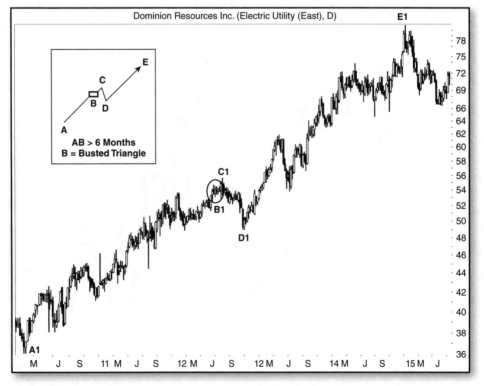

FIGURE 24.10 After an extensive rise, an upward breakout from a symmetrical triangle reverses, causing a failure.

The AB move is often, but not always, a long-term rise leading to the start of the symmetrical triangle (use the weekly scale for clarity). The breakout is upward, but the momentum fades quickly, sometimes in just days, to C, before the stock reverses. The rise is less than 10%, often less than 5%.

Price drops, busting the chart pattern at D. It seems that once the stock drops below the bottom of the triangle, flushing out traders, then price reverses and resumes its upward march to E. This reversal need not happen immediately as the stock chart shows.

Price rises from A1 to B1, where the symmetrical triangle lies buried in the weekly price chart. An upward breakout carries the stock to C1 and reverses, dropping the stock to D1. There it finds support and reverses again, eventually making its way to E1.

Traders assume that when a triangle appears after a long-term upward run, the run is about over. In this case, that is true, too, but the following decline from C1 to D1 is small compared to the extent of the run from D1 to E1. Also notice that triangle B1 is almost midway in the A1-E1 move.

- Triangles can act as half-staff patterns (that is, they can appear midway in the price trend).

The Downward Bust   Second in popularity among the triangle failures I looked at is another variation shown in **Figure 24.11**. It happened 15% of the time.

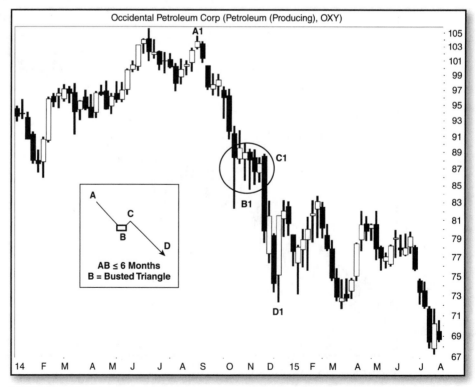

FIGURE 24.11   Price drops, breaks out upward from a triangle, but then resumes its downward move.

Price drops over the short-term from A to B. Price reverses at the triangle, but the upward breakout (C) fails. Price drops again, busting the upward breakout, and sending prices lower, to D.

The stock chart shows how the accident unfolds. The move down from A1 to B1 is fast in concert with tumbling oil prices. Because the chart is on the weekly scale, the symmetrical triangle (B1) is hard to see but it breaks out upward (C1).

A quick reversal takes price down to D1 and even lower after about a six-month pause.

Peak Reversal **Figure 24.12** shows a reversal at a price peak. This configuration occurred 15% of the time.

Price rises from A to B, but the move can be either short or long term. A symmetrical triangle appears at B and that leads to an upward breakout, C. This upward rise after the breakout is quick, taking price higher by less than 10% before it reverses.

The stock busts the triangle as price plummets from C to D.

The chart shows an example of this configuration on the weekly scale. In this case, the climb is a long-term one, from A1 to B1. You cannot see the upward breakout from the triangle, but it is there. Then the stock drops from B1 to D1 in dramatic fashion.

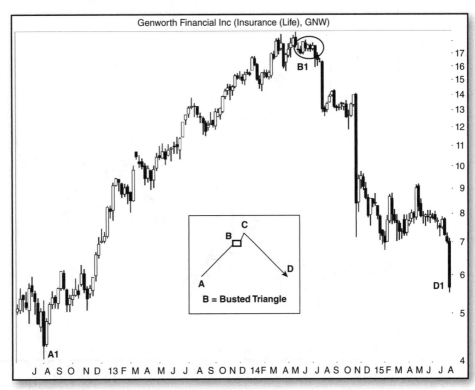

FIGURE 24.12 Price breaks out upward from a triangle but reverses after an upward run.

I owned this stock but sold it during the first big plunge after the triangle busted. I was not pleased with selling so far below the high, but it sure beats riding it down below $6.

Bottom-Fishing Fake Out   Figure 24.13 shows the last upward breakout failure. It occurred 14% of the time in the stocks I looked at.

The AB drop is a short one, typically six months or less. The BCD move is the same as the others in this section. The upward breakout from triangle B rises to C in a short move then reverses to bust the breakout, at D.

Once the reversal has shaken out traders, the stock flips again and rises in a strong push upward to E. Note that E need not be above A. I just drew it this way, and it so happens that the stock I chose also shows a good move.

The stock chart is on the weekly scale.

Price drops from A1 to D1. Near B1, a symmetrical triangle sends price breaking out upward, reversing, and busting. After the decline finishes, the stock recovers and makes a strong push higher to E1, regroups for many months before another strong push takes the stock higher still.

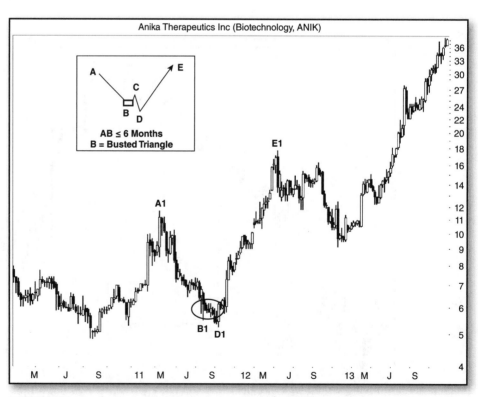

FIGURE 24.13   An upward breakout signals a reversal that did not hold.

Downward Breakouts

By looking at a number of charts with downward breakouts from symmetrical triangles, a pattern emerges. Rather, two patterns emerge, both associated with large declines.

The first appears in **Figure 24.14**.

The rise from A to B is often (but not always) a long-term rise (longer than six months). Because the triangle appears well along the uptrend, we can assume that the trend is nearer its end than its start. When a downward breakout occurs, look out below. The stock learns about gravity and drops, from B to C.

The stock chart shows a good example of this behavior. The inbound trend (A1-B1) will often appear more irregular than what I show here. Teradyne is unusual because of its steady climb.

The symmetrical triangle appears at B1 on the weekly scale, so it is hard to see. A downward breakout kicks the stock lower to bottom at C1 before a substantial bounce.

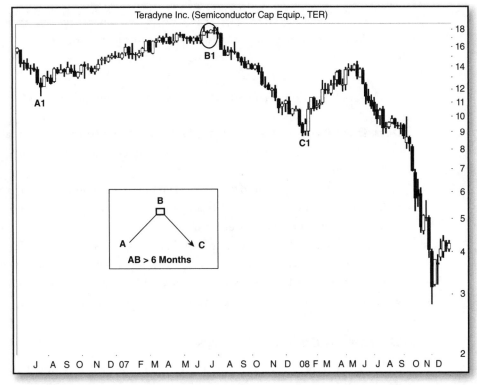

FIGURE 24.14 The stock peaks, forms a symmetrical triangle with a downward breakout, and the stock drops.

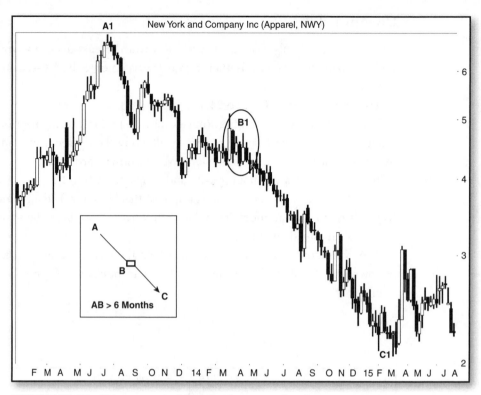

FIGURE 24.15   This symmetrical triangle acts as a continuation pattern.

This configuration occurred most often, 64% of the time.

Downtrend Continuation   **Figure 24.15** shows the second configuration that occurs 36% of the time in the 121 patterns I looked at before I filled my table with stock symbols.

Price forms a long-term downtrend, starting from A and dropping to B. The box at B represents the symmetrical triangle. A downward breakout from the triangle sends the stock on its way lower, to C.

The stock chart shows an example of this behavior. Price peaks at A1 and the stock begins to climb down from the summit. At B1, a symmetrical triangle appears (weekly scale, so it is hard to see) with a downward breakout. The bearish breakout joins with the existing downward price trend and the stock returns to base camp at C1.

Downward Breakout Failures

I found two types of failures in the 123 symmetrical triangles I looked at. The first configuration occurs 63% of the time. It has a shape similar to Figure 24.14. **Figure 24.16** shows the variation.

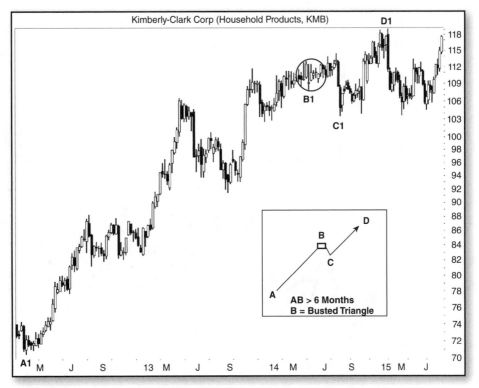

FIGURE 24.16 After a long uptrend, a symmetrical triangle breaks out downward but recovers quickly.

The stock climbs from A to B in a long-term move (more than six months) before a symmetrical triangle appears (B). The triangle breaks out downward and price drops, but only for a short time and a short decline (C). After that, the stock recovers and rises to D. The rise may not last long or it could set a new trend. The duration is unknown.

The stock chart shows an example of this configuration. Price climbs a wall of worry from A1 to B1. B1 is where the symmetrical triangle is, although it is hard to see on the weekly chart.

The triangle breaks out downward and reverses to bust the downward breakout, drops to C1 to bust it a second time and then rises to D1 to bust it a third time.

I do not know of a way to distinguish the scenario outlined in this chart versus the one outlined in Figure 24.14. Sorry.

Short-Term Trend Failure The inset in **Figure 24.17** shows the next configuration that occurs 37% of the time in the stocks I looked at.

Price from A to B is short term, meaning less than six months long. That distinguishes this configuration from the one shown in Figure 24.15. Price reaches the

FIGURE 24.17 Price trends downward over the short term before encountering a symmetrical triangle.

symmetrical triangle at B. The triangle breaks out downward, but price does not drop far, to C. When the stock recovers to D, it busts the downward breakout along the way.

The stock chart is not the best example of this configuration. Price peaks at A1 and trends down for a few months before creating the triangle at B1 (weekly scale). Although it may look like the triangle breaks out upward to D1, it actually has a downward breakout that lasts four days before returning to the triangle.

The rise to D1 busts the downward breakout. When price collapses to E, it busts the triangle for the second time. After that, the stock recovers.

■ Measure Rule

The measure rule helps predict how far price might rise or fall after the breakout from a chart pattern. It is not a guarantee, just a suggestion of how far price might move. Here is how to use it.

Figure 24.18 shows a symmetrical triangle with an upward breakout on the daily scale. Compute the height of the triangle. That means taking the low price at B

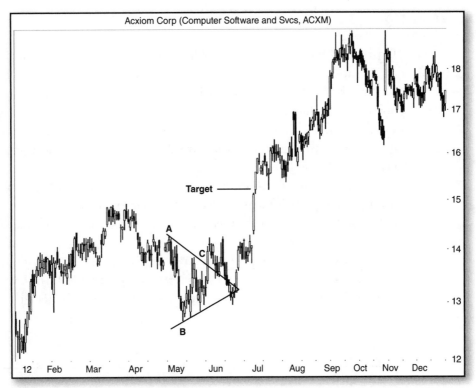

FIGURE 24.18 Use the measure rule to predict a target price.

(12.66) and subtracting it from the high price at A (14.27) for a height of 1.61. For upward breakouts, add the height to the price where the stock pierces the trendline on the day of breakout (near C, 13.61) for a target of 15.22.

For downward breakouts, subtract the height from the breakout price (13.61 − 1.61, or 12.00). If the predicted target is at or below 0, ignore it. The company will not likely go bankrupt.

Once you find the target, look for nearby overhead resistance or underlying support that might stop the stock. For swing and day trades, support, resistance, or the calculated target works well as sell points.

Price reaches the target 67% of the time for upward breakouts and 44% of the time for downward breakouts on the daily charts (not intraday).

If you cut the height in half and add or subtract that value from the breakout price, you get a closer target. The stock hits the closer target an average of 85% for upward breakouts and 72% for downward ones.

- The measure rule works 67% of the time for upward breakouts and 44% of the time for downward breakouts from symmetrical triangles.

Figure 24.19 shows an example of how to trade a symmetrical triangle.

The inset shows the stock on the daily scale, but the rest of the chart is on the weekly. The inset shows a symmetrical triangle with three touches of the top trendline (not including the breakout day when price zipped through the top trendline) and three touches on the bottom. The middle valley is close enough to the trendline to call it a touch. It is a valid symmetrical triangle because it meets all of the identification guidelines in Table 24.1.

The stock made an all-time high at A (trust me on this). With an upward breakout from the triangle at B, the stock does not need to rise far to soar into virgin territory (which it does soon after the breakout). Thus, this stock is a good candidate for Buy Setup 2.

Before A, the stock drops at least 20%, so A is the trend start. With the trend start about 16 months before the start of the triangle, it is not ideal. The triangle could be at the end of the uptrend or at least underperform its shorter inbound trend brothers.

FIGURE 24.19 This symmetrical triangle leads to a good trade when price clears overhead resistance.

If you were to buy this stock at the open a day after the breakout, it would fill at 48.44.

A stop placed a penny below the triangle's low price (45.17) would mean a potential loss of about 7%, which is acceptable (meaning it is not too high for me, but you be the judge).

Following the stock on the weekly scale shows that as price climbed, it followed an up-sloping trendline (the BC move). When the stock closed below the trendline, C, it was a sell signal. In many cases, it is not an automatic sell signal, but in this case, on the weekly scale, the signal was more reliable than on the daily charts.

If you sold at the next week's open, you would have received a fill at 63.05 for a gain of 30% in about 14 months.

Actual Trade

Figure 24.20 shows an actual trade I made using a downward breakout from a symmetrical triangle as the sell signal. Let me tell you about it. It gives me a chance to brag.

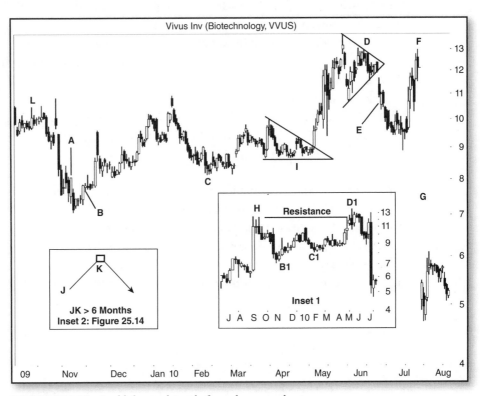

FIGURE 24.20   I sold the stock just before a large gap down.

I was looking at the stock in mid-October 2009 and wrote this in my notebook: "10/13/09. I was tempted to buy today but earnings are due in less than a month and the stock often tumbles a day later. Insiders are selling like crazy, not a good sign, 6 sales, no buys, since July alone, some for large amounts (35k).

"Based on a Fibonacci retrace of the recent move up, this is a buy. The stock dropped almost to the 50% Fibonacci line and is rebounding. Current candle (10/12, L) has a tall tail, indicating more down ahead."

After earnings came out (point A), the stock made a large move up that day but bottomed a day later.

I bought the stock a week later, at B. Here is what I wrote: "11/11/09. I believe this has retraced all it is going to so now is the time to buy. The stock has hit support setup by the bottom of the large gap and a prior peak in late July."

I received a fill at 7.80.

As the daily chart shows, the stock moved up nicely over the next several months. At D, a symmetrical triangle appeared. This was not a concern until it broke out downward. Uh-oh.

Because I am an end-of-day trader, I look at my stocks after the market's close. That was when I saw the downward breakout. I sold the stock the next day, at the market open. Here is my report, from my notebook: "Sold shares at the open, believing that this could pullback to the triangle bottom [it did, and climbed to F], but think that unlikely. I see this dropping to 9 [it did].

"Sell reason: Downward breakout from a symmetrical triangle with possible negative potential on FDA approval due to heart side effects. Got a great fill considering it opened at 10.56."

The sale filled at 10.71.

This is one of those trades that, even though I sold early, I am glad I got out with a 37% profit. At G, the U.S. Food and Drug Administration declined approval of their drug. The stock gapped open 58% lower.

Application What does the information in this chapter say about this triangle?

The triangle did not bust because price never closed above the top of the triangle, so Figure 24.5 does not apply. The stock was not breaking out to an all-time high (41.88) either, nor was price near it (forget Figure 24.6).

The weekly chart (Inset 1) of Figure 24.20 does not show the primary price trending higher since it is off the chart on the left, but it does trend higher from May

18, 2009 to May 18, 2010 (the trend one year before the pattern start). Thus, price rises over the long term and breaks out downward. Figure 24.14 is the perfect fit. It happened 64% of the time in the configurations I looked at.

Almost as likely was Figure 24.16, which came in at 63% of the time. Since the two probabilities (64%, 63%) are so close, they are no help.

Looking at Figure 24.20, the descending triangle at I should lend support to falling price. With the stock breaking out at 11.90 and assuming a drop to 9 (which is what I expected, from my notebook) where the triangle I is, that would be a decline of 24%, well beyond the 10% bust limit. So Figure 24.16 would not apply.

I show the inset to Figure 24.14 as Inset 2 in Figure 24.20. The long-term up move of the primary trend is JK with a downward breakout from the symmetrical triangle. A large decline should follow (and 24%, a drop to 9, is a large decline). That is what happened even though subsequent events took the stock down below 5.

■ Closing Position

I looked at Figure 24.1 and saw that the average rise is 40% from an upward breakout from a symmetrical triangle. That is far below the average 51% rise after a rectangle. Add in that 29% of symmetricals will bust an upward breakout, and I conclude that symmetrical triangles are nasty suckers. They appear frequently on the charts, but their performance and unknown breakout direction makes trading them difficult.

Perhaps the setups and configurations in this chapter will improve your trading performance should you decide to attempt trading a symmetrical. If you own a stock and a symmetrical appears, the configurations can suggest how well the postbreakout move will be. Then you can take appropriate action to preserve your capital.

Setup Synopsis

Figure 24.21 may help you identify the various types of trading setups. See the associated figure for an explanation.

"Occurs" in the figures means how often I found the configuration in the stocks I looked at. If two configurations apply to your situation, then the one with a more frequent occurrence (a higher percentage) is the one you should choose to follow.

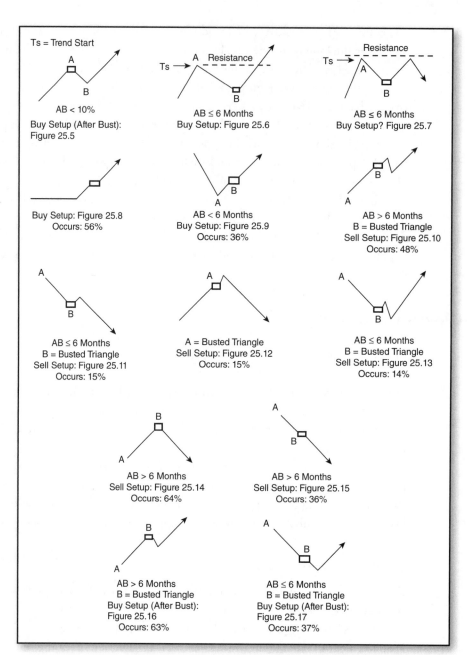

FIGURE 24.21 A collection of ideal trading setups and configurations.

CHAPTER 25

Vertical Run Down

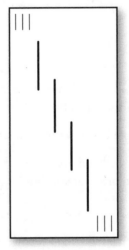

When a stock's price starts dropping like a stone, how worried should you be? To answer that question, this chapter explores a pattern I call a vertical run down. In this chapter, I refer to *vertical run* for simplicity. I mean vertical run down.

■ Behavior at a Glance

Figure 25.1 shows the typical behavior of a vertical run down pattern. Price tumbles in a vertical move that lasts a median of 7 days (left half of the figure). Then price bounces, and it takes a median of 17 days before price closes below the bottom of the vertical run.

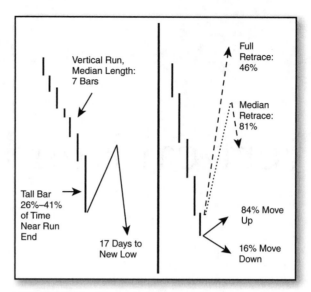

FIGURE 25.1 The typical behavior after a vertical run ends.

An unusually tall bar will appear at the end of the vertical run 26% of the time, or within one bar of the end 41% of the time.

■ An unusually tall bar will appear near the end of the vertical run 41% of the time.

The right half of the figure details the retrace, the behavior after the run ends. A full retrace (when price closes above the top of the vertical run) happens 46% of the time.

The median retrace is 81%. Half of the vertical runs down will see price retrace more than 81% and half will retrace less.

Eighty-four percent of the time, price bounces and retraces all or a portion of the vertical drop. The other 16% continue lower but at a slower pace than during the vertical run.

■ After a vertical run ends, price continues lower just 16% of the time.

■ Identification

Figure 25.2 shows an example of a vertical run down. The stock begins this vertical run down as it leaves a congestion area to the left of A. Then price plunges like a barrel over Niagara Falls. The move down is swift with little to no overlap from price bar to price bar.

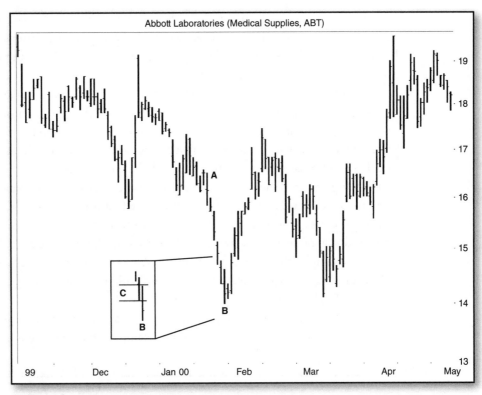

FIGURE 25.2 A vertical run down begins at A and ends at B.

At B, the downward plunge ends. Price moves sideways for a bar and then begins to retrace. In this example, the stock retraces the full height of the vertical run, returning to the price of A and continuing slightly higher.

Table 25.1 shows the identification guidelines for finding vertical runs.

TABLE 25.1	Identification Guidelines
Characteristic	**Discussion**
Price run	Price tumbles vertically, moving down in a swift and often short-lived plunge. The drop must be at least four bars long.
Overlap	The stock should not overlap price much from bar to bar.
Flag	For vertical runs only, a flag is an area within the vertical run in which price fails to move below a prior low for at least three consecutive days. Having a flag is not a requirement. Just be aware that price may pause for a time in a vertical run before resuming the plunge.
Run ends	The vertical move ends when the slope of the run changes dramatically. Often price begins to retrace or it may move sideways and form a knot of congestion.

Price Run. The vertical run down begins when the stock's price drops nearly vertically. This is what happens in Figure 25.2. At A, price transitions from sliding horizontally for almost two weeks to going vertical. By definition, the vertical drop must be at least four price bars long.

Overlap. The overlap from one price bar to the next is small during the vertical run. The average and median overlaps are both 28%. I show an example of two bars overlapping in the inset of Figure 25.2. C highlights the overlap between B and the prior bar. There is overlap in other price bars along the run (such as at A with the next bar), but mostly the stock tumbles with little or no overlap.

Flag. Figure 25.3 shows two congestion areas that I call flags at C and D (circled). They are not classic flag chart patterns, if you are familiar with them. Rather, vertical run "flags" are short breaks in the drop that retrace at least three consecutive days without dropping below a prior low before the downhill run resumes.

In this example, the vertical run begins at A and ends at B. Look at the flag circled at D. From the low at E, price retraces 3 days without making a new low below the bottom of E. This qualifies the pattern after E as a flag.

Another flag occurs at C. Price drops from A to F. Then price remains above the low posted at F for at least 3 days (4 in this example), qualifying it as a flag.

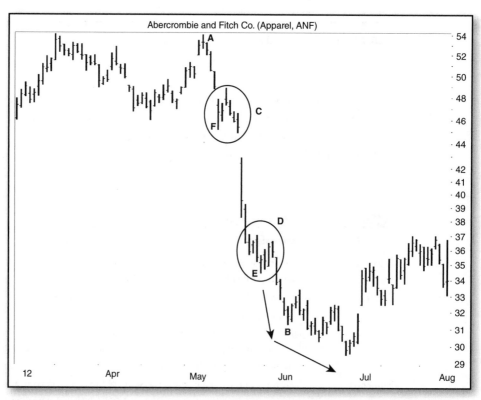

FIGURE 25.3 Two congestion areas, flags, appear (circled) along the vertical run AB.

The run ends at B, after which price has too much overlap to be called a vertical run.

Run Ends. Figures 25.2 and 25.3 show how a vertical run down ends. Simply, price stops dropping end over end.

Most of the time, a retrace will occur after the run ends. Both figures show this with Figure 25.2 having a pronounced retrace and Figure 25.3 showing the stock easing lower with lots of overlap from bar to bar after B. The two arrows illustrate the change in slope.

■ Retrace Findings

The following use bull market data (only) from July 1996 to January 2014. I found 2,036 vertical runs in 469 stocks. Here are some of the more important findings.

■ A price trend that begins above the start of the vertical run means a larger retrace.

When the trend start is above the top of the vertical run down, price retraces a median of 87%. When the trend start is below the top, the retrace measures a median of 68%.

■ Price retraces at a median velocity about one-third what it was during the run.

I wanted to know if the velocity of the run down is the same as the retrace velocity. Just looking at almost any chart will show that it is not. A vertical run has price dropping quickly, day after day with the price bars seldom overlapping. It is a swift decline, but the retrace does not share that vertical nature. Price recovers at a more sedate pace.

The median velocity in the vertical run is 63 cents per day. During the retrace, the velocity has a median of 17 cents per day. To put it another way, for every 1-day drop, expect a stock to take 3-4 days to recover.

■ Miscellaneous Statistics

Table 25.2 shows a frequency distribution of length, retrace, and duration.

TABLE 25.2	Frequency Distribution of Length, Retrace, and Duration										
(Bars)	4	5	6	7	8	9	10	11	12	13	>13
Length	10%	18%	17%	15%	12%	7%	5%	4%	3%	2%	7%
Cumulative	10%	29%	46%	61%	73%	80%	85%	88%	91%	93%	100%
Retrace	10%	20%	30%	40%	50%	60%	70%	80%	90%	>90%	Full
Retrace	2%	7%	10%	10%	8%	6%	4%	3%	2%	48%	46%
Cumulative	2%	9%	18%	28%	36%	42%	47%	50%	52%	100%	N/A*
(Days)	2	4	6	8	10	12	14	16	18	20	>20
Bounce High	25%	12%	11%	12%	6%	4%	5%	2%	1%	1%	19%
Cumulative	25%	37%	48%	60%	66%	70%	76%	78%	79%	81%	100%

*N/A: not applicable

The top third of the table shows what to expect for the length of the vertical run down, in price bars (trading days), not calendar days. The minimum bar length, by definition, is four. Just 10% of the vertical runs are that short. The median length is 7 bars.

If your run is 9 bars long, then just 20% of the runs I looked at were longer. Expect a reversal soon.

Retrace

The middle rows of Table 25.2 show how far price retraces (bounces) after a vertical run ends. The median is 81%, meaning that half retrace less and half retrace more. Almost half (46%) retrace the entire move down (that is, the "Full" retrace column).

For example, I found that just 10% of the vertical runs had retraces between 21% and 30% (shown in the 30% box). Twenty-eight percent (cumulative row, under 40%) of vertical runs retraced no more than 40%.

Bounce High

The lower third of the table shows how long it takes (calendar days) the stock to reach its highest price during the retrace. Think of this as the bounce high. It includes only those stocks that first closed below the bottom of the vertical run (and not above it).

A quarter (25%) of the patterns see price bounce and peak in 2 days or less. Those are likely the ones that did not retrace much at all (like the DEF pattern shown in Figure 25.4). The median is 7 days and the average is 14.

- After a vertical run down ends, price bounces and peaks in a median of 7 calendar days.

How is the information shown in this table useful? Imagine that you own a stock and a vertical run down has just taken your position to the cleaners. You need to raise cash because your girlfriend's birthday is coming, and she wants something sparkly, preferably in a platinum setting. How long should you wait to sell the stock?

Table 25.2 can help you decide. The length of the run can reassure you that the end of the downward run is near. That is, if the number of price bars in the run is 10, then there is a 15% chance (100% − 85%) that more of a downward move is coming (from the cumulative "Length" row).

Once the run ends, the stock is likely to retrace. If the stock has retraced 20% up the height of the vertical run, then there is a 91% chance (100% − 9%) that the stock will move higher (from the cumulative "Retrace" row).

If the bounce has lasted for 15 days and it made a new high yesterday (day 14) but not today, there is a 76% chance that yesterday's peak was the highest the stock was going to climb (from the cumulative "Bounce High" row). It might be time to sell.

- Use Table 25.5 to help determine how many price bars the vertical run will have, how far price will retrace, and how long it will take price to peak before trending lower.

Gaps

A vertical run can have price gaps. The gap type can indicate how long the run is likely to last. What type are they?

To answer that, I made a rule that a gap must be at least 25 cents wide, otherwise I assumed the vertical run did not have a gap.

Breakaway gaps occur at the start of the run, but because you do not know whether a vertical run exists until bar four, a breakaway gap has no significance. I ignored any gap before the third bar. That excluded breakaway gaps.

Continuation gaps occur near the middle of runs. The length of the run before a continuation gap can equal (or nearly equal) the length of the run after the gap.

How often does this happen for vertical runs? The following table shows the frequency. For example, a continuation gap will be within 5 percentage points of the middle 19% of the time. It will be within 10 percentage points of midway along the run 41% of the time.

Percentage Points from Middle	Frequency
±5	19%
±10	41%
±13.5	50%
±15	55%
±20	68%

Exhaustion gaps appear at the end of runs. If the vertical run has an exhaustion gap, then the next (adjacent) price bar should end the run.

I mapped the gap location and discovered that just 25% of them were exhaustion gaps. That is, the exhaustion gap occurred between the last 2 price bars at the end of the vertical run. The other 75% must be continuation gaps. I found that the median and average distance of the continuation gap was 59% down from the start of the run.

- Twenty-five percent of gaps in vertical runs are exhaustion gaps that appear one bar or less from the run's end. The other 75% are continuation gaps.

If a gap occurs after the third bar in a vertical run down, assume it is a continuation gap. The section on trading tactics discusses how to trade using this finding.

- Use continuation gaps to project how far the vertical run might last. Half of continuation gaps are within 13.5 percentage points of center.

TABLE 25.3   **Frequency Distribution of Tallest Bar Position**

	10%	20%	30%	40%	50%	60%	70%	80%	90%	>90%
Position	3%	12%	8%	8%	9%	6%	6%	11%	9%	26%
Cumulative	3%	15%	23%	32%	41%	48%	54%	65%	74%	100%

Tallest Bar Position

As I was finding vertical runs in my database, I noticed that the tallest price bar in the vertical run was at the end. That was not always the case, but it surprised me how often it was true.

I studied the location of the tallest bar in the run and **Table 25.3** shows the results.

Notice that the bin with the highest frequency is >90%. In other words, 26% of the vertical runs I looked at had the tallest bar at or near the end of the run. That is more than twice as many as the next closest bin.

If you allow the tallest bar to be no more than one bar away from the end of the vertical run (meaning it could be either of the last two bars in the run), then the frequency swells from 26% to 41%.

I compared bars at least twice as tall as the 1-month average and found that they appeared at a median of 75% of the way down the vertical run. If you see a vertical run with an unusually tall bar (on or after bar 4 since the run must have at least 4 bars), the run may be near its end.

- An unusually tall price bar (more than twice the one-month average height) may signal the end of the vertical run.

■ Configurations

Figure 25.4 shows two variations of what happens after a vertical run down ends.

The direction of the move after a vertical run down ends depends on whether the stock closes above or below the last bar in the vertical run. For example, vertical run A1-B1 has 4 price bars in the run. The last bar in the run, B1, has price first closing above the top of it at C1 (take my word for it since you will not be able to see closing prices in the chart). Thus, price retraces upward after the end of the A1-B1 run.

Vertical run D1-E1 is different. The last bar in the run is E1. This time, price closes below the bottom of E1 at F1. This vertical run sees price slide downward after the run ends.

Upward moves (retraces) like that shown after the A1-B1 vertical run occur 84% of the time. The E1-F1 move fills the other 16%.

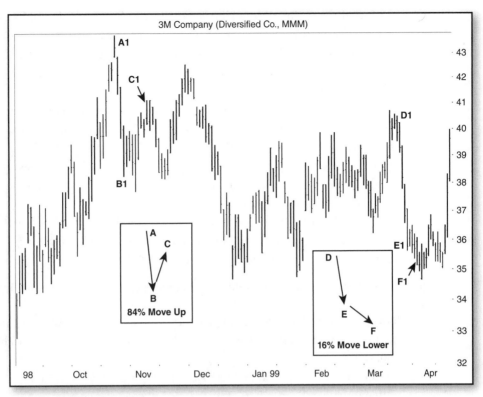

FIGURE 25.4 Two vertical runs appear in the stock of 3M with different trends after the run ends.

I highlight the behavior differences between the two vertical runs in the inset using similar letters and arrows.

■ Use the last bar in the vertical run to help determine the stock's new trend.

Trading Tactics

I split trading tactics into the four trading styles. For investors (buy and hold), a vertical run down does not pose much of a problem to long-term growth. Because price retraces the entire drop about half the time (46%), there is a decent chance that if you wait long enough, the stock will recover on its own.

You do have to be alert to a continued drop in a stock that could signal significant underlying problems at the company or with the business environment. But that can happen whether or not a vertical run appears in the stock.

Position Traders How often does the drop after the end of a vertical run signal a trend change? Answer: 20%.

■ Price makes a significant move lower (a drop of at least 20%) 20% of the time after a vertical run ends.

I found the ultimate low (the lowest low before a stock climbs at least 20%) and measured the drop from the bottom of the vertical run to the ultimate low. I found that 20% of the stocks dropped at least 20% below the bottom of the vertical run. The median drop after the vertical run ends was 10% and the average was 13%.

All of these numbers apply to vertical runs with downward breakouts, not ones with upward breakouts. A downward breakout occurs when price first closes below the bottom of the vertical run. An upward breakout occurs when price first closes above the top of the vertical run. (These breakout definitions are different from the last bar in the vertical run used to determine a retrace, as discussed for Figure 25.4.)

Since 80% of vertical runs do not suffer a trend change after a vertical run ends, it makes sense for position traders to hold onto the stock. Monitor it closely in case your stock is the exception and price continues lower.

- Position traders should hold onto a stock showing a vertical run down.

Swing and Day Traders   Swing and day trading are almost the same if you remove the time element. Both styles try to catch the move from swing low to high or swing high to low.

Here are a few tips on how to use vertical runs to your advantage. Let us begin with unusually tall price bars. **Figure 25.5** shows an example.

As price drops in the vertical run, an unusually tall price bar can signal the end of the run. The figure is an example of that at C.

Look at the height of the price bars in the month before the start of the vertical run. For this stock, the average bar height is $1.99 in the month before the start of the vertical run. Bar C is triple that height, or $6.05. When the tall bar appears, it is a good indication that the run is over, and that is what happens here.

Trading the Gap

Look at the gap in Figure 25.5. The gap must be at least 25 cents wide or else it does not count. The gap at B measures 33 cents, so it qualifies as a valid gap.

Assume that the gap is in the middle of the run. Let us use it to predict how far the stock is going to drop. The high price at A, the start of the run, is 87.28, and the *middle* of the gap is at 81.30 for a height of $5.98. That is, the distance from A to the middle of the gap at B. Projecting this height downward from the center of the gap gives a target of 81.30 − 5.98, or 75.32. The stock bottomed at D at 74.48. The target was off by just 1%.

Because it is rare that heavily traded stocks gap intraday (except at the open from the prior day), this gap technique is useless for day trading. For the daily charts, though, it can be helpful when setting a price to exit.

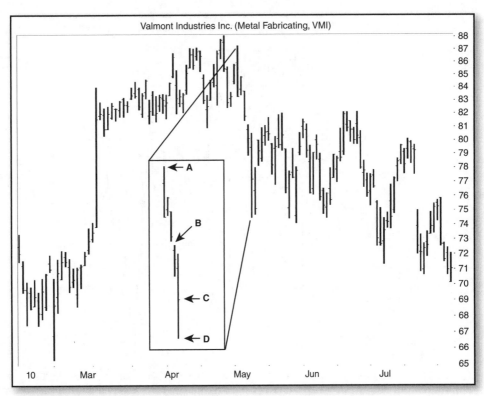

FIGURE 25.5 A tall price bar signals the end of the run and the continuation gap predicts how far the drop will last.

Using the Retrace Since 84% of vertical runs down retrace upward, and the median retrace is 81%, we can use those numbers to play the bounce after the vertical run ends.

Look at Table 25.2, the cumulative retrace row. If 36% of the samples retraced less than 50%, that means 64% retraced more. Thus, we can say that 64% of the time the stock will retrace at least halfway up the vertical run. Let us use the halfway point as the target.

Say we are interested in buying the stock shown in **Figure 25.6**. The gap at B is too small to qualify as a valid gap (22 cents, just short of the minimum 25 cents).

Bar C is a tall one, and we guess that the stock is going to turn. However, the next day, the stock continues dropping. In fact, the stock continues lower until E.

The gap at D is tall enough to qualify as a valid gap. However, continuation gaps often appear midway in the price run, so another 11-point drop is too big to be realistic. It is obvious that this must be an exhaustion gap.

The Entry Device I would place a buy order a penny above the high at E. This is one of the techniques I use to get into a day trade as soon as price reverses after a strong move down (but it also works for non–day trades).

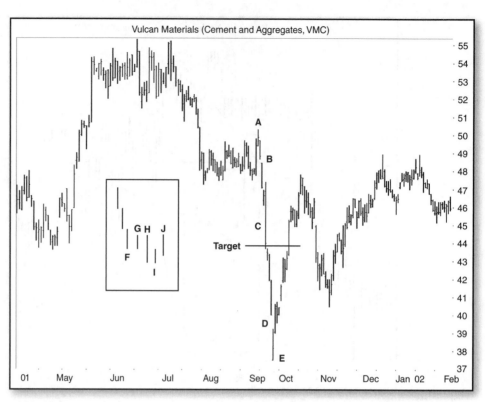

FIGURE 25.6 Because price retraces halfway up the vertical run 64% of the time, that becomes the target.

For day trades, after three price bars are in place (the start of a vertical run down which often precedes a strong rebound), I place a buy stop a penny or two above the prior price bar and trail it lower. When price reverses, my order executes, and I am in the trade as price bounces.

That entry device would work well here.

To clarify the entry, look at the inset of Figure 25.6 and assume this is a day trade. The three price bars that form a strong move down end at F. A strong rebound often follows, as I mentioned, but let us assume it does not. I place a buy stop a penny or two above F when bar G forms.

Then bars H forms. Because the top of G is below F, I lower the buy stop to a penny or two above G. Bar H takes price lower, leading to bar I. When bar J begins forming, I lower the stop to a penny or two above I. Bar J eventually takes out the stop, and I am in the trade.

The Retrace Exit When do you sell? For the retrace exit, look at the vertical run in September (Figure 25.6). I buy into the stock using the entry device just discussed.

The run begins at A (50.32) and ends at E (37.50). Halfway down the run is where the exit target goes. I place a sell order at the target. My stop loss would be a penny or two below the low at E.

As price rises, I trail the stop a penny or two below the prior bar's low (always raising the stop, never lowering it). When the stock reaches the target, the position sells for a tidy profit.

The trailing stop method works well when price bounces higher in a strong move up. At other times, you would do better to trail it farther away, maybe a penny or two below the low of two bars back instead of one, depending on the stock's volatility.

In this example, I would be into the trade at about 39.22 and out at 43.91 for a gain of 4.69 per share or almost 12% in less than 2 weeks.

■ Closing Position

The discovery of a tall price bar foretelling the end of a vertical run is as exciting as discovering the first bloom of spring. Well, you know what I mean.

Most often (84% of the time), price will bounce after a vertical run ends, and almost half the time (46%), the stock will recover all of the decline posted during the vertical run.

The techniques discussed in this chapter suggest how to handle the appearance of a vertical run and how price behaves after a run appears. That knowledge should help you trade and invest better.

CHAPTER 26

Vertical Run Up

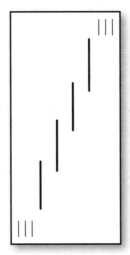

Your stock is red hot, climbing like a jet fighter with afterburners on. What happens after the vertical run ends? This chapter answers that question.

In this chapter, I refer to *vertical run* for simplicity. I mean vertical run up.

■ Behavior at a Glance

Figure 26.1 shows the typical behavior of a stock after a vertical run ends (daily scale). The left panel shows that the median vertical run up is 8 price bars long. After the run ends, price retraces. It takes a median of 18 calendar days before stocks close above the top of the vertical run. Half the stocks took less time and half took longer.

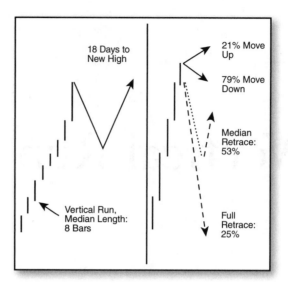

FIGURE 26.1 The direction price takes after the vertical run ends.

The right half of the chart shows that 79% of the time stocks retrace at least a portion of the vertical move, 21% continue higher (at a slower pace).

The median (midrange) retrace is 53%. That means half the stocks will give back less and half will give back more. A full retrace, where all of the gains from the vertical move disappear, happens 25% of the time.

- After a vertical run ends, price eventually continues higher 75% of the time (just 25% close below the bottom of the vertical run).

■ Identification

Figure 26.2 shows an example of a vertical run. The vertical run begins at A when price leaves a block of congestion and goes vertical, climbing with small amounts of overlap between the price bars. The run ends at B when price stops going vertical (in this example, it slides sideways for a time and then drops). In this case, price retraces all of the gain posted in the vertical run and more, ending lower, at C.

Table 26.1 shows the identification guidelines for finding vertical runs.

Price Run. Price should move higher at a good clip. I set an arbitrary minimum of 4 price bars in the run. The median length is 8 trading days (price bars) with an average of 11 days.

Overlap. Overlap is the amount of shared prices from price bar to bar. Two bars with 100% overlap will have the same high and low prices. Two bars with no overlap will not share any prices.

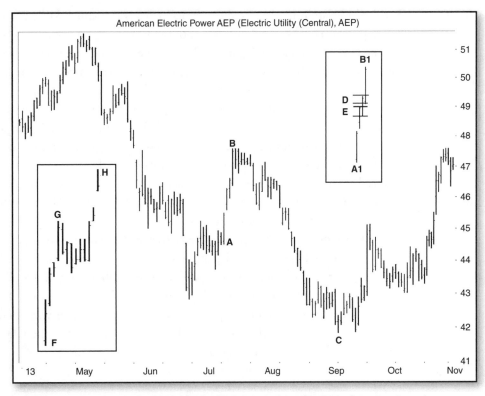

FIGURE 26.2 The stock gives back all of its gains in the vertical run from A to B on the way to C.

TABLE 26.1	Identification Guidelines
Characteristic	**Discussion**
Price run	Price makes a near vertical move for at least four price bars.
Overlap	The stock has minimal overlap from price bar to bar within the vertical run, but be flexible. The median and average overlap is 31%.
Flag	For vertical runs only, a flag is an area within the vertical run where price fails to move above a prior high for at least three consecutive bars. Fifteen percent of vertical runs have at least one flag. Having a flag is not a requirement. Just be aware that price may pause for a time in a vertical run before resuming the climb.
Run ends	The vertical run ends when price stops moving vertically.

The intent of highlighting overlap in the identification guidelines is to emphasize that price should be moving up swiftly, not meandering higher. Let the figures in this chapter be a guide to correct identification of vertical runs.

A frequency distribution shows that overlap ranges from 20% to 45% about evenly. Vertical runs will have overlap, but not an excessive amount. The average and median overlap in my database of vertical runs is the same: 31%. For example, the overlap for vertical run AB in Figure 26.2 is 16%.

The upper right inset of Figure 26.2 shows the same AB run marked as A1-B1. Overlap between price bars occurs at D and E, where two bars share a common price.

Flag. Most vertical runs (85%) will not show any flags. For a flag to occur in a vertical run, price should fail to make a higher high for at least 3 days (this flag definition is specific to vertical runs and should not be confused with flag or pennant chart patterns). Vertical run flags are the only kinds of congestion areas I counted (price can skid sideways or coast upward, having lots of overlap from price bar to bar, but I ignored those). Thus, congestion areas occur more frequently than 15% of the time.

In Figure 26.2, the inset with vertical run FH has a flag at G. Price after G fails to post a higher high for at least three days.

Look at **Figure 26.3** and compare the two rises AB and CD. Are they vertical runs?

The AB move has some overlap at the start (19% along the entire run), but it covers a lot of price territory in just a few days. The climb is vertical. The CD move rises just as far and yet it takes considerably more time. The price bars have lots of overlap from day to day and the entire pattern looks as if a powerful wind bent it. The AB move is straighter. The AB move is a valid vertical run up, but the CD move is not. The CD run has too much overlap.

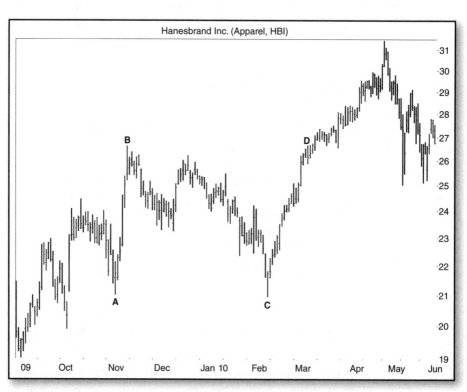

FIGURE 26.3   Are moves AB and CD vertical runs?

■ Miscellaneous Statistics

When the retrace occurs, does price drop as fast as it climbed during the vertical run? No. Only 33% of the vertical runs showed a faster retrace.

I measured the velocity and found that the median speed was 51 cents per trading day during the vertical run. After the run, price retraced at a median of 31 cents per trading day. That is 40% slower.

■ Price retraces slower than it climbs during the vertical run.

Table 26.2 shows a frequency distribution of the vertical run length, retrace amount, and how long it takes before price reaches its low during the retrace. Let us discuss them in order, beginning with length.

Suppose that you own a stock and it begins moving up in a vertical run. How long will the run last? The top third of the table provides a frequency distribution to help answer that question.

The minimum run length is 4 price bars, by definition (see Table 26.1). Just 9% of vertical runs end after 4 bars. The bins with the highest frequency span from 5 to 8 bars with a spike for exceptionally long runs (>13). Almost half the bars will fall in the 5 to 8 bar range.

■ A vertical run up usually lasts between 5 and 8 price bars.

Retrace

The retrace is the largest amount price drops after a vertical run ends and before price closes above the high posted in the vertical run.

Table 26.2 shows that most of the time, price retraces between 20% and 60%. Of course, that is a wide range, encompassing over half the samples. At the far right of the table, I show that 25% of the samples retrace the entire amount.

■ The most likely retrace after a vertical run up ends is between 20% and 60%.

TABLE 26.2	Frequency Distribution of Length, Retrace, and Duration									
(Bars)	**4**	**5**	**6**	**7**	**8**	**9**	**10**	**11**	**12**	**13**	**>13**
Length	9%	12%	15%	12%	10%	8%	6%	5%	4%	3%	16%
Cumulative	9%	21%	36%	48%	58%	66%	72%	77%	81%	84%	100%
Retrace	**10%**	**20%**	**30%**	**40%**	**50%**	**60%**	**70%**	**80%**	**90%**	**>90%**	**Full**
Retrace	3%	10%	12%	12%	11%	9%	6%	5%	4%	28%	25%
Cumulative	3%	13%	25%	37%	48%	57%	63%	68%	72%	100%	N/A*
(Days)	**2**	**4**	**6**	**8**	**10**	**12**	**14**	**16**	**18**	**20**	**>20**
Retrace Low	21%	13%	11%	11%	6%	5%	5%	2%	2%	2%	21%
Cumulative	21%	34%	45%	56%	63%	67%	72%	74%	77%	79%	100%

*N/A: not applicable

Retrace Low

The bottom third of the table shows a frequency distribution of how long it takes price to reach the lowest price in the retrace. In Figure 26.6, that would be the time it takes to reach G from E. To determine point G, I find the first close above the end of vertical run AE. That happens at H. Then I find the lowest low between E and H, which is G.

Returning to Table 26.2, the 2-day column shows that 21% of the samples take between 0 and 2 days to reach the low. Those vertical runs do not retrace much. They either continue higher at a slower pace or have a day or two of price dipping down before the rise resumes.

Over half the samples take between 0 and 8 days before the stock bottoms. Note that 21% of the samples take longer than 20 days.

- After a vertical run up ends, price retraces and reaches bottom often within 8 days, but many take over 3 weeks to bottom.

Gaps

There are two types of gaps that interest us in vertical runs: (1) continuation and (2) exhaustion gaps. Continuation gaps occur in the middle of the run and exhaustion gaps occur at the end of the run.

In my analysis of vertical runs, I ignored gaps less than 25 cents wide, but for this test, I also ignored vertical runs with more than 1 gap.

Analysis found that 66% of the gaps were continuation and 34% were exhaustion. Since we know that breakaway gaps occur at the start of runs when price breaks away from a congestion area, and vertical runs must be at least 4 price bars long, we can ignore any gaps that happen within the first 3 bars.

- Continuation gaps occur 66% of the time, and exhaustion gaps appear 34% of the time in a vertical run up.

Continuation gaps are supposed to appear in the middle of the runs, but do they? The following table shows how often a gap occurs within the percentage points of the middle of the run.

Percentage Points from Middle	Frequency
±5	17%
±10	34%
±13.5	44%
±15	48%
±20	65%

For example, 17% of the gaps appear within 5 percentage points of the middle of the run (that is, from 45% to 55% down from the top of the run). Over a third occur within 10 percentage points.

If you see a gap of at least 25 cents appear in a vertical run after the third bar, compute the distance from the start (bottom) of the run to the center of the gap. Project that height from the center of the gap to get a target. The projection will be correct 40% of the time within 5% and 73% of the time within 10%.

- Use a continuation gap to help predict a target price. This works 40% of the time, landing within 5% of the target.

Configuration Trading

Figure 26.4 highlights what happens after three vertical runs. Run AB shows a flag at C (circled). The vertical run begins with the last price bar in the congestion area at A, rises to C, where it pauses, and then resumes moving up to B. After B, price is not climbing as swiftly as it was from A to B (if you ignore flag C).

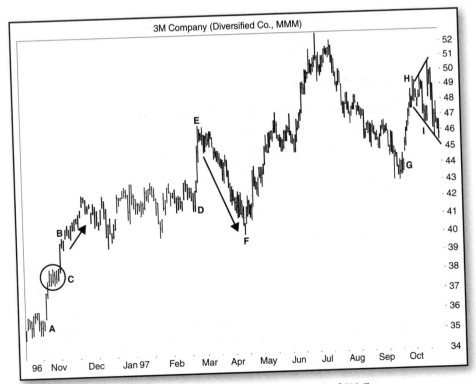

FIGURE 26.4 Three vertical run variations appear in the stock of 3M Company.

The second vertical run, DE, begins with the last price bar in the congestion area (D) and ends at E. This is the kind of run I like to see, one with no pauses along the way. Notice that after the vertical run ends, price collapses and retraces all of the way to F, giving back the gains made in the vertical run, and more.

Contrast the EF retrace with the rise after B (see arrows). Price after B continues to move up, rising in this fashion 21% of the time.

The vertical run from G to H shows lots of overlap (38%). I do not particularly like this vertical run because of that overlap, but it is still a valid run since the stock climbs at a brisk pace. After H, price forms a broadening top pattern (I), a mega-phone shape with peaks and valleys that widen over time.

■ Trading Tactics

Let us split trading tactics for vertical runs into trading styles. Investors or people that buy and hold can ignore vertical runs. Why? Because price usually recovers to make a new high after a vertical run. Just 1% of vertical runs see price take longer than 6 months to close above the top of the vertical run. Ninety-four percent take less than 3 months.

- After a vertical run ends, 94% of the time it takes price less than 3 months to make a new high.

Position Traders

Position traders will find that 22% of vertical runs suffer a trend change (retrace more than 20%). That is about 1 in 5 trades. Seventy-eight percent of the time you will do better holding on after a vertical run ends.

- Position traders should hold onto their stocks since a trend change is rare (occurring 22% of the time).

Swing and Day Traders

The advice for swing traders and day traders is the same for both styles.

Let us change the identification rules for vertical runs somewhat. Look for at least four price bars forming a vertical run with price moving higher without much overlap. Each day, price makes a new high. The appearance of the fourth bar qualifies the vertical run as a valid chart pattern. Bar four becomes the high water mark bar.

If the next day has a higher high, then it becomes the new high water mark bar. And so on as price climbs. The vertical run continues growing taller as long as price bars continue to make a high above the prior high water mark bar.

Let us say the day after the high water mark bar has a lower high. As long as that bar closes above the *low* of the high water mark bar, the vertical run remains intact. Wait for a new high water mark bar. If a new bar *closes* below the low of the high water mark bar, then the vertical run ends with the high water mark bar. Sell.

Here are the instructions.

1. Find a valid vertical run (at least 4 price bars with minimal overlap).
2. If price makes a higher high the next price bar, it becomes the high water mark bar.
3. If price *closes* below the low of the high water mark bar, then sell at the open of the next bar. Otherwise, go back to step 2.

That process may be confusing so let us look at the example in **Figure 26.5**.

Suppose you are swing trading the stock and price goes vertical. The vertical run begins at A. Bar four is at B, validating the vertical run (since a valid vertical run needs *at least* four price bars). Bar B is the high water mark, the highest high in the vertical run (so far).

The next day's high is below the high of the high water mark bar (B), but it also *closes* above the low of bar B. Do nothing. Several days pass without *closing* below B nor making a new high water mark until C. Bar C makes a higher high, so it becomes the new high water mark bar. A close below the low of bar C would signal a sale.

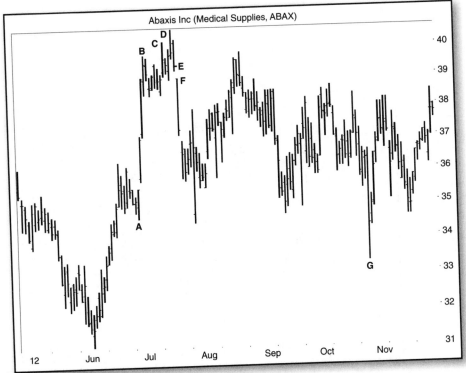

FIGURE 26.5   An example of how swing and day traders can profit from a vertical run.

The next two days do *not* close below the low at C nor do they post a higher high, so do nothing. Bar D makes a higher high, so it becomes the new high water mark bar. This time, bar E closes below the low of the high water mark bar (D). Sell at the open the next bar. That happens at the open of bar F.

This method allows you to hold a position as price continues making new highs after a vertical run ends but closes out the position when the trend reverses.

How often does this technique work? I tested it on the vertical runs in my database. I found that in a bull market, price drops below the sale price 96% of the time (meaning you save money by selling because price continues down).

The median drop is 4% and the average is 9% below the sale price. I measured this from the sell price (F in Figure 26.5) to the lowest low, G, before price rises to make a new high above the high water mark bar (D).

- Use the last price bar in the vertical run as a sell or hold signal.

Trading the Gap

Since we know that continuation gaps can (but no guarantee) appear midway in a vertical run, how can we use that information to help trade vertical runs? Look at **Figure 26.6** for one example.

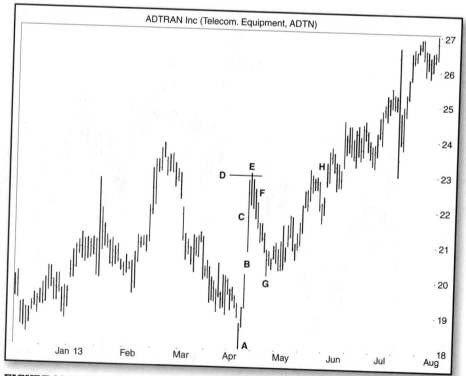

FIGURE 26.6   A gap appears midway in the vertical run up.

Suppose we own the stock and are swing trading it when vertical run AE appears. When bar C occurs, the run becomes valid since it has four price bars.

Measuring the distance from the start of the run (18) to the center of the gap at B (20.46) gives, $20.46 - 18 = 2.46$. Add that height to the middle of the gap gives $20.46 + 2.46 = 22.92$. Because 23 is a round number, we will use the 22.92 as our target to be just below where everyone else would sell. (Note: I am not using 22.92 to make this example work. I often trade 7 to 8 cents below a round number to avoid novices that trade at round numbers.)

We can place a sell order at 22.92 and bar E would take us out of the trade at horizontal line D.

Suppose we hope the run continues and use the 22.92 target as guidance, not as an automatic sell. When bar E appears, the stock hits our target, but we wait a day to see whether the stock continues higher.

The next day, the stock makes a lower high, so we assume that the vertical run is over and the stock is going to retrace. It is time to sell. At the next day's open (bar F), we sell and receive a fill at 22.46.

- Use a continuation gap to set an exit price.

Using a Trailing Stop

Figure 26.7 shows how effective a trailing stop can be. Imagine that you own the stock shown in Figure 26.7. Price drops down out of a consolidation region in May but soon begins recovering.

At B, you notice price is making a vertical run, which begins at A. Nervous about the trend reversing, you consider selling but then decide to use a stop-loss order to protect profits. Because price can tie the same low, you always place the stop a penny or two *below* the low, not *at* the day's low price. In this case, you place a stop a penny below the low at B.

After the close of day C, you raise the stop to a penny below bar C. After the close of bar D, you again raise the stop to just below D. You continue this method of raising the stop as price climbs in the vertical run, never lowering the stop.

Eventually, the stock retraces at E, hitting the stop-loss order placed at F. Yes, you are taken out well short of H, but you have successfully captured more profit than by selling at B.

In strong vertical runs, using a trailing stop works well. It does not always work, but it can help capture more profit without the worry of when to sell.

If you wish a more conservative exit method, try placing the stop two bars back. For example, when day D arrives, raise the stop to a penny or two below B. In this case, the two-day stop would keep you in the trade as price climbed to H. At H, the stop would be two bars back at G, eventually cashing out the trade at I.

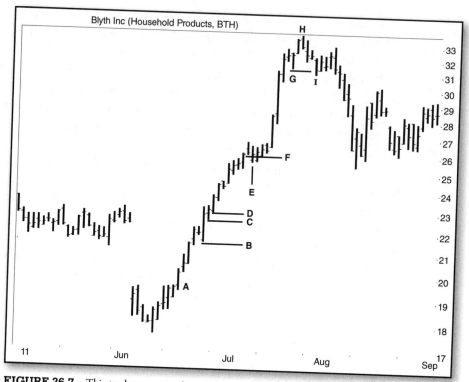

FIGURE 26.7 This trade uses a trailing stop.

The problem with the two-bar exit is that price can slide down much farther than in a one-bar exit, so you have the potential to give back more money.

■ Trail a stop one or two price bars behind to extend profits.

■ Closing Position

The vertical run up can leave traders and investors with their mouths hanging open, wondering how far price can rise. Often it rises farther and lasts longer than many expect.

I recall trading Insteel Industries in early 2006 when the stock made a vertical move upward. I bought and the move turned into a vertical run with price rising day after day. A volatility stop protected my backside during the rise.

I got frightened out of the move during a retrace after making 29%. The stock went on to almost double my buy price.

Would the knowledge from this chapter have helped? Sure. I see a tall price bar that correctly predicted the end of the vertical run (within a bar). If I switched from a volatility stop to a trailing stop, I could have made about 50 cents a share more.

Of course, I still left a lot on the table when the stock recovered and started posting new highs without me. Sigh.

By using the techniques in this chapter, I have shown how the typical stock behaves after a vertical run ends. Perhaps that knowledge will save you money or allow you to make more than you would otherwise.

Good luck, happy trading, and take care of each other.

average   The sum of the terms divided by the number of terms. The average of 1, 2, 3, 4, 5 is 3, or the sum of the numbers (15) divided by 5 (there are five numbers to average).

bearish countertrend   The stock closes lower but the index closes higher. The stock is making a bearish move against a rising market.

bear markets   From 1990 to October 2015, there were two bear markets in the Standard & Poor's 500 Index. The first lasted from March 24, 2000, to October 10, 2002, and the second lasted from October 12, 2007, to March 6, 2009.

benchmark close   The last close before an earnings announcement. See Chapter 8, "Earnings Miss."

big drop   A one-day drop of at least 1%, measured close to close, in the Standard & Poor's 500 Index.

big move day   The first trading session after the earnings announcement. See Chapter 7, "Earnings Miss."

big rise   A one-day rise of at least 1%, measured close to close, in the Standard & Poor's 500 Index.

breakeven failure rate   A percentage of chart patterns that fail to rise or decline more than 5% after a breakout. *Breakeven* assumes the 5% move will cover your cost of trading.

breakout   A close outside of the chart pattern's boundary, such as a trendline, or the chart pattern's top or bottom. Table G.1 shows the breakout location for chart patterns covered in this book.

breakout gap, breakout day gap   A gap that occurs on the breakout day. Usually a breakaway gap, one that shows high volume after leaving a consolidation area.

TABLE G.1	Chart Patterns and Their Breakout Locations
Chart Pattern	**Breakout Location**
Big M	A close below the lowest valley between the two peaks
Big W	A close above the highest peak between the two bottoms
Broadening Patterns	A close outside the trendline boundary
Double Bottoms	A close above the highest peak between the two valleys
Double Tops	A close below the lowest valley between the two peaks
Earnings Miss	See Table 8.1
Flags	A close outside the trendline boundary
Head-and-Shoulders Bottoms	A close above a down-sloping neckline, or a close above the high between the head and right shoulder for up-sloping necklines
Head-and-Shoulders Tops	A close below an up-sloping neckline, or a close below the low between the head and right shoulder for down-sloping necklines
Measured Move Down or Up	Not applicable
Pennants	A close outside the trendline boundary
Rectangles Bottoms and Tops	A close outside the trendline boundary
Straight-Line Run Down	Not applicable
Straight-Line Run Up	Not applicable
Triangles, Ascending	A close outside the trendline boundary
Triangles, Descending	A close outside the trendline boundary
Triangles, Symmetrical	A close outside the trendline boundary
Vertical Run Down	Not applicable
Vertical Run Up	Not applicable

bullish countertrend   The stock closes higher, but the index closes lower. The stock is making a bullish move against a falling market.

bull market   This is every date outside of the two bear markets. See *bear market*.

bust   A chart pattern busts when price breaks out in one direction, moves less than 10% before reversing and closing beyond the chart pattern in the new direction.

Figure G.1 shows rectangles A and A1 that *single*, *double*, and *triple* bust for upward and downward breakouts.

bust, double   A chart pattern double busts when price moves more than 10% after busting a chart pattern twice.

Figure G.1 (under "Bust") shows rectangle A single busting an upward breakout at F. Price rises to G where it busts the rectangle for the second time. The busting process ends when price rises at least 10% above the top of the rectangle (H).

Downward busts are similar. Price single busts the downward breakout at F1, reverses, and double busts the breakout at G1. When price closes at least 10% below the bottom of the rectangle (H1), the busting process stops.

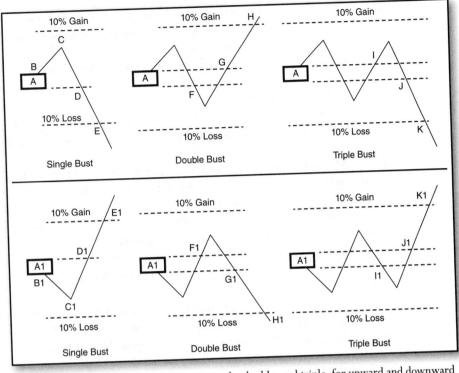

FIGURE G.1 The three types of busts: single, double, and triple, for upward and downward breakouts.

bust, single   A chart pattern single busts when price moves more than 10% after busting a chart pattern.

Figure G.1 (under "Bust") shows rectangle A single busting an upward breakout. The rectangle breaks out upward at B, rises less than 10% to C, and reverses. When the stock closes below the bottom of the rectangle at D, it busts the upward breakout. The busting process ends when price drops at least 10% below the bottom of the rectangle (E).

Downward busts are similar. Price breaks out downward from rectangle A1 at B1. Price drops to C1, reverses, and closes above the top of the rectangle at D1, busting the downward breakout. When price closes at least 10% above the top of the rectangle (E1), the busting process stops.

bust, triple   A chart pattern triple busts when price moves more than 10% after busting a chart pattern three times. I call three or more busts a triple bust.

Figure G.1 (under "Bust") shows rectangle A triple busting an upward breakout. The rectangle double busts the upward breakout at I, reverses, and busts it a third time at J. The busting process ends when price drops at least 10% below the bottom of the rectangle (K).

Downward busts are similar. Price breaks out downward from rectangle A1. Price double busts at I1, reverses, and triple busts the rectangle at J1. When price closes at least 10% above the top of the rectangle (K1), the busting process stops.

buy and hold   Often called investing. An investor buys a stock and holds it for many years, selling only when they need the money or the company goes private, bankrupt, or for some other significant reason.

calendar days   Calendar days include weekends and days when the markets are closed. Contrast with trading days. Most of the time statistics in this book use calendar days.

confirmation point, price, or level   Same as *breakout*.

congestion   A region at which price moves sideways with lots of overlap from day to day. Price does not maintain a consistent up- or downtrend during the congestion period.

consolidation   A region at which price moves sideways. The same as *congestion*.

continuation   When price breaks out in the same direction as it entered the pattern after ignoring overshoot and undershoot.

For example, if price enters the pattern from the bottom and exits out the top, the pattern acts as a continuation of the upward trend.

countertrend pattern   A pattern with an upward breakout in a bear market or a downward breakout in a bull market. The breakout direction is against the prevailing market trend.

countertrend stocks   Stocks that close in the direction opposite the market index. If the index closes higher, for example, a countertrend stock will close lower.

corrective phase   Part of a measured move up or down chart pattern, a region at which prices retrace a portion of the prior move.

day trade   A trader completes a trade (buys and sells) in one day.

event day   The day traders learn of an earnings miss.

event decline   The decline after an event day, often lasts for days.

failure rate   A measure of how many patterns fail to rise or decline a selected amount (like 5% or 10%). See *breakeven failure rate*.

flat base   A consolidation region in which a stock touches or nears the same price level multiple times over several weeks or months. Identification is usually easiest on the weekly scale. The bottom of a flat base appears level and sometimes forms the base of an impending up-move.

frequency distribution   A method of showing how often a value occurs using one of several nonoverlapping intervals.

gaps   A vertical space between two adjacent price bars: when today's low price is above yesterday's high or when today's high price is below yesterday's low.

inbound price trend   The price trend leading to the start of a chart pattern.

launch price   The price at which a stock begins a steep, often straight-line run that takes price to the first top or bottom of a big W or big M chart pattern.

measure rule   A way to determine a price target after the breakout from a chart pattern. Varies from pattern to pattern but is usually the pattern height added to (upward breakouts) or subtracted from (downward breakouts) the breakout price.

median   The middle value in a sorted list of values such that half the values are below the median and half above. If no middle value exists, the average of the two closest values is used. For example, in the list 10, 15, 30, 41, and 52, the median is 30 because there are two values on either side of it in a sorted list.

minor high A distinct price peak often separated from other peaks by at least a week.

minor low A distinct price valley usually separated from other valleys by at least a week.

neckline A trendline joining the valleys (armpits of a head-and-shoulders top) or peaks (armpits of a head-and-shoulders bottom). A close below or above the neckline, respectively, means a breakout.

overshoot When momentum carries price above the top of a chart pattern a few days (to a week or two) just before entering a chart pattern.

  Figure G.2 shows overshoot at E. The stock rises in a strong move higher and overshoots the top of the rectangle, F, briefly, before entering the rectangle.

partial decline After price touches a top trendline of a chart pattern, price declines but does not touch (or come that close to) a lower trendline before forming a distinct minor low and usually staging an immediate upward breakout. Partial declines must begin before the actual breakout and form after a valid chart pattern appears. Figure G.2 (under "Overshoot") shows a partial decline at C.

partial rise After price touches a lower trendline of a chart pattern, price rises but does not touch (or come that close to) the upper trendline before forming a distinct minor high and usually staging an immediate downward breakout. A partial rise must begin before the breakout and form near the end of a valid chart pattern. Figure G.2 (under "Overshoot") shows a partial rise at G.

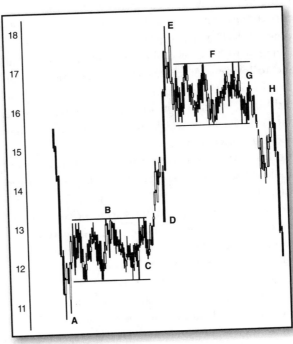

FIGURE G.2 Various parts of a chart pattern.

position trade Similar to a buy-and-hold position, except the trader is looking to exit before the trend changes. That would mean selling before a 20% decline in the stock or closing out a short sale before a rise of 20%.

primary trend As used in this book (only), it is the price trend one year before the start of a chart pattern, determined using closing prices. For flags and pennants, the primary trend is at least six months long but often measured over a period of a year.

pullback After a downward breakout, price returns to or comes very close to the breakout price or trendline boundary within 30 days. There should be white space between the breakout price and the pullback's lowest high to distinguish a stock that slides along the breakout price. Figure G.2 (under "Overshoot") shows a pullback at H for rectangle F.

reversal Price enters and exits the chart pattern from the same side. If price trends upward going into a chart pattern (from the bottom), a reversal will see price trend downward after leaving the chart pattern (exiting out the bottom). Both rectangles B and F in Figure G.2 (under "Overshoot") act as reversals.

swing trade A trader that buys near a swing low (minor low) and sells near the swing high (minor high), or the reverse. A swing trader tries to profit from the trade as price moves from high to low or low to high.

throwback After an upward breakout, price declines to, or comes very close to the breakout price or formation trendline within 30 days. There should be white space between the breakout price and the highest low during the throwback. Figure G.2 (under "Overshoot") shows a throwback (D) to rectangle B.

trading days Days when the markets are open.

trend change A swing of 20% in a stock or index. Often this is the close-to-close swing of the Dow Jones Industrials to signal a bull or bear market. I applied the same definition to stocks when finding the ultimate high or ultimate low.

trend followers Stocks that close in the same direction as a market index on a given day. If a market index closes higher, for example, a trend follower will also close higher.

trend high A minor high that begins or ends a price trend for flags and pennants. Similar to the ultimate high, except it marks the beginning or ending of the price trend, not a 20% price change.

trend low A minor low that begins or ends a price trend for flags and pennants. Similar to the ultimate low except it marks the beginning or end of the price trend, not a 20% price change.

trend start Beginning from the start of a chart pattern, it is the highest high or lowest low before which price drops or rises, respectively, at least 20%. For big M and big W patterns, look for the trend start before the launch price. Ignore any overshoot (E in Figure G.2, under "Overshoot") or undershoot (A).

For example, in Figure G.2, because the stock trends upward going into rectangle F, we will look for the lowest valley before which price rises at least 20%. That occurs at A since price rises before A from about 11 to over 15.

ultimate high After an upward breakout from a chart pattern, it is the highest peak before price declines by 20% or more, measured from the highest high to the close. Stop looking if price closes below the chart pattern's low or if data ends.

ultimate low   After a downward breakout from a chart pattern, it is the lowest valley before a minimum 20% price rise, measured from the lowest low to the close. Stop looking if price closes above the formation top or at end of data.

undershoot   When price suddenly drops for a few days to a week or two before the beginning of a chart pattern. Point A in Figure G.2 (under "Overshoot") is undershoot.

whisper number   The unpublished quarterly or annual earnings value that analysts expect.